# SOUTHEAST ASIA

*An Annotated Bibliography of Selected Reference Sources in Western Languages* • REVISED AND ENLARGED

Compiled by Cecil Hobbs
Head, South Asia Section

ORIENTALIA DIVISION • REFERENCE DEPARTMENT • LIBRARY OF CONGRESS

Washington : 1964

L.C. card 63–60089

For sale by the Superintendent of Documents, U.S. Government Printing Office
Washington, D.C., 20402- Price $1.00

# BIBLIOGRAPHICAL NOTE

Within the past two decades a growing interest has been shown in events happening within the countries comprising the region of Southeast Asia. Historians, anthropologists, economists, and political scientists as well as businessmen, newspaper columnists, and government officials have expressed a keen desire for more information and factual data regarding the peoples and culture of this portion of the Orient. To meet this demand books have been published in America and Europe which have brought to the consciousness of the people of the Western hemisphere the immediate importance as well as the long-term significance of Southeast Asia.

In 1952 the Library of Congress published the bibliographical compilation *Southeast Asia: An Annotated Bibliography of Selected Reference Sources,* with an analysis of each of the selected 345 entries, the majority of the items being published between 1942 through 1952.

The present publication comprising 535 entries, drawn from thousands of items, is an updating of that former compilation, with most of the books carrying imprints from 1952 through 1962. The original format has been preserved, thereby giving a critical appraisal in substantive language of the text, bibliography, maps, illustrations, statistical tables, and documents.

For typing the manuscript, special thanks are due Mrs. Aleice Haynes, Secretary of the South Asia Section.

CECIL HOBBS,
*Head, South Asia Section,*
*Orientalia Division.*

# Contents

# Southeast Asia—General

## GENERAL BACKGROUND

1. The Asia Who's Who. 3d ed. Hong Kong, Pan-Asia Newspaper Alliance, 1960. xii, 939 p.; index.  DS32.A8

*Text:* Among the 23 countries covered, these countries of Southeast Asia are included: Burma, Cambodia, Indonesia, Laos, Malaya, North Vietnam, Philippines, Singapore, Thailand, Vietnam. In each of these country sections, biographical sketches of leading personalities in various professions are provided.

Each section begins with the Government Cabinet Officers listed.

2. BUSS, CLAUDE ALBERT. Southeast Asia and the World Today. Princeton, Van Nostrand, 1958. 189 p.; bibliography, map, charts, index. (An Anvil original, no. 32)  DS503.B87

*Text:* This book is divided into two equal parts: a brief but careful analysis of the political, economic and social aspects and current problems of each of the countries in the region of Southeast Asia; and documentary speeches, treaties, and other items for collateral reading.

Among these documents these few representative ones are selected: 1. The Asian African Conference, Bandung, Indonesia, 1955. 2. Southeast Asia Collective Defense Treaty and Pacific Charter, 1954. 5. The acquisition of Singapore, 1819. 6. My last farewell—Dr. José Rizal, 1896. 8. Out of exile, 1934–1942—Soetan Sjahrir. 10. Pantja-Sila — the basic philosophy of the Indonesian State, 1945. 15. King Mongkut's personal letter to President Pierce, 1856. 20. Final declaration of the Geneva Conference on the problems of restoring peace in Indochina, 1954.

*Bibliography:* A few references enlarging on the text.

*Map:* Outline map of Southeast Asia.

*Charts:* Main lines of political change in Southeast Asia to 1500. Political change 1500–1900.

3. DOBBY, ERNEST HENRY GEORGE. Monsoon Asia. Chicago, Quadrangle Books, 1961. 381 p.; bibliography, illustrations, maps, tables, index.  DS10.D59

*Text:* Following a detailed review of the peculiarities of the area affected by the monsoon, outlining the setting and the major human influences, the emphasis of the study is on agriculture, the dominant activity of the people of Asia.

An examination, however, is made of the economic and political aspects of national geographies, including data from the latest U.N. reports and other sources to indicate new trends which are vital in international trade, industry, and even the political economy of Asia, Southeast Asia being considered in parts 3 and 5.

*Bibliography:* Includes articles and books pertaining to the political, economic and human geography of Asia.

*Illustrations* (selected) : Singapore from the air. Rice terraces of Indonesia. Rangoon from the air.

*Maps* (selected) : Distribution of natural vegetation in Asia; types of soil in monsoon Asia. Population densities. Distribution of religions. Distribution of economic animals and fish. Distribution of agricultural plants. Types of farming. Economic pattern of continental Southeast Asia. Bangkok and the coast of the Bight. The Kra Isthmus. Tin and rubber belt of Malaya.

*Tables* (selected) : Southeast Asia rainfall.

4. GINSBURG, NORTON SYDNEY, ed. The Pattern of Asia. Co-authors: John E. Brush and others. Englewood Cliffs, N.J., Prentice-Hall, 1958. 929 p.; illustrations, maps, tables, index.  DS5.G5

*Text:* Organized into six large sections, the third section comprised of chapters 15–21, deals with the countries of Southeast Asia.

Emphasis is given to the changing economic geography of the region, and attempts to illustrate the various problems and potentials of the Southeast Asia countries. The stated purpose is to provide a basic understanding of the processes of change which are radically transforming the Asian landscape.

Most of the countries are analyzed with reference to geography, agriculture, population, transportation, resources and industry. Aspects of politics and government are referred to only casually.

*Bibliography:* Each chapter closes with a "selected geographical bibliography".

*Illustrations:* Various pictures showing agriculture, transportation, housing, terrain and rivers.

*Maps* (selected): Southeast Asia. Southeast Asia, physiography. Land uses in the Philippines. Philippines: mineral resources. Land-use in Indonesia. Major ethnolinguistic groups, Malaya. Temperature and precipitation, Southeast Asia. Land uses in Malaya. Thailand, rice types and water conditions. Thailand, agricultural and forest regions. Land use in Indochina. Ethnolinguistic map, Cambodia. Land use in Burma.

*Tables* (selected): Land utilization in Southeast Asia. Philippine exports and imports. Filipino diet.

5. Hay, Stephen N., and Margaret H. Case. Southeast Asian History: A Bibliographic Guide. New York, Praeger, 1962. vii, 138 p.; map, appendix, indexes.      Z3221.H36

*Text:* An annotated list of about 700 books, articles and dissertations dealing primarily with the historical and political development of Burma, Cambodia, Ceylon, Indonesia, Laos, Malaya, North Borneo, Sarawak, Singapore, Philippines, Thailand, and Vietnam.

*Map:* Southeast Asia and Ceylon (Goode's Series Base Map).

*Appendix:* Book dealers handling books on Southeast Asia.

6. Irikura, James K. Southeast Asia: Selected Annotated Bibliography of Japanese Publications. New Haven, Southeast Asia Studies, Yale University, in association with Human Relations Area Files, 1956. xii, 544 p.; index. (Behavioral science bibliographies)      Z3221.I7

*Text:* Makes available to Western researchers books on Southeast Asia in the Japanese language, the first bibliography of this type ever to appear.

The 1965 items listed, date from the late 19th century through 1955, and are arranged under these geographical areas: Southeast Asia, General; Burma; Indochina; Indonesia; Malaya; Philippines; and Thailand. The subject clusters under each of these countries differ but usually cover culture, history, government, economy, foreign trade, foreign relations, geography, and other subjects. Each entry is given in both romanized Japanese and Japanese script. The annotations, given in a staccato style, are clear and concise.

7. Low, Francis. The Struggle for Asia. London, F. Muller, 1955. 239 p.; maps, index.      DS518.1.L68

*Text:* This is a background book designed primarily to give an overall, general view of the problems and tensions manifesting themselves in Southeast Asia and other parts of the Orient. It is not a detailed, scholarly study of any one given aspect—political, economic, or sociological—but endeavors to give the observations and analysis of various developments by one who lived in India for many years as a journalist, holding for a period of time the post of editor of the *Times of India.*

In the chapters summarizing the events in Southeast Asia, the author explains why and how nationalism has been confused, and intertwined with communism; why many of the Asian countries of the Colombo Plan boycotted SEATO; why the Manila Treaty (SEATO) is definitely limited in stemming the tide of communism in Southeast Asia.

In the concluding chapter, *The Crucial Issues,* a big question which is raised but not adequately answered is this: how can the Western democracies give of their best to help the Asian democracies which are struggling against communism and which do not wish to be involved in a Western-sponsored defense organization?

*Maps:* Associated States of Indochina. Southeast Asia.

8. Mahajani, Usha. The Role of Indian Minorities in Burma and Malaya. Foreword by H. N. Kunzru. Bombay, Vora, 1960. xxx, 344 p.; bibliography, tables, appendices, index. (Issued under the auspices of the Institute of Pacific Relations, New York)      DS595.M25

*Text:* A thesis prepared at Johns Hopkins University, deals with problems confronting Indian residents in Burma and Malaya in relation to economic life and the nationalist movements in those two countries. Traces the evolution of the direct and indirect roles of the Indian minorities in molding local nationalism;

discusses the causes of their political decline during the postwar years; and gives a sketchy representation of their future status as minorities within the two independent states of Burma and Malaya.

The study is divided into these nine parts: 1. The prewar anatomy of the Indian community in Burma. 2. Burmese nationalism and the Indian minority. 3. The problem of Indian labour and immigration in Burma. 4. The anatomy of the Indian community in Malaya. 5. The Japanese occupation of Burma and Malaya. 6. Indians in postwar Burma. 7. Indian problems in postwar Malaya. 8. Triple interaction of minority nationalism in postwar Malaya. 9. Conclusion.

*Bibliography:* List the primary and secondary sources consulted, and the persons interviewed for the study.

*Tables* (selected): Population in Burma. Immigration to Burma. Indians in Burma industry. Indians in Malaya. Immigration to Malaya. Population in Malaya.

*Appendices:* Constitution of Burma, 1947. Constitution of Malaya, 1957.

9. OEY, GIOK PO. Survey of Chinese Language Materials on Southeast Asia in the Hoover Institute and Library. Ithaca, Southeast Asia Program, Department of Far Eastern Studies, Cornell University, 1953. ii, 73 p. (Data paper no. 8)          Z3221.O33

*Text:* Confined largely to the modern period, the 20th century. Because the majority of the works embrace either the whole of Southeast Asia or a plurality of countries, the entries are arranged according to subject, and not by country. Among the subject groupings are: geography and general description, economic conditions, history, international relations, communism, Chinese periodicals and newspapers. A large bulk of the material covers the subject of Overseas Chinese, with fitting sub-subject breakdown: clans, and guilds, China government, education and others.

10. OSANKA, FRANKLIN MARK, ed. Modern Guerrilla Warfare; Fighting Communist Guerrilla Movements, 1941–1961. [New York] Free Press of Glencoe, 1962. xxii, 519 p.; bibliography, index.          U240.O8

*Text:* Concerned with recent developments in uses of guerrilla warfare, with particular emphasis on its employment by Communists in various situations—including Malaya, Philippines, Laos, and Vietnam in Southeast Asia. Shows how the Communists have skillfully utilized social, economic and political weaknesses as assets to guerrilla operations.

Among the nine sections, part four on the Philippines includes these chapters: 14. Huks in the Philippine by Major Kenneth Hammer. 15. Dual strategy for limited war by Major Boyd Bashore. 16. The Philippine anti-Communist campaign by Col. Tomás Tirona.

Part six on Laos and Vietnam consists of six chapters: 19. Indochina: the bleeding war by Paul Linebarger. 20. Indochina: the seven-year dilemma by Bernard Fall. 21. Guerrilla warfare by Col. Marc Geneste. 22. Red parallel: the tactics of Ho and Mao by Col. Robert Rigg. 23. The invisible front lines of South Vietnam by Denis Warner. 24. Laos: a phase in cyclic regional revolution by Anne Jonas and George Tanham.

Part seven presents Malaya with these chapters: 25. They call 'em bandits in Malaya by Paul Linebarger. 26. The guerrilla war in Malaya by James Dougherty. 27. Action in Malaya by Major Anthony Crickett.

*Bibliography:* A lengthy list of references on guerrilla and unconventional warfare.

11. PURCELL, VICTOR WILLIAM WILLIAMS SAUNDERS. The Chinese in Southeast Asia. London, Oxford University Press, 1951. 801 p.; bibliography, maps, tables, appendices, postscript, index. (Issued under the joint auspices of the Royal Institute of International Affairs and the Institute of Pacific Relations)          DS509.5.P8

*Text:* The first comprehensive account dealing with the Chinese in Southeast Asia, one of the minority groups which yields an important influence politically, economically and socially. Following a summary of the distribution of the Chinese in Southeast Asia, an account of their earlier contacts in the region and of some special aspects of Chinese society in Southeast Asia as a whole, there appear separate accounts of the Chinese in Burma, Thailand, Indochina, Malaya, British Borneo, Indonesia and the Philippines. Each of these country studies open with a statistical appraisal of the Chinese population and a historical sketch of the Chinese in the history of that country, and then discusses the subjects of economics, education and political parties as they relate to the Chinese in each particular country.

The study points up contemporary happenings and at the same time relates the historical development of the past two or three centuries. In relating the way in which capitalistic imperialism opened up the countries of Southeast Asia for the supply of raw materials to the Western industrial machine, one sees how Chinese labor loomed important in the tin mines and rubber plantations, and that Chinese merchants, artisans and traders were significant in developing trade and commerce in the large urban centers.

The author was a member of the Malayan Civil Service for nearly twenty-six years, during which time he was Protector of Chinese and Director-General of Information. At present he is a Lecturer in Far Eastern History in the University of Cambridge.

*Bibliography:* The thirty page bibliography lists the authorities cited in the text.

*Maps:* Principal places of origin in China of the Chinese in Southeast Asia. Ethnic Chinese showing areas of Chinese concentration. Southeast Asia, showing movements of monsoons.

*Tables:* Provide statistical data on ethnic Chinese in Southeast Asia, immigration, emigration, Sino-Siamese trade, Chinese population in each Southeast Asia country, 1947 census of Singapore and Malaya, Sino-Philippine trade, assessed incomes for 1948 in Singapore and Malaya.

*Appendices:* The southern dialects of Chinese by R. A. D. Forrest. A note on Chinese junks. Displaced overseas Chinese. The squatter problems in Malaya. Indians in Southeast Asia.

12. ROBEQUAIN, CHARLES EDOUARD. Malaya, Indonesia, Borneo, and the Philippines: A Geographical, Economic and Political Description of Malaya, the East Indies, and the Philippines. Translated by E. D. Laborde. Issued in cooperation with the International Secretariat, Institute of Pacific Relations. London, New York, Longmans, Green, 1954. xi, 456 p.; bibliography, illustrations, maps, diagrams, index.                    DS601.R752

*Text:* The author, a professor of colonial geography at the Sorbonne, is well known for his extensive knowledge of the physical and human characteristics of Southeast Asia as revealed in the earlier French edition in 1946, *Le monde malaise: Peninsule Malaise, Sumatra, Java, Borneo, Cèlèbes, Bali et les petites iles de la Sonda, moluques, Philippines.* This edition in English was made available through the translation of Professor Laborde, who is also known for his translation of Gourou's *The tropical world* (Longmans, Green, 1953).

While this book is essentially a geographical study guide to Malaya, Indonesia, and the Philippines, an examination and appraisal of European and American colonization in Southeast Asia are included. Frequent comparisons of the British, Dutch, and Hispano–American influences in Malaysia also appear. Parts 1 and 2, which present a geographical account of the region, discuss the physical divisions, oceanography, climate, fauna, flora, and distribution of population. Part 3, entitled Colonial expansion and its effect on the economic system, deals with commerce and trade, the development of scientific and peasant agriculture, the economic systems, and the problems associated with industrialization. Part 4, entitled Colonial achievement, considers the cultural and social aspects of the region—including medicine and health, education, and Christian missionary endeavor.

The study provides an account of the ethnological and religious forces prevalent in Sumatra and Java, with a clear account of Polynesian, Pre-Malay, Hindu, Arabic, Islamic, Chinese, and European roles. Partly dealt with is the Chinese problem in the Malay world.

*Bibliography:* A list of references about the history, geology, climate, vegetation, population, economics, agriculture and mining, with particular reference to Indonesia and the Philippines.

*Illustrations:* Scenes showing agriculture, shipping, housing, industries, and religious shrines.

*Maps:* Vegetation and crops of Indonesia. Population density in Indonesia and the Philippines. Malaya topography. Products of Malaya. Oostkunst plantations in Sumatra. Topography of Borneo. Topography of Luzon. Crops and minerals of the Philippines.

*Diagrams:* Volcanoes in Indonesia. Temperature and rainfall in Southeast Asia. Building styles in Indonesia.

13. SILCOCK, THOMAS H. The Commonwealth Economy in Southeast Asia. Durham, N.C., Published for the Duke University Commonwealth Studies Center, Duke University Press; London, Cambridge University Press, 1959. xix, 259 p.; bibliography, index. (Duke University Commonwealth-Studies Center. Publication no. 10)                    HC412.S58

*Text:* Present the pattern, development, problems and other aspects of the economy, principally in the countries of Malaya, Singapore, and Sarawak, with lesser references to North Borneo and Hong Kong. The overtones of political independence and how the newly independent areas have experienced or will experience substantial changes in economic structure are discussed.

Material consists of a series of lectures delivered at Duke University and an article which appeared earlier in the *Malayan Economic Review.*

*Bibliography:* A classified list of books and articles on the economy of Malaya and Singapore, divided into these divisions: population, structure, labor, organization, land and land tenure, capital, enterprise and business organization, currency and banking, national income, consumption patterns and social conditions, administration and taxation, transport, trade, rubber, tin, rice, other agriculture and cooperation, fisheries, industry and development, handicrafts and small industries.

14. SPENCER, JOSEPH EARLE. Asia, East by South: A Cultural Geography. New York, Wiley; London, Chapman and Hall, 1954. 453 p.; bibliography, illustrations, maps, charts, appendix, index. DS5.S6

*Text:* Divided into two specific parts, part one—Systematic geography—covers these elements in the physical environment and the cultural environment: climate, soils and plant culture, minerals, marine life, health and disease, languages, religion, law, architecture, and processes of modernization. Part two—The regional growth of culture—treats the individual countries of Southeast Asia, showing the evolution of group cultures according to the broad regional molds in which they have emerged.

*Bibliography:* A list of over 800 titles of books and articles are arranged in chapter sequence. Most items are after 1940 and are readily available in many American libraries.

*Illustrations:* Rice culture.

*Maps* (selected) : Rainfall, January and July. Soil regions. Plant growth. Malaria. Ethnic composition. Languages. Religions. Legal systems. Ricelands of Thailand.

*Charts:* Climate in various cities of Southeast Asia.

*Appendix:* Regional statistical data by political units.

15. THAYER, PHILIP WARREN, ed. Southeast Asia in the Coming World. With a foreword by William O. Douglas. Baltimore, Johns Hopkins Press, 1953. xii, 306 p.; index.
DS503.4.T45

*Text:* A record of the twenty-two papers which were delivered at a conference on Southeast Asia in Washington, D.C., in August, 1952, sponsored by the School of Advanced International Studies of the Johns Hopkins University. Politics, economics, culture and law are the four fields covered.

Some of the topics discussed include the following significant interpretations confronting these newly independent countries which are rapidly undergoing political, economic and social changes: Postwar problems in the Southeast Asia policy of the United States; Our friends and antagonists in Southeast Asia; Our responsibilities in Southeast Asia; National economic planning in Southeast Asia; Food and problems in Southeast Asia; Export-Import problems in Southeast Asia; Idological problems in Southeast Asia; Communism as a competing civilization in Southeast Asia; The future of adat law in the reconstruction of Indonesia; The impact of the new states of Southeast Asia on the development of international law; The position of Southeast Asia in the world community; Southeast Asia: proposals for the future.

Emphasis is placed upon the problems facing these countries during the decline of imperialism associated with the Western powers in the nineteenth and twentieth centuries and the current rise of Soviet imperialism.

# HISTORY, POLITICS, AND GOVERNMENT

16. BALL, WILLIAM MACMAHON. Nationalism and Communism in East Asia. 2d ed. rev. Carlton, Melbourne University Press, 1956. v, 220 p.; maps, index. DS518.1.B29 1956

*Text:* Cites these three contemporary political forces in Asia: (1) the revolt against foreign political control, against colonialism, against imperialism—all of which is the drive for self-determination and full national independence; (2) the social and economic revolt by people who have become more aware of the real meaning of their poverty and misery, excited by a heightened resentment of the gross inequalities which are observed al labout them; and (3) the racial revolt, or a determination that the destiny of their country shall be decided by themselves and not by westerners.

Discusses the problems which these three political forces create for the West in each of the countries of

Southeast Asia. The closing chapter presents three methods which are available to the West in the contest with communism in Southeast Asia; military, economic, and psychological methods.

*Maps:* Philippines, Indonesia and New Guinea. Southeast Asia mainland.

17. BONE, ROBERT C. Contemporary Southeast Asia. New York, Random House, 1962. 132 p.; bibliography, map, table. (Studies in political science, PS38) DS518.1.B6

*Text:* This paperback book, designed for collateral reading by the college student, is divided into two parts: first, the historical background section discussion of the political and social forces which were active in Southeast Asia in the past, and how these forces and events were either assimilated or modified thus causing certain problems to emerge; second, in analyzing the contemporary problems, consideration is given to governmental institutions, political ideologies, political parties, foreign aid, economics, and minorities.

*Bibliography:* Lists well known references on politics and government of Southeast Asia.

*Map:* Southeast Asia.

*Table:* Data on area, exports, population, minorities, religions, literacy, government, and political systems.

18. BRIMMELL, J. H. Communism in South East Asia: A Political Analysis. London, New York, Oxford University Press, 1959. 415 p.; bibliography, maps, index. (Issued under the auspices of the Royal Institute of International Affairs) DS518.1.B7

*Text:* Deals primarily with communism and the impact of the West on the countries of Southeast Asia. Indicates that in effect a struggle of three forces is in progress: of the nationalism and democracy learned from the West, of the ideas of state authoritarianism and planned economic development according to the Communist movement, and of the traditional concept of a community ordered in accordance with certain religious concepts. This struggle becomes all the fiercer because of the world conflict between the Western and Communist blocs.

Significant selected chapters are: The background to the Communist impact on Southeast Asia; Communist beginnings in Southeast Asia; The second Communist forward movement in Southeast Asia; the period of Communist confusion in Southeast Asia;

Southeast Asia during the cold war period. The Communist parties of Southeast Asia in the transition to peaceful coexistence; and New patterns and pressures in Southeast Asia.

*Bibliography:* Brief list of very well known books on communism in Southeast Asia.

*Maps:* Southeast Asia and its neighbors. Countries of Southeast Asia (both outline maps).

19. BUSS, CLAUDE ALBERT. The Arc of Crisis. New York, Doubleday, 1961. 479 p.; index.
DS33.3.B8

*Text:* Including the countries of Southeast Asia within the "arc of crisis" stretching from Pakistan to Japan, emphasis is given to the need of the underdeveloped nations in their battle against poverty, illiteracy and disease, and to the importance of American foreign policy confronted with the relentless Communist pressures—both Chinese and Russian—endeavoring to occupy the arc.

Selected chapters which consider these and other ideas are: What Asians say about us; People and poverty; Political revolution—nationalism in Asia; The Philippines and the United States; The uncommitted nations and the United States; Communist strategy for world revolution; Democracy in Asia; Asians and American aid; Information and propoganda; Americans in Asia.

20. BUTWELL, RICHARD A. Southeast Asia Today—and Tomorrow: A Political Analysis. New York, Praeger, 1961. x, 182 p.; bibliography, map, index. (Books that matter) JQ96.B8

*Text:* Provides an assessment of the political developments in the countries of Southeast Asia, with particular note to the changes in governments during the decade of independence. The closing chapters discuss the foreign policy of the individual countries with reference to SEATO and the cold war.

The nine chapters are: 1. Yesterday and today: Asian roots and European influence. 2. First choice of governments. 3. The search for the appropriate political system. 4. The political process. 5. The uses of government. 6. Persisting problems—and some changing policies. 7. The Communist challenge. 8. Foreign policy. 9. Facing the future.

*Bibliography:* Lists a few well-known books on Southeast Asia published within the past few years.

*Maps:* Sketch map of Southeast Asia.

21. CLUBB, OLIVER EDMUND. The United States and the Sino-Soviet Bloc in Southeast Asia. Washington, Brookings Institution, 1962. viii, 173 p.; bibliography, maps, appendices, index.　　　　　　　　　　　DS518.8.C57

*Text:* Addresses itself to the problems related to the formation of a broad U.S. foreign policy framework for Southeast Asia as a whole, U.S. foreign policy toward the nonaligned nations, a practical method with which to cope with Communist subversion, and the most effective way to channel economic assistance to Southeast Asia.

Contents: 1. The problem.　2. The Southeast Asian landscape.　3. Communist policies in Southeast Asia since World War II.　4. American policies in Southeast Asia since World War II.　5. Issues and alternative.　6. The task in perspective.

*Bibliography:* Books and articles used for the study.

*Maps:* Indochinese peninsula showing Viet Cong infiltration, in South Vietnam and Laos.　Outline map of Southeast Asia.

*Appendices:* 1. The Geneva Conference.　2. The Southeast Asia Collective Defense Treaty.　3. The Bandung Conference of Asian-African countries.　4. Statement of neutrality by the Royal Government of Laos.

22. CONLON ASSOCIATES, LTD. United States Foreign Policy: Asia. Studies prepared at the request of the Committee on Foreign Relations, United States Senate. No. 5. Washington, U.S. Govt. Printing Office, 1959. 157 p. (At the head of title: Committee print, 86th Cong., 1st sess.)　　　　　DS33.4.U6C6

*Text:* This volume is a combination of two former studies—*U.S. Foreign Policy in South Asia* and *U.S. Foreign Policy in the Far East and Southeast Asia,*—both of which were prepared for the U.S. Senate Committee on Foreign Relations.

Describes and analyzes major trends in Asia over the next decade and suggests courses of action in connection with American foreign policy. Transitory issues are avoided and the fundamental forces and trends in South Asia, Southeast Asia, and Northeast Asia are concentrated on. The purpose is to provide a simple, understandable, and forthright statement of America's basic foreign policy in Southeast Asia and other parts of Asia; and to examine the impact of the forces and current trends which tend to mold the basic policy aims of America in Southeast Asia and other areas of Asia.

Following the main findings and conclusions and recommendations pertaining to Southeast Asia, the main body of the report discusses these topics in connection with U.S. foreign policy in Southeast Asia: democracy and authoritarianism; role of the military; demographic facts and agrarian problems; impact of education; problem of economic developments; need for scientific action programs; problems of foreign policy and regionalism; and prospects of communism.

23. DEVERALL, RICHARD LAWRENCE–GRACE. Asia and the Democratic Revolution. Tokyo, Printed by International Literature Printing Co., 1952. ii, 243 p.　　　DS12.D4 1952

*Text:* A general discussion of communism and its drive to become established in all countries, prepared by the Representative-in-Asia of the Free Trade Union Committee of the American Federation of Labor. Chapter two, Asia is the battle ground, is concerned with communism in the countries of Southeast Asia.

24. EMERSON, RUPERT. From Empire to Nation: The Rise to Self-Assertion of Asian and African Peoples. Cambridge, Harvard University Press, 1960. x, 466 p.; bibliography, index.　　　　　　　　　　JC311.E49

*Text:* The central core of this study which serves as the unifying theme throughout is "the rise of nationalism among non-European peoples as a consequence of the imperial spread of Western European civilization over the face of the earth." Southeast Asia is a part of the author's purview, and thus shows how democracy of the free world—in distinct contrast to communism—has scored a triumph in that democracy has become the model to which the countries of Southeast Asia look in their drive for development.

Significant selected chapters are: Colonial policy and national movements; The West and non-Western nationalism; Colonialism as a school for democracy; Nationalism and democracy in non-colonial countries; Self-determination in plural societies; Traditionalism and communism; and The new nations and the international community.

*Bibliography:* Many references to books, periodical articles and newspaper items are included in the section on Notes.

25. EMERSON, RUPERT. Representative Government in Southeast Asia. With supplementary chapters by Willard H. Elsbree and Virginia Thompson. Cambridge, Harvard University Press, 1955. vii, 197 p.; index. JQ96.E5

*Text:* Relates the circumstances under which the new independent states in Southeast Asia—Indonesia, Burma, Malaya, Philippines, Thailand, and Indochina—launched their respective constitutional ventures of establishing the institutions and organization of representative governments. Points up the fact that cultural background, political tradition, mass literacy, plus the social disruption inherent from colonialism make the establishment of representative, democratic form of government no easy undertaking. Cites how communism encourages disruption, turmoil, and disintegration which the new states have had to fight against.

26. FIFIELD, RUSSELL HUNT. The Diplomacy of Southeast Asia, 1945–1958. New York, Harper, 1958. xv, 584 p.; bibliography, maps, appendices, index.    DS518.1.F47

*Text:* Describes and analyzes the new phase of international politics which has appeared in Southeast Asia with the emergence of the newly independent states of Southeast Asia during the postwar years: a new pattern of international relations between these new states and the world and among themselves.

Considering each country separately—Philippines, Indonesia, Burma, Thailand, Vietnam, Laos, Cambodia and Malaya—the important aspects of the foreign policy of each country as determined during the formative years from 1945 to 1958 are analyzed. The participation which these nations have taken with respect to the United Nations, the Colombo Plan, SEATO, the Bandung Conference and other Asian conferences is discussed with some detail.

*Bibliography:* Voluminous list of references, both monographs and articles, dealing with the political science aspects of Southeast Asia.

*Maps:* Outline maps of various parts of the region. Southeast Asia, international alignment, 1958.

*Appendices:* List of interviews, discussions, correspondence. Letter from Jawaharlal Nehru on Panch Shila. Final communique of the Asian–African Conference.

27. FURNIVALL, JOHN SYDENHAM. Colonial Policy and Practice; a Comparative Study of Burma and Netherlands India. New York, New York University Press, 1956. xii, 568 p.; bibliography, map, tables, appendices, index.
   DS485.B89F8 1956

*Text:* An evaluation of the British and Dutch experiments in colonial rule, presenting respectively extreme types of the alternative systems of direct and indirect rule. Reveals that the two basic principles of British colonial policy in the former Netherlands Indies was aimed at imposing restraints on economic forces by strengthening personal authority and by conserving the influence of custom. Contends that the weaknesses of British colonial administration in Burma can be traced to a common cause; namely, the disintegration of social life through the inadequacy of law to control the working of antisocial, economic forces. Endeavors to show how Burma, by adapting certain devices of Dutch administrative machinery, might apply the principle of controlling economic forces in the interest of social welfare in order to cure the ills of modern Burma and thereby lay the basis of a new and constructive policy.

Among the numerous subjects discussed in the thirteen chapters are: the early foundations of administrative practice in the judicial and revenue systems; economic progress as shown in communications, population growth, trade, western and native enterprise in agricultural and industrial production; the rise of nationalism; the development of local self-government; labor problems; educational policies, welfare and autonomy; and conditions of reintegration.

*Bibliography:* Lists briefly the articles used in the study.

*Map:* Burma, showing political divisions and tribal hill areas.

*Tables:* Statistical data on Burma's export and import trade. Trade of Indonesia, 1825–1937. Racial constitution of the Burma Army.

*Appendices:* Seaborne trade of Burma, 1869–1937, exports and imports. Distribution of seaborne trade of Burma, 1869–1937, exports and imports.

28. FURNIVALL, JOHN SYDENHAM. Progress and Welfare in Southeast Asia; a Comparison of Colonial Policy and Practice. New York, Secretariat, Institute of Pacific Relations, 1941. 84 p. (International research series*)
   JV241.F9

---

*[Other reports relating to Southeast Asia within this series are as follows: *The evolution of the Netherlands Indies economy* and *The structure of Netherlands Indian economy,* both by J. H. Boeke; *Modern Burma* by J. L. Christian; *Progress and welfare in Southeast Asia* by John S. Furnivall; *Transportation* by K. R. C. Greene; *Chinese in Thailand* by K. P. Landon; *Industrialization of the Western Pacific* by Kate Mitchell; *Pioneer settlement in the Asiatic tropics* by Karl Pelzer; *Industry in Southeast Asia* by Jack Shepherd; and *Thailand* by Virginia Thompson.]

*Text:* A brief study of the principal historical events, and the notable divergencies in the colonial policy of the Western nations—mainly Holland, Great Britain, and France—which had dominion over Indonesia, Malaya, Burma, and Indochina respectively for many, many years.

Emphasizes the idea that the main objective of all colonial powers is material advantage; that in essence the colonial relation between the Western power and the colony is economic. Shows that in all instances humanitarian ideas may be employed and the exploited country is rewarded with numerous benefits for the general welfare of the people but colonial policy is dominated by economic motives and is efficient in ratio to the economic circumstances in so far as they are favorable. This basic premise is supported by an elucidation of the economic factors by which the course of the colonial policies of the Dutch, British, and French in Southeast Asia have been conditioned.

Discusses at length the way in which colonial policy was carried out by direct administration on Western principles, that the government, ownership of capital, and the direction of the economic life were mostly in European hands, and, as a result, social disruption of the native social order brought about definitely in plural society. Includes a concise statement of the main features of the plural economy.

The closing portion, which points out certain contemporary problems, contends that the recent political reforms in the colonial areas in Southeast Asia have done little beyond obstructing government because the attempt was to install democratic machinery instead of creating democratic motive power.

29. HALL, DANIEL GEORGE EDWARD. A History of Southeast Asia. New York, St. Martin's Press, 1955. xvi, 807 p.; bibliography, illustrations, maps, appendices, index.
DS551.H15

*Text:* This extensive historical account of events during the past centuries in the countries of Southeast Asia are based upon lecture courses delivered to university classes in London, Rangoon, Singapore, Djakarta, and Bangkok. Whereas most histories on any country of Southeast Asia prior to this addressed themselves mainly to the European activities in Southeast Asia. This study is principally concerned with Southeast Asia itself. As a result, there are chapters on the island empire of Srivijaya in Indonesia; The Khmer kingdom of Cambodia; the empire of Pagan in Burma; the Malay powers from the fall of Malacca in 1511 to the end of the 18th century; the Kingdom of Laos from 1591–1836; Siam from 1688–1851; the reign of Bodawpaya and the first Anglo–Burmese War from 1782–1826; Siam under Mongkut and Chulalongkorn, 1851–1910; the economic aspect of European domination; the Japanese impact; after the war, 1945–50.

The forty-five chapters are divided into these four parts: 1. The pre-European period. 2. Southeast Asia during the earlier phase of European expansion. 3. The period of European territorial expansion. 4. Nationalism and the challenge of European domination.

*Bibliography:* Includes local chronicles, accounts contemporary to events in the 17th, 18th, and 19th centuries, references on each country, and biographies.

*Illustrations* (selected): Buddhist images, temples, monasteries, King Mongkut, U Nu, Bao Dai, Ho chi Minh, and President Sukarno.

*Maps* (selected): Prehistory of Eastern Asia. Spread of Islam. Dutch expansion in Java. The Franco-Siamese Question, 1893.

*Appendices:* Dynastic lists—Burma, Cambodia, Indonesia, Malaya, Thailand, and Vietnam.

30. HARRISON, BRIAN. Southeast Asia; a Short History. London, MacMillan, New York, St. Martin's Press, 1954. xi, 268 p.; bibliography, illustrations, maps, chart, index. DS511.H3

*Text:* After relating the early Chinese and Indian influences in various parts of the region—particularly in Indonesia and on the Indochinese peninsula, the succeeding chapters tell of the advent of Islam; the appearance of the Portuguese, Dutch and English trading companies from the West which established trade relations and brought about the beginnings of the colonial period; the growth of nationalism which was one of the symptoms of revolution in Southeast Asia emerging from the colonial era.

*Bibliography:* A few well-known books listed for further reading.

*Illustrations:* Borobodur. Angkor Wat. Chenderoh Dam in Malaya.

*Maps* (selected): Sites of early man in Java. States of the 1st and 5th centuries.

*Chart:* Main lines of political change in Southeast Asia to 1500.

31. Holland, William Lancelot, ed. Asian Nationalism and the West. A symposium based on documents and reports of the Eleventh Conference Institute of Pacific Relations. Contributors: George McT. Kahin, Philippe Devillers, T. H. Silcock, and Ungku Aziz. New York, Macmillan, 1953. viii, 449 p.; appendix. DS518.1.H6

*Text:* With the close relationship between the nationalist and Communist movements in Southeast Asia, three specific documents presented at the Eleventh Conference of the Institute of Pacific Relations at Lucknow, India, were revised and enlarged for this publication. These documents deal with various aspects of the nationalist movements in Malaya, Vietnam, and Indonesia, each being at a different stage of political evolution and subjected to varying external forces. Each of these principal sections discuss political parties, main problems faced by the governments, civil wars, postwar military activities and their interplay on political developments.

An opening chapter gives the highlights in Philippine and Burmese nationalism. The summaries of the Lucknow Conference discussions dealing with the political, economic, financial, and social problems comprise part four.

*Appendix:* Conference membership. List of conference papers.

32. Isaacs, Harold Robert, ed. New Cycle in Asia. Selected documents on major international developments in the Far East, 1943–1947. New York, Macmillan, 1947. xiii, 212 p.; index. DS518.1.I8

*Text:* A compilation of documents on the political activity between the Western Powers and various countries of the Far East. With reference to Southeast Asia, significant treaties, statements, manifestos, and other documents relating to Burma, Indochina, Indonesia, and the Philippines are included.

Among the documents are: Proclamation of Philippine Independence, July 4, 1946; White Paper on Burma, January 27, 1947; Declaration of the French Government on Indochina, March 23, 1945: Abdication of Bao Dai, August 25, 1945; Declaration of Independence of the Republic of Vietnam, September 2, 1945; Declaration of the Vietnam Government on the Franco-Vietnam Conflict, January 6, 1947; Plan for a Netherlands Commonwealth—radio address by Queen Wilhelmina, December 6, 1942; Political manifesto of the Government of the Republic of Indonesia, November 1, 1945; Declaration of the policy of the Netherlands Indies Government, by van Mook, November 10, 1945; Linggadjati (Charibon) Agreement, March 25, 1947.

Each section of documents is preceded with a brief outline of the political events within each of the countries concerned.

Serves as a supplement to the author's *No Peace for Asia* (New York, Macmillan, 1947).

33. Josey, Alex. Socialism in Asia. Singapore, Donald Moore, 1957. 112 p.; index. HX382.J6

*Text:* Presents an account of the development of socialism in the countries of Southeast Asia. Among the ten chapters these selected ones are cited: 2. Principles and objectives of Asian socialism. 4. The Bombay Congress. 6. An agrarian policy for Asia. 7. Economic development of Asia. 9. History of the Asian Socialist Conference. 10. Socialism and Malaya.

34. Kahin, George McTurnan, ed. Governments and Politics of Southeast Asia. Contributors: David A. Wilson, Josef Silverstein, Herbert Feith, J. Norman Parmer, Wells C. Klein, Marjorie Weiner and David Wurfel. Ithaca, N.Y., Cornell University Press, 1959. 531 p.; bibliographies, maps, charts, index. (Published under the auspices of the Southeast Asia Program, Cornell University) JQ96.K3

*Text:* Employing a broadly uniform pattern of organization and applying similar analyses to the political development and current processes in the six largest states of Southeast Asia, the chapters in each of the six parts present: the historical background, the contemporary setting, the political process, and the major problems of each country. Although the chapters on contemporary setting and major problems discuss agriculture, economy, and social organization, the main body of the study deals with the politics and government of these countries.

*Bibliography:* Suggested reading lists conclude each part.

*Maps:* Outline maps of each country shows railroads and principal products.

*Charts:* 1. Structure of government of Thailand in 1958. 2. Federation in Burma. 3. Structure of government in Vietnam.

35. KENNEDY, MALCOLM DUNCAN. A History of Communism in East Asia. New York, Praeger, 1957. ix, 556 p.; bibliography, indexes.

HX382.K4 1957

*Text:* Outlines the main developments in the rise of nationalism and the spread of communism in East Asia, with a section pertaining to the countries of Southeast Asia. Provides the reasons why these developments emerged and interprets the Communist tactics and conduct in strategically important or heavily populated regions with special reference to world affairs in general and of Russian policies in particular which have influenced Communist gains and setbacks in Southeast Asia.

Divided into these four parts: 1. The birth throes of nationalism and communism. 2. Revolutionary developments between the wars. 3. The Pacific War period. 4. Postwar developments.

*Bibliography:* Cites the documentary material, the firsthand works of former Communists, and general books used for the study.

36. MENDE, TIBOR. Southeast Asia Between Two Worlds. London, Turnstile Press, 1955. viii, 338 p.; maps, index. DS518.1.M45

*Text:* Discusses the problem of whether or not the new states in Southeast Asia are able to fill the vacuum created by the end of several centuries of Western domination, to construct developing political institutions, to maintain law and order, and to feed their populations.

Parts one and two deal with Indonesia and Burma, respectively; part three is about Pakistan; and part four discusses principally the economy of Southeast Asia as a whole.

*Maps:* Outline maps of Burma and Indonesia.

37. OLVER, A. S. B. SEATO; the Manila Treaty and Western Policy in South East Asia. London, Royal Institute of International Affairs, 1956. 24 p. Orientalia

*Text:* This presentation is one in a series of studies of various international pacts, conferences, and agreements which have been made available by the Royal Institute of International Affairs. It states both the value of SEATO, as the Manila Treaty is commonly called, and also historical developments—particularly the Chinese intentions toward the Southeast Asia countries—which brought about the pact as a buttress against communism. These and other topics are considered: Asian attitudes to a defense agreement; economic and technical assistance; Western economic policy; and Asian attitudes to the Manila Treaty.

38. PEFFER, NATHANIEL. Transition and Tension in Southeast Asia. [White Plains, N.Y. Fund for Adult Education,] 1957. ix, 287, p.; bibliography. DS510.7.P4 1957a

*Text:* Designed as a guide for discussion groups, in the college classroom or otherwise, selected problems which are manifest in the countries of Southeast Asia are outlined. Following the statement of a problem, there appears selected readings pertinent to the problem and country concerned.

Arranged for ten discussion sessions, the sections are: 1. Introduction. 2. Southeast Asia: powderkeg of the Pacific. 3. Burma. 4. Indonesia. 5. Indochina. 6. Thailand and Malaya. 7. The Philippines. 8. Can the West help? 9. International factors. 10. Conclusion.

*Bibliography:* A few well-known references.

39. RIGGS, FRED WARREN. The Ecology of Public Administration. Bombay, New York, Asia Publishing House, 1961. viii, 152 p.; index. (Issued under the auspices of the Indian Institute of Public Administration, New Delhi) JF1351.R5

*Text:* Two of these three lectures delivered at the Indian Institute of Public Administration examine in detail the patterns of public administration in the countries of Thailand and the Philippines in the context of their transitional phase from an agrarian to an industrial society. The wider background of a multiplicity of sociological, political and institutional factors is taken into account throughout the discussion.

The two chapters are: 2. Thailand: reflections on the traditional ecology. 3. Administrative change in the Philippines and Thailand.

40. ROMEIN, JAN MARIUS. The Asian Century; a History of Modern Nationalism in Asia. In collaboration with Jan Erik Romein. Translated by R. T. Clark; Foreword by K. M. Panikkar. Berkeley, University of California Press, 1962. 448 p.; bibliography, map, appendix, index. DS35.R583

*Text:* The dominant theme of this study is the historical development of the national movement in the countries of Asia in the twentieth century. Presents what the author believes to be the final cause of the temporary domination of Asia by Europeans from the West, and shows that when Asia became awakened and became "European," Asia rediscovered itself and at the same time took the significant step forward toward the realization of the unity of making of both East and West.

Following the introduction, these six periods appear: 1. The awakening of Asia, 1900–14. 2. The "deglorification" of the West, 1914–19. 3. Reaction and action, 1919–41. 4. Storm over Asia, 1941–45. 5. Fulfillment and disillusion, 1945–55. 6. The most recent past, conclusion, 1955–60. Chapters on the countries of Southeast Asia appear in each of these periods.

*Bibliography:* A few references on Southeast Asia are included in the list which deals with all of Asia.

*Appendix:* A chronological survey of principal historical events from 1830 to 1959.

41. ROSE, SAUL. Britain and Southeast Asia. Baltimore, Johns Hopkins Press, 1962. 208 p.; bibliography, maps, tables, index. (Britain in the world today) DS518.4.R6

*Text:* Traces historically the residency of the British in Southeast Asia from the time of the Anglo-Dutch struggle in the 15th century which forced the British out of Indonesia, through the British domination of Burma, Malaya, Singapore, and Borneo, until the Japanese occupation and the period of progressive withdrawal in the postwar years. Particular attention is given to the economic framework which emerged during the British regime in the 19th and 20th centuries.

*Bibliography:* A brief list of references of rather well-known postwar publications.

*Maps* (selected): English voyages up to 1600. British factories (commercial centers) in 17th and 18th centuries. British expansion, 1826–52. Malaya, 1914.

*Tables:* Imports and exports, 1947–58.

42. SACKS, MILTON. "The Strategy of Communism in Southeast Asia." *Pacific affairs*, September 1950, v. 23:227–247. DU1.I45 1950

*Text:* By the author of *Political alignments of Vietnamese nationalists* (1949), a former political analyst in the Office of Intelligence and Research in the Department of State.

Shows that communism in the countries of Southeast Asia is a coordinated movement with objectives to eliminate completely all Western influence and to establish immediately "people's democracies" which are Communist controlled. Presents some general historical observations with particular emphasis on the difference between nationalism and communism. Considers the strategic objectives and tactical operation of the manifold agencies of international communism concerned with Southeast Asia, with considerable emphasis on Communist activities in Indochina. Tells how the rise of Communist power in China has had a marked effect on the Chinese ethnic minorities living in highly organized and integrated communities within various areas of Southeast Asia. Indicates that the integrated nature of past Communist operations and the coordinated structure of the Communist organization in Southeast Asia is closely linked with the Asian and Australasian Trade Union Conference at Peking in late 1949.

43. SOUTHEAST ASIA TREATY ORGANIZATION. *Council.* SEATO; Record of Partnership, 1957–58. [n.p.] 1958. 33 p.; illustrations. UA830.S627

*Text:* An account of the works and accomplishments of SEATO in its third year. Describes the efforts of the member countries, individually and collectively, to make the Manila Pact an effective instrument for security against communism in Southeast Asia.

Includes these documentary items: Report of the Secretary General; An address by President Carlos Garcia of the Philippines entitled: "A larger role for Seato"; Final communique of the fourth meeting of the Council, March, 1958; The Manila Pact; The Pacific Charter; Protocol to the Southeast Asia Collective Defense Treaty.

44. STRAUSZ-HUPÉ, ROBERT, ALVIN J. COTTRELL, and JAMES E. DOUGHERTY. American-Asian Tensions. New York, Praeger, 1956. xiii, 239 p.; bibliography, index. (Foreign Policy Research Institute series, no. 3) DS35.S8

*Text:* Prepared under the auspices of the Foreign Policy Research Institute, University of Pennsylvania, the study proposes to determine the nature and extent of tensions between the U.S. and selected countries of Asia—India, Indonesia, Japan, and the Philippines.

In section one, Temper of neutralism, when discussing Indonesia as one country which has played a significant role in the development of a so called "neutralist" philosophy in international relations, these topics are considered: Resentment of American influence; Western colonialism and Communist imperialism; Chinese relations and American China policy; Differences in cultural patterns.

In section two, Trials of cooperation, when examining the relations between the U.S. and the Philippines and the pledge of the Philippines to support American defense measures in the Far East, these topics are presented: Philippine defense; American bases; U.S. tariffs; American aid; The Laurel-Langley Agreement; and Racial tensions.

*Bibliography:* Numerous book, periodical, and newspaper references are listed among the notes.

45. TANG, PETER S. H. The Nature of Communist Strategy in the Areas of Emerging Nations. A study delivered at the Fourth Annual Roundtable Conference, Institute of Ethnic Studies, Georgetown University, April 21, 1961. Washington, Research Institute on the Sino-Soviet Blov, 1962. 32 p. (Pamphlet series, no. 6)                    D847.T3

*Text:* Discusses the traditional Communist encouragement of national liberation movements and the Communist aid programs to provide credit or technical assistance to the new nations. Numerous references to Southeast Asia are given throughout the text.

46. THAYER, PHILIP WARREN, and WILLIAM T. PHILLIPS, eds. Nationalism and Progress in Free Asia. Introduction by Chester Bowles. Baltimore, Johns Hopkins Press, 1956. xvi, 394 p.; bibliography, index.      DS35.T5

*Text:* Comprised of lectures given at two conferences—one in Washington, the other in Rangoon—which had the purview of the areas of South and Southeast Asia and considered the rise of nationalism and the way in which these newly independent countries have progressed in a world of divided allegiances and growing tensions.

Among the more than 20 lectures given by various authorities, these pertain specifically to Southeast Asia: The United States looks at South and Southeast Asia by Walter Robertson; South and Southeast Asia look at the United States by R. S. S. Gunewardene; The European impact on Southeast Asia by D. G. E. Hall; Aftermaths of colonialism by Walter H. Mallory; The progress of nationalism by Rupert Emerson; Evolving political institutions in Southeast Asia by John Cady; The role of political parties in Indonesia by Soejatmoko; Problems of political integration in Southeast Asia by Brian Harrison; Burma: the political integration of linguistic and religious minority groups by Kyaw Thet; The development and utilization of labor resources in Southeast Asia by Abdul Aziz; Demographic influences on racial minorities by Victor Purcell; The United Nations and South and Southeast Asia by Sudjarwo Tjondronegoro; Policy choices of South and Southeast Asia by Sujono Surjotjondro; and Policy choices before the Western world by Patrick Walker.

*Bibliography:* References in footnotes.

47. THOMPSON, VIRGINIA, and RICHARD ADLOFF. The Left Wing in Southeast Asia. New York, William Sloane Associates, 1950. xiv, 298 p.; illustrations, map, appendix, index. (Published under the auspices of the International Secretariat, Institute of Pacific Relations)
                    DS518.1.T49 1950

*Text:* A study of political forces currently in operation in Indochina, Thailand, Burma, Malaya, and Indonesia. Offers the essential data for understanding the political developments of communism, nationalism, and related ideologies which have assumed various patterns in the countries of Southeast Asia. Shows that counter forces of Marxism and democracy have been at work in the countries within Southeast Asia for the past decade but the region of Southeast Asia is still one vast area of Asia which has not become Sovietized. In the process of examining radical, political trends in this region, the authors trace the relationship of Socialist and Communist organizations to international communism in each of the countries. Of the five countries discussed, it is shown that Indonesia and Indochina have been the only countries in Southeast Asia which have had long, intimate contacts with the Comintern.

Two leading queries discussed are: Why has socialism become strong in Burma and Indonesia, but relatively weak or nonexistent in Thailand, Vietnam, and Malaya? Why has the radical Trotskyism developed strongly in Vietnam, moderately in Indonesia, to a slight degree in Burma, and hardly at all in Malaya?

With reference to the international position of Southeast Asia, it is clearly delineated that the countries of Southeast Asia will follow one of three choices: To follow the lead of India in organizing on a regional basis within a United Nations framework; to accept Soviet leadership and become an integral unit in the Soviet sphere; or, to create a separate Asian regional entity with the purpose of promoting strictly regional interests and remaining aloof from the Soviet orbit or the Western power bloc.

*Illustrations:* Ho chi Minh, President Soekarno, and various political leaders in Southeast Asia.

*Map:* Outline map of Southeast Asia.

*Appendix:* Over fifty pages provide biographical sketches of U Aung San, Ho chi Minh, President Soekarno, Premier Pibul Songgram, and many other Southeast Asia political leaders.

48. THOMSON, IAN. Changing Patterns in South Asia. New York, Roy Publishers, 1962. 166 p.; bibliography, illustrations, map, index.                    DS509.3.T55

*Text:* An endeavor to identify and evaluate the major dynamic forces which are molding current Asia. Divided into four principal sections, section one deals with the social forces of nationalism, racialism, and idealism. Section two is concerned with the political factors at work: democracy, communism, socialism, and revolution. Section three is concerned with religion: Hinduism, Buddhism, Islam and Christianity, all of which are deeply rooted in the life of the people in various segments of the region. The last section is a summary as to how all these various factors contribute towards a focus or perspective. It appears that communism has lost some of its appeal to these people, and democracy has been more successful than was predicted a decade or two ago. Also, neutralism, as a principle, is a prominent and workable foreign policy with certain countries.

*Bibliography:* Mostly well-known secondary sources.

*Illustrations:* Dr. Leimena, Deputy Prime Minister of Indonesia.

*Map:* Outline map of Southern Asia.

[Also published under same title in London, by Barrie and Rockliff, 1961.]

49. THOMSON, IAN. The Rise of Modern Asia. New York, Pitman, 1958. xv, 265 p.; bibliography, illustrations, maps, appendix, index.                    DS35.T56 1958

*Text:* Divided into two main parts. Part one—The end of "Europe in Asia"—contains a chapter which traces the extension of European influence and colonization in the countries of Southeast Asia. Part two—Asia speaks for herself—has four chapters which discuss the independent nations of Southeast Asia which emerged after the Japanese occupation and the end of World War II. Particular attention is given to the Bandung Conference: the fundamental issues, its historic importance, and the Communist repercussions after Bandung.

*Bibliography:* A few well-known secondary sources.

*Illustrations* (selected): Prime Minister U Nu with Mao Tse-tung. Mao Tse-tung with Ho chi Minh. President Sukarno with President Nasser. Premier Chou En-lai with Premier Ali Sastroamidjojo.

*Maps:* Western approaches to Asia. South and Southeast Asia and Colombo Plan. Communist thrusts, 1955–57, from Moscow and Peking.

*Appendix:* Asiatic groupings: Colombo Plan and SEATO.

50. TRAGER, FRANK N. ed. Marxism in Southeast Asia: A Study of Four Countries. With contributions by Jeanne S. Mintz, I. Milton Sacks, John Seabury Thomson, David A. Wilson. Stanford, Calif., Stanford University Press, 1959. 381 p.; bibliography, index.

DS518.1.T7

*Text:* "This study has a threefold purpose: to identify the nature of Marxism in selected countries of Southeast Asia; to determine its relationship, avowed and hidden, to indigenous and similar ideologies; and to relate these findings to current political processes and activities, domestic and international, in the selected countries."

Following the four chapters which analyze Marxism in Burma, Thailand, Vietnam, and Indonesia, a closing chapter gives a historical overview and judgment as to the impact of Marxism on the region.

*Bibliography:* Divided into three parts—books and government documents; articles in newspapers and periodicals; newspapers and periodicals.

51. U.S. CONGRESS. HOUSE. COMMITTEE ON FOREIGN AFFAIRS. Report of the Special Study Mission to Pakistan, India, Thailand, and Indochina; comprising Chester E. Menow, Walter H. Judd, A. S. J. Carnahan, Clement J. Zablocki of the Committee on Foreign Affairs pursuant to H. Res. 113, a resolution authorizing the Committee on Foreign Affairs to conduct thorough studies and investigations of all matters coming within the jurisdiction of such committee. Washington, U.S. Govt. Print. Office, 1955. xi, 104 p.; maps, appendices. (83d Congress, 1st session. House report no. 412)                    DS518.1.U52

*Text:* Sections 5 and 6, dealing with Thailand and Indochina, provide introductory statements on general background of the economic situation and minority problems, and then give detailed information on the military and economic assistance given by the United

States to these two countries under the administration of STEM (Special Technical and Economic Mission) and MAAG (Military Advisory Assistance Group). Section 7 on findings and recommendations discusses Communist aggression in Southeast Asia.

*Maps:* Outline maps of the countries included in survey.

*Appendices:* Economic and technical agreements between the U.S. and Thailand and Indochina.

52. U.S. Congress. House. Committee on Foreign Affairs. Special Study Mission to Southeast Asia and the Pacific. Report by Walter H. Judd, Marguerite Stitt Church, E. Ross Adair, and Clement J. Zablocki.. Washington, U.S. Govt. Printing Office, 1954. viii, 107 p.; maps, tables.     DS518.1.U53

*Text:* An official congressional report of a mission to Southeast Asia headed by Congressman Walter Judd which undertook a study of U.S. policies, programs, and problems in Southeast Asia. Although the purview covered the entire Pacific area, all of the countries of Southeast Asia were visited by the group, and their findings dealt with the political situation, the military situation, internal security, the foreign policy in each of the countries. A section on U.S. military and assistance asks these questions: If U.S. assistance were stopped or sharply curtailed, could the programs be continued by the local government, or have there been substantial benefits to the U.S. from the air programs? Where U.S. military assistance programs are conducted, inquiries were made into the performance of equipment, the recipient's cooperation, and contribution in building a mutual defense program.

Two closing chapters emphasize the importance that the U.S. information and exchange of persons programs in Southeast Asia. The closing conclusions state that the Communist danger cannot be overestimated.

*Maps:* A map of each country precedes the various sections.

*Table:* U.S. aid to the countries of Southeast Asia from 1945 to 1953.

53. U.S. Congress. House. Committee on Foreign Affairs. Special Study Mission to the Middle East, South and Southeast Asia, and Pacific. Report by Clement J. Zablocki, John Jarman, Robert C. Byrd, Walter H. Judd, Marguerite Stitt Church, E. Ross Adair.

Washington, U.S. Govt. Printing Office, 1956. ix, 213 pp. maps.     DS518.U54

*Text:* Among the 26 geographical sections are accounts of the countries of Southeast Asia which were visited by the congressional study mission: Burma, Thailand, Vietnam, Cambodia, Malaya, Indonesia, and the Philippines. The political conditions, the economic situation, U.S. aid, foreign policy, and other aspects are considered in each of these countries. A findings and conclusions chapter emphasize the need for technical and economic assistance to these countries to combat communism in the area.

*Maps:* Outline maps of the Southeast Asia countries showing principal cities and provinces.

54. U.S. Department of State. American Foreign Policy; Basic Documents, 1950–1955. Washington, U.S. Govt. Printing Office, 1957. 2 vols.; maps, diagrams, index. (Publication no. 6446, General foreign policy series, 117.)     JX1417.A55

*Text:* This volume is a successor to *A decade of American foreign policy; basic documents, 1941–49,* a compilation of basic documents brought together by the Division of Historical Policy Research of the Department of State and the staff of the Senate Committee on Foreign Relations. Divided into twenty parts with appropriate headings for the documents relating to various parts of the world, parts 4, 5, and 14 include documents pertaining to Southeast Asia.

Among the treaties, statements, and agreements relating to the Southeast Asia countries, there are documents on the summary, of the Bell Mission in the Philippines, 1950, part 14; Treaty between the U.S. and the Philippines, 1951–52 (part 5); the revised U.S.-Philippine Trade Agreement, 1955 (part 14); the Communist threat in Indochina, 1950–53 (part 14); the Geneva agreements on the cessation of hostilities in Vietnam, Cambodia and Laos, 1954 (parts 4 and 14); aid for Indochina following the Geneva Conference, 1954–55 (part 14); the Manila Pact and Seato, 1954 (parts 5 and 14); communique of the Bandung Conference, 1955 (part 14); resolution about KMT troops in Burma, 1954 (part 14).

*Maps:* Indochina.

*Diagrams:* Basic security treaties of the U.S., including Southeast Asia countries.

55. Vandenbosch, Amry, and Richard A. Butwell. Southeast Asia Among the World Powers. Lexington, University of Kentucky

Press, 1957. vi, 336 p.; bibliography, map, index. DS518.1.V28

*Text:* An introductory chapter emphasizes that for centuries the region of Southeast Asia was an outpost of world politics severed from the main arena of conflict in world politics, being subject mainly to the rivalry between the Western powers, but now the Western world has become conscious of Southeast Asia and its importance in world politics. The succeeding country chapters deal individually with the countries comprising the region, discussing the struggle for independence, political developments, internal security, population pressure, neutralism, foreign policy, Communist tactics, Chinese minority, and related topics. A closing chapter describes the approach of American foreign policy toward the countries of Southeast Asia.

Contents: 1. Southeast Asia: contemporary power vacuum. 2. Indonesia: restless insular empire. 3. The Philippines: showcase of Western democracy. 4. Indochina: gateway to Southeast Asia. 5. Thailand: diplomatic and political phenomenon. 6. Malaya: a problem in nation building. 7. Burma: land of contradictions. 8. The international relations of Southeast Asia. 9. American policy in Southeast Asia.

*Bibliography:* General references pertaining to the six countries of the region.

*Map:* A rough outline map of Southeast Asia.

56. VLUGT, EBED VAN DER. Asia Aflame: Communism in the East. Foreword by Albert C. Wedemeyer. New York, Devin-Adair, 1953. xvi, 294 p.; illustrations, maps, appendices, index. DS518.1.V54

*Text:* Describes the influence of political, economic, and psychosocial forces in the evolution of strategic Communist plans and ambitions throughout Asia.

Three chapters deal with segments of Southeast Asia: 5. The Red attack on Indochina. 8. The Red attack on Southeast Asia. 9. The Red attack on Indonesia. Selected topics discussed in these respective chapters include: Ho chi Minh as the soul of the Communist party in Vietnam: the Communist menace from China with designs to penetrate Southeast Asia; Soviet tactics employed in Southeast Asia; British difficulties in Malaya; Communism in Indonesia following World War II; the tragic mistakes of the West with regard to the real situation in Indonesia and the consequent strengthening of Communism in the entire area.

*Illustrations* (selected): Group of Asians, showing Tan Malaka of Indonesia and Ho chi Minh of Vietnam. Dr. Hatta, Roem and Sjarifuddin of Indonesia in group picture.

*Maps:* Japanese propaganda map proclaiming the Japanese Empire established in Asia. Principal products produced in Southeast Asia. Various Indonesian racial groups.

*Appendices* (selected): Social structure of Asiatic countries.

57. WADE, WILLIAM W. U.S. Policy in Asia. New York, H. W. Wilson, 1955. 191 p.; bibliography, map. (The reference shelf, vol. 27, no. 6) DS35.W3

*Text:* Recognizing that events in Asia can be closely related to the U.S., one of the most controversial subjects on the American political scene is U.S. foreign policy toward the countries of Asia. This volume brings together facts and opinions expressed in the debate by reproducing articles which have appeared in American periodicals and newspapers. Among the articles which touch Southeast Asia are these: U Nu and his watchful nation by Robert Sherrod; Thai politics by James Michener; Ngo dinh Diem of Vietnam; The emergency (Malaya) by Saul Padover; Indonesia's Communists by Peggy Durdin; Magsaysay, dynamic example for Asia by J. P. McEvoy.

*Bibliography:* Lists articles and books dealing with U.S. foreign policy.

*Map:* The arc of free Asia: population 771 million.

58. WALES, HORACE GEOFFREY QUARITCH. Ancient Southeast Asia Warfare. London, Bernard Quaritch, 1952. 206 p.; illustrations, index. W31.W3

*Text:* An account of methods used in the countries of Burma, Thailand, Indonesia, and Malaya in ancient times. This study of the art of warfare reveals aspects of the national character and of the civilization which differ from those characteristics that find expression in the arts of peace, and thus an understanding of the peoples of Southeast Asia is broadened.

The historical references and citations in the text to wars between Burma, Siam, and other countries are incidental to the main subjects of methods employed in military conflict.

*Illustrations:* Plans of battle arrays.

59. WALES, HORACE GOEFFREY QUARITCH. The Making of Greater India. 2d ed. rev. and enl. London, Quaritch, 1961. 246 p.; illustrations, appendix, index. DS509.W3 1961

*Text:* This study deals with the process of acculturation of Indic cultural values in Southeast Asia. Gives consideration to the problem that, despite the successive Indic influence and other influences, the cultures of Java and Cambodia retained a distinctive character and were never just incongruous admixtures but are usually recognized as Indo-Javanese, Cham, or Khmer.

*Illustrations:* Khmer sanctuary of Wat Phu, Indochina. Megalithic sanctuary on Yang plateau, Java.

*Appendix:* The problem of Pre-Angkorian architecture.

60. WILLIAMS, LEA E. Overseas Chinese Nationalism; the Genesis of the Pan-Chinese Movement in Indonesia, 1900–1916. Glencoe, Ill., Free Press, 1960. xiv, 235 p.; bibliography, glossary, index. (Copyright by The Center for International Studies, Massachusetts Institute of Technology) DS632.C5W5

*Text:* Discusses the reasons why the Chinese resident in Indonesia, at first lacking cohesion and being politically inarticulate, eventually controlled an active political force in Indonesia and shared in the development of a vigorous nationalism. Such achievement came about through Chinese organizational skill and leadership of the nationalist movement. The study focuses attention on the efforts of the leaders of the overseas Chinese community in Indonesia to mobilize their people for Indonesian nationalism. Among the elements which the author gives as a reason for this success for nationalist mobilization is that of its "separateness" as a distinct population group. Without their separateness as a substantial base on which to develop nationalism, no Chinese nationalist movement would have evolved.

*Bibliography:* Includes titles of primary sources and secondary monographs and articles relating to Indonesia in the General State Archives and other Dutch government offices in The Hague.

*Glossary:* Dutch and Indonesia terms used in the text.

61. WINT, GUY. The British in Asia. London, Faber and Faber, 1954. 244 p.; index.
DS35.W56 1954

*Text:* Purposes to set down the historical events which happened during the period of British domination of certain countries of South Asia and Southeast Asia—principally India, but also Burma and Malaya—showing what impact took place on the politics, social organization, and to the temper of the mind in these countries. This historical survey of British power in Asia of part one includes chapters on: Traditional Burma; The British in Burma; Malaya; and The British Oriental civilization—which chapter discusses the features that influenced strongly the older societies in the British colonies.

Part two compares the Russian Empire in Asia with the British Empire in Asia. The emphasis is on the fact that the idea of communism was invented to have a rival appeal to nationalism as it arose in the countries of Asia.

Part three is an inquiry into what have been the consequences of the withdrawal of British power from Asia, and how the countries of India, Ceylon, Burma and Malaya have prospered after the British exodus.

## ECONOMICS
(including: Agriculture, Commerce, Industry, and Labor)

62. CONFERENCE ON AMERICAN TRADE WITH ASIA AND THE FAR EAST, INSTITUTE FOR ASIAN STUDIES, MARQUETTE UNIVERSITY, 1958. American Trade with Asia and the Far East. Robert J. Barr, editor. Milwaukee, Marquette University Press, 1959. xix, 317 p.; bibliographical references. (Marquette Asian studies, I) HF3119.C57 1958

*Text:* This volume is the first in a series, Marquette Asian Studies, published by the Institute for Asian Studies at Marquette University. The symposium consisting of 22 papers delivered at the Conference on American Trade with Asia and the Far East, explores the factors influencing the nature and volume of U.S. trade with the Asian countries. Three papers provide an analysis of American trade with three countries of Southeast Asia: American trade with the Philippines by Reed Irvine; Prospects for American trade with Indonesia by Douglas Paauw; and Trade and investment possibilities in Thailand by Ambassador Thanat Khoman.

63. *Far Eastern economic review; 1962 yearbook.* Hongkong, Far Eastern Economic Review, Ltd., 1961. 224 p.; illustrations, tables, appendices. HC411.F19

*Text:* Issued annually by the firm which publishes the weekly *Far Eastern economic review,* it provides a comprehensive review with reasonable detail of the economic development of 28 countries in Eastern Asia—

including everyone of the 13 countries of Southeast Asia—during the calendar year 1961, with prospects for 1962.

Opening with a review of the whole region, the principal trends and highlights which emerged during the year are discussed briefly. The main body of the survey comprises individual country reports, divided into seven standard sections: politics, economy, finance, trade, agriculture, industry, and power and transport. All of these sections, except the first, are packed with statistics and are said to be fairly up to date.

*Illustrations:* Heads of State in most Southeast Asia countries.

*Tables:* For many of the countries these statistical tables are provided: monthly economic indicators, foreign trade, industrial output, budget estimates.

*Appendices:* Currency conversion table. Index to advertisers.

64. FROEHLICH, WALTER, ed. Land Tenure, Industrialization and Social Stability; Experience and Prospects in Asia. Milwaukee, Marquette University Press, 1961. xv, 301 p. (Marquette Asian studies, II). HD856.F7

*Text:* This second volume of the Marquette Studies consist of the papers presented at an economic conference at Marquette University sponsored by the Institute for Asian Studies and the Department of Economics.

The symposium is an inquiry into the problem of land tenure and its relation to economic, political and cultural change confronting the economics of Asian nations.

The countries of Southeast Asia are considered in Chapter IV, Land reform and development in Southeast Asia, with these papers: Land reform and development in the Philippines by Hugh Cook; An economic development oriented land reform program for Vietnam by Richard Lindholm; Agricultural problems in the economy of Thailand by Paul Ellsworth; and Public policies, land tenure and population movements by Widjojo Nitisastro—this last paper pertains to Indonesia.

65. JACOBY, ERICH H. Agrarian Unrest in Southeast Asia. 2d ed. New York, Asia Publishing House, 1961. 279 p.; bibliography, maps, index. HD865.J3

*Text:* Presents an analysis of the multiple effects of economic dependence of those countries of Southeast Asia which have had to undergo colonial domination during the past century, and emphasizes the economic dislocation underlying the various forms of local discontent among the 150 million peoples of the region who are largely engaged in agricultural pursuits. Within each of the chapters dealing with the different countries, the foci of interest are: trends in population, land utilization, indebtedness, foreign investments, methods of agricultural cultivation, and related topics. The thesis of the closing chapter, Agrarian unrest and national movements, states that the movements for independence are deeply rooted in the basic economic and social conditions of the farming population. Well documented throughout.

*Bibliography:* Includes the titles of books and articles used in the text.

*Maps:* Southeastern Asia. Population density. Burma. Malay States. Indochina. The Philippines, northern and central islands. Siam.

66. JORDON, AMOS A. Foreign Aid and the Defense of Southeast Asia. With a foreword by William H. Draper. New York, Praeger, 1962. xvi, 272 p.; bibliography, maps, tables, charts, index. HC412.J63

*Text:* Written originally as a thesis at Columbia University under the title *Foreign aid and defense; United States military and related economic assistance to Southeast Asia,* this study analyzes how American military and economic aid programs are developed, administered and coordinated in foreign countries. Although seven countries are discussed—Pakistan, South Vietnam, Thailand, Cambodia, Laos, Taiwan, and the Philippines—concentration is directed to the two large scale recipients of American military and economic aid: Pakistan and South Vietnam. Besides detailed discussions of various types of military forces as deterrents to war in Southeast Asia, foreign exchange and export-import difficulties are exposed.

*Bibliography:* Long list of primary and secondary literature in the assistance field, including Mutual Security Program congressional hearings, Draper Committee reports, and staff papers.

*Maps* (selected): Threat of overt aggression against South Vietnam. American aid and defense facilities in Thailand.

*Tables* (selected): 1. U.S. assistance programs. 3. Key economic and defense indicators. 8. U.S. aid-mission personnel strengths in Southeast Asia.

*Charts* (selected): MAAG in South Vietnam. US-OM in South Vietnam.

67. MADAN, BALKRISHNA, ed. Economic Problems of Underdeveloped Countries in Asia. New Delhi, Indian Council of World Affairs, 1953. iv, 290 p.; tables, index.     HC412.M33

*Text:* The papers given at a symposium by scholars from various countries of Asia addressed to various economic problems being faced by the peoples of Asia: low standard living, poverty, malnutrition, inadequate medical facilities, high illiteracy, population increase and other problems.

These chapters provide data on Southeast Asia: Economic development in Burma by U That Tun; Economic development of Malaya by S. Nanjundan; Thailand, a developing economy by Joseph Gould; Philippine economic problems, progress and programmes by Salvador Araneto; and Economic problems in Indonesia and our way out by Sumitro Djoajhadikusumo.

*Tables:* Utilization of cultivated area, Malaya. Malaya's foreign trade by commodities. National income of Malaya, 1950. Thailand's national income, 1950. Budgets of the government of Thailand, 1950–52. Thailand's balance of trade, 1946–51. Thailand's international transactions, 1951. National income, 1950, Indonesia.

68. THOMPSON, VIRGINIA. Labor Problems in Southeast Asia. New Haven, Yale University Press; London, Oxford University Press, 1947. xviii, 283 p.; tables, index. (Published under the auspices of the International Secretariat, Institute of Pacific Relations)
HD8666.T456

*Text:* A survey of labor supply, labor organization, and postwar labor developments in Burma, Thailand, Indochina, Malaya, and Indonesia. Presents data on labor in each of these countries under these topics: general labor conditions; types of labor—agricultural, handicrafts, industrial, immigrant labor, forced labor; working conditions—wages, hours of work; health and safety regulations; workmen's compensation; housing; women and children; labor legislation; organized labor movement; postwar labor developments. Provides a synthesis of the labor laws and of the problems confronting the administration, management, and workers in dealing with the social revolution which manifested itself during the colonial period and will become more acute as the population expands.

Emphasizes the two major labor problems: (1) the unsatisfactory status of labor supply—with particular reference to modern production in industry where labor efficiency was law and the availability of the skilled mechanical worker was uncertain; (2) the ineffective labor movement as characterized by the seasonal character of much of the employment, labor migration, and the racial diversity of the labor force.

*Tables:* Factories and factory employees in Burma. Cottage industries in Burma. Incomes of Indonesian industrial workers. Strikes in Indonesia. Average daily wages of miners and factory workers in Indochina. Types of labor in Thailand. Unemployment in Thailand.

## SOCIAL CONDITIONS
(including: Anthropology, Education, and Health)

69. DU BOIS, CORA. Social Forces in Southeast Asia. St. Paul, University of Minnesota Press, 1949. 78 p.; map.     HN666.D8

*Text:* Presents certain significant observations and interpretations of the cultural changes which were set into motion within the countries of Southeast Asia by both the colonizers from the West and the Chinese immigrants. Characterizes the nature of cultural integration in the region before the time of intensive European colonialism and shows that integration was shaken by the philosophies of social humanism, nationalism, and Marxism. Maintains that the economic reintegration of Southeast Asian cultures will undoubtedly be in the direction of State socialism. Suggests that the Asiatic nation which would come to the front and take the leadership of Southeast Asia within the next decade will have to display its ability to lend genuine, economic assistance in competition with European countries.

Comprises three lectures delivered at Smith College in April 1947.

70. EELLS, WALTER CROSBY. Communism in Education in Asia, Africa, and the Far Pacific. Washington, American Council on Education, 1954. x, 246 p.; appendices, index.
LA133.E37

*Text:* Based upon firsthand conferences with representative educators in the various countries and upon current publications having educational data, the presentation shows how communism has infiltrated the field of education in all of the non-Communist countries of Asia. The Southeast Asia countries observed are: Singapore, Malaya, Thailand, Indochina, Burma, Philippines, and Indonesia—discussed in chapters three and four.

*Appendices* (selected): B. Foreign students in the United States from Asia. C. Participants under Fulbright and Smith-Mundt Acts from Asia.

71. LASKER, BRUNO. Human Bondage in Southeast Asia. Chapel Hill, University of North Carolina Press, 1950. 406 p.; bibliographical notes, appendices, index. (Published under the auspices of the Institute of Pacific Relations.)
HD4871.L3

*Text:* The key question to which the author addresses himself is: What part has human bondage played in the social development of Southeast Asia, and to what extent does its remnants and memories color present conditions and attitudes? Explores the lack of freedom from which these peoples have suffered, not only under colonial rule, but also just as much under that of their own princes, ruling families, and privileged classes. One of the few books to provide an essential background study of human bondage or servitude in its diverse forms, from which springs the motive power of the recent uprisings in Southeast Asia.

Detailed information is given on the continuance of slavery in a world where that institution has been legally abolished.

*Bibliography:* Bibliographical notes, arranged in chapter sequence, extend to 52 pages.

*Appendices:* Lengthy quotations from important sources dealing with slavery and labor problems.

72. MURDOCK, GEORGE PETER. Social Structure in Southeast Asia. Chicago, Quadrangle Books; London, Tabistock Publications, 1960. ix, 182 p.; bibliography, maps, tables, charts, index. (Viking Fund publications in anthropology. no. 29)
DS509.5.M8

*Text:* Comprised of papers delivered at a symposium on social structure in Southeast Asia held at the Ninth Pacific Science Congress in Bangkok, Thailand, in 1957. The analytic and descriptive studies presented cover thirteen separate social systems, including the patrilineal, the matrilineal, and the general type.

The subject matter related to Southeast Asia is presented in these chapters: Cognatic forms of social or-

ganization by George Murdock; The Mnong Gar of Central Vietnam by Georges Condominas; The Sagada Igorots of northern Luzon by Fred Eggan; The Eastern Subanun of Mindanao by Charles Frake; The Iban of Western Borneo by J. D. Freeman; The Javanese of south central Java by R. M. Koentjaraningrat.

*Bibliography:* Listing of fairly recent monographs and periodical articles on the anthropology of Southeast Asia.

73. SIMONIYA, N. A. Overseas Chinese in Southeast Asia: A Russian Study. Translated by U.S. Joint Publications Research Service. Ithaca, Southeast Asia Program, Department of Far Eastern Studies, Cornell University, 1961. iii, 151 p.; bibliography, tables. (Data paper no. 45)
DS509.5.S473

*Text:* This analyzes the role of ethnic Chinese in the economy of the Southeast Asian countries by a Russian writer who "unmasks the imperialist policy of opposition to the national minorities of the countries of Southeast Asia and the sowing of seeds of dissension among them, and also various bourgeois 'theories' related to this problem. The work points out the discriminatory policy of the reactionary governments of Thailand, South Vietnam and the Philippines vis-a-vis the Chinese population of these countries."

The three chapters are: 1. The historic roots of Chinese emigration and the general characteristics of the Chinese population in the countries of Southeast Asia. 2. The role of the Chinese bourgeoisie in the economic development of the Southeast Asian countries. 3. The role of the Chinese working class in the economic life of Southeast Asia.

*Bibliography:* Extensive footnotes to each chapter, and a list of Russian and English monographs and periodical articles.

*Tables* (selected): Number of Chinese in Southeast Asian countries. Population growth of the Malay Federation, 1931–56. Growth of Chinese population in Indonesia, 1860–1930. Growth of Chinese population in Thailand, 1825–1955. Malayans, Chinese and Indians employed in basic industries of the Malayan Federation, 1955.

74. THOMPSON, VIRGINIA, and RICHARD ADLOFF. Cultural Institutions and Educational Policy in Southeast Asia. New York, International Secretariat, Institute of Pacific Relations, 1948.

xii, 86 p. (Issued in cooperation with the Southeast Asia Institute and the Far Eastern Association) LA1141.T57

*Text:* Presents in an orderly manner data on primary education, secondary education, higher education, vocational and technical education, private schools, Chinese schools, adult education, the status of teachers, and educational problems as found in Burma, Thailand, Indonesia, Indochina, and Malaya. Under cultural activities, information is given about libraries, museums, cultural societies, and allied bodies.

75. THOMPSON, VIRGINIA, and RICHARD ADLOFF. Minority Problems in Southeast Asia. Stanford, Stanford University Press, 1955. viii, 295 p.; bibliography, index. DS509.5.T45

*Text:* The strategically placed, potentially disruptive, and possibly subversive ethnic minorities in the countries of Southeast Asia form the subject of this study. The two principal groups it considers are the immigrant peoples whose mother countries border the countries of Southeast Asia—the Chinese and the Indians.

Chapter one deals with Peking's attitude toward the Chinese in Southeast Asia, Peking's relations with Southeast Asian governments, the policies of the governments of Southeast Asia in regard to China, and the problems of population, the economy, education, and citizenship, as they pertain to the Chinese communities in each of the countries of Southeast Asia.

Chapter two, concerned with the Indian residents in Southeast Asia, presents data about their political activities, their work in banking, trade, industry, and labor, their cultural activities, and social welfare, and the intergovernmental relations between each of the Southeast Asian countries and India.

The second half of the volume surveys the indigenous minorities of Southeast Asia, including the Arakanese in Burma, the Malays of South Thailand, the Ambonese in Indonesia, and the Eurasians who are scattered throughout the regions.

A chapter entitled Buddhist vs. Buddhists shows clearly how closely intermeshed are politics and religion. This portion includes a discussion of the Viet Minh, the Issarak, and the Pathet Lao.

There is, finally, a brief report of the Christian minorities in Southeast Asia, and of the part played there by the Christian missions since the seventeenth century.

*Bibliography:* Brief list of secondary sources, and periodical titles.

# CULTURAL LIFE
(including: Fine Arts, Language, Literature, and Religion)

76. BERVAL, RENÉ DE, ed. "Présence du bouddhisme." *France-Asie*, Fev-Juin, 1959, nos. 153–157: 181–1024; bibliography, illustrations, maps, tables, glossary. DS1.F7 1959

*Text:* This voluminous compilation, which has been issued as a single volume from five consecutive issues of *France-Asie*, deals with many aspects of the Buddhist faith as found in all of the Buddhist countries of Asia.

Following introductory statements by Paul Mus, Giuseppe Tucci, and others, the study is divided into numerous sections which include these selected chapters pertaining especially to Southeast Asia: Gotama the Buddha by G. F. Allen; La doctrine du Kamma by Narada Mahathera; The meaning of orthodoxy in Buddhism, a protest by Bhikshu Sangharakshita; The fundamental principles of Mahayanism by Nalinaksha Dutt; The concept of freedom in the Pali canon by I. B. Horner; Asoka et l'expansion bouddhique by Jean Filliozat; Les Jâtaka et la littèrature de l'Indochine bouddhique by Ginette Terral-Martini; L'assistance médicale au Cambodge au XIIᵉ siecle by George Coedès; Buddhist trends and perspectives in Asia by Richard Gard; Expansion du bouddhisme en Asie by René de Berval; Introduction du bouddhisme au Vietnam by Maurice Durand; Le Bouddhisme au Vietnam by Mai tho Truyên; Le Bouddhisme en Endonésie by Louis-Charles Damais; Buddhism in Burma by U Hla Maung; Le Bouddhisme au Cambodge Panj Khat; Introduction de bouddhisme au Laos by P. B. Lafont; Le littérature bouddhique lal by Phouvong Phimmasone; Buddhism in Siam by Karuna Kusalasaya.

*Bibliography:* An extensive list of 44 pages giving references on these Buddhist subjects: The Buddah and Buddhisms; Pali and Sanskrit texts; Buddhist literature; Rites and rituals; Philosophy; Art and architectures; Buddhism in the various Southeast Asia countries; Dictionaries; and Manuscripts.

*Illustrations:* Among the more than 100 shown, these types are included—Buddhist images; Angkor Wat; Buddhist ceremonies; frescoes and paintings; temples; priests.

*Maps:* Religions in Asia. Itineraries of the Buddha. Buddhism in Asia.

*Tables:* Buddhist monuments.

*Glossary:* Buddhist terms with definitions.

77. CONGRESS FOR CULTURAL FREEDOM, Rangoon, 1955. Cultural Freedom in Asia. The proceedings of a conference held at Rangoon, Burma, on February 17, 18, 19 and 20, 1955, and convened by the Congress for Cultural Freedom and the Society for the Extension of Democratic Ideals. Tokyo, Rutland, Vt., Published for the Congress for Cultural Freedom by the C. E. Tuttle Co., 1956. 296 p.; illustrations, appendix.　　DS12.C63 1955

*Text:* Presents the more than 26 papers given by delegates to the Congress for Cultural Freedom held in Rangoon who came from many of the countries of Southeast Asia and Eastern Asia.

Divided into two principal parts. Part one, entitled The Condition of Cultural Freedom in Asia—a Review, includes these chapters relating to Southeast Asia: Resurgent Asia, a comprehensive view; The Filipino resurgence; The vitality of religion in Asia; Philippine music and contemporary aesthetics. Part two, The Problems of Cultural Freedom in Asia, includes these among the chapters: Colonialism and racial conflict; Colonialism and international cooperation in Asia; Freedom and economic planning; The economic development of Southeast Asia; Cultural minorities in Burma; Totalitarian threats to cultural freedom in Asia, an inventory.

*Illustrations:* Delegates from Burma, Indonesia, Laos, Pakistan, India, and other countries.

*Appendix:* List of the 34 delegates.

78. The East and West Must Meet; a Symposium. With an introduction by Benjamin Houston Brown. East Lansing, Michigan State University Press, 1959. ix, 134 p.
　　CB251.E17 1959

*Text:* A series of lectures delivered before the Cleveland Council on World Affairs in 1958, with the purpose of providing the people of one midwestern American city with a deeper awareness and understanding of Asian problems. Presents an examination of East-West relations in the broadest sense and considers what might be done to lower the barriers to understanding and cooperation.

Chapters: The cultural interplay between East and West by Cora Du Bois. The interplay of governments by John Sherman Cooper. Interplay between East and West: an Asian view by Ali Sastroamidjojo. The cultural interdependence of East and West. The inter-

play of East and West in philosophy and religion by Kenneth Morgan. Asian understanding—the citizen's responsibility by John D. Rockefeller III. Rival economic theories in India by John Kenneth Galbraith. A summing up by Barbara Ward.

79. INTERNATIONAL MISSIONARY COUNCIL. The Christian Prospect in Eastern Asia: Papers and Minutes of the Eastern Asia Christian Conference, Bangkok, December 3–11, 1949. New York, Friendship Press, for the International Missionary Council and the World Council of Churches, 1950. iv, 156 p.; appendix.　　BV3400.E3 1949

*Text:* This conference of 45 delegates from the countries of Southeast Asia and Eastern Asia, held under the joint auspices of the World Council of Churches and the International Missionary Council, is the first Asian conference of this type ever to be held.

Divided into four main parts. Section I. The contemporary situation, presents a picture of the way in which the Christian churches in Asia view the social, religious, and to a degree the political forces in their individual countries and the effect on the Christian Church. The country papers on Southeast Asia include Burma, Indonesia, Malaya, Philippines, and Thailand. The other sections are: II. The Christian challenge. III. The Bangkok conference speaks. IV. The minutes of the Eastern Christian Conference.

*Appendix:* Who's Who of the Conference.

80. LANDON, KENNETH PERRY. Southeast Asia, Crossroad of Religions. Chicago, University of Chicago Press, 1949. ix, 215 p.; bibliography, index.　　BL2050.L3

*Text:* Comprises the Haskell Lectures in Comparative Religion delivered at the University of Chicago in 1947. Two significant threads appear in the study; namely, (1) the developments and changes which issued in the different countries when Buddhism, Islam, and Confucianism made a lasting impact on the ways and the customs of the respective peoples they touched; and (2) notwithstanding the fact that the Burmans and the Siamese are devotees of the Buddha, while the Javanese and Malays are followers of Mohammed, a synthesis has taken place over the centuries whereby certain practices and beliefs of these regions have been recast and integrated with the ancient ceremonies and beliefs of the peoples of Southeast Asia. The final chapter, Westernization and modern trends in Southeast Asia, relates the acculturation which has taken place in Southeast Asia through the influence of missionaries, merchants, and colonial administrators from the West as well as by Westernized, indigenous persons.

*Bibliography:* Includes about 200 items dealing with history, literature, religion, and arts of the Southeast Asia countries.

81. LE MAY, REGINALD STUART. The Culture of Southeast Asia: The Heritage of India. Foreword by R. A. Butler. London, Allen and Unwin, 1954. 218 p.; bibliography, illustrations, maps, index. DS511.L4

*Text:* Describes the forces which have molded the culture of Southeast Asia, giving particular reference to the underlying principles of Buddhist and Hindu culture which came from India.

Following the introductory chapter giving a general survey of the beginnings of Indian colonization eastward from India, the succeeding chapters treat the planting of Indian culture in Burma, Thailand, Indonesia, Cambodia and other places, and how the fusion of the Indian and local genius is revealed in religious objects.

*Bibliography:* Lists books and articles dealing with art, sculpture, temples in the countries of Southeast Asia.

*Illustrations:* Over 200 pictures showing Angkor Wat, Borobodur, and temples and images in the various countries.

*Maps:* Relations and sea routes between India and Southeast Asia.

82. MORGAN, KENNETH W. The Path of the Buddha; Buddhism Interpreted by Buddhists. New York, Ronald Press, 1956. x, 432 p.; bibliography, map, glossary, index.
BL1420.M6

*Text:* This volume, one of a series initiated by the National Council on Religion in Higher Education to promote better understanding of non-Christian religions, presents an account of Buddhism in the words of leading Buddhists in various Buddhist countries of Asia. The presentation is not a study in comparative religion but a straightforward presentation of the life and teachings of the Buddha, the spread and development of Buddhism during the past 2,500 years, and the beliefs, attitudes, and religious practices of Buddhists

in Southern Asia including Burma, Thailand, and Cambodia.

The various writers depict graphically the daily life of the monks, the techniques of Buddhist meditations, popular customs and traditions at religious shrines, Buddhist art and scriptures, and many other aspects of that religious faith. The wide variations in Buddhist theory and practice as found in the various sects are also related.

*Bibliography:* Besides including general secondary works on the two branches of Theravada and Mahayana Buddhism, translations of Buddhist writings are listed.

*Map:* The Buddhist world.

*Glossary:* Includes many of the principal terms in Buddhism, and, although it does not intend to be exhaustive, will aid the student who is beginning his study of Buddhism.

83. THOMAS, WINBURN T., and RALPH B. MANIKAM. The Church in Southeast Asia. With an introduction by Frank T. Cartwright. New York, Friendship Press, 1956. xvi, 171 p.; bibliography, map. BR1178.T45

*Text:* Provides a reliable summary account of the Christian movement in the various countries of Southeast Asia, with particular attention to the way in which the managerial responsibility and authority have passed from the hands of Westerners to the nationals of the countries.

*Bibliography:* A few general books with particular reference to Christian missions in Southeast Asia.

*Map:* Topographical map of Southeast Asia.

84. WALES, HORACE GEOFFREY QUARITCH. Prehistory and Religion in Southeast Asia. London, Bernard Quaritch, 1957. 180 p.; bibliography, illustrations, index. GN851.W3

*Text:* Shows how the prehistoric cultures of Southeast Asia have affected the development of religion in the region. It is an attempt at reconstruction of the earlier religious phases in Southeast Asia as it was practiced during the Palaeolithic, the Neolithic and the Bronze Age.

*Bibliography:* Bibliographical footnotes.

*Illustrations:* Pen sketches of sacrificial altars, drums, temples, and other items used in worship.

**85.** YALE UNIVERSITY. SOUTHEAST ASIA STUDIES. Ethnic Groups of Northern Southeast Asia. New Haven, Connecticut, 1950. iii, 175 p.; bibliographical references, map, tables, index.

DS509.2.Y2

*Text:* Presents information about the principal ethnic groups living in the northern parts of Burma, Thailand, Indochina, and the southern part of China. The classification of the various racial groups is based primarily on linguistic affiliations, but in some instances other cultural criteria are used to identify the people—all of which are readily found in the alphabetical name index. As far as possible, data provided about each ethnic group deals with location—giving general regional distribution and ethnic affiliation; population; village sites—*i.e.,* topographical location; economy—as to subsistence base and degree of dependence on trade and on outside groups; language—stating the major linguistic stock to which the tribal language belongs, and any significant dialectical relationships; religion—as to affiliation with a world religion, and data on types of animistic beliefs; contacts—*i.e.,* degree and kind of relationship with and attitudes toward neighboring racial groups; and names—*i.e.,* the terms used to identify the group, both by members of the groups and by others outside of the group. A brief introductory statement precedes each of the four major sections of the study.

*Bibliography:* Bibliographical references conclude each major section of the text.

*Map:* Ethnic groups of northern Southeast Asia (color), scale–1:2,500,000, showing the major ethnolinguistic groups and the minor population groups.

*Tables:* List proper names of the numerous racial groups discussed.

# II

# Burma

## GENERAL BACKGROUND

86. BURMA (UNION). ECONOMIC AND SOCIAL BOARD. Pyidawtha, the New Burma. A report from the government to the people of the Union of Burma on our long-term programme for economic and social development. Rangoon, 1954. 128 p.; illustrations, map, tables, charts.  HC437.B8A52

*Text:* An official report outlining the basic findings in an intensive study of Burma's resources, present and potential, needed for the economic and social development of independent Burma. This development program, designed to extend for at least six years, included these major fields: agriculture, forestry and fishing, transportation, telecommunications, power development, minerals, industrial development, small scale industries, health, education, housing, and social welfare—all of which are discussed in brief chapters.

*Illustrations:* Typical scenes which show how the development program is being carried out in the various segments.

*Maps:* Colored maps showing railways, highways, power projects, mines, oil fields, and irrigation projects.

*Tables* (selected): National production and consumption. Irrigation.

*Charts* (selected): Major fields of economic development. International trade. Land resources. Agricultural production. Industrial program.

87. FERRARS, MAX, and BERTHA FERRARS. Burma. London, Sampson Low, Marston, 1900. xii, 237 p.; illustrations, map, appendices, index.  DS485.B81F3

*Text:* Although published in 1900, a one-volume work unsurpassed as a pictorial representation of Burmese social life and customs. The textual account is vivid in its description of Buddhist monastic life, religious orders and worship, agriculture, home industry, children's games, the drama, music, festivals, the village system, various social groups, Burmese royalty, and British administration. Would serve as a companion volume to *The Burman: his life and notions* by Shway Yoe [Sir James George Scott]. Transliterated Burmese terminology used profusely throughout the text and included in the index.

*Illustrations:* Excellent photography illustrating customs, religious festivals, religious practices, industries, handicrafts, racial groups, domestic life, and numerous other topics.

*Map:* Burma and adjacent countries, showing ancient settlements and shrines.

*Appendices:* Chronology of Burma. Structure of the Burmese language. Notes on Burmese music. Statistical data on population, crime, and trade. Burmese measures of time, length, capacity, weight, and money. Specimens of Burmese music.

88. SCOTT, SIR JAMES GEORGE. Burma; a Handbook of Practical Information. 3d ed. rev. London, Alexander Moring, 1921. x, 536 p.; bibliography, illustrations, map, appendices.  DS485.B81S28

*Text:* An exceptionally well-organized handbook divided into seven parts: The country and climate; Government; Industries; Archeology, architecture, art, music; Religion; Language and literature; and Hints to visitors or new residents—which in turn include the chapters: Geology and minerals; The races of Burma; Education; The forests of Burma; Mines; Agriculture; Trade; Transport; Currency; Art—sculpture, wood carving; and Buddhism.

*Bibliography:* Includes a number of references on the early history of Burma.

*Illustrations:* Depict religious shrines; racial groups; types of dwellings, and scenes of the country.

*Map:* Political divisions in Upper and Lower Burma.

*Appendices:* Divisions and districts of Burma; The Shan States; List of the commoner beasts, birds, reptiles, smaller fishes; List of common trees, shrubs, plants, grasses, flowers.

89. SCOTT, SIR JAMES GEORGE, and J. P. HARDIMAN. Gazetteer of Upper Burma and the Shan States. Rangoon, Govt. Printing, 1900–1901. 3 vols. in 5; illustrations, maps, glossaries, and vocabularies, indices. DS485.B8S4

*Text:* An indispensable reference work presenting facts about Burma during the regime of the Burmese kings and the early years of British administration. First two volumes contain information on physical geography, Burmese history during the reigns of King Mindon and King Thibaw, causes for the Third Anglo-Burmese War, Shan States, Kachin hills, Chin hills, Burmese palace customs, geology and economic mineralogy, revenue administration, population and trade, and government and administration under the Burmese kings. Last three volumes comprise a descriptive gazetteer of places in Upper Burma. Burmese and Shan script used throughout the text.

*Illustrations:* Pictures of Shan, Chingpaw (Kachin), Chin, Wa, Akha, Karenni, Palaung, and other racial groups; mode of dress; handicrafts, plan of Mandalay Palace and buildings; and scenes throughout Upper Burma.

*Map:* Upper Burma to accompany the gazetteer.

*Language:* Comparative vocabularies of Shan, Lahu, Chingpaw, Wa, Lisu, and other languages of tribal groups in Upper Burma—in Pt. I, Vol. 1. Glossary of Burmese words—in Pt. I, Vol. 2 and Pt. II, vol. 3.

90. TINKER, HUGH. The Union of Burma; a Study of the First Years of Independence. 3d ed. London, New York, Toronto, Oxford University Press, 1961. xv, 424 p.; bibliography, maps, tables, glossary, appendix, index. (Issued under the auspices of the Royal Institute of International Affairs)
DS485.B81T52 1961

*Text:* This study brings together the historical and social aspects which have developed in Burma during the postwar years, as observed and interpreted by a teacher at the School of Oriental and African Studies at the University of London. The account reflects the considerable degree of social change and disintegration in Burma as an aftermath of World War II, the continuing civil war, and the Chinese nationalist (KMT) invasion. As a historian, the author presents an orderly sequence of the principal developments in Burma during the postwar period. In describing the Pyidawtha (Welfare State) plan for social, cultural, economic, and political development

of the new Burma, he presents individual chapters dealing with religion, education, agriculture, trade, defense, and foreign relations.

*Bibliography:* Besides the secondary sources of a general nature, official publications issued since independence are listed.

*Maps:* Civil war in Burma: rebels, 1949. Civil war in Burma: KMT, 1953. Union of Burma, political divisions. Burma, economic development up to 1955.

*Tables* (selected): Government income and expenditure, 1949–54. Schools, teachers, pupils, 1952–55. Rice production, 1938–49. Rice, world allocation, 1946–49. Rice sales, 1949–54. Trade unions, 1946–52.

*Glossary:* Meanings of Burmese words used in the text.

*Appendix:* Twelve pages provide short biographical sketches of men and women prominent in various fields in Burma.

91. TRAGER, FRANK N. ed. Burma. Editor: Frank N. Trager. Assistant editor: Janet Welsh. Copy editor: S. Bernard Thomas. Chief bibliographer: John K. Musgrave, Jr. Cartographer: Robert S. Huke. New Haven, Printed by Human Relations Area Files, Inc., [1956]. 3 vols., maps, table. (Human Relations Area Files, Inc. Subcontractor's monograph, HRAF 37) DS485.B81T68

*Text:* Brings together a wealth of basic information on most aspects of Burma as presented in 29 chapters. Selected chapters include: 1. Historical setting. 2. The character of society. 4. Social structure and social values. 5. Religion. 8. Education. 10. The languages of Burma. 17. The Constitution and government. 19. Labor movement. 21. Why the insurrection failed. 22. Foreign policy. 23. Planning for economic development. 24. Agricultural development. 25. Industrial development. 26. Domestic and foreign trade.

*Maps:* 22 maps depict land reform, rainfall patterns, population growth, distribution of racial groups, Sino-Burmese boundary, transportation, mineral reserves and other topics.

*Tables* (selected): Exports by country. Rice export trade. Timber export trade. Distribution of labor. Factories and employment. Sources of organized credit. Budgeted expenditures and government.

# HISTORY, POLITICS, AND GOVERNMENT

92. ALLIED FORCES. SOUTHEAST ASIA COMMAND. Report to the Combined Chiefs of Staff by the Supreme Allied Commander Southeast Asia, 1943–1945, Vice-Admiral The Earl Mountbatten of Burma. London, H. M. Stationery Office, 1951. xi, 280 p.; maps, charts, appendices. D767.6.A53 1951

*Text:* A detailed introduction relates the way in which the Southeast Asia Command was formulated at the Quebec Conference in the spring of 1943, defines the boundary of China-Burma-India theater, the functions and responsibilities of the Commanders-in-Chief, the organization for planning, lines of communications, and supply bases, disposition of naval, land, and air forces, and strength of Japanese forces.

The strategy and operations which took place from October 1943 through September 1945 are intimately related with numerous colored maps showing troop movements.

The third section on civil affairs in Burma discusses the Allied Military Administration which was in control, food shortage, inflation, price controls, restoration of the educational system, organization of the Burma National Army, and the transfer of administrative departments.

*Maps* (selected): 1. Boundaries of SEA Command. 6. Malarial zones of Burma and Assam. 11, 12 and 13. Attempted invasion of India. 20. Japanese lines of communications with Burma. 21. Strategic air targets in SEA Command. 27. Ledo Road. 33. Capture of Rangoon. 35. Japanese surrender. 36. Extended boundaries of SEA Command. 37. Burma—Divisions and Districts.

*Charts* (selected): Chain of Command, SEA Command. Japanese organization and dispositions.

*Appendices* (selected): A. Extracts from the final report of Quadrant (Quebec) Conference. C. Directive by the Prime Minister to S.A.C.S.E.A. F. Policy towards the Burmans. 6. Instrument of surrender of Japanese in SEA Command. 3. Topography and climate of Burma. 7. Psychological warfare. 9. Senior officers of SEA Command. 10. Strength of forces in SEA Command. Gazetteer for Burma.

93. AUNG SAN, U. Presidential Address Delivered by Major-General Aung San at the Second Session of the Supreme Council A.F.P.F.L.,

Held on the 16th May, 1946. Rangoon, Printed at The New Light of Burma Press, 1946. 38 p. Orientalia

*Text:* An important address delivered by Burma's first postwar premier a little over a year prior to his assassination in July 1947. This document was the blueprint which subsequently guided Burma's economic development, notably in the Villa Sorrento planning and the two-year plan of economic development for Burma.

Deplores the sad prospects for peace, internationally and internally, in the near future. Reviews anew the sad plight of Burma's agrarian situation and indicates concrete measures that the P.V.O. (People's Volunteer Organization) units should take to meet the problems. Challenges openly the inability of the British administration to cope with Burma's postwar economic problems.

94. BURMA (INDEPENDENT BURMA, 1943–1945). Burma's New Order Plan. Rangoon, Bureau of State Printing Presses, 1944. 77 p.; appendices. JQ443.A5 1944

*Text:* Outlines the administrative structure of the Burma Government during the time of the Japanese occupation. Presents the plan as conceived by U Ba Maw, at that time Burma's Nainggandaw Adipadi, or Head of the Government, for an administrative program relating to the basic requirements of the civilian population during wartime, to the establishment of Burma's wartime relations with Japan, and to Burma's national development as to agriculture, industries, communications, health, finance, labor, civilian defense, and the nation's general economic program. Describes the duties of the various boards which were set up for the program: The Economic Board which was concerned with all economic questions connected with production, supply, and distribution; The Publicity and National Welfare Board concerned primarily with publicity and education; and The Finance and Revenue Board concerned with currency, insurance, budget, and monetary affairs. The chapter entitled Second review of the working of the new order plan, includes the four-front plan for joint civil-military action in regard to the civilian war situation.

*Appendices:* Includes documents which were presented by the Burmese Independence Preparatory Commission to Japan—Memorandum on enemy properties. Memorandum on economy and industry. Memorandum on transportation and communications. Memorandum on finance and monetary system.

95. BURMA (UNION). COMMITTEE FOR THE RE-
ORGANIZATION OF THE ADMINISTRATION. The
First Interim Report. Rangoon, Govt. Printing and Stationery, 1949. vii, 50 p.; appendices.                                    Law

*Text:* An official report to the Ministry of Home
Affairs, through the Economic Planning Board, presenting proposals for the reorganization of the existing system with a view to achieving a new plan of government administration after Burma's independence.

Following a brief statement of the general principles
which guided the Committee's deliberations, three
chapters tell about the composition of the government
organization and authority in the village, town, township, and district councils. Recommendations for the
transformation of the former system along democratic
lines, with the minimum delay consistent with continuity of administration, conclude the report. Valuable data regarding the historical development
of government administration in Burma appears
throughout the report.

*Appendices:* The Democratic Administration Act
(1948), which evolved from the Committee's report.
Note of dissent to the Democratic Administration Bill,
as prepared by U Khin Maung Gale, a member of the
Committee.

[Note: The Committee's *Final report* was published in 1954.
Rangoon, Govt. Printing, 1954]

96. BURMA (UNION). DEPARTMENT OF INFORMA-
TION AND BROADCASTING. Kuomintang Aggression Against Burma. Rangoon, Govt.
Printing, 1953. 221 p.; illustrations, maps,
appendices.             DS485.B892A567

*Text:* Discusses the KMT problem which has manifested itself in upper Burma since 1949, and has com-
manded the attention of the United Nations General
Assembly.

Divided into three parts. Part one outlines the history of the KMT aggression, with particular reference
to the diplomatic methods and military operations for
effecting the withdrawal of the Chinese from the
frontier areas of Burma. Part two gives the relevant
proceedings of the U.N. General Assembly as it pertains to this Sino-Burma problem. Part three relates
the KMT action as seen by outside observers, particularly journalists, who provide a brief résumé of world
opinion on the problem.

*Illustrations:* U Myint Thein, leader of the Burmese
delegation to the U.N., and other members on the

delegation. Chinese troops in training in upper
Burma.

*Maps:* Shows routes by means of which the KMT
forces entered and infiltrated into Burma.

*Appendices:* Documents sent within the KMT organization, in both Chinese and English. Organization and formation of KMT troops in Burma.
Disposition and strength of KMT troops inside Union
territories. Implementation plan of the Four-Nation
Military Commission for the evacuation of KMT
forces from Burma.

97. BURMA (UNION). DIRECTORATE OF INFORMA-
TION AND BROADCASTING. Is Trust Vindi-
cated? A Chronicle of the Various Accomplishments of the Government Headed by
General Ne Win During the Period of Tenure
from November, 1958 to February 6, 1960.
Rangoon, 1960. 567, iv, p.; illustrations,
tables, charts, appendices, index.

DS485B892A567 1960

*Text:* An account of what was done during the Ne
Win regime to establish law and order when lawlessness was rampant and to improve the national security
when the economic plight of the country was rapidly
becoming more acute. Summarizes the official action
taken by the military to stem the tide of lawlessness—
political insurgents, economic insurgents, and footloose
criminals; to revitalize the government's administration; and to alter government agencies for improving
the social and economic life of the nation.

Thirty chapters are divided into these four sections:
I. Administration; II. National economy; III. Social
service; IV. States; and relate the activity of the
various ministries in the Ne Win Government.

*Illustrations* (selected): Agricultural projects, irrigation, road repairs, resettlement program, dam projects,
military training, publications, and pictures of various
Ministers.

*Tables* (selected): Decrease in insurgent strength.
Insurgent surrenders. Loans and interest. Industrial
Development Corporation. Insurance. Rehabilita-
tion Brigade.

*Charts* (selected): Crime. Population. Defense Services Institute. Income and expenditure.

*Appendices* (selected): 1. The national ideology and
the role of the defense services. 2. U Nu's broadcast
on September 26, 1958. 3. Exchange of letters (U
Nu and General Ne Win). 4–8. Addresses of General Ne Win. 9. List of Defense Services officials.

98. Burma (Union). [Ministry of Information]. Burma and the Insurrections. [Rangoon] 1949. 63 p.; maps, appendices.

DS485.B892A52 1949

*Text:* A recent account depicting the political activities and the severe Communist insurrection which has continued since the spring of 1948. Discusses the Red Flag Communists; White Flag Communists; the People's Volunteer Organizations; The Socialists; Labor agitation and strikes; The U Nu Plan; The Yebaw Plan of Leftist Unity; The Army meeting; and the KNDO insurrection.

*Maps:* Areas dominated by the Communist insurgents. Areas dominated by the White PVO insurgents. Areas dominated by the Karen insurgents.

*Appendices:* Resolutions adopted at the Conference of the All-Burma Peasants Union (Burma Communist Party). The Fourteen Point Programme. Manifesto of the Joint Political Committee. Chronological statement of the Communist insurrection in Burma. Chronological statement of the White PVO insurrection in Burma.

99. Burma (Union). [Ministry of Information]. KNDO Insurrection. 2d ed. [Rangoon] 1949. ii, 59 p.; appendices.

DS485.B892A53 1949

*Text:* Part I gives a brief description of the Karen people and their religion, culture, origin, population, social and economic conditions. Part II describes Karen politics before the war and during the Japanese occupation and the postwar period. Part III provides data about the Karen insurrection—the formation of the Karen Nationalist Defense Organization (KNDO) by the Karen National Union (KNU), the early coup d'état in Tenasserim, the Karenni States, the Karen secret radio station, the Karen army, source of arms and ammunition, and peace overtures.

*Appendices:* KNDO insurrection in chronological order. Statement of cases of dacoities committed on large scale by KNDO insurgents. Atrocities committed by the KNDO.

100. Cady, John Frank. A History of Modern Burma. Ithaca, Cornell University Press, 1958. xiii, 682 p.; bibliography, illustrations, map, glossary, index. DS485.B86C2

*Text:* This volume sets forth in an orderly manner those events that happened in the political arena of Burma during the nineteenth and twentieth centuries.

Although an early chapter gives a quick and hasty view of the social and economic aspects of "old Burma," *i.e.,* prior to British domination, basically the author does not include in his purview the developments and trends in the social aspects and cultural institutions of Burma during the past century and a half.

A sympathetic attitude is shown when interpreting the carefully assembled facts related to the strong Burmese nationalist point of view as manifested in the intense desire for Burma's independence, and when evaluating the demands and controls imposed on the Burmese by Britain as a controlling Western power.

The work is divided into four parts. Part one—Old Burma and its Disappearance, relates the time of the Burmese kings when patronage of Buddhism was a basis of loyalty to the Burmese king; when there was a central system of administration coupled with despotism; and when the Burmese kingship came to an end after the three Anglo-Burmese wars. Part two—British Colonial Rule, analyzes the British form of administration, and the changes that evolved as a result of British business practices and influence. Part three—The Renaissance of Burmese Nationalism, comprises the principal discussion of the entire work, since it tells about the steps that led to the Constitution of 1935. Part four—Re-emergence of Independent Burma, deals with the war period and the Japanese occupation, the problem of postwar British policy, the Nu-Attlee Treaty, the Communist rebellion in 1948, and the prospects and problems that Burma faces today.

*Bibliography:* References are organized according to primary and secondary sources relevant to political Burma.

*Illustrations:* Shwe Dagon Pagoda. U Ba Baw, General Aung San, Premier Nu.

*Map:* Burma (Frontispiece)

*Glossary:* Word list of Burmese terms used in the text.

101. Desai, Walter Sadgun. History of the British Residency in Burma, 1826–1840. Rangoon, University of Rangoon, 1939. xiv, 491 p.; bibliography, tables, appendices, index.

DS485.B88D4

*Text:* Describes Anglo-Burmese relations from the close of the first Anglo-Burmese War (1824–25) up to the early years of the reign of the Burmese monarch, King Tharrawaddy (1837–46). Relates in detail the attempt on the part of the British Indian Government to maintain, without resort to war, diplomatic relations with the Government of Burma by means of a permanent residency at Ava. Henry Burney, the British Resident in Burma (1830–38), is portrayed as an outstanding and highly important personality in this period of Burma's history. Throughout the volume considerable light is thrown on the reigns of two Burmese kings, Bagyidaw and Tharrawaddy, of the Alaungpaya Dynasty.

*Bibliography:* Includes unpublished documents and other works used in this study.

*Tables:* List of the principal British subjects in Burma, 1838.

*Appendices:* Text of the Yandabu Treaty of Peace after the first Anglo-Burmese War. Letters from the Council of India to King Tharrawaddy and Ministers of the Burma Government.

102. FURNIVALL, JOHN SYDENHAM. The Governance of Modern Burma. 2d ed. enl., with an appreciation by Frank N. Trager and a supplement on the Ne Win administration by John Seabury Thompson. New York, International Secretariat, Institute of Pacific Relations, 1960. 154 p.     JQ444.F8 1960

*Text:* Completed not too long before the author's death, this work presents some penetrating observations of how the form of government inherited from the days of British rule might be adapted to the political, social, and economic conditions of the new, independent Burma. Discusses the difficult problem facing postwar Burma of creating unity in a disintegrated social order and thus fit the people for the social and economic life in which they have been absorbed recently.

103. FURNIVALL, JOHN SYDENHAM. "Twilight in Burma." *Pacific affairs,* March 1949, v. 22: 3–20; June 1949, v. 22:155–172.

DU1.I45   1949

*Text:* Prepared by one who served many years in the Civil Service of Burma, who is an author of different studies dealing with Southern Asia, and who was for many years an advisor to the Government of Burma.

Presents a historical account of the fast moving events which have occurred in Burma during the postwar years—from May 1945, when the British reoccupied Rangoon, to 1948, when Burma gained her independence through the withdrawal of British rule.

Analyzes the basic factors determining the course of current events in Burma, with particular reference to

the Karen and Communist insurrections. States that law and order were maintained during the British regime by a foreign military force and that anarchy naturally appeared in the country when that foreign control was removed. It is shown that Burma is faced, therefore, with the stupendous task of creating a new social order, a national society that will comprehend all of the racial elements in an organic whole.

104. HARVEY, GODFREY ERIC. History of Burma From the Earliest Times to 10 March 1824, the Beginning of the English Conquest. With a preface by Sir Richard Carnac Temple. London, New York, Longmans, Green, 1925. xxxi, 415 p.; bibliography, illustrations, maps, tables, appendix, index.

DS485.B86H3

*Text:* A thorough analysis of historical events and trends in Burmese history from the Kingdom of Pagan in the middle of the 11th century to the Alaungpaya Dynasty in the early part of the 19th century prior to the British era in Burma. Based on inscriptions and manuscripts made available for the first time by the Burma Research Society. Important Chinese, Portuguese, Dutch, and English state papers are also used as source material.

*Bibliography:* Eighteen pages listing the principal sources used in the study, together with the location symbols indicating where these books are available.

*Illustrations:* Comparative representation of the Burmese and Pyu scripts in the Myazidi inscription.

*Maps:* Burma about 700 A.D.; The Kingdom of Pagan, 1044–1287. Shan Dominion, 1287–1531. Burma under the Toungoo Dynasty, 1531–1752. Burma in 1824.

*Appendix:* Extensive explanatory notes which amplify the text.

*Tables:* Chronological table (c. 500 to 1885). Genealogical tables of the Burmese kings and chieftains.

[An abridgement of this volume appeared in 1947 under the title *Outline of Burmese History* (Bombay, Calcutta, Longmans, Green)].

105. JOHNSTONE, WILLIAM CRANE. Burma's Foreign Policy: A Study in Neutralism. Cambridge, Harvard University Press, 1963. ix, 339 p.; bibliography, appendices, index.

DS485.B892J6

*Text:* An analysis of the foreign policy of Burma since independence in 1948 which examines the basic concepts accepted by the leaders of Burma in their formulation of national foreign policy during the cold war. The study in no way pretends to be a comprehensive account or review of Burma's foreign relations from 1948 to the present, but rather focuses upon those concepts which have caused Burma to adopt a policy of neutralism.

Contents include eight chapters: 1. Introduction. 2. The formative period, 1948–53. 3. "Positive neutralism," 1954–58. 4. Political malaise—and its aftermath, 1958–62. 5. Burma's relations with Communist China. 6. Burma's participation in the United Nations. 7. After fourteen years—an evaluation. 8. Neutralism: visable policy or fatal trap?

*Bibliography:* Voluminous bibliographical footnotes citing newspapers, articles, and books used in the study.

*Appendices:* 1. Burma research project papers. 2. Sino-Burma border treaty and non-aggression treaty. 3. "A hard look at Mr. Tender," by U Law Yone. 4. The Burmese way to socialism (Manifesto of Burma Revolutionary Council, Rangoon, April 30, 1962).

106. JOHNSTONE, WILLIAM CRANE. Observations on Contemporary Burma. Santa Monica, Rand Corporation, 1960. v, 70 p. (Research memorandum, RM–2535–RC)
Q180.A1R36 no. 2535

*Text:* Discusses the political and economic stability of postwar Burma, with particular emphasis on the influence which the armed forces have had on Burmese politics and the strong anti-communist attitude which has emerged.

Contents: 1. Burma's foreign policy. 2. The political crisis of 1958–59. 3. The Communist role in the crisis. 4. The Ne Win government. 5. The political crisis and foreign policy. 6. The Communist role in Burma. 7. Some final observations.

107. MAUNG MAUNG, U. ed. Aung San of Burma. Introduction by Harry J. Benda. The Hague, Published for Yale University, Southeast Asia Studies, by Nijhoff, 1962. 162 p.; illustrations, appendix. DS485.B89M3

*Text:* This biographical sketch of Burma's most popular hero, national leader, and one who worked hard for Burma's independence, is more than a picture of a man who aided in shaping the new Southeast Asia; it is also a moving account, ofttimes with complex historical events, of the days when Burma was struggling to bring forth the status of an independent nation.

This unorthodox but well-designed biography, consisting mainly of brief accounts by persons who knew Aung San intimately, is presented in five parts. Part one, The making of Aung San, describes many facets of the Aung San's personality and experiences, during his student days and reveals those abiding qualities which were to make him a living inspiration to those who were to outlive his assassination. Part two, War and resistance, display graphically the transformation of a young student charged with ideals into a determined soldier, an adroit politician and a wise leader. Part three, The winning of Burma's freedom, consists of gleanings of articles and writings which show the personal zeal with which Aung San labored to make Burma independent. Part four, The wisdom of Aung San, brings together from many sources speeches and statements the General made on behalf of his country. Part five, Appreciation, contains statements which place the man in a right perspective.

*Illustrations:* Letter from Aung San to Ba Maw, then a hostage of the Japanese army. Aung San at successive stages from a student to a leader at the Panglong Conference.

*Appendix:* Who's Who of persons associated with Aung San.

108. MAUNG MAUNG, U. Burma in the Family of Nations. 2d rev. and enl. ed. Amsterdam, Djambatan, 1957. xi, 243 p.; bibliography, map, appendices, index.
DS485.B86M3 1957a

*Text:* This diplomatic and legal history of Burma in the modern period depicts in a lucid and most interesting manner the important aspects of Burma's history and provides an assessment of earlier and contemporary events which occurred during the time of the Burmese kings, the British era, the Japanese occupation, and the subsequent years of liberation and independence.

The twelve orderly chapters are: 1. Burma background. 2. The British advent. 3. Missions, residency, and war. 4. Burma; coming out season. 5. The eclipse. 6. Law and administration under the British. 7. Constitutional changes. 8. War and occupation. 9. Liberation and independence. 10. The Constitution. 11. Burma since independence. 12. Burma in the family of nations.

*Bibliography:* Among many well-known sources, a few lesser known references are included.

*Map:* Outline map showing states within the Union of Burma.

*Appendices* (selected) : 1. Treaty of Yandabo, 1826. 2. Commercial Convention between France and Burma, 1873. 6. Constitution of Burma, 1943. 7. Burma, statement of policy of His Majesty's Government, 1945. 9. Treaty between United Kingdom and Burma, 1947. 11. Burma independence Act, 1947. 13. Treaties and conventions to which Burma became a party as part of the British Empire. 16. Reparations and economic cooperation agreement between Burma and Japan, 1954.

109.  MAUNG MAUNG, U.  Burma's Constitution. 2d rev. and enl. ed.  Foreword by J. S. Furnivall.  The Hague, Nijhoff, 1961.  xviii, 340 p.; bibliography, illustrations, map, appendices, index.                           Law

*Text:* Divided into two parts.  Part one is historical as it traces the genesis of the Constitution and outlines the constitutional progress of Burma under British rule, the changes under Ba Maw during the Japanese occupation, and the developments until the attainment of independence by the Anti-Fascist People's Freedom League.  Part two is analytical as it examines each part of the Constitution, item by item, and explains it in laymen's language.  The chapters in part two are: 1. Form of State.  2. Fundamental rights. 3. Peasants and workers.  4. Directive principles of state policy.  5. The President.  6. Parliament.  7. The union government.  8. The union judiciary.  9. The states.  10. Amendment of the constitution.  11. International relations.  12. General provisions.  13. Transitory provisions.  14. End of an era.

*Bibliography:* Bibliographical footnotes to numerous official documents.

*Map:* Burma's border with China.

*Illustrations* (selected) : 1. Bogyoke Aung San and family.  3. U Nu and other student strikers.  7. Japanese decorating Burmese leaders.  11. Governor Rance's Executive Council.  14. U Nu signing Nu-Attlee Agreement.  16. General Ne Win's cabinet.  17. Union Government, April 4, 1960.  18. Burma-China Boundary Treaty signing.

*Appendices:* 1. Opinion on annexation of Burma.  2. Constitution of Burma under Japanese occupation. 3. The Panglong Agreement.  4. Draft Constitution approved by AFPFL Convention.  5. Members of the Constitution Drafting Committee's Constituent Assembly, 1947.  6. Motion to adopt Draft Constitu-

tion.  7. Constitution of the Union of Burma (1947). 8. Constitution Amendment Act, 1961.  10. Boundary Treaty between Burma and China, October 1, 1960. 11. Chronology of events.

110.  MAUNG MAUNG, U.  A Trial in Burma; the Assassination of Aung San.  The Hague, Nijhoff, 1962.  117 p.; illustrations, appendix.                           DS485.B89M32

*Text:* A historical presentation of one of the most important trials in Burma's history—the trial of U Saw and others who killed Bogyoke Aung San and other members of the Executive Council of the Burma Government in July 1947, just prior to the independence of Burma in January 1948.

The carefully prepared account of this event which altered the course of postwar events in Burma is based on the primary records of the criminal trial.  The very interesting and reliable narrative of events is divided into these seven parts: 1. Aung San's hour.  2. U Saw and his men.  3. The trial.  4. The approver's story. 5. U Saw's story.  6. Speeches and decisions.  7. The long journey.

*Illustrations:* U Aung San, U Saw, and others at the London talks in January 1947.  The justices who conducted the trial.  Scenes of the trial.

*Appendix:* Full account of the judgment of the Special Tribunal on the Secretariat assassinations.

111.  MYA SEIN, DAW.  Administration of Burma: Sir Charles Crosthwaite and the Consolidation of Burma.  With a foreword by Sir Archibald Douglas Cochrane, Governor of Burma.  Rangoon, Zabu Meitswe Pitaka Press, 1938.  xxvi, 206 p.; bibliography, illustrations, maps, index.      Microfilm 5774JQ

*Text:* An authoritative work supplementary to Harvey's *History of Burma* and Furnivall's *An introduction to the political economy of Burma.*  The introduction and the chapter Historical background provide a brief summary of Burmese historical events after 1044.  This study of constitutional history in Burma includes sections on the general administration in pre-British Burma, village administration before and after 1885, and the system of taxation during the time of the Burmese kings.  Burmese terminology for government officials and activity are included.  Frequent quotations are made from U Tin, an official in the Burmese court and a noted authority on Burmese history.

Among the large number of documentary source

material used in this study are the *sittans,* i.e., the results of the revenue inquests, undertaken in the reigns of the Burmese kings Nyaungyan, Anaukpetlun, Thalun, Sinbyushin, Bodawpaya, and Thibaw. Numerous quotations from original Burmese sources are given in the Burmese script. The bibliography is especially valuable for the primary sources listed.

The writer was the representative of the All-Asian Women's Conference to the League of Nation's Committee on Nationality, 1931, and Woman Delegate to the Burma Round Table Conference, 1931–32.

*Bibliography:* Includes titles of unpublished primary sources.

*Illustrations:* The palace of King Bagyidaw at Ava. Costumes of the Wungyi, Sayadawgyi, and other members of the Burmese court. U May Oung.

*Maps:* Burma under the Pagan Dynasty, 1244–87. Burma under the Toungoo Dynasty, 1571–1752. Burma under the Alaungpaya Dynasty, 1755–1885. Present-day Burma.

112. NU, *U.* Towards Peace and Democracy. (Translation of Selected Speeches by the Hon'ble Thakin Nu, Prime Minister of the Government of the Union of Burma.) [Rangoon] Ministry of Information, 1949. 237 p.
DS485.B892N8

*Text:* Comprises thirty-four speeches delivered by Burma's Prime Minister from July 1947 to August 1949. Within the collection is the important statement (no. 16), made on May 25, 1948, in which the famous "fifteen points" are set forth as the basis of a unification program designed to rally the country around the united strength of Leftism. In the address entitled The nature of leftist unity (no. 18) the "fifteen points" are discussed in considerable detail. Other addresses are: Communist allegations (no. 4); The policy of state socialism (no. 6); I choose democracy (no. 10); Review of the general situation (no. 25); and To the Karen nationals (no. 28).

113. PE MAUNG TIN, *U.,* and GORDON HANNINGTON LUCE, tr. The Glass Palace Chronicle of the Kings of Burma [. . . Mahayazawindawgyi]. London, Oxford University Press, 1923. xxiii, 179 p.; map. (Issued by the Text Publication Fund of the Burma Research Society) DS485.B87M3

*Text:* A portion of the original 1829 Royal Chronicle, *Hmannan yazawin*—parts three, four, and five—translated into English. Portrays Burmese history as it concerned the activities of the kings from the Tagaung Dynasty through the illustrious Pagan Dynasty. The story of Hinayana Buddhism during Anawrahta's kingship and the two centuries of Pagoda building is one which holds the reader's attention. A concise introduction describes the chronicle and the primary sources which were examined. Unfortunately there is no index.

*Map:* Map of Burma showing cities referred to in the text.

114. PYE, LUCIAN W. Politics, Personality, and Nation Building; Burma's Search for Identity. New Haven, Yale University Press, 1962. xx, 307 p.; index. JQ442.P9

*Text:* This erudite study from the Center for International Studies at the Massachusetts Institute of Technology will be of particular concern for the political scientist as it provides insights into and interpretations of the political events and new governmental structure which have evolved during Burma's emergence as a non-colonial, self-governing nation.

The nineteen chapters are divided into these six divisions: I. The problem of nation building. II. The traditional order and the varieties of change. III. The political culture: the spirit and calculations of Burmese politics. IV. The socialization process. V. Political acculturation and reactions to changes in identity. VI. Epilogue.

115. SYMES, MICHAEL. Michael Symes; Journal of His Second Embassy to the Court of Ava in 1802. Edited with introduction and notes by Daniel George Edward Hall. London, George Allen and Unwin, 1955. 270 p.; appendices, index. DS485.B81S92

*Text:* Pertains to historical events in Burma during the early 19th century prior to the Anglo-Burmese wars. Besides the valuable historical documents which describe the British mission to the Burmese capitol for the purpose of reopening diplomatic relations with the Burmese, this volume is of particular value because of the lengthy introduction and notes by Professor Hall, formerly of the School of Oriental and African Studies at the University of London. The Symes documents are far better understood in the light of this introduction which discusses the beginnings of Anglo-French rivalry in Burma; Burma during the period 1792–95; and Captain Hiram Cox's mission in 1796–98.

*Appendices:* Correspondence between Col. Symes and Burmese Government officials and officers of the British Government.

116. WOODMAN, DOROTHY. The Making of Burma. London, Cresset Press, 1962. ix, 594 p.; bibliography, maps, appendices, index.

DS485.B86W6

*Text:* Divided into five parts. Part one provides a view of Burma prior to British colonial rule, with particular reference to trade with China, and an account of events culminating in the First Anglo-Burmese War; part two describes a prelude to Empire, including the Second Anglo-Burmese War; part three relates the final annexation of Burma with the Third Anglo-Burmese War and the quieting of Chinese antagonism through the Anglo-Chinese Convention of 1894; parts four and five deal with the resistance encountered in upper Burma and controversial frontier issue with China only recently settled and fixed between Burma and China.

Selected from the nineteen chapters are: 1. Early travellers in Burma. 2. The first British traders. 3. Rivals on India's eastern frontier. 4. The First Anglo-Burmese War. 6. Developing trade. 7. The Second Anglo-Burmese War. 9. All roads lead to China. 11. Trade and the Third Anglo-Burmese War. 12. Appeasing China. 13. Britain, China, and the Irrawaddy. 14. Britain, France, and the Mekong. 15. Pacifying the Kachins. 16. The story of Chin resistance. 17. Absorbing the Shan States. 19. China and Burma's frontier.

*Bibliography:* An extensive list of primary sources, manuscript collections located in the India Office Library. Also unpublished theses prepared at London University, and parliamentary publications on the three Burmese wars, commercial relations, and Sino-British relations.

*Maps* (selected): Burma–China border in the 17th-century. Chinese frontier according to Government of India Survey. Frontier agreement of 1897. Chin Hills. Kachin Hills. Political divisions of Burma. Sino-Burmese border agreement, 1960.

*Appendices* (selected): Documents exchanged between Governor-General Dalhousie and Commodore Lambert. Account of the guerrilla leader Mayat Htoon. Articles on the Iselin Commission. The Hpare incident in 1900. Boundary agreement between China and Burma, 1960. Treaty of friendship and non-aggression between China and Burma, 1960. Boundary treaty between China and Burma, 1960.

# ECONOMICS

(including: Agriculture, Commerce, Industry, and Labor)

117. ANDRUS, JAMES RUSSELL. Burmese Economic Life. Stanford, Stanford University Press; London, Oxford University Press, 1947. xxii, 362 p.; maps, table, index.

HC437.B8A65

*Text:* A survey of basic facts and statistics of Burmese economy, with particular emphasis on the decade from 1937, when Burma was separated from India, to 1947. The author provides a careful treatment of the development of Burma's agriculture, forestry, minerals, trade, transportation, and public health, and supplies data on handicrafts, cooperatives, labor, and public finance. Two closing chapters are entitled: Economic consequences of the Japanese occupation, and The future of Burmese economy. Extensively documented.

The author, formerly a Professor of Economics at the University of Rangoon, combines economic proficiency with an insight into social conditions of the country.

*Maps:* Nine geographic areas of Burma. Political divisions and their economic products.

*Tables:* Provides statistical data on rainfall and temperatures, population, timber and mineral production, trade and commerce, transportation, government expenditures, and other subjects discussed in the text.

118. BAXTER, JAMES. Report on Indian Immigration. Rangoon, Govt. Printing and Stationery, 1941. vii, 192 p.; maps, table, charts, appendices. JV8509.B94B35

*Text:* Official report of the Commission of Inquiry appointed by the Government of Burma to examine the question of Indian immigration into Burma. Commonly referred to as the Baxter report. The inquiry deals with the volume of Indian immigration prior to World War II and the extent to which it was seasonal, temporary, or permanent; the occupations in which the Indians were mainly employed, and whether in such employment Indians either had displaced Burmans or were replaced by Burmans; in light of the statistics obtained and other relevant factors, the need of any system of equating the supply of Indian unskilled labor to Burman requirements. Selected chapters are: Growth of Indian population; Occupations of Indians; Indians in agriculture; and Special enquiry into industrial labor.

*Maps:* Burma, scale–1″ to 64 miles. Burma, showing the distribution of districts of Indians, scale–1″ to 64 miles. Burma, showing distribution of Indians by districts as a percentage of total population, scale–1″ to 64 miles.

*Tables:* Distribution of workers in major industries in Burma. Seasonal variation in employment. Indian population in Burma. Imports and exports. Distribution of Burmans and Indians in Burma. Occupation and race of laborers. Industrial establishments.

*Charts:* Distribution of various races in Burma. Burma's foreign trade.

*Appendices:* Include statements showing sea-passenger statistics. Graphs showing value of foreign trade and Indian migration. Tables indicating age and sex distribution of population. Abstracts revealing various aspects of industrial labor.

119. BINNS, SIR BERNARD OTTWELL. Agricultural Economy in Burma. Rangoon, Govt. Printing and Stationery, 1948. iii, 192 p.; tables, appendices. HD2075.B8B5

*Text:* A foundation document presenting a plan for the reconstruction of agriculture in Burma. Stresses the fact that compared with agriculture in Burma all other economic factors are of minor importance since basically the economic reconstruction of the country must be founded on agriculture and that the fundamental necessity of such reconstruction is the stability of the agricultural population and the use of good agricultural methods. Emphasizes the necessity for the reintegration of Burmese village life as another important factor in bringing about the successful economic reconstruction of Burmese agriculture; namely, that a sound Burmese economic structure can be developed and a healthy agricultural industry can flourish best on the foundation of the Burmese village as a social as well as an administrative unit which needs to be re-established. Shows that the ills of agriculture in Burma appeared primarily because of the fundamental defects in the social economy, which must be removed in order to cure the defects of agriculture.

Describes with considerable detail the most urgent matters in connection with agricultural reconstruction in Burma; namely, to provide for new tenancy legislation, thus preventing the former inadequate Tenancy Act from automatically being enforced again; to make available immediate credit facilities for the farmers; to bring about legislation to control money lenders as an essential element in the reconstruction of the credit system; to prevent land from falling into the possession of nonagriculturists; to constitute a controlling body to deal with the administration and the organization of an efficient agricultural education department.

Other subjects dealt with are: the cooperative movement, soil erosion, labor, insurance, village welfare, and statistics.

The author was for many years in the Burma Civil Service and has made close observations of Burma's agricultural problems.

*Tables:* Rice production in Burma and other countries of Asia. Wages of agricultural laborers. Balance sheet of cultivators in various parts of Burma, showing expenses and receipts of owners and tenants.

*Appendices:* Long-term credit; the position up to the evacuation in 1942. Procedure for ensuring the effectiveness of the Land Alienation Act. Draft bill to regulate the possession of agricultural land by nonagriculturists. Outline scheme for a collective cooperative farm. Draft Tenancy Bill. Village township and district banks. Draft bill for the control of money-lending.

120. BURMA (UNION). MINISTRY OF AGRICULTURE AND FORESTS. The Land Nationalization Act, 1948. Rangoon, Govt. Printing and Stationery, 1948. 41 p. Law

*Text:* A highly important document to the student of economic conditions in present-day Burma. Prior to the Act itself (no. 60 of 1948), addresses by Thakin Tin, Minister for Agriculture and Forests, and by Thakin Nu, the Prime Minister, delivered in support of the nationalization of land in Burma, are recorded. Includes data on the history of agrarian legislation, indebtedness of Burmese farmers, status of landlords, the cooperative system, and other aspects of the agrarian problem.

121. BURMA (UNION). MINISTRY OF FINANCE. Economic Survey of the Union of Burma, 1961. Rangoon, Govt. Printing, 1961. vii, 114 p.; tables, graphs. HC437.B8A37

*Text:* An annual publication which gives a succinct report on the principal economic trends for the previous year in Burma. Following an account of the production by major sectors of the economy, the foreign trade, and finance and credit, the development progress by major government programs is related in the fields of agriculture, irrigation, forestry, mining, transportation, communications, power, industry, health, and education. International assistance programs are summarized in closing.

*Tables:* Statistical data in most of the fields referred to above.

*Graphs:* Depict the production in the major sectors.

122. FURNIVALL, JOHN SYDENHAM. An Introduction to the Policial Economy of Burma. 2d rev. ed. edited by J. Russell Andrus. Rangoon, Burma Book Club, 1938. xv, 293 p.; maps, tables, appendices.

HC437.B8F8 1938

*Text:* A study of the economic life and problems in Burma, as written by a former Commissioner of Settlement and Land Records well acquainted with Burmese economic life prior to and during the British régime. Until his death, the author was one of the few Britishers who had been retained as advisors to the Burma Government. Significant chapter headings indicate the scope of the study: The wealth of Burma; Crop and cultivation; Rural economy under Burmese rule; Landowners, cultivators, and labourers in Lower Burma . . . Upper Burma; Capital and debt; Trade and industry. Unfortunately there is no index.

*Maps:* Map of Burma, showing rice cultivation by districts. Sketch map of dry zone.

*Tables:* Maritime trade of Burma (1932–36). Areas under dry crops in 1936–37. Area of expansion of cultivation of rice. Sea-borne passengers entering and leaving Burma. (See also appendices.)

*Appendices:* Some Burmese revenue records, bilingual. Statistical tables on rice cultivation and exports on the number of rice mills, and on the growth of population from 1830 to 1931.

123. INTERNATIONAL LABOR OFFICE. Report to the Government of Burma on the Development of Co-operatives. Geneva, 1955. 197 p.; charts. HD3540.A3B85

*Text:* A study made by four cooperative experts of the United Nations Expanded Programme of Technical Assistance on the development of various types of cooperatives in Burma. The 31 chapters are grouped into the 8 parts: 1. Introduction. 2. General. 3. Cooperative education. 4. Agricultural producers' cooperatives. 5. Consumer's cooperatives and the conversion of the civil supplies department into a national cooperative wholesale. 6. Industrial coopera-

tion. 7. Fishery and miscellaneous cooperatives. 8. Summary of accomplishments and recommendations, implementation, and follow up.

*Charts:* The cooperative movement, June 1951. Suggested operational structure of the U.B.C.W.S. (Union of Burma Cooperative Wholesale Society).

124. KNAPPEN-TIPPETTS-ABBETT-MCCARTHY, ENGINEERS. Economic and Engineering Development of Burma, Comprehensive Report. Prepared for the Government of the Union of Burma [by] Knappen-Tippetts-Abbett-McCarthy, Engineers, in association with Pierce Management, Inc., and Robert R. Nathan Associates, Inc. New York, 1953. 2 vols.; maps, tables, charts, diagrams.

HC437.B8T54

*Text:* Volume one of this extensive and significant postwar publication, often referred to as the KTA report, opens with an introductory statement about national organization for coordinating, administering and manning the development programs. Succeeding chapters provide the findings of the research done relative to agriculture, irrigation, the transportation system, railways, seaports, inland waterways, ocean shipping, highways, and airways. Volume two deals with findings, summary, and recommendations about telecommunications, electric power, interrelation of industries, mineral industries, manufacturing, development of small-scale industry, forestry and other industry, and the coordinated plan.

*Maps* (selected): Natural and artificial vegetation of Burma. Average annual rainfall. Density and population by districts, 1941. Lands topographically suited to agriculture. Irrigation development. Mu river irrigation project. Yamethin District soil map. Port of Rangoon. Outport of Akyab. Navigated inland waterways. Petroleum pipeline. Burma highways. Civil communications system. Mineralized areas. Reserved forests of Burma.

*Tables* (selected): Land use in Burma. Forests of Burma. Rice output. Agricultural production. Program for increasing agricultural production. Irrigation in Burma. Hydropower sites. Public electricity supply. Industrial uses of the principal raw materials of Burma. Schedule of projects in development program.

*Charts* (selected): Ministerial organization, Government of the Union of Burma. Government agencies concerned with agriculture. Organization of Agricultural Department. Ministry of Transport and Communications. Highway Department of Burma. Union of Burma Airways. Department of Telecommunications. Mineral Resources Development Corporation. Projected industrial development of Burma.

*Diagrams* (selected) : Kalewa coal project. Saw mill, plan and equipment layout. Steel products plant Pharmaceutical plant.

125. MYO HTUN LYNN, *U.* Labour and Labour Movement in Burma. Rangoon, Department of Economics, University of Rangoon. 1961. 168 p., tables, appendices. HD6815.B2M9

*Text:* This volume, originally a thesis submitted to the University of Rangoon, is the first in a series of publications on applied economics relating to Burma to be issued by the Department of Economics with the aid of the Asia Foundation. The material presented is a part of the considerable amount of research work done on various aspects of the Burmese economy at the University.

The status and development of the labor movement in Burma is presented in these chapters: General theory of trade unionism and its application to the situation in Burma. The history of the Burmese labour movement. Case studies of important trade unions. Labour and state. Labour and the industry. Labour force in Burma. Wages, hours of work and the standard of living. The labour boss system of employment.

*Tables:* Total labor force and union members. Distribution by race of male earners. Occupations in Burma. Factories in Burma. Seasonal wages in selected districts in Burma. Local wage-scale study. Average monthly incomes of all permanent workers in selected industries.

*Appendices:* List of registered trade unions in Burma according to industrial categories, 1953. Finance of trade unions in the Rangoon area, 1953.

126. TUN WAI, *U.* Economic Development of Burma from 1800 till 1940. Rangoon, Department of Economics, University of Rangoon, 1961. 136 p.; bibliography, tables. HC437.B8T8

*Text:* Expanded from a thesis written originally at Yale University, this study presents a clear concept of the economic development of Burma in the 19th and 20th centuries. Divided into these six chapters: The structure of the Burmese economy under Burmese kings around 1800; The economic relation and structure of the two parts of the economy—upper Burma under Burmese rule, and lower Burma under British rule, 1852–85; The colonization of the delta, 1869–1900; Annexation of upper Burma—growth and change in structure of the integrated economy, 1886–1929; The effect of the great depression on the economy; and The structure of the Burmese economy in 1940.

*Bibliography:* References dealing with Burmese economics, divided into three parts: official reports and publications, general works, and periodical literature.

*Tables:* Burma's foreign trade. Standard of living. Population. Price level of finished products.

127. WALINSKY, LOUIS JOSEPH. Economic Development in Burma, 1951–1960. New York, Twentieth Century Fund, 1962. 680 p.; maps, tables, charts, appendices, index. HC437.B8W2

*Text:* The general manager and chief economist of Nathan Associates, economic consultants to the Government of Burma, presents the comprehensive long-term economic and social development program for Burma. Divided into six parts: Part I, is devoted to background material of a general nature; Part II, The eight-year development program; Part III, Implementing the program in a changing economic setting—an overview; Part IV, Implementation by major sectors and projects; Part V, Major problems in program implementation; Part VI, Conclusions and appraisals.

*Maps:* Physical Burma. Development projects.

*Tables* (selected) : 1. Distribution of workers in various fields. 12. Government and private capital. 18. Rice exports. Proposed imports. 24. Consumer price index. 32. Capital expenditures for agriculture and irrigation. 75. Union Government budget, 1953–60. 84. U.S. Project loan agreements.

*Charts:* Organization of the Central Government. The development program for Burma.

*Appendices* (selected) : 1. Premier reports to the people: the national economy. 2. Our goal and our interim programme. 3. Investment policy statement. 4. The Union of Burma Investment Act, 1959. 6. Subjects considered by the Economic and Social Board. 8. Selected economic indicators in Burma, 1938–60.

# SOCIAL CONDITIONS
(including: Anthropology, Education, and Health)

128. HANSON, OLA. The Kachins: Their Customs and Traditions. Rangoon, American Baptist Mission Press, 1913. x, 225 p.; illustrations, table, appendices, index. DS485.B85H3

*Text:* Presents in a lucid and orderly manner information about origin of the Kachins; dialects of the Kachin language; and domestic life; appearance and dress; racial characteristics; habits and customs; government and law; industries; social life; mythology and traditions; religious concepts; and natal, marriage, and funeral ceremonies. The intricate question of Kachin relationship and family names is elucidated.

*Illustrations:* Numerous views of Kachin dwellings. Religious ceremonies and practices. Occupations.

*Table:* Kachin dialects.

*Appendices:* Terms of relationship. Family names.

129. HOBBS, CECIL CARLTON. Christian Education and the Burmese Family. Unpublished thesis, Department of Education, Colgate-Rochester Divinity School, Rochester, N.Y., 1942. ix, 259 p.; bibliography, appendices, index. Microfilm 6866 BV

*Text:* An investigation of the family in Burma, depicting certain historical and current environmental factors which are closely related to the Burman family unit. Part two, which deals with Burmese history and sociology, endeavors to untangle and summarize the history of the Burmese people and to provide an account of the social structure in which the Burman family developed. Part three presents an appreciative critique of Burmese Buddhism as a living religion and its relation to the members of the Burman family. Part four discusses the Burman family as it exists today.

Selected chapters: Ethnological problem of Burma origins; The social structure of early Burmese society in which the family existed; Burmese royal family and marriage; Matriarchal system in early Burmese society; Development of Buddhism in Burma; Buddhism and woman; Factors in the structure of society affecting Burmese family life; The position of Burmese women; Burmese marriage customs; Property and divorce; Religious instruction and the Buddhist family; Customs and traditions within the Burmese family life; and An evaluation of the Burman—personal and social.

*Appendices:* Wethandya—one of the lives of the Buddha. The *Dhammathat,* the ancient Burmese law code—which deals with inheritance, marriage, divorce, and other subjects related to the family life of the Burman.

[A portion of this study has been issued in provisional form under the title, *The Burmese family: an inquiry into its history, customs, and traditions* (Washington, 1952)].

130. KICKERT, ROBERT WARREN. The Political Organization of Some Minority Groups in North Burma and Assam. Wien, 1958. 269 l; bibliography, maps. Microfilm 7214JQ

*Text:* A thesis written at the University of Vienna dealing with these racial groups: Kachins, Nagas, Apa Tanis, Nisu, Akas, Abors, Mishmis, Lushais, Lakhers, Kukis, and Chins. Particular attention is given to the political organization, the methods and measures by which these semiliterate groups handle internal and external affairs. Together with evaluations of political concepts, considerable ethnological data on economy, social customs, family life, agriculture and other aspects of village life are also included. In English and German.

*Bibliography:* Books and periodical articles on these racial groups.

*Maps* (selected) : Racial groups in Burma. Districts in Burma.

131. KOOP, JOHN CLEMENT. The Eurasian Population in Burma. New Haven, Yale University, Southeast Asian Studies, 1960. 66 p.; bibliography, tables. (Cultural report series, no. 6) DS485.B85K6

*Text:* This Cultural Report will be of value to the sociologist and demographer who have so little source material dealing with the population problems of postwar Burma. It combines these two studies originally published in Rangoon: *Preliminary survey of the social and economic condition of the Eurasian people in Rangoon* and *A demographic Study of the Eurasian population in Rangoon in 1949.*

*Bibliography:* List of references, some unpublished, used in the study.

*Tables:* Deal with age distribution, earnings, migration, population, sex composition, name changing, and other subjects.

132. MARSHALL, HARRY IGNATIUS. The Karen People of Burma: A Study in Anthropology

and Ethnology. Columbus, The University, 1922. xv, 329 p.; bibliography, illustrations, glossary, index. (The Ohio State University Bulletin, v. 26, no. 13. Contributions in history and political science, no. 8)

DS432.K2M3

*Text:* A scholarly and readable account of the Karens, an important racial minority in Burma. Deals particularly with the Sgaw branch of the Karen people. The thirty chapters present in a thorough fashion a study on their domestic life, social life, religious life, and racial development.

*Bibliography:* A brief list of references, which includes general works dealing with Burma as a whole.

*Illustrations:* Pictures of Karen customs, houses, dress, agricultural methods, musical instruments, and other matters referred to in the text.

*Glossary:* Lists all Karen words used within the text.

133. [SCOTT, SIR JAMES GEORGE]. The Burman: His Life and Notions, by Shway Yoe [pseud.]. 3d ed., rev. London, Macmillan, 1910. xii, 609 p.; index.    DS485.B81S4

*Text:* Presents a thorough account of the everyday life and customs of the Burman, from the First Years in chapter one, to Death and burial in the last chapter. Sixty-four chapters describe: Burmese religious practice and belief; marriage customs; domestic life of people; monastic life of clergy; ceremonies related with rice cultivation, ploughing, and harvesting; festivals, drama, and dancing; astrology and superstitions; King Thibaw and the royal palace; ministers of state, Burmese army, judicial system, land revenue during the era of Burmese kings. Although long published (1st ed. in 1882), it remains a basic reference work.

134. VAJDA, EMIL HAROLD. Burmese Urban Characteristics: A Size-of-Place of a Southeast Asian Urban Population. Unpublished thesis. Chicago, University of Chicago Library, 1960. 329 l.; bibliography, map, tables, charts.    Microfilm 6779HN

*Text:* A study which aids greatly in filling the large gap of information about the population of Burma—at least one important aspect, the urban population of the country. Much of the data given is based on the *1953 census of population* published in Burma in 1955.

The eight chapters of the presentation are: 1. Introduction. 2. Urbanization and community size.

3. Cultural pluralism and the age-sex composition. 4. Marital status. 5. The household: a place to live and a place to work. 6. Regional variation. 7. Burmese—United States comparisons. 8. Summary and conclusion.

*Bibliography:* Lists books, articles, and census of India pertaining to Burma.

*Map:* Burma.

*Tables* (selected): Urban population, 1891 to 1953. Estimated Indians, Pakistani, and Chinese in Southeast Asia. Population in Rangoon and Mandalay, 1891–1953. 1953 distribution of the Burmese urban population by regions. Cities and towns by region and size of place, urban Burma, 1953.

*Charts* (selected): Illustrate the statistical data given in the tables.

## CULTURAL LIFE
(including: Fine Arts, Language, Literature, and Religion)

135. ANDERSON, COURTNEY. To the Golden Shore; the Life of Adoniram Judson. Toronto, Little, Brown, 1956. xiii, 530 p.; bibliography, illustrations, index.    BV3271.J7A5

*Text:* A historical and dramatic account of the life and work of the first Protestant missionary resident in Burma (1813–50), who, among his various achievements, translated the entire Bible from the original Hebrew and Greek languages into the Burmese language and produced a dictionary and grammar of the Burmese language.

136. BURMA RESEARCH SOCIETY. Fiftieth Anniversary Publications. Rangoon, Printed at Sarpay Beikman Press, 1960 and 1961. 2 vols.; illustrations, map.    In process

*Text:* Volume one is comprised of papers read or prepared for the 50th Anniversary Conference held in Rangoon in 1960. Selected titles are: 4. King Mindon's funeral by W. S. Desai. 6. The romanization of Shan by S. Egerod. 8. Tone and intonation in Western Bwe Karen by E. J. Henderson. 9. Some adapted Pali loan-words in Burmese by U Hla Pe. 10. Laryngeals and the development of tones in Karen by R. B. Jones. 11. Financing the small manufacturing establishments of Burma by U Khin Than Kywe. 14. Botanical survey of the Southern Shan States by Mohinder Nath. 16. The Ostend East India Company and the fate of its servants in Burma. 20. A review of economic planning in Burma by U Thet Tun.

Volume two consists of articles which appeared in former issues of the Society's *Journal* during the past 50 years. Selected articles are: 2. Shin Uttamagyaw and his Tawla—a nature poem by U Ba Han. 4. An Arakanese poem of the 16th century by M. S. Collis. 5. Early newspapers in Burma by C. A. Cuttriss. 6. The early revenue history of Tenasserim—land revenue by J. S. Furnivall. 10. The beginnings of Christian missionary education in Burma, 1600–1824 by U Kaung. 12. A new translation of Letwethondara's famous Ratu by U Khin Zaw. 19. The ancient Pyu by G. H. Luce. 23. The Burmese novel by U Pe Maung Tin. 27. Burmese books printed before Judson by B. R. Pearn. 31. The Burmese drama by J. A. Stewart.

*Illustrations:* Persons present at the 50th Anniversary Conference. Presidents of the Society for the past 50 years.

*Map:* Southern Shan States, botanically surveyed.

137. HTIN AUNG, U. Burmese Drama; a Study, With Translations, of Burmese Plays. Oxford University Press, 1937. viii, 258 p.; appendices, index. PL3971.H7

*Text:* A thesis written at the University of Dublin which presents a highly useful introduction to the largely unexploited field of Burmese literature. The work falls into four parts: the rise of a vernacular literature; the origins and development of Burmese drama; biographical sketches of outstanding Burmese playwrights; and Burmese dramatic practice.

*Appendices:* Contain in translation a partial text of twelve principal Burmese dramas. A full translation of each of four dramas: *Daywagonban, Parpahein, Paduma, The water seller.*

138. HTIN AUNG, U. Burmese Folk Tales. London, Calcutta, Oxford University Press, Indian Branch, 1948. xxxii, 246 p.
GR305.H78

*Text:* A classified collection of folklore commonly known by the Burmans, gathered by the author in various villages in Upper and Lower Burma. Approximately seventy-five stories are classified into four groups of folktales: animal tales, romantic tales, wonder tales, and humorous tales. A long introduction describes in considerable detail the main kinds of

Burmese folk literature—folktales, folklegends, and Buddhist birth stories—and points out significant facts regarding the *naga,* the *galon,* and other beings in Buddhist mythology and *nat* worship. Only collection of Burmese folktales, either in English or in Burmese, which has been published.

139. HTIN AUNG, U. Burmese Law Tales: The Legal Element in Burmese Folk-Lore. London, New York, Oxford University Press, 1962. x, 157 p.; bibliography. Law

*Text:* This volume, a sequel to the author's earlier anthology entitled *Burmese folk tales* (Calcutta, Oxford University Press, 1948), has brought together 65 folk tales, each of which tells about some aspect of Burmese law or law practice and interpretation.

Besides the tales and the analysis of each tale, a signal worth is the concise introduction of Burmese law as these topics are discussed: Burmese social and legal theory, the development of Burmese law and the rise of a Burmese legal literature, justice under the Burmese kings, Burmese law of civil wrongs, Burmese *pyat htons* in Burmese legal literature.

*Bibliography:* An excellent listing of published works on Burmese law, will particular attention to Burmese Buddhist law.

140. HTIN AUNG, U. Folk Elements in Burmese Buddhism. London, New York, Oxford University Press, 1962. xiii, 140 p.; bibliography. BL1453.H75

*Text:* Originally delivered in a series of annual lectures to the Burma Research Society in Rangoon, this study presents a permanent record of the oral lore of the pre-Buddhist cults in Burma, which has never been collected before, even in the Burmese language. Analyzes the folklore elements which are to be found in present-day Burmese Buddhism, and traces their origins in the native cults which were flourishing in the middle of the 11th century during the time of Anawrahta.

*Bibliography:* A brief list of references on Buddhism in Burma and the thirty-seven nats.

141. KHIN ZAW, U. "Burmese music (a preliminary enquiry)." *Journal of the Burma Research Society,* Dec. 1940, p. 387–466.
DS485.B79B8

*Text:* A brief but trustworthy account describing the historical influence of China, Thailand, and India on the music of Burma. The technical use of various instruments is given in detail. Music examples and four complete Burmese classical songs in staff notation for piano and violin and oboe are included. The only work in English dealing solely with Burmese music.

142. RAY, NIHAR-RANJAN. An Introduction to the Study of Theravada Buddhism; a Study in Indo-Burmese Historical and Cultural Relations From the Earliest Times to the British Conquest. Calcutta, University of Calcutta, 1946. xvi, 306 p.; bibliography, appendix, indices. BL1445.B95R3

*Text:* Traces the early history of Buddhism in Burma from the time of the alleged Asoka mission to Burma to the early 19th century, as reconstructed from archaeological, epigraphic, and literary sources—with extended reference to Buddhism in old Prome, Pegu and Thaton, importance of Pagan, and the reformation during the 14th and 15th centuries. Relates the character of Burmese Buddhism during its early development, the relation of the *Sangha* or clergy to the Burmese kings, the literary and scholarly activities of the Buddhist monks, and the role which the monks played in their relation to the life of the people.

*Bibliography:* Includes many references to primary source material, in the Burmese language.

143. STEVENSON, ROBERT CHARLES, and FREDERICK HOWARD EVELETH, comp. The Judson Burmese-English Dictionary. Rev. and enl. ed. Rangoon, American Baptist Mission Press, 1921. 1123 p.; appendices.

PL3957.J834 1921

*Text:* A dictionary, prepared originally by Adoniram Judson, revised and enlarged to include a considerable number of new words not contained in former editions. These special features are included: many of the words have examples showing their use; both the written and colloquial forms of expression are exemplified; Buddhists religious and metaphysical terms are amplified by excerpts from different authorities; and the exact pronunciation of many words is given.

*Appendices:* Illustrative and explanatory notes to the words in the text. Burmese proverbs and quaint sayings. Formal and colloquial phraseology contrasted. Antonyms.

# III

# Thailand

## GENERAL BACKGROUND

144. BLANCHARD, WENDELL, ed. Thailand, Its People, Its Society, Its Culture. In collaboration with Henry C. Abalt, Aldon D. Bell, Mary E. Gresham, Bernard G. Hoffman, Jean H. McEwen, John H. Schaar. New Haven, HRAF Press, 1958. x, 528 p.; bibliography, maps, tables, charts, index. (Country survey series)                           DS566.B5

*Text:* As a volume in the Country Survey Series published by the Human Relations Area Files, this study presents an interpretive and integrated description of various aspects of Thailand. The sociological, political and economic characteristics of Thai society are discussed under these selected chapter headings: 3. Geography and population. 4. Ethnic groups and languages. 5. Religion. 6. Dynamics of political behaviour. 8. Structure of government. 11. Foreign policies. 12. Basic features of the economy. 15. Organization of labor. 16. Agriculture. 17. Industry. 20. Social organization. 21. The family. 22. Education. 24. Social values, attitudes and patterns of living.

*Bibliography:* A lengthy list divided into social and cultural, political, and economic sections.

*Maps* (selected): Landforms and drainage. Vegetation. Population density. Major ethnic groups.

*Tables* (selected): 1. Languages spoken. 2. Ceremonies and rites current. 5. Thai daily newspapers. 14. Production of principal crops. 13. Composition of Thai labor force.

*Charts* (selected): Constitutional structure of Thai government. Bangkok social structure. Thai school system. Lunar calendar.

145. CAUVIN, RAYMONDE. Thaïlande; essai photographique commenté. Brussels, Elsevier, 1958. [174 p.] bibliography, illustrations, maps, chart.                           DS566.C3

*Text:* A volume of black-and-white and colored photographs which depict the people, customs, temples,

religious life, cremation ceremony, handicrafts, dance, and numerous other subjects found in Bangkok and in upper Thailand. Each picture is accompanied by a clearly stated annotation, and longer descriptive statements are given about the capital, Bangkok; Buddhism, temples, elephants; and northeast Thailand.

*Bibliography:* General list of references.

*Illustrations:* Show canals, Bangkok streets, transportation scenes, houseboats, sellers, dress, temple architecture, dance varieties, bazaar scenes, festivals, Buddhist monks, agricultural scenes, industries and the Parliament.

*Maps:* Thailand.

*Chart:* Chronological table of the history of Thailand and the world.

146. CREDNER, WILHELM. Siam, das Land der Tai; eine Landeskunde auf Grund eigener Reisen und Forschungen. Stuttgart, J. Engelhorns, 1935. xvi, 422 p.; bibliography, illustrations, maps, tables, charts, diagrams, appendices, index.                           DS565.C92

*Text:* An exhausive study of Thailand since 1935 which has become a valuable secondary source for scholars. Although the presentation opens with extensive accounts of the geology, geography, topography, and climate, succeeding chapters deal adequately with the cultural, sociological, political, and economic aspects of Thailand—with considerable emphasis on agriculture, mining, fishing, and various industries.

*Bibliography:* Lists 336 items pertaining to the subjects discussed in the text.

*Illustrations:* Views of schools, transportation, canals, buildings, temples, images, mining, industries, and landscapes in hill country.

*Maps:* Ethnological divisions of Thailand, scale—1:10,000,000. Geology, scale—1:10,000,000. Morphology, scale—1:10,000,000. Rainfall in Thailand, scale—1:10,000,000. Linguistic map of Thailand and adjacent countries—scale—1:10,000,000. Principal cities in Thailand—scale—1:8,000,000. Political divisions bordering on Thailand, scale–1:10,000,000. Rice and timber trading companies, scale–1:10,000,-000. Thailand's foreign trade, scale–1:10,000,000. Bangkok, scale–1:50,000.

*Tables:* Languages. Rice cultivation. Imports and exports.

*Charts and Diagrams:* Geological strata. Rice exports and domestic consumption.

*Appendices:* Rainfall in different centers of Thailand. Thai weights and measures. Statistical analysis of exports from Thailand.

147. GRAHAM, WALTER ARMSTRONG. Siam. London, Alexander Morning, 1924. 2 vols. Bibliography, illustrations, map, appendices, indices.                              DS565.G8 1924

*Text:* Provides a mine of information regarding: geography—general divisions, country and towns, and climate; flora and fauna; geology and minerals; racial groups of Thailand; history; social organization—titles, rank, and classes; educational system; language and literature; government—various ministries; industries—agriculture, irrigation, forestry, mining, and rice-milling; commerce and trade—exports and imports, and customs; communications and transport—waterways, roads, and railways; art, archeology, and architecture; music and dancing; religion—Buddhist festivals and ceremonies.

*Illustrations:* Rama V, King Chulalongkorn. Rama VI, King Mongkut. Racial groups. Roads. Various industries. Religious temples.

*Map:* Map of Siam, showing railways and important cities.

*Appendices:* List of animals, plants, and minerals—each with English and Siamese equivalents. Trade statistics. Tables of currency, weights, and measures.

148. PENDLETON, ROBERT LARIMORE, and ROBERT C. KINGSBURY. Thailand: Aspects of Landscape and Life. New York, Duell, Sloan and Pearce, 1962. xv, 321 p.; bibliography, illustrations, maps, tables, charts, index.
DS566.P4 1962

*Text:* The product of a world famous soil technician who served in the countries of Southern Asia for over four decades, and became an authority on tropical soils, particularly laterite—a bricklike material found in the tropics. Noted for his service to the Governments of India, Philippines, Thailand, and the FAO of the United Nations, this work includes much of his research and findings in the fields of agronomy and agricultural economics during his extended residence in Thailand to the time of his death there in 1957.

Following the opening chapters which give an excellent summary of Thai history, the geography, agriculture, and economy are discussed in the following chapters: Physiography and geology; Soils, natural vegetation, and animal life; Climate and water economy; The agrarian landscape: irrigation, rice agriculture, and farm systems; The agrarian landscape: subsidiary crops, animal husbandry, and fishing; The utilization of forests; Mineral deposits and their development; Power, industrial potential, and manufacturing; Transportation, communications, and trade.

*Bibliography:* Each chapter closes with a brief list of references on the topics of the chapter.

*Illustrations:* Paddy fields, housing, rice cultivation, irrigation, timber industry, mining, bazaars, canals.

*Maps:* Physiographic regions. Drainage and river systems. Reconnaissance geology. Soils of the central valley and southeast coast. Soils of Khorst. Soils of the peninsula. Soils of the north. Teak forests. Mean monthly rainfall. Mean monthly temperature. Cropped area. Agricultural survey regions. Flooding and irrigation of the Bangkok plain. Irrigation development. Lowland rice cultivation. Village types. Metallic minerals. Mining industry. Ports of the peninsula.

*Tables* (selected): Use of irrigation. Major irrigation projects. Rice cultivation. Rural indebtedness. Major subsidiary crops. Rubber holdings. Animals on Thai farms. Major commercial minerals. Manufacturing industries. Thailand's trade with the United States.

*Charts:* Climate of Bangkok.

149. The Siam Directory, B. E. 2492–93, 1949–50. Bangkok, Thai Company [1950?]. (Various paging)                              DS563.S53

*Text:* Includes numerous historical documents: Constitution of Thailand, as signed in March 1949; Anglo-Siamese Treaty of Commerce and Navigation, ratified February 19, 1938; Treaty of Friendship, Commerce, and Navigation between Siam and the Netherlands, ratified November 2, 1938; and different peace treaties between Thailand and Great Britain, China, the Netherlands, and Australia. Chronologies for 1948 and 1949 list principal events in Thailand. Name-lists include government officials, universities and schools, associations and societies, Thai royalty, banks, and business firms.

150. SIAM SOCIETY. The Siam Society; Selected Articles From the Siam Society Journal. Bangkok, 1954. 8 vols. (Vol. 1–2. Fiftieth anniversary commemorative publication.) DS562.S5

*Text:* During the half-century since the Siam Society was founded in 1904, scores of articles on anthropology, archaeology, religion, history, the arts, languages, and many other cultural aspects of Thailand have been published in the Siam Society Journal.

The Society's commemorative publication consists of eight volumes containing reprinted articles by O. Frankfurter, Prince Damrong, W. A. Graham, and other famous writers and authorities which appeared during the past fifty years. Among these many articles, these few are cited: in volume one—King Mongkut; Immigration of Mons into Siam; The story of the records of Siamese history; in volume two—Sacred images of Chiengmai; Siam's tribal dresses; The shadow-play as a possible origin of the masked-play; Traditional Thai painting; in volume three—Siam in 1688; Pre-historical researches in Siam; Kingship in Siam; Siam and the pottery trade in Asia; in volume four—The early postal history of Thailand; King Mongkut as a legislator; The reconstruction of Rama I of the Chakri Dynasty; in volume seven—The introduction of Western culture in Siam; Historical account of Siam in the 17th-century; Early Portuguese accounts of Thailand; in volume eight—The French foreign mission in Siam during the 17th-century; The mission of Sir James Brooke to Siam, September 1850; Early trade relations between Denmark and Siam.

151. THOMPSON, VIRGINIA. Thailand, the New Siam. New York, Macmillan, 1941. xxxii, 865 p.; bibliography, map, appendices, index. (Issued under the auspices of the Secretariat, Institute of Pacific Relations. International research series.) DS565.T63

*Text:* The most exhaustive historical study on Thailand which has appeared since Graham's two-volume book, *Siam*, was revised in 1924. Divided into three parts: Part one deals with geography; racial groups; history—with emphasis on the events during the reigns of Chulalongkorn and other kings of the Chakkri Dynasty in the era of transition of the 19th century and early 20th century and the period of the constitutional regime after 1932; foreign relations—with lengthy accounts of Franco-Siamese and Anglo-Siamese relations during the past two hundred years; government administration in the central government, provinces, and municipalities; judicial system, crime, and law enforcement; and, national defense. Part two is concerned with land tenure; population; natural resources; agricultural techniques, products, and marketing; domestic and foreign commerce; handicrafts; mechanized and state industries; transportation, communications, and housing; finance; and labor. Part three gives data about religion—with accounts of Thai Buddhism and Christianity; structure of Thai society; social problems; public health—with particular reference to tropical diseases; art, drama, music, language, and literature; education; and the press.

*Bibliography:* An extensive bibliography (20 pages) arranged alphabetically by authors.

*Map:* Shows Thailand's strategic position in the Southeast Asia mainland.

*Appendices:* Major foreign companies in Siam. Siamese newspapers and periodicals. Bibliographical notes.

# HISTORY, POLITICS, AND GOVERNMENT

152. CHAKRABONGSE, PRINCE CHULA. Lords of Life: The Paternal Monarchy of Bangkok, 1782–1932. With the earlier and more recent history of Thailand. New York, Taplinger, 1960. 352 p.; bibliography, illustrations, chart, index. DS578.C48

*Text:* The author, a grandson of Thailand's great king, Chulalongkorn, is known for his former works *The twain have met* (London, Foulis, 1957), *Brought up in England* (London, Foulis, 1943) and other books in Thai on 19th-century Western history.

This recent work, based primarily on published and unpublished Thai sources in English and French, is a full history of the Chakkri Dynasty from the time of the founding of the House of Chakkri by General Chakkri as Rama I in 1782. This dynasty guided Thailand for 150 years to 1932, when a bloodless revolution gave birth to a limited monarchy. Biographical data is provided for the kings from Rama I to the present Rama IX and for important princes and ministers who served in significant advisory capacities.

Shows how a breakdown of the Thai limited society took place as Western influence manifested itself and as the kings, especially from King Mongkut to the present, began to assess and become interested in Western values.

*Bibliography:* Divided into three parts: French, English, and Thai; the latter including Thai sources not listed elsewhere.

*Illustrations* (selected): Rama I. Rama II. Rama III. King Mongkut. King Chulalongkorn and family. Prince Damrong. Prince Chakrabongse. Rama VI. Luang Pradit. King Prajadhipok. King Bhumibol Adulyadej. Prince Wan Waitayakorn. Field Marshal Sarit Dhanarajata.

*Chart:* The House of Chakkri, showing descent through the Queens.

153. CHAKRABONGSE, PRINCE CHULA. The Twain Have Met; or, An Eastern Prince Came West. London, Foulis, 1957. 299 p.; bibliography, illustrations, map, chart, index.
DS570.6.C5A32

*Text:* An autobiography of a grandson and great grandson respectively of two illustrious Thai monarchs King Chulalongkorn and King Mongkut. To the historian the chief interest of this autobiography lies in the chapters devoted to the history and politics of Thailand as viewed through a personal knowledge of the author's family history which provides a clear and authoritative story of these two kings who carried out reforms most revolutionary and brought into existence an independent and modernized State.

Following the historical section, the account relates that the Thai royal family had physical ties with Russia because the author's father, while being educated in Russia, married a Russian woman, the author's mother. Other chapters reveal the significant impact of Western civilization, particularly English school life, on a Thai boy brought up in a very different world from Thailand.

*Bibliography:* Lists the books cited in text.

*Illustrations* (selected): Rama I. King Mongkut. King Chulalongkorn and his family. Scenes of English royalty. Author and his English wife.

*Map:* Thailand.

*Chart:* House of Chakkri showing descent through the queens.

154. "Constitution of the Kingdom of Thailand." In *The Siam directory, 1960.* Bangkok, (96 Mansion 2, Rajdamnern Ave.), 1960. p. A3–A4.
DS563.S53

*Text:* Signed by Field Marshall Srisdi Dhanarajata, leader of the Revolutionary Party, this is the 1959 Constitution given on January 28, B. E. 2502 (1959) after the seizure of power in October 1958. This document is to serve as the Interim Constitution until the promulgation of a new Constitution being drafted by the newly set up Constituent Assembly.

155. CROSBY, SIR JOSIAH. Siam, the Crossroads. London, Hollis and Carter, 1945. vi, 174 p.; illustrations, map, index.
DS571.C7

*Text:* An authoritative study by one who spent practically a quarter of a century in Thailand in the British Foreign Service.

Section one, The country and the people of Siam, relates the origins, history, art, religion, and national characteristics. Section two, Old Siam, tells of conditions prior to the *coup d'état* in 1932, when a constitutional form of government emerged. Section three, Siam and the Great Powers, discusses Thailand's foreign relations with England, France, Japan, and China. Section four, The present-day Siam, has chapters on the Revolution of 1932, chauvinism in the new Siam, and the boundary dispute with Indochina. Section five, War, relates how war came to Thailand. Section six, Looking forward, discusses the problems of military and economic security.

*Illustrations:* Coronation ceremony of King Rama VI. Signing of the Anglo-Siamese Pact of Nonaggression. Typical scenes within Bangkok.

156. GORDON, ERNEST. Through the Valley of the Kwai. New York, Harper, 1962. 257 p.; illustrations, map.
D805.J3G65

*Text:* Relates the experiences of prisoners of war, Americans and others, who built the "railroad of death" along the River Kwai in Thailand under torturous circumstances during the Japanese occupation of Southeast Asia. Strong religious overtones are manifested throughout the moving narrative.

*Illustrations:* Live drawings depicting the conditions in the Chungkai Camp and other prison camps.

*Map:* The railroad of death through the Valley of the Kwai.

157. GRISWOLD, ALEXANDER B. King Mongkut of
Siam. New York, Asia Society, 1961. 60
p.; bibliography, illustrations.    DS518.G7

*Text:* This well-documented historical treatise presents the highlights in the life of a Siamese monarch who proved himself to be one of the very few Asian leaders of the 19th century who could match in skill and diplomacy the Western empire-builders bent on increasing their holdings in all parts of Southeast Asia.

Tells about the opening of diplomatic relations with England, France, and America to generate a life-giving flow of Western trade with Thailand; introducing printing presses, modern currency, administrative reforms in government; employing foreign advisors, encouraging Westerners with their schools and hospitals; and, as a devout Buddhist, initiating reforms in the religious field—all to achieve the objective to transform Thailand into a modern, progressive state.

*Bibliography:* Various references are distributed throughout the notes.

*Illustrations:* King Mongkut.

158. GURNEY, NATALIE. History of the Territorial
Dispute Between Siam and French Indochina, and Post-War Political Developments
in the Disputed Territories. A thesis submitted to the Walter Hines Page School of
International Relations, Johns Hopkins University, 1950. vi, 192 p.; bibliography, map,
appendices.    DS575.G8

*Text:* Divided into three parts. Part one traces the history of the border dispute between Thailand and her neighbors, Laos and Cambodia, a problem which colored the foreign relations of Thailand for most of the past century. As a part of the background, relevant geographical, ethnic, social and international factors are provided.

Part two, based on previously unorganized and unanalyzed French, Thai, and American sources, gives a picture of political developments within Laos and Cambodia from the beginning of the Japanese occupation up to the postwar years. Particular attention is given to the nationalist movements in these two countries, especially the effect of the Japanese and Chinese upon the development of these nationalist movements.

*Bibliography:* Includes general histories and commentaries, periodical articles, and references to interviews.

*Map:* Territorial settlements on Indochinese peninsula based on OSS map, 1945.

*Appendices:* Treaty of 1893 between Siam and France. Franco-Siamese convention of 1904. Treaty of 1907 between Siam and France. Tokyo Convention, 1941. Population statistics of provinces ceded to Siam, 1941. Recommendations of Franco-Siamese Commission of Conciliation, 1947. Constitution of Laos, 1947. Treaty between France and Cambodia, 1949.

158a. INSOR, D. Thailand; a Political, Social and
Economic Analysis. New York, Praeger,
1963. 188 p.; bibliography, illustrations, appendix, index.    DS566.I5

*Text:* Following the opening chapters which are concerned with a description of Bangkok as the capital, climate, housing, health, labor and religion, the core of the work deals with Thai politics—the influence of the military, corruption, the part which Pibun and Pridi played in political change, communism, and the combating power in the present regime of General Sarit. The chapter on foreign affairs deals with Cambodia, Vietnam, Karens of Burma, the KMT, and Thailand's commitment to U.S. aid. Closing with a quick view of Thailand's economic change, emphasis is given to the part which the overseas Chinese play in trade and the economic life of the nation, the importance of agriculture, the government ventures in industry, and the financial status of the country.

*Bibliography:* Completely well-known secondary source material.

*Illustrations:* Typical views of housing, canals, bazaar shops, and religious shrines.

*Appendix:* Chronology of selected historical events in old Ayuthaya and Bangkok, 1785–1962.

159. LANDON, KENNETH PERRY. Siam in Transition; a Brief Survey of Cultural Trends in the
Five Years Since the Revolution of 1932.
Shanghai, Kelly and Walsh, 1939. 328 p.;
bibliography, map, appendices, index.
DS584.L3

*Text:* Describes modern trends in the country of Thailand as manifested just prior to and after the bloodless revolution in 1932, which transformed the absolute monarchy into a form of government approaching a democracy. The study shows the changes which have taken place in the Siamese way of life and indicates how the people were beginning to adjust themselves to a technological world.

The author discusses the political, economic, ethnic,

educational, medical, and religious trends, together with the trends in methods of communication, crime, family life, recreation, and arts and crafts. In the first two chapters which deal with Siamese politics, clear data are given relating to the causes, leaders, results of the 1932 revolution, and abdication of King Prajadhipok in 1935. In the section dealing with economic trends is a detailed outline of the economic program as formulated by the Ministry of Economic Affairs, newly established in 1933. The closing chapters dealing with religion describe the traditional Hinayana Buddhism in older Thailand and provide a summary of the modifying influences in modern Siamese religion.

*Bibliography:* An extensive list including many titles (transliterated) of Siamese works.

*Maps:* Map of Siam, scale–1:6,000,000, shows railways, highways, and principal cities.

*Appendices:* The decree proroguing the People's Assembly. Act concerning communism. A discussion of the Siamese family. King Prajadhipok's abdication announcement. National economic policy of Luang Pradist Manudharm. Economic Administration Act. Report of the Commission on the Alleged Communism of Luang Pradist Manudharm.

160. MARTIN, JAMES V., JR. A History of the Diplomatic Relations Between Siam and the United States of America, 1833–1929, 1929–1948. Unpublished thesis, Fletcher School of Law and Diplomacy, Tufts College, 1948. 2 vols.; bibliography, map, appendices.

Microfilm copy E–21

*Text:* Traces the numerous events of over a hundred years and presents in a coherent manner an account of the economic and political relations between the country of Thailand and the United States. Volume one discussed in detail the Roberts Treaty and the opening of Siamese-American diplomatic relations, the first attemps to establish commercial relations, the problems related to extraterritoriality, the unfruitful Balestier Mission, the repercussions of the American Civil War and its aftermath, and the "open door" policy and treaties of concillation in the 20th century. It relates how certain Americans—Sickles and Holderman, as official representatives; Matton, Bradley, and McFarland, as missionaries; and, Westengard and Sayre, as advisors—assisted Thailand to attain her status as a sovereign state among the nations. Volume two deals with the period from 1929 to 1948.

*Bibliography:* Extensive list of primary and secondary sources used in the study.

*Appendices:* Include documents relevant to the Commercial Treaty, 1833. The Harris Treaty, 1856. The Treaty and Protocol between the United States and Siam, 1920. The Extradition Treaty between the United States and Siam, 1922. The Treaty of Friendship, Commerce, and Navigation between the United States and Siam, 1938.

161. MINNEY, RUBEIGH JAMES. Fanny and the Regent of Siam. London, Collins, 1962. 382 p.; map, illustrations, chart.

DS582.P7M5 1962a

*Text:* This historical novel, as a sequel to *The English governess at the Siamese court* by Anna Leonowens, is an account of Anna's son Louis who is in the service of King Chulalongkorn. This historical treatise, providing valuable insights into the social life and other events in Thailand during the reign of King Chulalongkorn, is based on official documents, private diaries and letters, and interviews with persons closely related to the Leonowens and Knox families.

*Map:* Bangkok in 1878. Siam.

*Illustrations* (selected): Fanny Knox. Surivong Bunnog. Anna Leonowens, King Chulalongkorn.

*Chart:* Family tree of the Knox and Leonowens families.

162. MOFFAT, ABBOT LOW. Mongkut, the King of Siam. Ithaca, Cornell University Press, 1961. 254 p.; bibliography, illustrations, appendices. DS581.M6

*Text:* Describes "one of the great Asians of the nineteenth century" who, although he reigned in Thailand only 17 years (1851–1868), showed real statesmanship in guiding Thailand through the conflicting pressures and territorial ambitions of Western Powers without bowing to European domination.

The stated purpose is not to present a conventional biography of the King or a historical account of the reign of Rama III, but is merely to sketch the man with pertinent selections from the King's own writings. A number of King Mongkut's letters, decrees, judgments and state papers appear here for the first time in English.

*Bibliography:* Lists the books and articles cited in the source notes.

*Illustrations:* King Mongkut in royal regalia. King Mongkut's signature. A daguerreotype of King

Mongkut sent to President Pierce. A photograph of King Mongkut sent to Pope Pius IX. King Mongkut in Western uniform.

*Appendices:* Exchange of presents between President Pierce and King Mongkut, and between Queen Victoria and King Mongkut. An account of the illness and death of the consort of King Mongkut. Anna Leonowens as historian.

163. REEVE, W. D. Public Administration in Siam. London, Royal Institute of International Affairs, 1952. vi, 93 p.; tables, index. (Published in cooperation with the International Secretariat, Institute of Pacific Relations)

JQ1742.R4

*Text:* An examination of the system of administration as found within the government of Thailand, telling about its development since the establishment of the limited monarchy in 1932, and, in light of the merits and defects of the system, giving recommendations for possible improvements.

Following a brief introductory account of the geography, communications, economy, social factors, and prominent events in the recent constitutional history of Thailand, the discussion includes information regarding the following subjects: national debt and sources of revenue; kind of government which existed during the absolute monarchy before 1932 and during the limited monarchy in accordance with the Constitution of 1932; use of foreign advisors; organization of ministries and departments; territorial framework of the administration; legal and judicial system; education; public health and the cooperative movement; civil service under the absolute monarchy, and under the constitutional régime; and, the principal problem of bribery and corruption which has become acute in the years after World War II.

*Tables:* Statistical information about expenditure and revenue of the Thai government.

164. SKINNER, GEORGE WILLIAM. Leadership and Power in the Chinese Community of Thailand. Ithaca, Published for the Association of Asian Studies by Cornell University Press, 1958. xvii, 363 p.; bibliography, tables, charts, appendices, index. (Monographs of the Association of Asian Studies)

DS570.C5S55

*Text:* The first of a series of research projects planned to study the ethnic Chinese who form a substantial and significant minority people of Southeast Asia. Furthermore, this study is one of the very first known field studies of urban community leadership to be conducted in an oriental society.

The economic, political, and social impact of the Chinese in Thai society are related with great detail in these nine chapters: 1. History and community: the background of Chinese leadership in Thailand. 2. The men and their past: social characteristics of Chinese leaders. 3. Values and influences: the basic of elite and leader status. 4. Authority and alignments: the political dimensions of community leadership, 1951–52. 5. Leaders and business: the shape of economic power, 1951–52. 6. Control and the inner circle: the structure of power, 1952. 7. Assimilation and leadership: a rapprochment of expediency. 8. Stability and change: Chinese leadership through three years, 1952–55. 9. Politics and security: trends in the alignment of power, 1952–56.

*Bibliography:* Majority of sources cited are in Chinese, published in Bangkok or Singapore.

*Tables:* 41 in all, covering wealth, educational attainment, prestige and wealth, politico-economic power, Chinese associations, political orientation, and other subjects.

*Charts:* Power blocs. Leadership structure.

*Appendices:* A. Tables, on various subjects considered in text. B. Methodological notes.

165. SUTTON, JOSEPH L., ed. Problems of Politics and Administration in Thailand. Bloomington, Institute of Training for Public Service, Department of Government, Indiana University, 1962. 205 p.; bibliography.

JQ1745.I5

*Text:* A study made in Bangkok by the Indiana University group associated with the establishment of the Institute of Public Administration at Thammasat University. Discusses the actual forces and processes that constitute Thai government as presented under these topics: Political and administrative leadership by Joseph L. Sutton; The public service by Edgar L. Shor; Provincial government and administration by Frederick J. Horrigan; Municipal government and administration by John W. Ryan; Economic development by William J. Siffin; Interest and clientele groups by Fred W. Riggs; and Improving public administration in Thailand by Joseph B. Kingsbury.

*Bibliography:* References are cited in notes following each chapter.

166. U.S. Department of State. Office of Strategic Services. Research and Analysis Branch. Territorial Conflicts Between Thailand and French Indochina. [Washington] 1945. iv, 150 p.; bibliography, maps, appendices. UB250.U33

*Text:* A study of the role of Thailand in the colonial expansion of France on the Indochinese peninsula from 1863 to 1941, including data on geographic, economic, and ethnic factors involved in a long series of conflicts between Thailand and Indochina regarding disputed areas along the international border.

Details concerning the geographic, economic, and ethnic relationships in the disputed areas serve as an introduction to the historical data in the chronological account of the territorial conflicts from the time when the French assumed control of Cambodia, an area claimed by Thailand, to the occasion when Thailand utilized the opportunity offered by French colonial weakness and Japanese aggression to reopen the border question and by treaty claimed suzerainty over certain border territory in Indochina. The closing chapter, Recapitulation, discusses the wish of the Thai Government to retain the territories acquired in 1941, but explains that Thailand would welcome a review and investigation of the whole border problem by an international commission.

Published British and American diplomatic documents and manuscript material from the U.S. Department of State archives provide the basic sources for the study.

*Bibliography:* Lists briefly the official documents, French sources, and other references used in the study.

*Maps:* Thailand and French Indochina territorial changes, 1867–1907 (color), scale–1:4,000,000. Thailand and French Indochina territorial retrocessions, 1941 (color), scale–1:4,000,000. Thailand and French Indochina ethnic groups (color). Selected route across the Indochinese peninsula (color)—showing railways, selected water routes, selected roads, selected caravan trails, and transportation bottlenecks.

*Appendix:* Treaties of 1867, 1898, 1904, and 1907 between France and Thailand. An English translation of the Franco-Thai treaty of 1941, as summarized in the *Tokyo Gazette.*

167. Vella, Walter Francis. The Impact of the West on Government in Thailand. Berkeley, University of California Press, 1955. 317–410 p.; bibliography, index. (University of California publications in political science, vol. 4, no. 3) JQ1742.V4

*Text:* An account of government in Thailand in the 19th and 20th centuries with particular reference to the way in which the absolute monarchy, the centralized bureaucracy, provincial administration, and the class system were all affected by new Western techniques, the spread of Western political ideas, and finally the influence of the democratic ideal.

The six chapters are: 1. The traditional pattern of government. 2. The adoption of Western techniques in government by the monarch, 1851–1910. 3. Democratic trends, 1910–32. 4. The establishment of the constitutional regime, 1932–38. 5. The decline of constitutionalism, 1938–52. 6. Prospects for democratic government.

*Bibliography:* 3 parts—sources in the Thai language; books and pamphlets; and periodical articles.

168. Vella, Walter Francis. Siam Under Rama III, 1824–1851. Locust Valley, N.Y., Published for the Association for Asian Studies by J. J. Augustin, 1957. ix, 180 p.; bibliography, illustrations, maps, appendix, index. (Monographs of the Association for Asian Studies, 4) DS580.V4

*Text:* This volume is the first critical study in English of that part of Thai history dealing with the reign of Rama III, King Phra Nang Klao, of the Chakkri Dynasty. The aspects covered during this twenty-seven year period from 1824 to 51, represent a Thailand which is considerably different from the Thailand which was developed in the next reign during the years of King Mongkut. It was during Rama III's time that one is able to read about a king who was looked upon as being semidivine, and one who held absolute power; a social order with a wealthy aristocracy existing simultaneously alongside a large peasant farmer population living in a semivassal status; a reform movement in the national faith of Buddhism, led by Prince Mongkut, to conform to ideas of Western science; a marked development in the arts; and a nation which had the minimum contact with the Western world.

Besides this general picture of a feudal society, the author's original research with vernacular sources in the Thai language makes it possible to know about the court intrigue, the King's administrative problems, and the foreign policy of Thailand in her relation to her tributary vassals of Laos, Cambodia, and certain Malay sultanates. An insight is gained into those policies by which Thailand was to be successful eventually in preserving her freedom in her foreign relations with the Western powers of Britain and France, and thus to become the only country in Southeast Asia not to succumb to Western expansion.

*Bibliography:* List of books and periodical articles in the Thai language and Western languages, many of the Thai titles being listed for the first time in a published bibliographical list.

*Illustrations:* Rama III. Buddha image in Wat Parinnayok.

*Maps:* Malay vassal states, 1824, in relation to Siam. Siam and its Laotian vassal states, 1824. Cambodia, 1824, in relation to Siam. Siam and its vassals, 1851.

*Appendix:* Important events in the history of Siam.

169. WILSON, DAVID A. Politics in Thailand. Ithaca, Cornell University Press, 1962. xiv, 307 p.; bibliography, tables, chart, appendices, index. (Published under the auspices of the Southeast Asia Program, Cornell University.)

JQ1745.W5

*Text:* Provides an analysis of the general characteristics of Thai political relationships, with an effort to portray them as the fundamental, concrete experiences of Thai politicians. Points up the prominent dynamic aspects of the structure of institutional behaviour, and thereby examines Thailand's Constitution. Throughout the study the gradual and sudden changes which have taken place due to the interplay of cultural, social and legal forces are sketched.

Contents: 1. Historical background. 2. Economic and social setting. 3. Authority and kingship. 4. National leadership. 5. The Cabinet and bureaucratic government. 6. Military bureaucracy. 7. The difficulties of the National Assembly. 8. Political organizations. 9. Coups and constitutions. 10. Conclusion.

*Bibliography:* Divided into three parts: newspapers and periodicals, laws and documents, and general books.

*Tables:* 1. Prime Ministers in the constitutional period. 2. Summary of constitutional history, 1932–61.

*Charts:* The inculcation of character in the army academy.

*Appendices:* Political chronology, 1932–59. Constitution (interim) of the Kingdom of Thailand, 1959.

170. WOOD, WILLIAM ALFRED RAE. A History of Siam From the Earliest Times to the Year A.D. 1781, With a Supplement Dealing With More Recent Events. Rev. ed. Bangkok, The Siam Barnakich Press, 1933. 300 p.; illustrations, map, appendix, index.

DS571.W6 1933

*Text:* Relates the salient facts of Thai history down to the time when Rama I of the present Chakkri Dynasty ascended the throne in the late 18th century. The closing chapter provides the highlights of the reign of Rama I through that of Rama VI.

For some years the author was the British Consul-General at Chiengmai.

*Map:* Kingdom of Siam.

*Illustrations:* H.R.H. Prince Damrong Rajanubhab. The seven kings of the Chakkri Dynasty.

*Appendix:* Table showing the Pali form of some of the names of persons and places used in the book.

# ECONOMICS

(including: Agriculture, Commerce, Industry, and Labor)

171. ANDREWS, JAMES MADISON. Siam, 2nd Rural Economic Survey, 1934–1935. Bangkok, Bangkok Times Press, 1935. viii, 396 p.; map, tables, appendices.     HD2111.S5A5

*Text:* A survey performed by a Professor of Anthropology at Harvard under the joint auspices of the Government of Thailand and Harvard University. Deals with factual information on economic conditions in rural Thailand.

The analysis of the incomes, expenditures, and inventories of over 1,700 rural Thai households in forty villages of the agricultural districts provides detailed information about farm costs; future of agriculture; fishing; livestock; handicrafts; labor; trade; annual incomes; expenditures for food, clothing, and housing; and operating profits, agricultural credits, and economic development.

*Map:* Siam, showing villages studied.

*Tables:* Farming costs. Income from crops. Annual and capital expenditures for fishing. Income from fishing. Income from handicrafts. Income from labor. Income from trade. Expenditures for food, clothing, and housing. Annual income. Distribution of annual expenditure. Capital expenditure. Capital income. Debts, interest rates, and loans.

*Appendices:* Members of the committee convened by the Ministry of Economic Affairs. Members of the survey party.

172. INGRAM, JAMES C. Economic Change in Thailand Since 1850. Stanford, Stanford University Press, 1955. vii, 254 p.; bibliography, map, tables, appendices, index. (Issued under the auspices of the International Secretariat, Institute of Pacific Relations)
HC497.S515

*Text:* Based largely on an examination of official files of the Government of Thailand, this revised thesis has the distinction of being the first book to describe in any detail the economic changes that have taken place in that country in the last century.

Following an introductory chapter of general historical background, the writer describes the economy of Thailand at the time of Rama IV or King Mongkut. It was during the reign of this Thai monarch that an Anglo-Thai treaty was negotiated in 1855, thus linking Thailand to the world economy and exposing her to outside influences from which she had been largely isolated. It is shown that this and subsequent events led eventually to widespread use of money and exchange based chiefly on world markets, and to a racial division of labor.

The remainder of the book is organized on a topical rather than a chronological basis. Rice, Thailand's principal export, is the subject to two of the eleven chapters, with special attention to the Thai Government's role in the rice industry. The other topics include non-rice imports and the development of home-market industries, currency and exchange, sources of government revenue, government expenditures to strengthen the nation's economy, the effects of American aid during the years following World War II. On the whole, it is made clear that Thailand is an excellent example of a country which, during its economic development, has changed—and is still in the process of changing—from a predominantly subsistence and barter economy to a money economy.

*Bibliography:* A selected list of references on Thai economics, including numerous official Thai documents.

*Map:* Thailand, showing railroads and principal cities.

*Tables:* Siam's exports in 1850. Rice exports, 1857–1961. Population by official census, 1911–47. Teak, tin, rubber and rubber exports, 1867–1951. Revenue sources, 1892–1950.

*Appendices:* Regions in Thailand. Government receipts and expenditures. Statistics of foreign trade. Exchange rates, 1850–1951.

173. U.S. DEPARTMENT OF COMMERCE. Thailand: A Market for U.S. Products, by Paul A. Mayer. Washington, 1962. viii, 92 p.; illustrations, maps, tables, graphs, appendices.
In process

*Text:* Provides current market information on Thailand and describes that country's present import pattern, distribution and marketing facilities, and import regulations and trade practices.

*Illustrations* (selected): Yan Hee Dam. Kong Toi harbor. Aerial view of Bangkok.

*Maps:* Thailand. Bangkok business district. Thailand transportation system.

*Tables:* Indicated by * in appendices.

*Graphs* (selected): 1. Thailand's population growth. 2. Thai imports. 5. Foreign trade. 6. Thailand's leading suppliers.

*Appendices:* *A. Laws, regulations, programs, and other factors affecting Thailand's market potential, including Thailand's six-year economic development plan. *B. Selected statistical information. C. Commercial information: American companies with offices, distributors, or agents in Thailand.

# SOCIAL CONDITIONS
(including: Anthropology, Education and Health)

174. COUGHLIN, RICHARD J. Double Identity; the Chinese in Modern Thailand. Hong Kong, Hong Kong University Press, Oxford University Press, 1960. xi, 222 p.; bibliography, maps, tables, index. DS570.C5C6 1960

*Text:* Based on a thesis prepared at Yale University, *The Chinese in Bangkok, a study of cultural persistence,* this account is focused on the contemporary group-life of the Chinese in Thailand (principally Bangkok) with particular attention given to their community structure, principal institutions, and their economic and political interests. The principal characteristic of these overseas Chinese is their ability to participate as dual members in their own Chinese community and in Thai society.

These chapter headings suggest the scope of the study: 2. Immigration and its control. 3. Chinese community life. 4. Home and family life. 5. Temples, spirits and festivals. 6. Economic organization and interests. 7. Chinese schools and education. 8. Citizenship and political interests.

*Bibliography:* Lists well-known secondary sources about Chinese in Southeast Asia.

*Maps:* Thailand and her neighbors. Provinces and ports of Chinese emigration.

*Tables* (selected): Population changes of Chinese aliens. Chinese schools in Thailand and Bangkok.

175. DE YOUNG, JOHN E. Village Life in Modern Thailand. Berkeley & Los Angeles, University of California Press, 1955. vii, 225 p.; bibliography, illustrations, maps, tables, appendices, index. (Institute of East Asiatic Studies, University of California.

HD940.5.D4

*Text:* In this descriptive study, attention is focused on the vast area of Thailand to the north and northeast of Bangkok. More than two-thirds of Thailand is included in this region, and in it live eighty percent of the rural peasants. In the long-settled, compact villages, a self-subsistent rice economy is practiced, and dependence on secondary crops is a forced necessity. The discussion of the agricultural and economic patterns brings out the important fact that commercialized rice cultivation during the present century has wrought important changes in the social and economic life of the peasants.

Sociologists will find interesting the chapters dealing with Thai village organizations, the typical daily activities of a Thai farming family, the social interrelationships, and the religious beliefs and practices cherished by the Thai Buddhists.

*Bibliography:* Lists of titles of books and periodical articles giving general background information on Thailand.

*Illustrations:* Views related to living conditions, farming methods, and the religious life of the people.

*Maps:* Geographic areas of Thailand. Typical village layouts. Plan of a village wat.

*Appendices:* Tables on population growth, on birth and mortality rates, on land area in various provinces, and population by major regions. Chart of provincial and district government. List of Thai official holidays.

176. GRAHAM, HENRY M. Some Changes in Thai Family Life, a Preliminary Study. Bangkok,

Institute of Public Administration, Thammasat University, n. d. 61 p. HQ686.5.G7

*Text:* With no comprehensive study of Thai family life available, this preliminary account provides an insight into Thai family problems, conflicts, patterns of thinking and doing. Most all the information given was obtained from personal interviews with Thai people, for the most part well-educated persons.

Selected portions of the three principal chapters are education, standard of living, mate selection, child rearing, financial conflicts, conflict about religion, and increased struggles with standards of living.

177. JUMSAI, MANICH. Compulsory Education in Thailand. Paris, UNESCO, 1951. 110 p.; map, appendices. LC136.J8

*Text:* Following a statement about Buddhist influence on education, the interest of Siamese kings in education, and the emergence of the modern period of education, a historical account of the development of education in Thailand, with specific references to the Palace system from 1871 to 87, the State system of education from 1887 to 1921, and the beginnings of compulsory education from 1921–32 is presented. Concluding chapters give data on the advances in compulsory education after the revolution in 1932 and discuss the general problems of primary education.

*Map:* Thailand, showing routes and railways.

*Appendices:* Names of the kings of the Chakkri Dynasty. Names of successive ministers of education. A chronology of events pertaining to education in Thailand.

178. KAUFMAN, HOWARD KEVA. Bangkhuad; a Community Study in Thailand. Locust Valley, N.Y., published for the Association of Asian Studies by J. J. Augustin, 1960. ix, 235 p.; bibliography, illustrations, glossary, appendices, index. (Monographs of the Association of Asian Studies, 10) DS568.K3

*Text:* As volume ten of the Monographs of the Association for Asian Studies, this village study is centered in a rice growing area of central Thailand. A general introductory chapter discusses the geography, ethnohistory, agriculture, education, religious practices, and Buddhist sects. Following chapter two which outlines the community structure of Bangkhuad, the succeeding chapters discuss economy, government and law, education, the Wat (monastery), daily life, and religious concepts and ceremonies.

*Bibliography:* A brief list of well-known Western-language references.

*Illustrations:* Line drawings of articles used in the village.

*Glossary:* List of Thai words with meanings used in text.

*Appendices* (selected): Thai proverbs. Superstitions. Activities and customs. Weights and measures.

179. KINGSHILL, KONRAD. Ku Daeng—the Red Tomb; a Village Study in Northern Thailand. Chiangmai, Prince Royal's College. Distributed by The Siam Society, Bangkok, 1960. xiii, 310 p.; bibliography, illustrations, maps, tables, glossary, appendices, index.

HN750.5.K5

*Text:* Provides ethnographical data gathered in a village in the Chiangmai plain in northern Thailand with particular attention to the problems of cultural change and receptivity, the village status hierarchy, and the role of the Buddhist religious institutions.

Various social, economic, political, and religious aspects of this Thai village are presented in these chapters: 2. Environment and population. 3. The village economy. 4. The family. 5. Education. 6. Age and sex roles. 7. Government. 8. Religion in Ku Daeng. 9. Religious expression. 10. Acculturation.

*Bibliography:* Includes many references in the Thai language on Buddhism in Thailand.

*Illustrations:* 112 views of village life: housing, fishing methods, rice cultivation, religious festivals, village customs, and other practices.

*Maps:* 1. Thailand and neighboring countries. 2. Sarapi District. 3. Ku Daeng village.

*Tables:* Indicated by * in appendices.

*Glossary:* Thai words used in text are given in both Thai sceipt and transliteration.

*Appendices* (selected): B.* Distribution of population by age and sex. D. Kinship terminology. L. Prestige rating.

180. LANDON, KENNETH PERRY. The Chinese in Thailand. London, New York, Oxford University Press, 1941. xi, 310 p.; bibliography, appendices, index. (A Report in the International research series of the Institute of Pacific Relations)

DS570.C5L3

*Text:* Examines the social and economic conditions and the legal status of the Chinese people resident in Thailand. Evaluates the various measures introduced by the Government of Thailand; to limit the size of the Chinese community by means of government control of immigration; to control the activities of the Chinese in major and minor industries, with special reference to commerce and trade; to bring about a rigid control of Chinese schools, which for the most part were founded to preserve the foreign culture of a minority population; and to perpetuate the Chinese language and Chinese nationalism. The closing chapter, entitled Chinese in politics, discusses the part that Chinese secret societies played in Thai politics, the way in which Chinese newspapers served Chinese political purposes, and the restrictions by Thai law which were placed upon the Chinese in voting, participation in politics, and holding public office.

*Bibliography:* List of books, reports, and periodicals pertaining to the subjects discussed in the text.

*Appendices:* Excerpts from the treaty of friendship, commerce, and navigation between Siam and Japan (1938). Excerpts from the Constitution of Siam (1932). The principles of the People's Party, which overthrew the monarchy in 1932.

181. SEIDENFADAN, ERIK. The Thai Peoples. Book I. The Origins and Habitats of the Thai Peoples, With a Sketch of Their Materials and Spiritual Culture. Bangkok, Siam Society, 1958. 177 p.; bibliography, illustrations, maps.

DS560.S4

*Text:* A presentation which describes the historical origins of the Thai people in western central Asia, from where they trekked across China and later settled in the tropical areas to the south in Thailand.

These eight chapters describe the various Thai groups located in different parts of Thailand: 1. The origin of the Thai. 2. The various Thai groups and their physical types. 3. The northern and central Thai. 4. The western Thai. 5. The eastern Thai. 6. The southern Thai. 7. The non-Thai peoples of Thailand. 8. Thailand, the land of the Thai.

*Bibliography:* Cites books and articles pertaining to the ethnological characteristics of the Thai.

*Illustrations:* Numerous pictures of the racial types, houses, and religious monuments.

*Maps:* Approximate Thai habitats in China, ethnological sketch maps of Thailand and Laos.

182. SKINNER, GEORGE WILLIAM. Chinese Society in Thailand; an Analytical History. Ithaca, Cornell University Press, 1957. xvii, 459 p.; bibliography, maps, tables, charts, index.

DS570.C5S54

*Text:* Presents a historical account of the role which the Chinese have played in Thailand from the seventeenth century to the present day.

The early history from the time of the Ayuthia and Thonburi periods into the reigns of the Chakkri Dynasty is presented in the chapters dealing with the Chinese in old Siam; Chinese migration and population growth to 1917; the Chinese position in the Thai economy through the reign of Chulalongkorn; and Chinese society in Siam from the reign of Nangklao through the reign of Chulalongkorn.

The modern period is dealt with in the last five chapters on Transition to nationalism and cohesion; Demographic trends, 1918–55; Chinese life in Thai society to 1938; The Second World War and its aftermath; and Chinese under the second Phibun administration, 1948–56.

*Bibliography:* Includes lengthy list of books, Western and Chinese, as well as articles and newspapers used or cited in the text.

*Maps:* Outline map showing regions and major towns. Emigrant areas in China from which Chinese came to Thailand. Central Thailand showing railroads, river systems, and towns. Index of Chinese concentration.

*Tables* (selected): Chinese immigrants, and emigrants in Thailand, 1882–1917 . . . 1918–55. Chinese population in Thailand—prior to 1917. Distribution by region of Chinese nationals, 1919–47. Occupational stratification of Thai and Chinese ethnic groups.

*Charts:* Growth of China-born population in Thailand, 1882–1955. Chinese emigrants and immigrants in Thailand, 1882–1917 . . . 1918–55.

183. TIRABUTANA, PRAJUAB. A Simple One; the Story of a Siamese Girlhood. Ithaca, Southeast Asia Program, Department of Far Eastern Studies, Cornell University, 1958. 40 p.

DS568.T55

*Text:* A short autobiographical account of the childhood of a young Thai woman who was born and reared in a provincial town in northeast Thailand not far from the border of Laos. Presents a most readable and illuminating account of the experiences of a Thai child in typical Thai surroundings which are not completely divorced from Western influences. Her reactions to these influences of the West and the effect on her thinking and actions is most revealing.

The narrative was written at the time when the author was learning English in a Unesco Fundamental Educational Center in Ubol. The style, organization, and English usage were not altered in order to preserve the thought and style of the writer.

184. UNITED NATIONS EDUCATIONAL, SCIENTIFIC, AND CULTURAL ORGANIZATION. CONSULTATIVE EDUCATION MISSION TO THAILAND. Report of the Mission to Thailand, February 10 to March 5, 1949, by Sir John Sargent and Pedro T. Orato. Paris, 1950. 56 p.; bibliography, illustrations, map, tables, charts, appendices. (UNESCO publication No. 630)

LA1221.U5 1949

*Text:* Presents the observations and recommendations based on a brief study of the educational situation in Thailand by a mission authorized by the Fundamental Education Division of UNESCO. The chairman of the Mission which prepared the report, commonly referred to as the Sargent-Orato report, was Sir John Sargent who headed an educational mission in 1947 for the study of education in India.

The mission ascertained first the numerous problems which confront the schools of Thailand: compulsory attendance, curriculum, teacher education, examinations and evaluation of the student's accomplishments, and adult and university education. Second, the mission indicated how the schools of Thailand could best cooperate with the various departments of government in promoting the common welfare of all the people. Specific recommendations are made for implementing the best educational principles with which to meet the current problems in Thailand.

*Bibliography:* A brief list of books for general background reading on Thailand.

*Illustrations:* Photographs of school buildings, school groups, and vocational school activities.

*Maps:* Map of Thailand, prepared for the Thai Department of General Education.

*Tables:* Statistics on the number of schools, teachers, and enrollment. Qualifications for teachers in higher vocational schools. Data about adult evening classes.

Subjects within the curricula of elementary and pre-university classes.

185.  YOUNG, OLIVER GORDON. The Hill Tribes of Northern Thailand: A Socio-Ethnological Report. [Bangkok] Prepared under the auspices of the Government of Thailand and the cooperation of the U.S. Operations Mission to Thailand, 1961. 120 p.; illustrations, maps, tables, chart.           DS569.Y63

*Text:* Based on the personal observations and knowledge of one who has been associated with the Lahu and other tribes of northern Thailand and Burma for many years. The lifelong acquaintance of the author with the habits, patterns of living, customs, and traditions of these hill peoples, enables this brief account to fill a great need for this kind of information.

Discusses the affiliation, location, population, language, religion, villages, physical description, economy, social customs, and village government of these tribes: Akha, Lahu, Lisu, Meo, Yao, Kha, Mu, Htin, Kha Haw, Yumbri, Skaw Karen, P'wo Karen, B'ghive Karen, Taungthu, and Haw.

*Illustrations:* Facial features, houses, clothing and decorations, dances, and other features of the people.

*Maps:* General maps showing migration, distribution, and farming areas of the hill peoples. Individual maps showing location of each tribe discussed.

*Tables* (selected): 1. Population. 2. Location by provinces. 3. Population and causes of death. 6. Agricultural products. 7. Income. 8. Ethnolinguistic affiliations.

*Chart:* Origins of the hill tribes of northern Thailand.

## CULTURAL LIFE
(including: Fine Arts, Language, Literature, and Religion)

186.  ANUMAN RAJADHON, PHYA. Life and Ritual in Old Siam: Three Studies of Thai Life and Customs. Translated and edited by William J. Gedney. New Haven, HRAF Press, 1961. 191 p.; illustrations.           DS568.A7

*Text:* This compilation comprises three related articles prepared in the original Thai language by a Thai writer who is intimately acquainted with traditional Thai culture and is a devout student of Thai history, literature, and language.

The titles of the three papers are: 1. The life of the farmer. 2. Popular Buddhism in Thailand. 3. Customs connected with birth and the rearing of children.

*Illustrations:* Drawings and photographs of farm implements, village weddings, ordinations, and hair cutting.

187.  BENEDICT, RUTH. Thai Culture and Behavior; an Unpublished War-time Study Dated September, 1943.* Ithaca, Southeast Asia Program, Department of Far Eastern Studies, Cornell University, 1952. 2, iii, 45 p.; bibliography. (Data paper no. 4)           DS568.B4

*Text:* An investigation of the Thai way of life and regularities of their customary behavior by a prominent cultural anthropologist, well known for her *Patterns of culture* (Boston, Houghton Mifflin, 1943) and *Race: science and politics* (New York, Viking Press, 1945). Describes the interrelated sociological and psychological aspects of Thai culture manifested in Thai dealings with other national states in economic matters, in religious practices, and in practices within the family, and shows what patterns of Thai behaviour emerges. The account tells about the customs related not only to the royal court and government officials but particularly to the life of the common people who comprise about 90 percent of the Thai population. While the author has relied largely on printed books for information, data on childlife and practices of adults were secured from Thai persons in the United States.

Divided into two parts: Part one deals with historical background, religion and animism, and the principal characteristics of adult life; Part two considers the customs connected with Thai children and some general characteristics of Thai life—the enjoyment of life, the "cool heart," and male dominance.

*Bibliography:* Lists the books consulted during the study.

188.  CARTWRIGHT, BASIL OSBORN. The Student's Manual of the Siamese Language. Bangkok, Printed by the American Presbyterian Mission Press; London, Luzac, 1915. vii, 320 p.; appendices.           PL4163.C35

*Text:* Divided into three parts. Part one discusses the characters and their various combinations in the Thai language. Also, the five distinct tones used in the Thai language are discussed with considerable de-

---

*[Originally published by the Institute for International Studies, Inc., New York, in 1946 for limited distribution.]

tail. Part two treats the elements of Thai grammar, and numerous exercises illustrate grammatical construction. Part three deals with Thai orthography.

Brief English-Thai and Thai-English vocabularies conclude the handbook.

*Appendices:* Common Thai liable to be confused. A complete list of all the Thai designatory particles.

Notes on Thai names and titles.

[This work was originally published with the title *An elementary handbook of the Siamese language* (Bangkok, Printed at The American Presbyterian Mission Press; London, Luzac, 1906)].

189. INDIANA UNIVERSITY. The Arts of Thailand: A Handbook of the Architecture, Sculpture and Painting of Thailand (Siam). Edited by Theodore Bowie. Bloomington, Indiana University Press, 1960. 219 p.; bibliography, illustrations, map, index.     N7321.I5

*Text:* This volume is a description of various selected works on Thai art, the property of museums in Thailand and of private persons or institutions, both Thai and American, in an exhibit on display in eight American institutions from October 1960 to March 1962 under the joint honorary patronage of the United States and Thailand. Besides the carefully prepared notes for the catalog by Subhadradis Diskul, two worthy treatises on the fine arts of Thailand appear in the chapters: The architecture and sculpture of Siam by Alexander B. Griswold and A note on Thai painting by Elizabeth Lyons.

*Bibliography:* A brief list including works of these scholars of Thai art and archaeology: Coedès, Döhring, Griswold, Le May, and others.

*Illustrations* (selected): Images and objects in stone and marble. Figures in stucco and terra cotta. Bronze figures and heads. Objects in bronze, brass, and lead. Gold, jewelry, niello, and silver objects. Ceramic works. Objects in wood. Paintings. Illuminated manuscripts.

*Map:* Archaeological map of Thailand.

190. LE MAY, REGINALD STUART. A Concise History of Buddhist Art in Siam. Cambridge, England University Press, 1938. xxi, 165 p.; bibliography, illustrations, maps, index.
N7321.L4

*Text:* Furnishes a connected and comprehensive account of the art of Thailand and includes information on the intimately related arts of Burma, Cambodia, and other neighboring countries. From out of the complexity of the streams of foreign cultural influence which appear concurrently in different parts of Thailand, the study shows important aspects of Siamese art over a period of about 1,500 years. Particular attention is given to the different forms of Buddhist art which flourished in Thailand from the early part of the Christian era to the end of the 16th century. Shows the influence which the art of India and Ceylon have had in certain areas of Southeast Asia. Delineates in broad outline the different schools of art in different historical periods which have penetrated Thailand and left their impress upon that country—the Dvaravati (Môn-Indian) period, the Kingdom of Crivijaya and the Indo-Javanese school; the Khmer period, the Chiengsen school and the Suk'ot'ai school.

*Bibliography:* Contains two principal lists: those works dealing with Indian and allied art and history as a groundwork for the study of Buddhist art in Thailand; those works which deal with art and history and have a direct bearing on the forms of art found in Thailand.

*Illustrations:* Photographs of the different phases through which the art forms in Thailand have passed, including examples from India, Ceylon, Burma, and Cambodia for purposes of comparison.

*Maps:* Sea routes between India and the Indochinese peninsula. Siam and adjoining countries.

191. MCFARLAND, GEORGE BRADLEY. Thai-English Dictionary. Stanford University, Stanford University Press; London, Oxford University Press, 1944. xxi, 1019, 39 p.; bibliography, appendices.     PL4187.M18 1944

*Text:* A voluminous work which presents each word with the Thai script, transliteration, and English equivalent. The lengthy introduction discusses the following aspects of the Thai language: consonants, vowels, tones, numerical designatory particles, word arrangement, and typographical signs.

*Bibliography:* Lists about fifty books which were used in the preparation of this dictionary, and also the symbols of reference used in the text.

*Appendices:* One thousand common Thai words most used. Scientific Thai terms used for birds, fishes, and flora.

192. [MANUNET BAHNAN, PHYA, ed.] Siamese Tales, Old and New: The Four Riddles and Other Stories. Translated by Reginald [Stuart] Le May, with some reflections on the tales. London, Noel Douglas, 1930. 192 p.  GS312.M3

*Text:* One of the very few books translated into a Western language which allows a Thai person to speak for himself and shows firsthand, by means of the fifteen stories given: the Thai outlook on life, his capacity for humor, the values within his philosophy of life, the place of magic and superstition in his thinking, and the use of proverbs in Thai literature.

The portion entitled Reflections gives the author's observations of Thai village life, Thai-Buddhist practices, types of Thai literature, and many other subjects—all drawn from the author's experience when he was Advisor to the Thai Government in the Ministry of Commerce and Communications.

The editor of these folk tales was a former Judge of the International Court in Bangkok.

193. Thailand Culture Series. Bangkok, National Culture Institute, 1953– Illustrations, maps, charts, music scores.  DS568.T5

*Text:* Up to 1955 these seventeen studies on various aspects of Thai culture were issued: 1. The cultures of Thailand by Phya Anuman Rajadhon. 2. A brief survey of cultural Thailand by Phya Anuman Rajadhon. 3. Thai literature and Swasdi Raksa by Phya Anuman Rajadhon. 4. Thai architecture and painting by Silpa Birasri. 5. Loy Krathong and Songkran festivals by Phya Anuman Rajadhon. 6. Chao Thi and some traditions of Thay by Phya Anuman Rajadhon. 7. Phra cedi by Phya Anuman Rajadhon. 8. Thai music by Phra Chen Duriyanga. 9. Thai images of the Buddha by Luang Boribal Buribhand. 10. Thai Buddhist sculpture by Silpa Birasri. 11. The knon (masked Play) by Prince Dhaninivat Kromamün Bidyalabh. 13. The story of Thai marriage custom by Phya Anuman Rajadhon. 14. Modern art in Thailand by Silpa Birasri. 15. The preliminary course in training in Thai theatrical art by Dhanit Yupho. 16. Life in Bangkok by Witt Siwasariyanon. 17. Thai language by Phya Anuman Rajadhon.

*Illustrations:* Pagodas, Buddhist images, dramatic art, and many other ideas considered in the various pamphlets.

194. WALES, HORACE GEOFFREY QUARITCH. Siamese State Ceremonies, Their History and Function. London, Bernard Quaritch, 1931. xiv, 326 p.; illustrations, index.  DS568.W3

*Text:* An analytical description of the religious festivals and court ceremonies which have played an important part in Siamese history and still remain the most characteristic features of Siamese social life. Despite the fact that most of the royal ceremonies discussed in this work—the coronation, tonsure, and, cremation ceremonies connected with the kingship—as well as agricultural ceremonies, and other miscellaneous state ceremonies are Hindu in origin and continue to manifest much Brahmanical ritual, the author shows that Buddhism is now the real religion of both the people and kings of Thailand, as has been the case for many centuries.

Buddhism is considered in the study only in so far as it is necessary to understand the Buddhist practices introduced by pious kings in connection with the state ceremonies. Only one purely Buddhist festival is discussed—the Kathina—which illustrates that aspect of Siamese kingship in which the king is the protector of the people's faith. In analyzing the various rituals, the author shows the value of any given custom or rite for the continuity of culture. Particularly, the author expresses concern for the actual sociological value of the rite as shown by the effect which it has on the life and status of the Siamese community.

The principal sources of information were Siamese literature and the author's personal observations when he was in the Lord Chamberlain's Department, Court of Siam.

*Illustrations:* Temples, thrones, and regalia used during the ceremonies.

195. WELLS, KENNETH ELMER. Thai Buddhism, Its Rites and Activities. Bangkok, Distributors: Christian Bookstore, 1960. 320 p.; bibliography, illustrations, index.

  BL1445.T5W4 1960

*Text:* Portrays Buddhist practices and traditions as followed by the people and the organized clergy of Thailand in conducting daily ceremonies of worship in temples, in sponsoring religious fairs and festivals, in assisting with ceremonies of state, and in promoting education, both religious and secular. Numerous Siamese texts are used for commentaries on Siamese ceremonies and for the Pali chants and responses. There is virtually nothing in Western works about the chants.

A companion volume to *Siamese Ceremonies; Their History and Function* by Horace Geoffrey Quaritch Wales (1931).

*Bibliography:* Includes an extensive list of books in the Thai language and numerous titles of books and articles in Western languages.

*Illustrations:* Various temples and ceremonies.

196. WENNING, RUDOLF, and A. F. SOMM. Thailand. Photographs by Michael Wolgensingen. English version by H. Carmichael. Zurich, Éditions Silva, [1961?] 121 p.; illustrations. DS566.W413

*Text:* Translation of *Wunderland Siam* (Zurich, Éditions Silva, 1959).

The text provides information on such subjects as Buddhism and Buddhist practices, races and tribes, language, calendar, festivals, temples, handicrafts, theater, music, politics, and economic affairs, and photographs give a graphic introduction of Thailand to the person becoming acquainted with this colorful country of Southeast Asia.

*Illustrations:* Show all the subjects noted above, and many other aspects of Thai life and culture.

197. YUPHO, DHANIT. Thai Musical Instruments. Translated from the Thai by David Morton. [Bangkok, Printed by Siva Phorn, Ltd., 1960] xi, 104 p.; illustrations. ML541.T5Y8

*Text:* Following a brief historical statement of the time when the Thai people were resident many centuries ago in southern China, a short account tells how the various Thai instruments received their names.

The instruments discussed comprise three groups: percussion instruments made of wood, metal, and skin or leather; the wind instruments; and the stringed instruments played either with a plectrum or a bow. Altogether fifty-six instruments are described with considerable detail.

Includes a phonetic system used by the translator in the translation.

*Illustrations:* Photographs and line drawing show the individual instruments and ensembles playing the three types of instruments.

# IV

# Cambodia, Laos, and Vietnam

## GENERAL BACKGROUND

198. BERIAULT, RAYMOND. Khmers. Montréal, Les Éditions Leméac, 1957. 256 p.; illustrations.
DS557.C2B4

*Text:* A general descriptive account of the history and cultural aspects of Cambodia, with particular reference to Angkor Wat. The chapter headings are: Le Cambodge moderne; et son histoire; et son peuple; et sa religion bouddhique; et ses ruines archéologiques; et la présence de la France; et son avenir.

*Illustrations:* Views from the everyday life of the Cambodian people in the city and countryside. Angkor Wat.

198a. BERVAL, RENÉ DE. Kingdom of Laos; the Land of the Million Elephants and the White Parasol. In collaboration with Their Highnesses Princess Phetsarath and Souvanna Phouma, and others. Translation by Mrs. Teissier du Cros, Alexander Allan, John W. Fisher, E. R. Pratt. Saigon, France-Asie, 1959. 506 p.; bibliography, illustrations, musical scores, map, tables. DS557.L2B43

*Text:* Originally the French edition was published in 1956 under the title *Présence du royaume Lao.* Divided into thirteen principal sections, the text covers the broad subjects of geography, history, arts, ethnography, religion, medicine, language and literature, annals of Lan Xang, folklore, education, economy, and external relations. Within these larger sections are these selected topics: Two accounts of travels in Laos in the 17th-century, by Paul Levy; Profane and religious festivals by Rene de Berval; Legends and fables by Banyen Levy; Laotian writings by Louis Finot; The Laotian calender by Tiao Maba Upahat Phetsarath.

*Bibliography:* References to monographs and articles in various languages, mostly French, are listed on 17 pages.

*Illustrations* (selected): H. M. Sisavong Vong, King of Laos. Savang Vatthana, Crown Prince of Laos.

Prince Boun Oum. Prince Phetsarath. Prince Phoui Sananikone. Katay Don Sasorith. Luang Prabang. Carved temple doors. Musical instruments. Arts and crafts. Festivals. Buddhist images.

*Musical Scores:* Folk songs from Luang Prabang and Vientiane.

*Map:* Economic map of Laos.

*Tables:* Kings, filiations and chief events, 1316–1955. Characteristics of the Buddha images.

199. BURCHETT, WILFRED G. North of the Seventeenth Parallel. Delhi, People's Publishing House, 1956. 258 p.; illustrations.
DS557.A7B8

*Text:* An Australian journalist's observations in North Vietnam and evaluations of South Vietnam soon after the fall of Dien Bien Phu, the critical battle which soon brought to a close the French-Vietnamese conflict. Following a sketch of Ho chi Minh, the account tells what was done in North Vietnam to establish the government, to distribute land to the farmers, and to improve the economic conditions of the country. The account is sympathetic to the Communist regime in North Vietnam.

*Illustrations:* President Ho chi Minh. Secretary-General Truong Chinh. General Vo Nguyen Giap. Vice Premier Pham van Dong.

200. BUREAU OF SOCIAL SCIENCE RESEARCH. Information and Attitudes in Laos. Washington, 1959. v, 122 1; map, tables. DS557.L2B85

*Text:* A public opinion survey conducted in all the twelve provinces of the country of Laos by Laotians in the Laotian language. The persons questioned provided data on these topics: awareness of change in Laos; awareness of foreign aid; sources of news and communications; voting behaviour and candidate selection; leadership; conceptions of mutual responsibilities between citizen and government; attitudes toward the Royal Government of Laos; and attitudes toward foreign nations. A convenient section giving summary of findings is provided in the first part of the study.

The survey was made early in 1959, five years after the provinces of Sam Neua and Phong Saly had been integrated under the Royal Government.

*Map:* Outline map showing provinces and capitals.

*Tables:* Gives questions asked in questionnaire, and the percentages of positive, negative, and other answers to these questions.

201. CHICAGO UNIVERSITY. Area Handbook on Laos. General editor: Norton S. Ginsburg. Editor: Gerald C. Hickey. Authors: Albert Androsky, Gerald C. Hickey, Ann Larimore, Naomi Noble, Hong phuc Vo, Mitchell Zadrozny. Cartography: J. Beyer, L. Grotewold, A. Larimore. Chicago, University of Chicago, for the Human Relations Area Files, 1955. xiii, 328 p.; bibliography, maps, tables, charts. (Human Relations Area Files, subcontractor's monograph, HRAF-23)

DS557.L2C5

*Text:* The stated purpose of this handbook is twofold: (1) to provide useful information concerning Laos, and (2) to transmit some understanding of the systems of organization and complex patterns which characterize Laotian society.

These twelve chapters analyze various segments and problems in Laos: 1. The characteristics of the society. 2. The history of Laos. 3. The resource base of Laos. 4. Transportation routes, services and equipment. 5. The population characteristics of Laos. 6. Communication. 7. Religion and education in Laos. 8. Government administration in Laos. 9. Agriculture. 10. The Laotian economy. 11. Laotian culture: a focus on the village. 12. The ethnic minorities of Laos.

*Bibliography:* Brief lists of book and article titles are given for the various chapters.

*Maps* (selected): 2. Stages of French intervention in Indochina. 5. Average annual rainfall. 6. Forest and mineral resources. 8. Physical regions of Laos. 10. Laotian airfields and air service routes. 11. Road and rail network. 14. City of Vientiane. 15. Ethnolinguistic groups. 17. Ethnic groups in each province. 18. Economic production.

*Tables:* Statistical data on exports and imports, tin production, forest production, rice production, and other economic aspects.

*Charts* (selected): Political structure of Laos. Temperature and rainfall.

202. DANNAUD, JEAN PIERRE. Cambodge. Photo-
203. graphies de Cahery, R. Cauchetier, R. Coutare, Nguyen monk Dan, J. P. Dannaud, G. Defive, P. Ferrari, [1956]. 158 p.; illustrations, map. DS557.C29D3 1956a

*Text:* A volume of colored and black-and-white photographs which depict the people, customs, geography, religious practices, industries, and numerous other aspects of Cambodia. Brief descriptive accounts accompany the pictures and the subject fields represented.

*Illustrations:* Show village life, dress, monks, harvesting, fishing, children, ceremonies, city streets, worship, art and architecture.

*Map:* Pictorial showing rivers, railroad and cities.

204. HONEY, P. J., ed. North Vietnam today: Profile of a Communist Satellite. New York, Praeger, 1962. vi, 166 p.; tables.

DS557.A7H65

*Text:* An account of the only fully constituted Communist state in Southeast Asia. An introductory chapter, of no small length, sets forth the basic background facts about the Democratic Republic of Vietnam or about the historical events which have led to the present situation in North Vietnam—including data about opposition to the Communist regime, and the living conditions in North Vietnam.

The succeeding chapters, which originally appeared in the *China Quarterly**, present these aspects of North Vietnam: The struggle for the unification of Vietnam by Philippe Devillers; The position of the DRV leadership and the succession to Ho Chi Minh by P. J. Honey; Power and pressure groups in North Vietnam by Bernard Fall; Intellectuals, writers and artists by Nhu Phong; Indoctrination replaces education by Gerard Tongas; A bowl of rice divided: the economy of North Vietnam by William Kaye; Collectivisation and rice production by Hoang van Chi; Vietnam—an independent viewpoint by Nguyen ngog Bich; Local government and administration under the Viet-Minh, 1945–54 by George Ginsburgs.

*Tables:* 1. Economic planning. 2. Gross value or production. 3. Government expenditure. 4. Soviet-bloc aid. 5. Agricultural cooperation. 6. Food and farming.

---

*[January–March, 1962 issue, under the title "North Vietnam, a special survey."]

205. HUARD, PIERRE ALPHONSE, and MAURICE DURAND. Connaissance du Vietnam. Paris, Imp. Nationale; Hanoi, Ecole Française d' Extrême-Orient, 1054. iii, 356 p.; bibliography, illustrations, maps, tables, indices.

DS557.A5H8

*Text:* A survey of various aspects of the culture of Vietnam: history, religion, literature, music, living habits, transportation, communications, and other topics.

Contents (selected): 1. Aperçu géographique du Vietnam. 2. Histoire succinte du Vietnam. 4. Genèse de la culture vietnamienne. 7. Calendrier et fêtes. 8. Structure mentale des Vietnamiens traditionels. 12. Les transports et des communications. 20. Musique et chant. 21. La littérature vietnaminenne.

*Bibliography:* Short lists follow each chapter relating to that chapter.

*Illustrations:* Line drawings to show housing, clothing, musical instruments, handicrafts, and social customs.

*Maps:* Vietnam: north, central and south.

*Tables:* Vietnamese calendar.

206. HUMAN RELATIONS AREA FILES. Laos; its People, its Society, its Culture. New Haven, HRAF Press, 1960. 294 p.; bibliography, maps, tables, index. DS557.L2H8

*Text:* As the eighth volume in the Survey of World Cultures of the HRAF, this volume brings together the principal historical, economic, social and cultural aspects of Laos.

Selected subjects treated in the 21 chapters are: history, geography, population, ethnic groups, languages, religion, social structure, education, art, literature, patterns of living, politics, government, communications, foreign relations, economy, labor, health, financial system, agriculture, industry, trade, national attitudes.

*Bibliography:* Brings together monographs and articles on Laos, arranged by authors.

*Maps:* Historical references. Relief and drainage. Rainfall. Ethno-linguistic groups. Structure of Government of Laos. Provinces of Laos.

*Tables* (selected): Laotian rulers. Population estimates. Ethnic composition of population. Students in schools. Government salaries. Medican facilities. Exports and imports by commodities. U.S. project aid. U.S. aid to Laos, 1958–59.

207. KENE, THAO. Bibliographie du Laos. Vientiane, Ministère de l'éducation nationale. Comité littéraire lao, 1958. 68, 7 l.

Z3238.L2K4

*Text:* Presents titles in the French language, arranged by author, and although not arranged by subject, there are items on anthropology, archaeology, botany, history, and the arts.

208. LEVI, SYLVAIN, ed. Indochine. Paris, Sociéte d'Editions Geographiques, Maritimes et Coloniales, 1931. 2 vols.; bibliography, illustrations, map, tables, charts, appendix. (Exposition Coloniale Internationale de Paris. Commissariat Général) DS521.L4

*Text:* Deals with the history, culture, and government of Indochina as viewed by authorities in various subject fields. Volume one is comprised of articles by writers on these different subjects: A descriptive account of the geographical features and racial groups by Charles Robequain; The languages and civilizations by J. Przyluski; Ancient and modern history by Louis Finot and Andre Masson; The religions of Hinduism, Buddhism, Taoism, and Islam as practiced by the Cambodian, Laotian, and Cham peoples by Paul Mus; An extensive presentation of Annamese literature by M. G. Dufresne; Cambodian literature by George Cœdès; Cham literature by Paul Mus; and, Art and archaeology by Victor Golonbew.

Volume two describes the government organization: army and navy, post and telegraph, finance, economic affairs, agriculture, mines and industries, and, libraries and archives, including l'Ecole Française d'Extrême-Orient.

*Bibliography:* Lists many references used in the study, arranged by subjects.

*Illustrations:* River, canal, and mountain views. Temples, including Angkor Vat. Cambodian sculpturing. Cambodian dance. Aerial view of Hanoi. Rice cultivation. Racial types.

*Map:* Principal mineral production in 1929.

*Tables:* Population density in Indochina in 1930. Population of principal cities in 1938. Foreign population in Indochina. Movement of European population. Immigration and emigration of Chinese.

*Charts:* Production and exports of zinc. Annual production of mines in Indochina.

*Appendix:* Statistical data relative to population and racial groups.

209. MASPERO, GEORGES, ed. Un empire colonial français, l'Indochine. Paris, Brussels, Les Editions G. Van Oest, 1929. 2 vols., bibliography, illustrations, maps, indices.
DS534.M35

*Text:* A symposium dealing with various subjects related to Indochina as presented by numerous outstanding specialists.

Selected chapters are: Géographie physique by E. Chassigneux; Géographie humaine by J. Brunhes; Langues by H. Maspero; Histoire générale by G. Maspero. Histoire archéologique by G. Maspero. Moeurs et coutumes des pays annamites by J. Przyluski; Moeurs et coutumes de l'ancien Cambodge by M. Le Gallen; Moeurs et coutumes de l'ancien Laos by G. Maspero; Religions hindoues by G. Cœdès; Religions annamites et non annamites by R. P. Cadière; Littérature du Cambodge et du Laos by G. Maspero; Littérature annamite by G. Cordier; Historique de l'organisation et de l'administration francaise by G. Lamarre; Organisation actuelle de l'Indochine by G. Lamarre; L'exploration scientifique de l'Indochine by A. Chevalier; Agriculture, exportation agricole, forêts, caoutchouc, recherches scientifiques, industrie, mines by H. Brenier; Travaux publics, routes, chemins de fer, ponts by F. Cazenave; and Sites pittoresques, artistiques, et archéologiques by P. Pasquier.

*Illustrations:* Excellent photographs depict customs, dress, religious practices, Buddhist art and achitecture, handicrafts, racial groups, village life, agriculture, railroads and bridges, and numerous other subjects.

*Bibliography:* An extensive bibliography provides references for each of the preceding chapters.

*Maps:* L'Indochine politique aux environs de 960 A.D. Indochine physique (color), scale. –1:4,000,000. Carte linguistique (color) scale. –1:4,000,000. Indochine politique (color); scale. –1:4,000,000. Carte économique (color). Cochinchine économique (color). Tonkin économique (color). Voies navigables de la Cochinchine. (color). Digues du Tonkin (color). Indochine touristique (color) Carte pluviométrique.

210. SITHIBOURN, SITHAT. Biographies des personalités du royaume du Laos. Vientiane, Edition Lao presse, 1960. unpaged; illustrations.
DS557.L26A18

*Text:* Provides biographical data about leading personalities in the Lao Government, including the positions they have held and the honors received.

*Illustrations:* Photographs of persons for which biographical data is given.

211. STEINBERG, DAVID J. Cambodia; Its People, Its Society, Its Culture. In collaboration with Chester A. Bain, Lloyd Burlingham, Russell G. Duff, Bernard B. Fall, Ralph Greenhouse, Lucy Kramer and Robert S. McLellan; revised for 1959 by Herbert H. Vreeland. New Haven, HRAF Press, 1959. 351 p.; bibliography, maps, tables, charts, index. (Survey of world cultures)
DS557.C2S8 1959

*Text:* As the fifth volume in the Survey of World Cultures of the Human Relations Area Files, this volume—although not the product of original research—is a collection and synthesis of the most authoritative material contemporary at the time of writing about the principal historical, economic, social and cultural aspects of Cambodia.

Selected subjects, treated in the 22 chapters are: history, geography, population, ethnic groups, languages, religion, social structure, government, foreign relations, economy, labor, financial system, agriculture, industry, trade, health, education, arts, patterns of living, national attitudes.

*Bibliography:* Titles of books and articles on Cambodia, arranged by authors.

*Maps:* Settlement distribution. Ethnic groups. Transportation network. Agricultural products.

*Tables* (selected): Population and ethnic groups. Newspapers. Two year plan. Government budget. Rice production. Cooperatives. Industrial settlements. Exports and imports. Public education.

*Charts:* Structure of central government. Cambodian holidays. Corresponding Buddhist and Western dates.

212. THOMPSON, VIRGINIA. French Indochina. London, Allen and Unwin [1937]. 517 p.; bibliography, map, index.
DS541.T5

*Text:* An extensive survey of the history, economy, and culture of a highly important colony of the French in the Orient. Aims to present cross sections of the problem of French colonization in Indochina; French administration of the country, agricultural production, natural resources, labor, commerce, currency, communications, capital and credit, and ownership of land. Shows the cultural interpenetration of the different cultivations—Annamese (Vietnamese), Cambodian, and Laotian by a detailed study of history, literature, art, psychology, religions, language, music, and political organization.

The influence of French ideas and institutions is a thread which runs throughout the study, and it is clearly shown that the most far-reaching transformation of native life has resulted from the involuntary absorption of Western ideas. Native life was modified especially by French activity in the fields of politics, education, and Christian missions.

The last chapter, Reaction to the French colonization of Indochina, contains a good summary of the development of nationalism in Indochina. Well indexed.

*Bibliography:* Includes over 300 items.

213. U.S. DEPARTMENT OF STATE. OFFICE OF STRATEGIC SERVICES. RESEARCH AND ANALYSIS BRANCH. Programs of Japan in Indochina, with index to biographical data. Assemblage no. 56, 2d ed. of Assemblage nos. 26, 40. Honolulu, 1945. 369 p. (R. and A. no. 3369)  Microfilm 1554

*Text:* Comprises the Federal Communications Commission intercepts of shortwave broadcasts, except those of a purely military nature, from Radio Tokyo and affiliated stations, December 1941 to May 24, 1945, as well as from the Office of Strategic Services sources.

Following a brief section with general information, the volume is divided into five principal divisions: politics, war measures, economics, social conditions, and biographies.

In the division dealing with political matters, there are sections relating to: administrative reorganization; officials in the various provinces; native and minority population; national movements sponsored by Japan; international relations with Japan, China, France, and Thailand; and, propaganda.

War measures include data on mobilization, defense measures, Annamite women in war; internees, decentralization of population, and general military situation.

The economic division presents information about: economic agreements with Japan; economic control and administration; labor; foreign trade with Japan, Manchukuo, and Thailand; land and property rights; agriculture—controls, program for increased production and self-sufficiency, food cooperatives, acreage and exports, rice production, and various agricultural products; forestry; fishing; industry and manufacturing—chemical industries, fuel, rubber, electrical power

and mining; transportation—roads; railways; sea and river travel; air travel; communications; and finance—banks, currency exchange, bonds and taxes.

Social conditions include information about cultural institutions, fine arts, language, education, publications, religion, scientific research centers, youth movements, and public health and welfare.

The index to biographical data, concluding the document, is classified according to Japanese and French names and names of native peoples.

214. U.S. INTERNATIONAL COOPERATION ADMINISTRATION. Republic of Vietnam. Report on rural–urban water supply development. New York, Hydrotechnic Corporation, Consulting Engineers, 1960. 3 vols. in 2; illustrations, tables.  Orientalia

*Text:* The objectives of the study are to determine the water supply needs of 50 municipalities in Vietnam, to establish a comprehensive program for developing an adequate supply of safe drinking water in each town, and to recommend an administrative organization to operate the systems on a self-sustaining basis.

*Illustrations:* Street scenes, raw water canals, treatment plants, dams and water reservoirs.

*Tables* (selected): Municipal water rates required. Summary of revenue study. Total water production. Annual costs for operation and maintenance.

*Appendices* (selected): Direction of the Viet Cong by North Vietnam. The Viet Cong organization in North and South Vietnam. Translations of confessions of Viet Cong agents. Medical equipment from North Vietnam and the Communist bloc. Party leadership of front organizations.

215. U.S. NATIONAL SCIENCE FOUNDATION. Scientific Facilities and Information Services of the Republic of Vietnam, by John O. Sutter. Honolulu, Published for the National Science Foundation by the Pacific Scientific Information Center, 1961. 36 p.; map, appendices, index. (Pacific scientific information, no. 3)  In process

*Text:* Tells about the present status of the limited scientific research and information in South Vietnam—particularly in the fields of medicine, archeology, and oceanography. It is to be noted that because of the country's split as a result of the Geneva Agreement in 1954, the number of scientific institutions open to the non-Communist world was radically affected. The personnel picture of scientists in South Vietnam underwent a rapid change and in varying degrees several new institutions are producing Vietnamese scientists.

Four chapters discuss general background data on South Vietnam, scientific manpower and training, scientific research institutions, and scientific information activities.

*Map:* Outline map of Southeast Asia mainland.

*Appendices:* Instructions of higher learning providing science teaching and research. Research institutes. Scientific publications. Scientific societies.

216. UNIVERSITY OF CALIFORNIA, LOS ANGELES. DEPARTMENT OF ANTHROPOLOGY. LAOS PROJECT. Bibliography of Laos and Ethnically Related Areas by John McKinstry. [1961?] 91 p. (Laos project paper no. 22)
In process

*Text:* A compilation of approximately 1,000 references on all aspects of Laos, but heavy in anthropology and ethnology. Includes articles from numerous periodicals and encyclopedias as well as titles of books.

217. UNIVERSITY OF CALIFORNIA, LOS ANGELES. DEPARTMENT OF ANTHROPOLOGY. LAOS PROJECT. Government, Politics and Social Structure of Laos: a study of tradition and innovation by Joel H. Halpern. [1961?] i, 199 p.; bibliography, map (Laos project. Paper no. 21*)
In process

---

*[Other papers on Laos issued by this Project prepared by Joel Halpern, except noted otherwise, are as follows: no. 1, The role of the Chinese in Lao society, 1959; no. 2, Capital, savings and credit among Lao and Serb peasants; a contrast in cultural values; no. 3, Population statistics and associated data; no. 4, Geographic demographic and ethnic background on Laos; no. 5, An annotated bibliography on the peoples of Laos and northern Thailand; no. 6, American policy in Laos; no. 7, Laotian educational statistics; no. 8, Government statistics; no. 9, Laotian agricultural statistics; no. 10, Laotian health statistics; no. 11, Economic and related statistics; no. 12, Village life in Vientiane Province (1956–57) by Howard K. Kaufman; no. 13, The Meo of Xieng Khouang Province by George L. Barney; no. 14, The village of Ban Pha Khao Vientiane Province by Tsuneo Ayabe, ed. by Joel Halpern; no. 15, Ethnic groups in the valley of the Nam Song and the Nam Lik—their geographical distribution and some aspects of social change by Keiji Iwata; no. 16, Minority groups in northern Laos, especially the Yao, translated by Keiji Iwata; no. 17, The natural economy of Laos; no. 18, The rural and urban economies; no. 19, Laotian health problems; no. 21, Government, politics, and social structure of Laos: a study of tradition and innovation; no. 22, Bibliography of Laos and ethnically related areas, by John McKinstry.]

*Text:* An examination of the fundamental patterns of the structure of Lao government on national and local levels, and correlates these findings with traditional family structure and observations on Lao character and behavior. Particular attention is given to the role which religion, foreign influence and secular education have as they pertain to changing value systems and to individual mobility. Although an analysis of the current turbulent political situation in Laos is not given, consideration is given to the interaction and clash of the three types of governmental systems—the traditional Royal, the Western parliamentary, and the Communist oriented.

*Bibliography:* References to Laos included in footnotes.

*Map:* Outline map of Laos showing provinces and capitals.

## HISTORY, POLITICS, AND GOVERNMENT

218. AMERICAN FRIENDS OF VIETNAM. A Symposium on America's Stake in Vietnam. New York, 1956. 110 p. appendices.
DS557.A5A15

*Text:* The edited record, representing many points of view and difference on specifics, of the first public conference on Vietnam held in Washington in June 1956, following the formation of the American Friends of Vietnam in late 1955 made up of public spirited citizens concerned with South Vietnam and the Free World.

Divided into two major parts: Vietnam's internal problems, and Vietnam's international position, these selected addresses are cited: America's stake in Vietnam by Senator John F. Kennedy; United States policy towards Vietnam by Walter S. Robertson; Vietnam's economy by Leo Cherne; The ICA in Vietnam by Frederick Bunting; Refugee resettlement by Joseph Harnett; Vietnam's capabilities by Joseph Buttinger; The 1954 Geneva Conference: An assessment by Hans J. Morgenthau; A review of American policy in Asia by Rep. Walter H. Judd; Vietnam's defense capacity by John O'Daniel; and Vietnam in world affairs by Milton Sacks.

*Appendices* (selected) : Messages from American Ambassador to Vietnam, G. Frederick Reinhart and President Ngo dinh Diem. Vietminh response to the Washington Conference. Conference sponsors.

219. BUREAU OF SOCIAL SCIENCE RESEARCH. Political Awareness in Laos, January–February, 1959. Washington, 1959. 45 l., tables. In process.

*Text:* Based on nearly 2,000 interviews with Laotian people conducted in all twelve provinces of Laos, it provides a cross-section survey of the political outlook, information and opinion of the Lao people about politics, government, and society conditions. The topics dealt with: personal problems; government and foreign aid; news and communications; voting and political preferences; town and village leadership; Lao government aid; obligations of the citizen toward his government; government crisis of January, 1959; foreign nations.

Serves as a supplement to Information and attitudes in Laos.

*Tables:* Provides questions and tabulation of replies.

220. BUTTINGER, JOSEPH. The Smaller Dragon; a Political History of Vietnam. New York, Praeger, 1958. 535 p.; bibliography, illustrations, maps, chronology, index. (Books that matter)   DS557.A5B8

*Text:* Certain aspects of Vietnamese history have been published in a few books written in the Vietnamese and French languages, but this work is unique in that it is the first political history of Vietnam to appear in English.

Furthermore, notwithstanding the value of two other recent books—*Le Viet-Nam histoire et civilisation* by Le Thanh Khoi and *La geste francaise en Indochine* by George Taboulet, this study brings fresh documentary information taken from French Government files which were kept secret until late 1955.

The author writes a history which would "not only be a useful book for the student and scholar, but also that would hold the attention of people who are interested in Vietnam for purely political reasons." The professor, classroom student, or the average citizen who desires to understand the significance of a divided and troubled Vietnam in current international affairs will find this study valuable.

The account covers more than two thousand years of Vietnamese history, with particular treatment of how Vietnam has been a bulwark against Chinese penetration into and conquest of Southeast Asia for hundreds of years during the pre-colonial period. The study provides insight into the forces which shaped Vietnam's mentality and gives a knowledge of the circumstances which enabled the Vietnamese to survive and avoid absorption into the Chinese empire.

*Bibliography:* An extensive bibliography (51 pages) arranged in two sections: history and civilization. Annotations of the principal sources are included.

*Illustrations:* Alexander of Rhodes. François Pallu. Pierre Poivre. Pigneau de Behaine. Prince Nguyen Canh. Phan thang Giang. Admiral Rigault de Genouilly. Admiral Bonard. Admiral Dupré. Francis Garnier.

*Maps:* Burma, Thailand, and Vietnam. Population density in Vietnam. Distribution of population. Empire of Funan. Nam Viet. Warring kingdoms, 400 B.C. Cambodian Empire. March to the south. Phases of French conquest.

*Chronology:* Major Vietnamese historical events summarized from 1900 to 1957.

221. CHAMPASSAK, SISOUK NA. Storm Over Laos; a Contemporary History. New York, Praeger, 1961. x, 202 p.; illustrations, appendices. (Books that matter)   DS557.L28C5

*Text:* Written by one who was the representative of Laos to the International Control Commission, who served as Secretary General of the Council of Ministers, and who held a Cabinet post under Premier Phoui Sananikone. Presents an account of events in Laos since 1845, concentrating especially on those events after the Geneva Conference of 1954. Endeavors to show the various stages of the advance of international communism in Laos in its overall plan of the conquest of Southeast Asia.

Biographical information about and political views and activities of Prince Souphannouvong, the Pathet Lao leader; of Phoui Sananikone and Souvanna Phouma, both Prime Ministers of Laos, are discussed candidly.

*Illustrations* (selected): Signing of the 1957 agreements. Prince Souphannouvong. Prince Souvanna Phouma. Meo refugees. Prince Souvanna Phouma and Pham van Dong, Prime Minister of North Vietnam.

*Appendices:* Selected documents from the Geneva Conference, 1954. Statement of Phoui Sananikone in Geneva. Annex no. 1 to Royal Government memorandum of April 12, 1954. Testimony of escapees from Sam Neua.

222. CŒDÈS, GEORGE. Les États hindouisés d'Indochine et d'Indonésie.* Paris, E. de Boccard, 1948. xi, 466 p.; maps, charts, glossary, indices. DS514.C6

*Text:* Deals with the acculturation process of certain aspects of Hindu culture as integrated into the civilizations of Cambodia, Thailand, Burma, and Indonesia. In the main it is a comprehensive history of the Hindu and Buddhist influences in these areas, and describes the ethnological foundations of pre-Hindu Southeast Asia. Special attention is given to Cambodia, Champa, Angkor, and other portions of Indochina which were indianized by successive waves of immigrants from India, as related in the following chapters: 4. La seconde hindouisation de l'Indochine et de l'Insulinde; 5. Le démembrement du Fou-nan; 7. Fondation de la royauté angkorienne . . . ; 10. La dynastie cambodgienne de Mahidharapura . . . . The introduction of Indian culture into the Indonesian archipelago is discussed in chapters four, six, seven, nine, and ten.

*Maps:* Carte génerale de l'Inde, de la péninsule Indochinoise, et de l'Insulinde, scale–1:20,000,000ᵉ. Péninsule Indochinoise, scale–1:7,500,000ᵉ. Cambodge, scale–1:2,000,000ᵉ. Groupe d'Angkor, scale–1:80,000ᵉ. Insulinde, scale–1:10,000,000ᵉ.

*Charts:* Tableau généalogique des rois du Cambodge. Tableau généalogique des rois de Mojapahit.

*Glossary:* Brief list of terms used in the text.
*Indices:* Geographical place names. Names of persons. Religious terms. Sources used in the study.

*[Formerly published under the title *Histoire ancienne des états hindouisés* (Hanoi, Impr. d'Extreme-Orient, 1944)]

223. COLE, ALLAN BURNETT, ed. Conflict in Indo-China and International Repercussions; a Documentary History, 1945–1955. Published under the auspices of the Fletcher School of Law and Diplomacy, Tufts University, and the Southeast Asia Program, Cornell University. Ithaca, Cornell University Press, 1956. xxix, 265 p.; bibliography, map, appendices. (The Fletcher School studies in international affairs) DS550.C6

*Text:* Presents documentary texts previously published and unpublished, relative to the role of North Vietnam, South Vietnam, and Laos in the history of colonialism and international relations in general.

The documents cover treaties, protocol statements, speeches of heads of governments, letters, declarations, foreign policy statements, manifests, constitutions, decrees, ordinances, and agreements. This compendium of key documents are grouped into these five historical phases of the Vietnamese conflict which led to the Geneva Conference: 1. Negotiations and developments to the outbreak of hostilities, March 1945–May 1947. 2. Deepening conflict and formation of a rival Vietnam, May 1947–December 1949. 3. Spreading international dimensions of the conflict, January 1950–December 1952. 4. International crisis and the Geneva agreements, January 1953–November 1954. 5. Developments following the Geneva agreements, December 1954–July 1955.

*Bibliography:* A list of rather well-known secondary reference sources.

*Map:* Outline map showing Thailand, Laos, Cambodia, North Vietnam and South Vietnam.

*Appendices:* 1. Chronology of events in and concerning Indochina. 2. Statistics on French expenditures of personnel and money in Indochina; and on United States aid to France and to South Vietnam.

22.4 DEVILLERS, PHILIPPE. Histoire du Viet-Nam de 1940 à 1952. 3d ed. Paris, Editions du Seuil, 1952. 479 p.; illustrations, map, index. DS557.A5D45

*Text:* The author, a professor at Collège Libre des Sciences Sociales et Economiques, presents the events in North and South Vietnam for the short period from 1940 to 1952 in 27 chapters divided into three parts. Among these chapters are those which discuss: the Japanese occupation of Vietnam, the Viet Minh and the Chinese, the Dalat Conference of 1945, Gen. Giap and Bao Dai and the war in Vietnam, the Viet Minh army, the rise of Ho chi Minh, and the Bollaert mission.

*Illustrations:* Ho chi Minh and French officers.
*Map:* Sketch map showing North and South Vietnam.

225. DUNN, WILLIAM BROTHERS. American Policy and Vietnamese Nationalism, 1950–1954. Unpublished thesis, University of Chicago, Chicago, Ill., 1960. 317 l.; bibliography. Microfilm 6726E

*Text:* A thesis which examines the American attempt to cope with Vietnamese nationalism since World War II, particularly dealing with events and trends which took place between 1948 and 1954. Relates how the effort to "contain communism" during the Communist attempt to take over Southeast Asia pushed into the background the sympathies for the nationalist goals of the Vietnamese. Shows how eventually American policy went to the extent of supporting a vast military effort on the assumption that forcible destruction of the Communist leadership within the Vietnamese nationalist movement would bring the nationalist sentiments into alliance with the West. The question as to the validity of that assumption is the real core of the study.

The ten chapters are: 1. Wartime involvement and postwar detachment. 2. The policy of detachment challenged. 3. The American response to the challenge, 1947–48. 4. The "Bao Dai experiment." 5. Vietnam and the new Far Eastern policy, 1950. 6. American support for Vietnam, 1950–53. 7. A season of false assumptions, January–March, 1954. 8. A season of crises, April–July, 1954. 9. After Geneva: a new approach. 10. Vietnamese nationalism and American policy.

*Bibliography:* Lists the French, English, and American public documents, books, and periodical articles which were used in the study.

226. ENNIS, THOMAS E. French Policy and Development in Indochina. Chicago, University of Chicago Press, 1936. vii, 230 p.; bibliography, map, tables, appendices, index. DS541.E5

*Text:* Describes the French penetration of the different provinces of Indochina and discusses the economic, social, and administrative problems which arose between the time of the French military occupation in the middle of the last century and before World War II. The character and extent of the Indochinese resistance to French domination is delineated to a certain degree. Shows the conflict which evolved out of the clash between the French individualistic philosophy and the Indochinese collectivistic principles. A brief comparison of the colonial policies and achievements of the Dutch in Indonesia and the French in Indochina is provided in the introduction. Chapter 8, The unrest in Indochina, describes the strong nationalistic spirit in Indochina and the activities of communism in this French colony.

*Bibliography:* A long list of primary sources, secondary sources, official and semiofficial publications, and newspapers.

*Map:* Outline map on flyleaf shows the political divisions in Indochina.

*Tables:* Mineral concessions in 1931. Railroads—extent and cost. Trade between the United States and Indochina. Imports and exports by countries. Rice and rubber exports.

*Appendices:* Treaty of November 17, 1787. Letter of Louis XVIII to the Emperor of Annam. Francis Garnier in Annam. Speech of Jules Ferry, October 30, 1883. General features of communism in Indochina.

227. FALL, BERNARD B. Political Development of Vietnam, VJ Day to the Geneva Cease-Fire. Unpublished thesis. Syracuse, Syracuse University, 1954. 3 vols.; bibliography, illustrations, maps, charts, appendices. (University Microfilms, publication no. 11, 867)

Mic AC–1 no. 11, 867

*Text:* A well documented analysis of the Vietnam problem presented in three volumes: 1. The Viet Minh regime. 2. State of Vietnam. 3. International aspects of the Vietnam problem. Volume one contains these seven parts: 1. The birth of the Democratic Republic. 2. The Republic at war. 3. The party in power. 4. Fighting a total war. 5. Economic problems. 6. Agrarian policy. 7. Summation.

Volume two, State of Vietnam, has nine parts: 1. The "national solution." 2. From "autonomy" to "independence." 3. "State of Vietnam." 4. The transition. 5. The ethnic minorities. 6. Politics and religion in Vietnam. 7. The struggle for the countryside. 8. Social problems. 9. "State of Vietnam."

Volume three, International aspects of the Vietnam problem, discusses the part which France and other Western powers shared in the political struggle in Vietnam. The four parts are: 1. France and Vietnam—politics and policies. 2. A decade's dilemma—American policy in Vietnam. 3. As seen from Moscow. 4. Britain, the Commonwealth, and the Asian area.

*Bibliography:* Lengthy list of references used—books, official documents, unpublished items and articles in English, French, Vietnamese, and Russian languages.

*Illustrations:* Ngo dinh Diem. Scenes of agricultural life.

*Maps* (selected): Communal elections in North Vietnam, 1953. Territorial organization of the armed forces of Vietnam, 1954. Administration in North Vietnam, 1953. Security control in North Vietnam, 1953. Feudal sects in South Vietnam.

*Charts:* Program of mass literacy in North, Central, and South Vietnam.

*Appendices:* Constitution of the Democratic Republic of Vietnam.

228. FALL, BERNARD B. Street Without Joy: Indochina at War, 1946–54. Harrisburg, Pa., Stackpole Co., 1961. 322 p.; bibliography, illustrations, maps, appendices.    DS550.F3

*Text:* Although not a history of the war in Vietnam, it does reveal graphically the way in which guerrilla warfare in the jungle by the Viet Minh, supported by the Chinese, eventually defeated the French who were impeded by their traditional heavy military equipment. The account does reveal many facts and interpretation of facts of how the war started and came to the tragic end of dividing the country of Vietnam at the 17th parallel.

Besides being based on official French papers and military files, personal experiences during actual field research in Vietnam was a rich source of information.

*Bibliography:* A military bibliography on Indochina, divided into 6 parts: Strategy and general background; land warfare, Guerrilla warfare; Aerial warfare; Naval warfare; The enemy.

*Illustrations:* Views of military operations. Scenes in the Dien Bien Phu area.

*Maps* (selected): Operations in North Vietnam, 1950–52. Battle of Vinh Yen. Defense of Mao Khé. Battle on the Day River. Battle of Hoa Binh. The struggle for the highlands. Operation Lorraine (Cao Mai). Guerrilla warfare in Indochina. Communist prisoners of war camp system. Death march routes. Dien Bien Phu, Rebellion in Laos, 1959–60. Guerrilla warfare in Vietnam, 1953–60.

*Appendices:* Glossary of abbreviations. Comparisons between French and U.S. losses.

229. FALL, BERNARD B. The Viet-Minh Regime; Government and Administration in the Democratic Republic of Vietnam. Ithaca, Southeast Asia Program, Department of Far Eastern Studies, Cornell University, 1954. ix, 143 p.; bibliography, illustrations, maps, charts, appendices. (Data paper no. 14. Issued jointly with the Institute of Pacific Relations)    JQ815.F3

*Text:* Outlines and interprets the events surrounding the birth and development of the Communist regime in North Vietnam from 1941 to 1954. The presentation is divided into these six parts: 1. The birth of the Democratic Republic of Vietnam. 2. The Republic at war. 3. The party in power. 4. Fighting a total war. 5. Economic problems. 6. Agrarian reforms. Within these parts, the subjects of constitutional structure, local administration, courts, Vietnam Workers

Party, psychological warfare, foreign relations, religion, Vietnam People's Army, taxation system, small farmer, and reforms are discussed.

*Bibliography:* Significant references on North Vietnam in English, French, Vietnamese, and Chinese.

*Illustrations:* Vo Nguyen Giap. Truong Chinh. Pham van Dong. Ton duc Thong. Hoang quoc Viet—North Vietnam leaders.

*Maps:* 1. Political situation in North Vietnam, September, 1945. 2. The Viet-Minh Army in North Vietnam. 3. Viet-Minh economy in North Vietnam. 4. Political military situation in Indochina.

*Charts:* 1. The Viet-Minh judiciary. 2. The Vietnam Dang Lao Dong (Workers' Party). 3. Organization of the Vietnam People's Army. 4. Viet-Minh revenue system.

*Appendices:* 1. Constitution of the Democratic Republic of Vietnam. 2. Organization of a village in the Viet-Minh zone. 3. "The achievements of the year 1953 and the tasks which we shall have to fulfill in 1954." 4. Summary glossary of Viet-Minh administrative and political terms.

230. GENEVA. CONFERENCE, 1954. Conférence de Genève sur l'Indochine (8 mai–21 juillet 1954). Procès-verbaux des séances, propositions, documents finaux. Paris, Impr. nationale, 1955. 470 p.; appendices.*
    DS550.G37

*Text:* Presents primary documents—speeches, proposals, reports, declarations, and related papers—which were considered at the 31 sessions of the Geneva Conference from May 8 to July 21, 1954 after Dien Bien Phu.

*Appendices* (selected): International control and guarantees. Final documents of the Conference: Accords for the cessation of hostilities in Vietnam, Laos and Cambodia. Declaration of the Government of Laos and Cambodia for elections. Final declaration of

[*See also: Geneva. Conference, 1954. *Documents relating to the discussion of Korea and Indochina at the Geneva Conference, April 27–June 15, 1954.* London, Stationery Office, 1954. vii, 168 p.

Geneva. Conference, 1954. *The final declaration of the Geneva Conference on Indochina [and] Chou En-lai's statement at the final session of the Geneva Conference.* n.p., 1954. 7 p.

Geneva. Conference, 1954. *Further documents relating to the discussion of Indochina at the Geneva Conference, June 16–July 21, 1954.* London, Stationery Office, 1954. 45 p. (Papers by command. Cmde. 9239)].

the Geneva Conference on the establishment of peace in Indochina.

231.  HALPERN, ABRAHAM MEYER, and H. B. FREDMAN.  Communist Strategy in Laos.  Santa Monica, California, Rand Corporation, 1960. xiii, 162 p.; maps, index.  (Rand Corporation.  Research memorandum RM–2561)
Q180.A1R36

*Text:* Analyzes the military action in Laos in 1959 as the Communist political reaction to the internal political developments in Laos following the Geneva Agreement in 1954.  Following the historical summary of events in Laos from 1954–58 in the first chapter, succeeding chapters observe carefully the Asian Communist foreign political behaviour at the time of the crisis in 1959 when the Sananikone cabinet was in power.

*Map:* Show strategic positions held by the Pathet Lao, the Royal Lao Army, and significant assaults.

232.  JUMPER, ROY, and NGUYEN THI HUE.  Notes on the Political and Administrative History of Viet Nam, 1802–1962.  [Saigon], Michigan State University Viet Nam Advisory Group, 1962.  227 p.; bibliography, tables.
DS557.A5J8

*Text:* This account of the evolution of Vietnamese political and administrative history is organized into three specific periods: 1. From 1802 to the French occupation, which relates the problems of the Nguyen emperors and their efforts to reunify Vietnam under a central authority located at Hue.  2. From the French intervention to World War II, deals with the French occupation and the introduction and fusion of Western ideas and organization during the colonial period.  3. The political and administrative evolution of Viet Nam, 1940–62, relates the political and governmental changes brought about by independence.

*Bibliography:** Lists in footnotes the references cited in text.

233.  LE THANH KHOI.  Le Viet-Nam, histoire et civilisation.  Paris, Éditions de Minuit, 1955. 587 p.; bibliography, maps, table, index.
DS557.A5L47

*Text:* Following introductory chapters dealing with the geography, climate, population and ethnic minori-

ties, the ten succeeding chapters present the principal divisions of Vietnamese history from prehistoric times to the present time, and various aspects of Vietnamese culture.

The chapter headings are: 1. Les origines.  2. La conquête chinoise.  3. La fondation de l'etat.  4. Les gloires et les crises.  5. Grandeur et décadence de la monarchie.  6. La sécession du nord et du sud.  7. La reconstitution de l'unité.  8. De l'isolement a l'ouverture.  9. La colonisation francaise.  10. Le Viet Nam nouveau.

*Bibliography:* Eight pages listing numerous references on geography and people, the prehistory period, the Sino-Vietnamese period, the monarchy period, and the contemporary period.

*Maps* (selected): 16.  Maps showing Vietnam in the 4th-century, the 11th-century, the 14th-century, the Empire of Le Thanh-tony, the conquest of South Vietnam by Nguyen, and the formation of present day Vietnam.

*Table:* Chronological table of the history of Vietnam.

234.  LÉVY, ROGER, GUY LACAM, and ANDREW ROTH.  French Interests and Policies in the Far East.  New York, International Secretariat, Institute of Pacific Relations.  1941.  xi, 209 p.; map, tables, appendices, index.  (I.P.R. inquiry series)
DS518.2.L4

*Text:* Part one, prepared by Roger Levy, Chargé de Cours, Ecole Nationale de la France d'Outremer, deals with the cultural and economic activities of the French in the Far East during the past one hundred years, and includes a supplement by Guy Lacam on the economic relations of Indochina with southern China.  Part two describes the transition stage of Indochina from 1938 to 1941, and shows how the intensification of Japanese pressure brought about an urgent change in French foreign policy in the Far East, particularly in Indochina.

*Map:* Shows geographical relations of Indochina to the rest of Southeast Asia.

*Tables:* Trade statistics pertaining to Indochina.

*Appendices:* Include the following documents: Agreement concerning the nonalienation of the Island of Hainan (March 5, 1898).  Convention concerning the relations between China and France with regard to French Indochina and the adjacent Chinese provinces, and annexes to this Convention (May 16, 1930).  Arrangement between Japan and France for the provi-

---

*[As a supplement to the above, the *Bibliography on the political and administrative history of Vietnam, 1802–1962, selected and annotated* was issued in the same year].

sional regulation of the exchange of products between Japan and Indochina (May 13, 1932). Treaty of amity, commerce, and navigation between France and Siam (December 7, 1937). Commercial and customs agreement between France and Siam concerning Indochina.

235. LINDHOLM, RICHARD WADSWORTH, ed. Vietnam: The First Five Years; An International Symposium. Lansing, Michigan, Michigan State University Press, 1959. xi, 365 p.; tables, index.                     DS557.A6L5

*Text:* A symposium which endeavors to interpret various aspects in the development efforts in free Vietnam. The study is divided into seven parts.

Part one, A new state of Southeast Asia, includes the chapters: Nationalism vs. colonialism and communism; The miracle of Vietnam; and The political background of Ngo dinh Diem.

Part two, The refugee problem, presents the chapters: The role of friendly nations; the role of the U.S. Navy; The work of the Roman Catholic groups; and A critique of the program for the economic integration of refugees.

Part three, The Chinese and other minorities, includes the chapters on The Chinese in Vietnam; A survey of Chinese occupations; and The tribesmen.

Part four, Education for development, has two chapters: The challenge in education, and The National Institute of Administration.

Part five, Industrial and agricultural development, presents these chapters: Economic setting; Experiment in planning economic and social development; Agrarian reform; Industrial development efforts; A general report on industrial development; and Early steps toward an industrial development bank.

Part six, Aspects of Vietnamese finance, includes the chapters: Monetary reorganization and the emergence of central banking; The foreign exchange policy of Vietnam; Tax reforms in Vietnam; American aid and its financial impact.

Part seven, Some evaluations of the Vietnam experiment presents two chapters: A summary of Vietnam's political and economic progress; and General consideration of American programs.

Many of the chapters are in turn evaluated by critics in commentary sections.

*Tables* (selected): Classification of Chinese occupations in Free Vietnam. Ethnic minorities in Vietnam, 1958. Progress of education in Vietnam. Per capita income of South and Southeast Asian countries. Rice yield per hectare for Asian countries. Land ownership patterns. American aid. Economic and technical assistance with estimated expenditure, 1956–57.

236. MUS PAUL. Vietnam, sociologie d'une guerre. Paris, Éditions du Seuil, 1952. 375 p.; map. (Collections Esprit. "Frontière ouverte")
                                  DS557.A5M77

*Text:* The author, who has been associated with Indochinese studies for many years as a member of Ecole Française d'Extrême-Orient and other interested oriental bodies, presents a valuable sociological study of the Vietnamese people in the years following World War II.

Significant selected chapters are: 1. Geopolitique vietnamienne. 2. Mandat du ciel et politique vus d'un village vietnamien. 3. De la Féderation indochinoise à la liberation vietnamienne. 7. Cosmologie du marxisme et guerres coloniales. 9. Paysage ethnologique du conflit. 11. L'élite vietnamienne aux approches du conflit. 18. Marxisme et traditionalisme. 19. L'Occident et les chances d'un marxisme asiatique. 24. Sociologie et reconstruction au Vietnam.

*Map:* Map of Vietnam showing location of hill peoples.

237. NGUYEN DUY TRINH. Government Report on the Three Year Plan of North Vietnam, 1958–1960. New York, U.S. Joint Publications Research Service, 1959. 58 p.; tables, (JPRS:632–D)            AS36.U56 no. 632

*Text:* This official report of the Government of North Vietnam appeared in the December 11, 12, 13, 1958, issues of Nhan Dan, the official newspaper of Vietnam published in Hanoi. The report which concerns itself with a three-year plan for economic development and reform, and for cultural development in North Vietnam, considers agricultural cooperatives, state-owned industries, transportation, communications, trade and commerce, finance, education, publishing, foreign aid.

*Tables:* Foodstuff production, 1960. Crops increase, 1957–60. State-owned industries production. Investments by the government.

238. NGUYEN THAI. Is South Vietnam Viable? Manila, Printed by Carmelo and Bauermann, 1962. xii, 314 p.; bibliography, maps, charts.
                                       In process

*Text:* A former Diem government official endeavors to assess the present situation in South Vietnam under the Diem regime, together with predictions of what will happen in the future. States that Diem's survival is due to American foreign aid and support, and the tremendous dislike by the Vietnamese for Communist dictatorship. Emphasizes that the present regime in South Vietnam, in the long run, is not capable of developing Vietnam into a modern nation and of fighting communism successfully. Emphasis is placed on the opinion that the United States must force drastic reforms in South Vietnam if the country is to be saved from a Communist takeover.

Chapter headings: 1. Administrative leadership, the key to South Vietnam's political crisis. 2. Administrative problems inherited by Ngo dinh Diem in 1954. 3. Concepts of government in the Ngo dinh Diem regime. 4. The invisible family government. 5. Administrative consequences of Diem "government of men." 6. Conclusion—toward a viable form of government of men in the Republic of Vietnam.

*Bibliography:* Deals primarily with government and politics in Vietnam. Government official documents, Vietnamese works, and newspapers are listed.

*Maps* (selected): Government of the Republic of Vietnam: field administration and local government.

*Charts:* Main periods of Vietnam's history. The Presidency and dependent agencies. Government of the Republic of Vietnam: central administrations.

239. NGUYEN THAI BINH. Vietnam, the Problem and a Solution. (Paris?) Vietnam Democratic Party, 1962. 145 p.; illustrations, map.
DS557.A6N49

*Text:* Although propaganda in nature, this treatise is severely critical of both the Ho chi Minh regime in North Vietnam and the Ngo dinh Diem regime in South Vietnam. Describes in detail the Democratic Party of Vietnam—its party organization, its creative program to bring about the reunification of the two Vietnams, and its advocacy of a change of government in South Vietnam. Articles, columns, and reports giving the reactions of the American press to the Diem government are included.

*Illustrations:* President Ngo dinh Diem, Ngo dinh Nhu, and others in the Diem government.

*Map:* Outline map of Southeast Asia mainland.

240. NGUYEN VAN THAI, and NGUYEN VAN MUNG. A Short History of Vietnam. Saigon, Published for the Vietnamese-American Association by the Times Publishing Co., 1958. xiii, 350 p.; bibliography, maps, charts.
DS557.A5N48

*Text:* This compilation, the first English history of Vietnam written by Vietnamese and based on Viet-

namese sources, is presented in 40 chapters within these six parts: 1. Vietnam in the pre-recorded era. 2. Under the foreign yoke. 3. Toward independence. 4. Rivalry and partition. 5. Reunification of the country. 6. Prelude to independence.

*Bibliography:* A brief list of rather well-known references.

*Maps* (selected): Vietnam in 1953. China under the Five Dynasties. Annam under the Tran Dynasty and the Nguyen wars. Vietnamese expansion southward.

*Charts* (selected): Under the foreign yoke (Chinese). The various dynasties from the Ngo Dynasty to the Nguyen Dynasty.

241. ROBERTS, STEPHEN HENRY. "Indochina." In History of French Colonial Policy (1870–1925). London, P. S. King, 1929. p. 419–498; bibliography, map, index. (Studies in Economics and Political Science. London, School of Economics and Political Science. Monograph no. 95)
JV1811.R6

*Text:* Divided into two parts the study presents a discussion of the theoretical principles of French colonial policy together with a comparison of French colonization with that of other Powers. The regional survey, which presents each French colony in turn, gives the full details of the history and position of the French as they put into practice the French colonial theory in Indochina.

The account of the French activities in Indochina is divided into seven parts: preliminary stage up to 1885; people and their civilizations; early struggles of French colonial principles from 1885 to 1895; Paul Doumer, Governor-General, from 1897–1902; native policy after the Doumer period; economic development in the early 20th-century—agricultural products, industry, communications, and trade; and conclusion.

*Bibliography:* Includes official and nonofficial documents.

*Map:* Development of French Indochina, showing cultivated land and railway system.

242. SASORITH, KATAY D. Le Laos; son evolution politique, sa place dans l'Union française. Paris, Editions Berger-Levrault, 1953. 1953. 155 p.; illustrations, maps, appendices.
DS557.L2S3

*Text:* Presents a brief account of the history and political evolution of Laos with particular reference to the French advent in 1893, the Japanese occupation during World War II, and the Franco-Laotian agreement in 1949 which brought Laos eventually into the Associated States of Indochina. The closing chapter tells of the political and economic future of Laos.

*Illustrations* (selected): His Majesty King Sisavong-Vong. Flute player. Laotian dancers. Chao Boun Oum de Champassak.

*Maps:* Indochina states. Laos, showing provinces.

*Appendices:* 1947 Constitution of Laos. Exchange of letters between King Sisavong-Vong and President Auriol. 1949 Franco-Laos protocol. Statements of President Auriol and King of Laos at protocol signing. 1949 decree of the Prime Minister of the Provisional Government of Laos. Lao-Issara Resistance Movement dissolved. Political status of Laos in 1938.

243. SHAH, IKBAL ALI, SIRDAR. Viet Nam. London, Octagon Press, 1960. xv, 232 p.; map, index.  DS557.A5S46

*Text:* Divided into 11 parts, these subjects are among those discussed: the divided Vietnam; Communist movement in Vietnam; the philosophy of President Ngo dinh Diem; problem of feeding the nation; development and resettlement in South Vietnam; economic life and steps towards greater prosperity; the educational system; the artistic appreciation and folklore.

*Map:* Vietnam and her neighbors.

244. TANHAM, GEORGE K. Communist Revolutionary Warfare: The Vietminh in Indochina. New York, Praeger, 1961. x, 166 p.; bibliography, map. (Books that matter)
DS557.A5T3

*Text:* As no. 96 in the series of Praeger publications in Russian history and world communism, this volume "focuses primarily on military aspects of the war and attempts to provide insight by means of an analysis of Vietminh military doctrine, tactics, and organization as revealed during the 1945–54 war in Indochina." Considerable emphasis is laid on the Communist revolutionary warfare tactics in the political, economic, military, and psychological means to win the minds of the Vietnamese people. The Vietminh guerrilla-type warfare has enabled the Communists to retain mobility in a difficult jungle terrain and facilitated the gathering of intelligence information, and thus showed that the West must learn that guerrilla operations of the Vietminh type will continue to be important even in a nuclear age. The closing chapter emphasizes the idea

that if the free world is to prevail against the Communist drive, and is to give solid assistance to the countries of Southeast Asia in their own independent development, it is imperative that the West understand the appeal and tactics of the Communists.

*Bibliography:* A specialized list of monographic titles together with articles and bulletins which deal with the military and other aspects of the Vietnamese war.

*Map:* Indochina before the truce of 1954.

245. U.S. CONGRESS. SENATE. COMMITTEE ON FOREIGN RELATIONS. Report on Indochina: Report of Mike Mansfield on a Study Mission to Vietnam, Cambodia, Laos. Washington, U.S. Govt. Printing Office, 1954. v, 48 p.; map, appendices.  DS550.U513

*Text:* A member of the Senate Foreign Relations Committee reviews the situation in Vietnam very soon after the Geneva Agreement, in August 1954, terminated the war in Indochina and divided Vietnam into North Vietnam and South Vietnam. The effect of the 17th parallel, the exchange of prisoners, the refugee problems, and the political crisis in South Vietnam are reviewed. Brief summaries of conditions in Laos and Cambodia also are provided. Emphasizes the need for military and economic aid to sustain South Vietnam free and independent from Communist North Vietnam.

*Map:* Outline map showing the two zones of divided Vietnam, Cambodia, and Laos.

*Appendices:* 1. Agreements of the Geneva Conference on Indochina. 2. Biographies of various personages in Indochina.

246. U.S. CONGRESS. SENATE. COMMITTEE ON FOREIGN RELATIONS. Vietnam, Cambodia, and Laos; report by Senator Mike Mansfield. Washington, U.S. Government Printing Office, 1955. v, 19 p.; map.

DS550.U515.

*Text:* A congressional report by a member of the Senate Foreign Relations Committee who visited the three countries which formerly comprised French Indochina. Following a presentation of his findings on the political situation, the economic conditions and the international relations of these countries, it was concluded— at the time of the report—that the tide of totalitarian communism, which was on the verge of overrunning Vietnam and other parts of Southeast Asia, had been slackened due to the Diem government in opposition to the Ho chi Minh regime in the north.

247. U.S. Department of State. The Situation in Laos. Washington, 1959. ii, 23 p.; map.
DS557.L2U46

*Text:* An account which reviews the background of the events of the international conflict in Laos from 1954 up to late 1959; describes the action of the Royal Laos Government to fulfill its international commitments and to preserve its independence and identity; and reveals the Communist opposition which is ever present in the country.

*Map:* Outline map of Laos showing provinces and principal towns.

248. U.S. Department of State. Office of Intelligence and Research. Outline of Basic Treaty Relationships Between France and the Associated States of Indochina. Washington, 1952. i, 24 p.; appendices. (IR 5758) In process

*Text:* Outlines the basic treaty relationships between France and the Associated States of Indochina—Vietnam, Cambodia, and Laos—in accordance with the Baie d'Along Agreement (1948), The Franco-Vietnamese Agreement (1949), The Franco-Cambodian Agreement (1949), and The Franco-Laotian Agreement (1949). The discussion gives the general nature of and summarizes the important points contained in the agreements between France and Vietnam— foreign relations, military status, police services, immigration, domestic finance, trade and commerce, transportation and communication, economic planning, foreign exchange, cultural and educational matters, social welfare, labor, public health, and status of French personnel in Vietnam. The Franco-Cambodian and Franco-Laotian agreements are not discussed in detail.

*Appendices:* Lists the Franco-Vietnamese, the Franco-Laotian, the Franco-Cambodian Implementing Conventions (1949–50), and the Interstate Conventions (1950).

249. U.S. Department of State. Office of Intelligence and Research. Political Alignments of Vietnamese Nationalists. Washington, 1949. vii, 176 p.; bibliography, map, charts, 2 appendices, index. (OIR report no. 3708) Microfilm DS18

*Text:* A study dealing with the nationalist movement in Vietnam and the role which the movement of communism is playing in Vietnamese political change.

Following a brief statement on the origins of the nationalist movement, the study is divided into four principal parts: Nationalist movements, 1918–41; Vietnam during World War II; Nationalism in power; and, Nationalist alignments since the outbreak of the French-Vietnam war.

Within these respective parts there is a wealth of information regarding the early political parties, the religious movement of Caodaism—which has wielded political influence—the revolutionary nationalist parties, the development and activities of the Indochinese Communist Party, the Trotskyist movement, the Japanese-supported nationalist parties, the party alignments under direct Japanese control, the underground activities of the nationalist movements during the war years, the seizure of power by the nationalists and the installation of a "People's Revolutionary Government" headed by Ho chi Minh, and the establishment of the Vietnam National Assembly. Includes the principal political and military events since official diplomatic relations between the French and Vietnam Governments were terminated in December 1946; namely, activities of parties in the Vietnam Government camp, the role of the Trotskyist movement since the war, the Bao Dai restoration movements, the French sponsored regimes, and the establishment of the Provisional Vietnam Central Government in early 1948.

*Bibliography:* Brings together the small amount of publications dealing with this subject.

*Map:* Indochina (color), scale–1: 5,656,000; provides boundaries, capitals, and transportation information.

*Charts:* Describe the intricacies of: (1) International connections of Indochinese Communist Party in 1930; (2) Development of Communist organizations in Indochina, 1921–31; (3) History of the Vietnam Nationalist Party; and, (4) Development of Communist organizations in Indochina, 1931–45.

*Appendices:* Chronology of principal events in Indochina from 931 A.D. to July 1949. Index of Vietnamese proper names.

250. U.S. Department of State. Office of Public Services. A Threat to the Peace: North Vietnam's Effort to Conquer South Vietnam. Parts I and II. Washington, 1961. vi. 53, 102; illustrations, maps, charts, appendices. (Dept. of State publication 7308. Far Eastern series, 110) DS557.A6U48

*Text:* Divided into two parts. Part one outlines the conflict between North Vietnam and South Vietnam based on documentary evidence exposing the activities of the Viet Cong in both parts of Vietnam. Much of the evidence of Communist activities is based on specific cases dealing with infiltration of agents, infiltration of military personnel, introduction of supplies from the north, and Laos as a base and route of the Viet Cong.

Part two is a separate publication consisting of appendices referred to in part one.

*Illustrations:* Captured Viet Cong. Written confessions. Reproduction of various Viet Cong documents, typed and handwritten.

*Maps:* Outline map showing places in North and South Vietnam where the Viet Cong are active. Maps in connection with various cases discussed in part one.

*Charts:* Political organization of the Viet Cong. Inter-province organization of the Viet Cong. Organization of central research agency of the Viet Cong. Organization of typical Viet Cong intelligence center. Special targets for penetration by Viet Cong intelligence agents.

251. VIETNAM. Violations of the Geneva Agreements by the Viet-Minh Communists. Saigon, 1959. 158 p.; illustrations, appendices.
DS557.A6A45

*Text:* Five years after the Geneva Conference which brought about the partition of Vietnam, the Government of South Vietnam set forth the provisions of the Geneva Agreements which have been violated by the Viet-Minh Communists, grouping such violations in these three categories: 1. Military matters; 2. Civilian population; and 3. Problem of internal subversion.

*Illustrations:* Photostats of letters, resistance loan bonds, people's court scenes.

*Appendices:* Translations in English of various documents referred to in the text.

252. VIETNAM. CONSTITUTION. The Constitution of the Republic of Vietnam. Saigon, Secretariat of State for Information, 1956. 40 p.; table, chart. Law

*Text:* Divided into these two parts: I. The history and philosophy of the Constitution; II. The text of the Constitution.

Part one discusses: The presidential message; The Constitutional Commission; The preamble; Basic human rights and duties; The check and balance of powers; The President of the Republic; The Legislative Assembly; The judicial function; The National Economic Council; and The spirit of the Constitution.

Part two, the text, is thus divided: Basic provisions; Rights and duties of the citizens; The President of the Republic; The National Assembly; The judges; The Special Court of Justice; The National Economic Council; The Constitutional Court; Amendment of the Constitution; General provisions.

*Table:* Composition of the 15-member Constitutional Commission.

*Chart:* The Constitutional Court.

253. VIETNAM. MINISTRY OF INFORMATION. The Problem of Reunification of Vietnam. [Saigon] 1958. viii, 105 p. DS557.A6A58

*Text:* Brings together the statements, communiques, and official messages of the government of the Republic of Vietnam on the subject of the reunification problem. This compilation also contains a study of the Geneva Agreements of 1954 and documents on the Ba Lang and Luu My incidents and the peasant revolt in Quynh Luu in North Vietnam.

254. VIRAVONG, MAHA SILA. History of Laos. New York, U.S. Joint Publications Research Service, 1958. 147 p. (JPRS (NY) 712)
AS36.U57 712

*Text:* Translated from *Phong savadon Lao,* volume one, this summary account of Lao history from ancient times to the 19th-century when Thailand dominated Laos, is presented in seven parts: 1. History of the Lao race. 2. The birth of the Lao race. 3. The ancient kingdom of the Lao. 4. The Lao kingdom of Nong Sae or Nan Tchow. 5. The Lan Xang kingdom. 6. The division of the Lao kingdom into three kingdoms. 7. The kingdom of Laos after the loss of its independence.

255. VO NGUYEN GIAP. People's War, People's Army: The Viet Công Insurrection Manual for Underdeveloped Countries. Foreword by Roger Hilsman. Profile of Giap by Bernard B. Fall. New York, Praeger, 1962. 217 p.; illustrations, map. (Praeger publications in Russian history and world communism, No. 119) DS557.A7V6

*Text:* A facsimile edition of a series of articles by the Viet Minh military Commander-in-Chief in book form under the same title *People's War, People's Army,* published by the Foreign Languages Publishing House, Hanoi, 1961.

There are four principal parts: The Vietnamese people's war of liberation against the French imperialists and the American interventionists (1945–54). People's war, People's Army. The great experiences gained by our Party in leading the armed struggle and building revolutionary armed forces. Dien Bien Phu.

The biographical sketch of Giap shows how he became a Communist and later the highest military leader in the Viet Minh.

*Illustrations:* General Vo Nguyen Giap, Ho chi Minh.

*Maps:* Outline map showing North Vietnam and South Vietnam. Defeat of the Navarre Plan.

256. WOODRUFF, LLOYD WILBUR, and NGUYEN NGOC YEN. The Study of a Vietnamese Rural Community: Administrative Activity. Annex: Village Government in Viet-Nam, a Survey of Historical Developments by Nguyen xuan Dao. [Saigon?] Michigan State University, Viet-nam Advisory Group, 1960. 2 vols.; bibliography, maps, tables, appendices.

JS7225.V5W6

*Text:* As one of three parallel studies in the fields of economics, anthropology, and sociology, and public administration prepared by the Michigan State University Group staff in South Vietnam under the sponsorship of the National Institute of Administration, this volume is concerned with the historical development and the present condition of village administration in South Vietnam. The problems of village administration in the central lowlands and delta region are compared in these selected chapters: 2. Administrative organization. 3. Village organization. 4. Financial affairs. 6. Political and personal security. 7. The settling of disputes. 8. Ceremonies and celebrations. 9. Activities of the village council.

The annex, *Village government in Viet-Nam*, provides a summary of administrative change in the Vietnamese village from the earliest period to the present time. Major political events in the history of Vietnam are cited as they relate to administrative change. Particular attention is given to the influence of China and the historical expansion southward.

*Bibliography:* Cites official documents, books, articles, and pamphlets dealing with Vietnamese public administration.

*Maps:* South Vietnam, showing provinces and capitals. Khanh-Hau village.

*Tables* (selected): Tax payments of landowners. Village expenditures. Village revenues.

*Appendices* (selected): Khanh Hau village budget. Excerpt from the "Declaration of the Government of the Republic of Vietnam relative to the problem of unification," 1958.

# ECONOMICS

(including: Agriculture, Commerce, Industry, and Labor)

257. BERNARD, PAUL. Le Problème économique indochinois. Introduction by René Bouvier. Paris, Nouvelles Éditions Latines, 1934. lxii, 424 p.; bibliography, map, tables, charts.

HC442.B42

*Text:* A survey of economic conditions in Indochina prior to World War II, with particular reference to the period of the depression after 1932. Within the twenty-five chapters these subjects are discussed: population, foreign trade, finance and credit, cultivation of rice, economic development of Indochina under French influence, and, problems involved in a more constructive economic program for the country.

*Bibliography:* Brief list of references related to the study.

*Map:* Population in the Tonkin area.

*Tables:* Products imported from China. Imports and exports of principal merchandise. Rice production. Comparative budgets of various Indochinese states.

*Charts:* Organizational scheme of agricultural and industrial credit systems.

258. CHILD, FRANK C. Essays on Economic Growth, Capital Formation, and Public Policy in Viet-Nam. Saigon, Michigan State University Viet-Nam Advisory Group, 1961. ii, 138 p.; bibliography, tables. HC443.V5C5

*Text:* Concerned with a constructive economic development policy, this study emphasizes various aspects of the Vietnamese economy in these five chapters: 1. Economic growth, capital formation, and public policy. 2. A growth model for Vietnamese national income. 3. Economic prospects for Vietnam. 4. Deficits, inflation, and growth potential. 5. Where to invest and who should do it.

*Bibliography:* Bibliographical footnotes.

*Tables* (selected): Selected economic indicators. National income estimates. Foreign aid. Commodities eligible and ineligible for ICA aid.

259. ESTEBE, PAUL. Le Problème du riz en Indochine. Toulouse, Impr. F. Boisseau, 1934. 326 p.; bibliography, map.    HD9066.I52E8

*Texts:* Selected chapter headings include: Part I.—Les conditions actuelles de la production: 1. L'Indochine et la crise rizicole. 2. Technique de la production du riz en Cochinchine. 3. Riziculture et credit. 4. Le problème de l'assainissement financier de la situation rizicole. 5. Crédit foncier à long terme et Office de colonisation. 6. Mesures secondaires d'assainissement. Part II—Les conditions actuelles de la vente: 7. Commerce et exportation. 8. Abaissement de la taxe de sortie. 9. Abaissement des tarifs douaniers. 10. Destabilisation de la piastre. Part III—L'Avenir du riz: 11. L'Augmentation de la production. 12. Culture intensive. 13. Culture extensive. 14. La question indochinoise.

*Bibliography:* Brief list of references pertaining to rice production.

*Map:* Rice cultivation in Cochinchine, scale–1:1,500,-000ᵉ.

260. GAUTHIER, JULIEN. L'Indochine au travail dans la paix française. Paris, Eyrolles, 1949. 323 p.; bibliography, illustrations, maps, tables, charts, diagrams.    HC442.G3

*Text:* This well-documented volume provides economic data on Indochina. Numerous graphs, diagrams, and statistical tables amplify the text.

Divided into five principal divisions which are as follows:

I. Considerations générales sur l'Indochine et l'intervention française: 1. Vue d'ensemble—debuts de l'occupation; 2. Moyens d'execution des grands programmes d'aménagement de l'Indochine.

II. Equipment économique de l'Indochine, voies de communication et liaisons extérieures: 1. Routes et voies ferrées; 2. Voies navigables et ports fluviaux; 3. Ports et travaux maritimes; 4. Liaisons postales et télégraphiques—liaisons aeriennes, navigation aerienne.

III. Aménagement agricole de l'Indochine: 1. Le riz en Indochine; 2. Aménagement du delta tonkinois; 3. Aménagement agricole de l'Annam; 4. Aménagement de la Cochinchine; 5. L'hydraulique agricole au Cambodge; 6. L'hydraulique agricole au Laos.

IV. Aménagement des villes et des stations de repos l'eau potable et l'électricité en Indochine: 1. Les villes et les grands centres; 2. Les stations climatiques; 3. L'eau potable en Indochine; 4. L'électricité en Indochine.

V. Développement économique de l'Indochine: A. Apercu de la production indochinoise—1. Agriculture, èlevage et pêche; 2. Industrie; B. Commerce et transports—1. Transactions terrestres et fluviales aperçu du commerce intérieur; 2. Navigation maritime; 3. Commerce extérieur; C. Liaisons postales, télégraphiques, aériennes et radiotélégraphiques.

*Bibliography:* Lists the principal documents consulted in the study.

*Maps:* Provide information on roads, railroads, dams, waterways, agriculture, and electricity plants.

*Tables:* Statistical data on agricultural production, electricity plants, exports and imports, and other subjects considered in the text.

*Charts and Diagrams:* Irrigation schemes.

*Illustrations:* An excellent series comprising views of the cities of Hanoi and Saigon; bridges and railroads; canals, waterways, and dams, and coastlines and lighthouses.

261. GOUROU, PIERRE. Land Utilization in French Indochina. [New York, Institute of Pacific Relations] 1945. vii, 588 p.; maps, tables.    Microfilm 1572HD

*Text:* A translation of the author's *L'Utilisation du sol en Indochine Française*, published by the Centre d'Etudes de Politique Etrangère, publication no. 14, Paul Hartmann, Paris. The author is Professor of Geography in the Faculty of Lettres, University of Bordeaux.

Divided into three parts. Part one deals with information on physiography, climate and soils, and includes a discussion of the physical conditions governing land utilization. Part two discusses population distribution as an index to land utilization. Part three presents rural economic activities as found in agriculture, fisheries, exploitation of forests, and rural handicraft industries. A closing chapter examines the standards of living of the rural population.

Unfortunately the English edition of this important study has no index.

*Maps:* Numerous sketch maps relating to population, agriculture, forests, and geographical features of Indochina.

*Tables:* Statistical data pertaining to the subjects discussed in the text.

262. ROBEQUAIN, CHARLES. The Economic Development of French Indochina. Translation by Isabel A. Ward. London, New York, Oxford University Press, 1944. vii, 400 p.; map, tables, index. (Issued under the auspices of the International Secretariat, Institute of Pacific Relations)    HC442.R613

*Text:* A translation of the author's book entitled *L'évolution économique de l'Indochine française* (Paris, Hartmann, 1939), which is most valuable since the French edition was published in 1939 when World War II broke out and only a few copies were distributed outside France before the German occupation.

Shows the changes effected in the economy of Indochina as a result of the French occupation. The organization of the information consists of: I. General factors in Indochina's economic development—people, communications, economic theories, and capital and its circulation; II. New economic developments—French colonization, changes in native agriculture, industry, foreign trade, and conclusion. A supplementary chapter by J. R. Andrus and Katrine Green provides some of the principal economic developments in Indochina since the French edition appeared.

*Map:* Outline map on flyleaf, showing roads and railroads.

*Tables:* Deal with population, government budget expenditures, capital investments, rice cultivation, and foreign trade.

263. U.S. AGENCY FOR INTERNATIONAL DEVELOPMENT. The American Aid Program in Cambodia; a decade of cooperation, 1951–1961. Phnom Penh, 1961. 64 p.; illustrations, charts.    HC443.C3U4

*Text:* Presents in a graphic manner the ways in which over one billion dollars were utilized in the U.S. foreign aid program to strengthen the economy, social life, and living standards of Cambodia from 1951 to 1961.

The account relates the assistance given in the fields of education, agriculture, public health, police, public works, commodity imports, and military assistance.

*Illustrations:* Views of projects in all the above fields of assistance.

*Charts:* Educational statistics. American aid to Cambodia, 1951–61.

264. U.S. CONGRESS. HOUSE. COMMITTEE ON FOREIGN AFFAIRS. Mutual Security Program in Laos. Hearings Before the Subcommittee on the Far East and the Pacific of the Committee on Foreign Affairs, House of Representatives, Eighty-Fifth Congress, Second Session. May 7 and 8, 1958. Washington, U.S. Govt. Printing Office, 1958. iii, 78 p.; tables.    UA12.U5 1958a

*Text:* Presents the testimonies of representatives of the U.S. General Accounting Office, State Department, and the International Cooperation Administration about the conditions in Laos in the spring of 1958, with particular reference to the management or mismanagement of the whole ICA program in that country, the use of U.S. foreign aid from 1951 to 1958 as the core of the economic and technical assistance program to Laos, Cambodia, and Vietnam.

*Tables:* Composition of dollar funds and local currency in the aid program for the years, 1955, 1956, and 1957.

265. VIETNAM. INSTITUT DE LA STATISTIQUE ET DES ÉTUDES ECONOMIQUES. Bulletin économique du Viêt-Nam. Saigon. Vol. 1 appeared in Jan. 1950.    HC443.V5V552

*Text:* A bilingual serial publication in the Vietnamese and French languages. The Vietnamese title is: *Việt-Nam kinh-tê tâp-san;* and the Vietnamese issuing office is Viên Thông-kê và Khâo-cúu Kinh-tê Viêt-Nam. There are three principal divisions in each issue: namely, Economie du Viêt-Nam; Etudes et informations; and, Bulletin statistique mensuel—all of which provide data pertaining to agriculture, forests, industry, and labor.

The *Bulletin statistique mensuel du Viêt–Nam,* formerly issued as a separate publication, is now a part of this new publication.

## SOCIAL CONDITIONS
(including: Anthropology, Education and Health)

266. BILODEAU, CHARLES, SOMLITH PATHAMMAVONG, and LE QUANG HONG. Compulsory Education in Cambodia, Laos and Vietnam. Paris, Unesco, 1955. 157 p.; bibliography, tables, appendices. (Studies on compulsory education, 14)    LC136.I55B5

*Text:* These three studies are part of a series of publications intended to provide an account of the manner in which free and compulsory education might be applied in Cambodia, Laos and South Vietnam. Each is based on an earlier report given at the Regional

Conference on Free and Compulsory Education held in Bombay in December 1952. The treatises, prepared by well-qualified persons in the educational field in their countries, emphasize the efforts of the government and teachers to develop an adequate system of education and at the same time is in harmony with the national culture.

*Bibliography:* Book titles, largely in French, give data on education in these countries.

*Tables* (selected): Educational statistics for Cambodia. Elementary education in Vietnam.

*Appendices:* Decree concerning compulsory education in Cambodia. Statistics relating to primary education in Vietnam. Decree of 20 January 1952 making primary education compulsory in Vietnam. Decree . . . concerning the campaign against literacy in Vietnam.

267. CONFERENCE ON SOCIAL DEVELOPMENT AND WELFARE IN VIETNAM. New York, 1959. Problems of Freedom: South Vietnam Since Independence. Edited by Wesley R. Fishel. Introduction by Mike Mansfield. Contributors: Joseph Buttinger and others. New York, Free Press of Glencoe; East Lansing, Bureau of Social and Political Research, Michigan State University, 1961. xiv, 233 p.; bibliography, maps, tables, appendices, index.

HN700.V5C6 1959a

*Text:* Consists of the papers and addresses given at a conference of scholars, businessmen, government officials, and journalists which evaluate and shed light on the many aspects of the process and problems of developing a truly free Vietnam following the partition of Vietnam in 1954. The papers emphasize the way in which the tide of totalitarian communism was slackened and the social revolution which has brought about a new society, produced a higher standard of living, improved health and living conditions, initiated the second largest land reform program in free Asia, developed a broad and far reaching cooperative movement, and called forth a pioneering spirit of the people which has transcended all that has been accomplished.

The eleven chapters describing this social change are: 1. The consequences of partition by Robert Nathan. 2. Problems of democratic growth in free Vietnam by Wesley Fishel. 3. Personalism in Vietnam by John Donnell. 4. Vietnam's concept of development by Vu van Thai. 5. Problems of education in Vietnam by Edgar Pike. 6. The ethnic minorities in the Republic of Vietnam by Joseph Buttinger. 7. Opening of new lands and villages: the Republic of Vietnam's

land development program by William Henderson. 8. Stresses and strains in a developing administrative system by John Dorsey, Jr. 9. Agrarian reform in the Republic of Vietnam by Wolf Ladejinsky. 10. The growth of agricultural credit and cooperatives in Vietnam by Tran ngoc Lien. 11. The social and economic characteristics of the work force in Saigon by James Hendry.

*Bibliography:* References to books and articles given in footnotes at end of some chapters.

*Maps* (selected): American assistance since 1953 to June 1959 under education projects. Expansion and improvement of technical vocational education. Distribution of ethnic groups in Vietnam. Land development (rural resettlement). Agrarian reform area subject to transfer. Agricultural cooperatives. Improved irrigation and water control. Improvement of nursing and allied education. Malaria eradication.

*Tables* (selected): Evolution of the educational system in Vietnam from 1949 to 1959. Land development program.

*Appendices:* 1. Tabular data on the characteristics on the work force in Saigon by James Hendry. 2. Limitations of the survey of the characteristics of the work force in Saigon by James Hendry. 3. Health progress in Vietnam by Craig Lichtenwalner.

268. FALK, CHARLES JOHN. Educational Survey of Central Vietnam. Saigon, U.S. Operations Mission to Vietnam, 1957. 78 l., appendices. (Field study no. 4, F.Y. 1956)

LA1181.F3 1957

*Text:* One of a series of field studies prepared by the Education Division of U.S.O.M. to Vietnam to gather data on the educational and cultural situation in South and Central Vietnam. This study deals with historical background, educational administration, higher education and secondary schools, elementary schools, private schools, teacher training, and educational problems.

*Appendices:* A. Community pilot schools. B. Population studies in Central Vietnam.

269. FALK, CHARLES JOHN. Higher Education in Vietnam; Provisional Report. Saigon, U.S. Operations Mission to Vietnam, 1956. 89 l.; appendices. (Field study no. 5, F.Y. 1956)

LA1183.F3 1957

*Text:* A survey of higher education with considerable emphasis on the National University of Vietnam—the origin and development of the university and its parent institutions, plans for university education, and foreign aid. Other sections deal with higher schools of pedagogy, institute of government, higher schools of technology, and cultural and research institutions.

*Appendices:* A. Vietnamese education at terms. B. University statutes and regulations. C. Curriculum of the medical school. D. The Institute of Government.

270. GOUROU, PIERRE. The Peasants of the Tonkin Delta: A Study of Human Geography. New Haven, Human Relations Area Files, 1955. 2 vols.; bibliography, illustrations, maps, diagrams, index. DS557.T7G62 1955

*Text:* Originally published in 1936 by Editions d'art et d'histoire in Paris, *Les Paysans du Delta Tonkinois,* it deals with the physical surroundings, the peasant population, and the means of existence of the Tonkinese peasants in North Vietnam.

The eleven chapters are: The relief of the delta; The climate; Water; History of the peopling of the delta; The population density; The population movements; the villages; The houses; Agriculture; The village industrial; Exchange transactions.

*Bibliography:* A long list of articles and monographs relating to the preceding chapters.

*Illustrations:* Types of houses; high altitude views of villages; village industries.

*Maps* (selected): Rainfall map; Dikes in the Tonkin Delta; Region of Dai Cong; Foundation dates of villages in Nan Dinh. Population density; Types of village in Tonkin Delta; Rice fields; Industrial population; Industrial villages.

*Diagrams:* Cross-sections of house boats and other living quarters.

271. HOANG VAN CHI, ed. and tr. The New Class in North Vietnam. Saigon, Cong Dan, 1958. 165 p.; illustrations DS557.A7H6

*Text:* Translated articles written by persons of the elite living in North Vietnam and originally printed in Vietnamese newspapers and periodicals within the Communist controlled zone of North Vietnam provide insights into the nature of communism as found in northern Vietnam. Some of these articles have been selected from opposition papers which were allowed to appear in Hanoi in 1956.

Prefatory to the translated articles is a general survey of the situation in Communist North Vietnam, and a sketch of the progress of communism in Vietnam since 1941.

*Illustrations:* Cartoons which appeared in *Nhan Dan* and other papers.

272. HUMAN RELATIONS AREA FILES. Vietnamese Ethnographic Papers, by L. Cadiere, and others. New Haven, 1953. unpaged; illustrations, map, tables, charts. (Behavior science translations) DS557.A5H83

*Text:* This collection of writings on ethnology pertaining to Vietnam is comprised of these nine papers: 1. The dynastic urns of the palace in Hue, historical note, by L. Cadiere. 2. The dynastic urns of the palace of Hue, technique of manufacture by P. Chonet. 3. The blackening of teeth in Eastern Asia and Indochina by Pierre Huard. 4. Annamese costume by A. J. Gorin. 5. The "Thuoc me" mysterious drugs of the thieves of Annam by Albert Sallet. 6. Medicine and doctors according to the Annamese code by E. Jeanselme. 7. Suicide in Annamese society by Vu cong Hoe. 8. Some statistical data on suicide in Vietnam by T. Smolski. 9. Annamese astrology by G. Dumoutier.

*Illustrations:* Annamese furnace of kiln. Figures of astrology.

*Map:* Areas where teeth are blackened.

*Tables:* Frequency and methods of suicide.

*Charts:* Mortality by suicide.

273. TRAN VAN TRAI. La Famille patriarcale annamite. Paris, P. Lapagesse, 1942. 360 p.; bibliography, appendix. (Université de Paris—Faculté des Lettres) HQ673.T7

*Text:* A well-documented thesis, prepared at the University of Paris, dealing with marriage customs, rites and practices in Vietnam. The contents is divided into five principal divisions: Considérations générales sur la famille patriarcale annamite; Le mariage; Les droits et les devoirs nés du mariage; La naissance; and, Les idées et les coutumes relatives à la mort. The conclusion presents an evaluation of the family in Vietnam.

*Bibliography:* Numerous Vietnamese works are listed.

*Appendix:* L'accord sur les recommandations aux membres de la famille des Thái.

# CULTURAL LIFE
(including: Fine Arts, Religion, Language, and Literature)

274. BENEDICT, PAUL K. "Languages and Literatures of Indochina," *Far Eastern Quarterly*, Aug. 1947, v. 6:379–389.   DS501.F274 1947

*Text:* A discussion of the Khmer (Cambodian), Annamese, Cham, and Lao languages, the so-called "indigenous" and "naturalized" languages of Indochina which are used in the three principal cultural and political divisions of the country.   Presents data about the "immigrant" languages which are largely concentrated in the mountainous areas of northwestern Tonkin.   Includes information about Chinese and Indian influences on the languages and literature of Indochina—especially on the Vietnamese language in Vietnam and the Cambodian language in Cambodia.

275. GIRONCOURT, GEORGE DE. "Recherches de géographie musicale en Indochine." Extrait du *Bulletin de la Société des Etudes Indochinoises.* Tome 17, no. 4–4ᵉ trimestre, 1942. 174 p.; bibliography, illustrations, musical scores, map, indices.   ML3758.I5G5

*Text:* A detailed study of music among various peoples in Indochina and Thailand, with special attention given to musical instruments made from metal, bamboo, and other kinds of wood.   Discusses the relation of music to mythology, the influence of the climate on music, and the use of music in religious rites, marriage ceremonies, and other customs.

*Bibliography:* A valuable list of references on the subject of music in Indochina.

*Map:* Indochina and Thailand showing the places where the research was done for this study.

*Illustrations:* Various types of musical instruments. Different racial peoples and their dress.

*Musical scores:* Illustrate the various kinds of music used.

276. GOBRON, GABRIEL.   History and Philosophy of Caodaism: Reformed Buddhism, Vietnamese Spiritism, New Religion in Eurasia.   Translated from the original French by Pham-xuân Thai. [Saigon?] 1950.   189 p.; illustrations, appendix.   (Published under the auspices of His Excellency Trân quang Vinh, Major-General, Commander-in-Chief of the Caodaist Troops, Minister of the Armed Forces of the Government of Vietnam)   BL2055.G613

*Text:* One of the very few accounts in English of the development of Caodaism, a religious movement which was founded in Indochina in 1926 by Ngâ vân Chiêu.   Relates how the provincial governor received a message from a spirit named Cao Dai to establish a new religion which would incorporate the good features of all religions including Buddhism, Confusianism, Taoism, Christianity, and the cult of ancestors.   Outlines the beliefs, fundamental principles, forms of worship, and rituals of a movement which claims over two million followers.

*Illustrations:* General Trân quang Vinh.   Lê vãn Trung, the first Caodaist Pope.   Scenes from the celebration during 61st anniversary of H.H. Hô Pháp.   Principle temple of Caodaism in Phnom Penh.

*Appendix:* Biographical account of Ngô vãn Chiêu, the founder of Caodaism.

277. GROSLIER, BERNARD PHILIPPE.   Indochine; carrefour des arts.   Paris, A Michel, 1961. 281 p.; bibliography, illustrations, maps, charts, appendices, index.   (L'Art dans le monde—mondements historiques, sociologiques et religieux: Civilisations non européennes)   N7311.G7

*Text:* Nothwithstanding that Angkor Wat holds a central place in this volume because of the graphic description and commentary of that ancient edifice, the total purview includes the art, architecture, and civilizations of all the countries sharing the so-called Indochina mainland.   Considerable valuable early historical data is provided for the historian.

The chapter headings are: 1. Pre- et proto-histoire. 2. L'apport de la Chine et de l'Inde: naissance de l'Indochine.   3. La formation des états indianisés l'Empire du Fou-nan.   4. L'Indochine préangkorienne: l'empire du Tchen-la.   5. La fondation d'Angkor.   6. L'hégémonie Khmère.   7. L'Indochine a l'ombre d'Angkor.   8. Le classicisme Khmer: Angkor Vat.   9. L'apothéose d'Angkor.   10. La dislocation des états sous le signe du bouddhisme du renoncement. 11. L'Indochine au pouvoir des Thai et sous le signe du bouddhisme de renoncement.   12. La prise du pouvoir des vietnamiens et l'intrusion de l'Europe.

*Bibliography:* Book titles are arranged as they pertain to the various chapters.

*Illustrations:* Colored plates of various views in Angkor Wat.

*Maps:* Physical structure of Indochina. History in Indochina. Indochina coastline. Plan of Angkor.

*Charts:* Chronological tables of history in Southeast Asia.

*Appendices:* Technical terms used in text. Names of monuments.

[Also issued in English: *The art of Indochina, including Thailand, Vietnam, Laos and Cambodia.* New York, Crown Publishers, 1962].

278. HALPERN, JOEL MARTIN. Aspects of Village Life and Culture Change in Laos. Special report prepared for the Council on Economic and Cultural Affairs, Inc. Pre-publication copy. New York, Council on Economic and Cultural Affairs, 1958. iii, 143 p.; bibliography, illustrations, map, tables, glossary.
HN700.L3H3

*Text:* Brings together data from published and unpublished materials on agricultural, economic, and related problems in Laotian village life, and examines some of these problems with a view to seeking solutions which will eventually bring about improved economic and social conditions in the villages of Laos. To give perspective to the findings, comparative data from neighboring Thailand is presented.

The chapters discussing Laotian village life are: Geographic and ethnic setting; The natural economy; Other aspects of rural economy; Rural health problems; and Government and education.

*Bibliography:* A couple of pages listing book and article titles.

*Illustrations:* Housing, people, agriculture, dress, travel, markets, schools in Laos.

*Map:* Outline map showing provinces.

*Tables* (selected): Population. Rice yields. Livestock sacrifice. Market prices. Employment. Transportation. Health problems. Schools.

*Glossary:* Lao terms used in text.

279. LE VAN HUNG *Mrs.,* and LE VAN HUNG. Vietnamese-English Dictionary; With the International Phonetic System and More Than 30,000 Words and Idiomatic Expressions. Paris, Editions Europe-Asie, 1955. vi, 820 p.; bibliography.
PL4376.L55

*Text:* A compilation in which it is not difficult to distinguish the derivatives or compound words from the root words. Diacritical marks are used to indicate the uniform tones and the modulated tones.

*Bibliography:* Lists Vietnamese, Chinese, and English dictionaries.

280. REINHORN, MARC. Dictionnaire laotien-français. Paris, Centre Militaire d'Information et de Specialisation pour l'Outre-Mer, 1959. 5 vols.
PL4251.L3R4 1959

*Text:* Compiled by the scholar in charge of Laotian matters at the École Nationale des Langues Orientales Vivantes, the compilation is one of the most extensive ever produced. Volume one includes a summary analytical account of the grammar and other aspects of the structure of the Lao language.

281. TRAN VAN TUNG. Le Viet-Nam et sa civilisation. Paris, Éditions de la Belle Page, 1952. 117 p.
In process

*Text:* The author, Conseiller de l'Union Française and Vice Président de la Commission de l'Information, is a poet and an essayist who wrote *Rêves d'un campagnard annamite* (Paris, Mercure de France, 1940) and *L'Annam, pays du rêve et de la poésie* (Paris, J. Susse, 1945).

The nature of the study is indicated by the subjects discussed: Forces spirituelles; Littérature et poésie; L'Ame du peuple à travers ses chants; Pensées et proverbes; Trung-Troc et Trung-Nhi; Art et artisanat; Psychologie du têt; and La Pensée guide l'action.

# V

# Malaysia

(including: Singapore, Sarawak, Brunei and Sabah)

## GENERAL BACKGROUND

282. BRUNEI (STATE). Annual Report, 1960. Kuala Belait. Printed at the Brunei Press, 1962. 182 p.; illustrations, map, tables.

DS646.35.A26 1960

*Text:* General handbook providing recent data on population, labor, finance, commerce, agriculture, communications, history and government administration in this small State neighboring Sarawak and North Borneo.

*Illustrations:* Industry, handicrafts, Malay dance, and office buildings.

*Map:* Outline map of Brunei State.

*Tables* (selected): Population. Rainfall. Rubber production. Revenue. Education. Crime.

283. CHEESEMAN, HAROLD AMBROSE ROBINSON. Bibliography of Malaya; Being a Classified List of Books Wholly or Partly in English Relating to the Federation of Malaya and Singapore. London, New York, Published for the British Association of Malaya by Longmans, Green, 1959. xi, 234 p.; index.

Z3246.C5

*Text:* Provides book and article entries in these subject fields: agriculture, forestry, and horticulture; animals, archaeology, and prehistory; bibliographies and lists; biography and memoirs; education; fiction; health and medicine; history; law; linguistics; mining and geology; miscellaneous; peoples of Malaya; plants, poetry; religion, Second World War in Malaya; trade and economics; and travel.

284. CHICAGO. UNIVERSITY. Area Handbook on British Borneo. General editor: Norton S. Ginsburg. Editors: Irving Kaplan and Chester F. Roberts. Authors: Bettyann Carner, Lois Grotewold (cartographer), Zelda B. Hauser, Irving Kaplan, Chester F. Rob-

erts, C. Lester Stermer, John E. Trotter. Chicago, University of Chicago, for the Human Relations Area Files, 1955. xi, 443 p.; bibliography, maps, tables, charts, glossary. (Human Relations Area Files, Inc. Subcontractor's monograph, HRAF 14)

DS646.3.C5

*Text:* The stated purpose of this study is to provide useful information concerning North Borneo under the British, and to transmit the greatest understanding of the systems of organization and complex patterns of activities which characterize the people of Borneo. These twelve chapters analyze various segments and problems of the society: General character of the society; British Borneo, a historical outline; The resource base; Transportation in North Borneo; Demography and settlement; Communications in North Borneo; Education; Public health and welfare; Political organization; Economic organization and activities; The Chinese in British Borneo; and Indigenous Peoples of British Borneo.

*Bibliography:* Brief lists of book and article titles are given for the various chapters.

*Maps* (selected): Southeast Asia. British Borneo. Territorial expansion, Sarawak and North Borneo. Physical regions. Land utilization and natural resources. Air transportation, 1953. Land and water transportation, 1953. British Borneo, population, density. Major indigenous communities. Chinese dialect communities. Points of political control. Location of indigenous peoples.

*Tables* (selected): Major ethnic groups in British Borneo. Proposed legislature organization, Sarawak. Area and population distribution. Chief exports. Sarawak government revenue.

*Charts:* Temperature and rainfall. North Borneo government structure. North Borneo courts. The courts of Brunei. Sarawak courts.

*Glossary:* Malay words used in text.

285. GINSBURG, NORTON SYDNEY, and CHESTER F. ROBERTS, JR. Malaya; with the collaboration of Leonard Comber, Burton Stein, C. Lester Stermer and John E. Trotter. Seattle, University of Washington Press, 1958. 533 p.; bibliography, maps, tables, index. (Publications of the American Ethnological Society) DS592.G55

*Text:* Based on *Area Handbook on Malaya*, product of a research project performed in 1955 under contract to the Human Relations Area Files, by a staff of social scientists at the University of Chicago. Describes and evaluates the environmental, social, economic, and political characteristics of Malaya and Singapore. Analyzes the pluralistic character of Malayan society, composed of three major ethnic groups—Malay, Chinese, and Indian communities. Presents selected key problems facing Malaya as a whole: communications between the various communities because of the extreme linguistic heterogeneity; the political aspirations in a plural society; and the need for a balanced and accelerated economic development.

Titles of the twelve chapters are: 1. The Malayan peninsula. 2. Past and present. 3. Demographic patterns. 4. Patterns of settlements. 5. Systems of transportation and telecommunications. 6. Communication in a plural society. 7. The Malays in Malaya. 8. The Chinese in Malaya. 9. The Indians in Malaya. 10. The economic system. 11. Political organization and development. 12. A recapitulation.

*Bibliography:* Lists books and articles dealing with various aspects of Malaya.

*Maps* (selected): Political divisions. Density of population. Population change. Major cities and towns. Transportation facilities. Major ethno-linguistic groups. Chinese dialect communities. Land uses. Elections returns, 1955.

*Tables* (selected): Population. Major ethnic groups. Literacy. Newspapers. Rubber estates. Agricultural land uses. Trade, by commodity.

286. GREAT BRITAIN. COLONIAL OFFICE. State of Brunei; annual report, 1957. Kuching, Govt. Printing Office, 1958. viii, 216 p.; illustrations, map, tables, appendices. DS646.35.G7

*Text:* Divided into three parts. Part one gives a general review for the year; part two, the real core of the book, provides data on population, labor, finance, and taxation, commerce, industry, legislation, public works, communications, and other topics; and part three, outlines the geography, history and colonial administration of this small sultanate.

*Illustrations:* Brunei Town mosque under construction. Laying pipelines to marine oil well. Brunei airport. Bridge over Telambu River.

*Map:* State of Brunei, 1956.

*Tables* (selected): Statistics of migration. Revenue and expenditure. Schools and pupils.

*Appendices:* Imports, 1956 and 1957. Exports, 1956 and 1957. Glossary of vernacular terms. Rainfall. Proposed forest reserves. Statement of revenue. Crime statistics, 1957. British residents, 1907–56.

287. HUMAN RELATIONS AREA FILES. North Borneo, Brunei, Sarawak (British Borneo). New Haven, 1956. xi, 287 p.; bibliography, maps, tables, diagrams, index. (Country survey series, no. 2) DS646.3.H8

*Text:* As the second volume in the Country Survey Series of the HRAF, this volume presents an overall view of the principal aspects—historical, economic, social, and cultural—of these small countries sharing the island of Indonesia's Kalimantan.

Selected subjects treated in the 24 chapters are: history, geography, ethnic groups, languages, government, public order, communications, economy, finances, labor, agriculture, industry, trade, social conditions, education, art, and religion.

*Bibliography:* Monographs principally on social and cultural, political and economic aspects.

*Maps:* Territorial expansion, Sarawak and North Borneo. British Borneo in its regional setting. Borneo, population density. Borneo, administrative units. Borneo, population change. Location of indigenous peoples, Borneo. Major indigenous communities, Borneo. Chinese dialect communities, Borneo. Borneo, points of local control. Physical regions, Borneo. Land utilization and natural resources, Borneo. Air transportation, Borneo. Telecommunication systems, Borneo. Land and water transportation, Borneo.

*Tables* (selected): Indigenous peoples of Borneo. Census groupings. Chinese dialect groups distribution. Literacy in Borneo. Newspapers in Borneo. Revenue in Sarawak. Sarawak's distribution of labor force.

*Diagrams:* Structure of Sarawak government. Judicial structure of Borneo.

288. MALAYA (FEDERATION). Annual Report, 1956. Kuala Lumpur, Govt. Press, 1957. 495 p.; bibliography, illustrations, tables.

J618.R162

*Text:* Contents: 1. General review. 2. The people. 3. Employment, wages, and labour organisation. 4. Finance and taxation. 5. Currency and banking. 6. Trade and industry. 7. Production. 8. Social services. 9. Legislation and the legal department. 10. Justice, police, and prisons. 11. Public utilities. 12. Transport and communications. 13. Information services, broadcasting, and printing. 14. The armed forces of the Federation. 15. Cooperative development and registration of societies. 16. The campaign against the armed forces of the Malayan Communist Party.

*Bibliography:* A checklist of references including official reports and secondary sources.

*Illustrations* (selected) : Tunku Abdul Rahman Putra. Sir Donald MacGillivray. Drafting of the United Kingdom-Federation of Malaya Defense and Mutual Assistance Agreement.

*Tables* (selected) : Deal with population, immigration, revenue, taxes, banking, rubber, rice, fishing, hospitals, crime, Communist casualties.

289. MORAIS, JOHN VICTOR, ed. The Leaders of Malaya and Who's Who, 1959–60. 3rd ed. Kuala Lumpur, Printed by Khee Meng Press, [1960?]. xiv, 466 p.; illustrations, appendices. DS595.5.L4

*Text:* Contains biographical information about men and women who have served and are currently serving in Malaya. Divided into four principal parts: Rulers of the Malay States and Governors of Penang and Malacca; Who's Who in Federation Government; Who's Who in Federation and Singapore; Who's Who in North Borneo, Sarawak, and Brunei.

*Illustrations:* H. M. The Yang Di-Pertuan Agong. State Sultans. Malaya and Singapore government officials. Other persons in Malaya and Singapore.

*Appendices:* Malayan national honors. Federal and State orders and decorations. Malayan representatives abroad. Members of Senate. House of Representatives. Diplomatic corps. Political parties.

290. SARAWAK. Annual Report, 1960. Kuching, Sarawak Govt. Printing Office, 1961. 234 p.; bibliography, illustrations, maps, tables, appendices, index. DS646.36.A3

*Text:* Provides information in handbook style regarding the population, labor, finance, commerce, legislation, communications, education, health, industries, geography, and government administration of this British colony which for many years had been under the control of James Brooke and his successors.

*Bibliography:* Special studies and general books on Sarawak.

*Illustrations* (selected) : Governor of Sarawak, Sir Alexander Waddell. Long Akah airstrip in the Ulu Baram. Rice cultivation. Shell refineries. Stephen Yong, Secretary-General of Sarawak United People's Party.

291. TREGONNING, KENNETH G. North Borneo. London, H. M. Stationery Office, 1960. xiii, 272 p.; bibliography, illustrations, map, glossary, index. (The Corona library)

DS646.33.T69

*Text:* This is the initial volume in the Corona Library, a series of illustrated volumes under the sponsorship of the British Colonial Office dealing with the United Kingdom's dependent territories—the way their peoples live, and how they are governed. This series of books is designed to fill the gap between the official Blue Books on the one hand and occasional writings on the other.

This first volume of the Corona Library covers the history, industry, social life and customs, geography and general description, natural resources, education, commerce and trade, and other topics on Borneo.

*Bibliography:* A brief list of secondary references.

*Illustrations* (selected) : Site of proposed hydroelectric dam on the Padas River gorge. Chinese village at Sandakan. New Karamunting road under construction. Keningau hospital. Various racial types of Borneo. Mt. Kinabalu. Various industries.

*Maps:* North Borneo (in color), by Directorate of Overseas Surveys.

*Glossary:* Meanings of Malay words used in text.

292. U.S. NATIONAL SCIENCE FOUNDATION. Scientific Facilities and Information Services of the Federation of Malaya and State of Singapore by John O. Sutter. Honolulu, Published

for the National Science Foundation Center, by the Pacific Scientific Information, 1961. 43 p.; maps, tables, appendices, index. (Pacific scientific information, no. 2)

In process

*Text:* Presents in brief compass information about the present status of scientific research and scientific information facilities in Malaya and Singapore. Relates that the centers particularly in the fields of botanical, agricultural and medical research started by British scientists are still functioning but the personnel is gradually changing.

Four chapters provide brief discussions of general background of Malaya as to natural environment, Malayan society, and the government; science education in the Malayan school system; scientific institutions and their facilities; and science information activities as to publications and international scientific relations.

*Maps:* Political divisions of Malaya. Ethnic groups of Malaya.

*Tables* (selected): Urban population. Federation government. Organization for research and development in Malaya. Education in Malaya.

*Appendices:* Institutions of higher learning providing science teaching. Research institutes in Malaya. Research institutes in Singapore. Scientific publications of Malaya and Singapore. Scientific societies in Singapore and Malaya.

## HISTORY, POLITICS, AND GOVERNMENT

293. BAKER, MICHAEL H. North Borneo: The First Ten Years, 1946–1956. Singapore, Malaya Publishing House, 1962. xiii, 154 p.; bibliography. (Singapore studies on Borneo and Malaya, no. 1)

In process

*Text:* Originally prepared as a thesis at Stanford University following field work in a timber center in North Borneo, was issued as the first in a series of Singapore Studies on Borneo and Malaya.

Endeavors to show what has been made of the opportunity for achieving political and economic advancement when North Borneo passed from the aegis of the British North Borneo Company to the direct rule of Great Britain.

The contents is presented in these ten chapters: 1. Geography and resources. 2. The people. 3. The historical background. 4. Constitution and adminis-

trations. 5. Social services and public utilities. 6. Trade, labour and industry. 7. Agriculture. 8. Communications. 9. Postscript and prospect. 10. Conclusion.

*Bibliography:* Bibliographical footnotes and sources are distributed throughout the text.

294. CHIN, KEE ONN. Malaya Upside Down. 2nd ed. Singapore, Printed by Jitts and Co., 1946. 208 p.; tables, glossary, appendices, index.

D802.M2C5 1946

*Text:* An account of Malaya during the occupation by the Japanese, with an analysis of the way in which the Japanese authorities enslaved the population—Chinese, Malay, and Indian—and exploited the wealth of the country in the interests of Japan. Presents data regarding certain abnormal elements which appeared in the wartime economy: looting and robbery, inflation, bribery, corruption, and, gambling. Shows the ways in which Japan endeavored to Japanize the people of Malaya through the schools, Japanese language, Japanese customs, Japanese national festivals. In one chapter, the Indian National Army and Subhas Chandra Bose are discussed at length. Tells of the Japanese policy towards Malayan Communists.

*Tables:* Inflation values, 1941–45. Taxes levied, 1945. Bank deposits, 1945. Prices for everyday commodities.

*Glossary:* Brief list of common Japanese language terms used in Malaya.

*Appendices:* Notes about the anti-Japanese movement in Malaya. Imperial rescript declaring war on United States and Great Britain. Imperial rescript ordering surrender of forces.

295. COUPLAND, SIR REGINALD. Raffles of Singapore. 3d ed. London, Collins, 1946. 144 p.; bibliography, map, index.

DS646.26.R3C65 1946

*Text:* An authoritative biographical account of one of the most influential men who served in the East India Company during the 19th century. Portrays the remarkable administrative ability of this assiduous worker who served in both Penang and Java. Relates the interesting story of how Raffles founded Singapore, an act which led to the establishment of one of the finest ports in the Far East and influenced the extension of British control throughout the States of the Malay Peninsula.

The author is Professor of Colonial History at the University of Oxford.

*Bibliography:* Brings to light numerous primary sources.

*Map:* The Malay archipelago.

296. COWAN, CHARLES DONALD. Nineteenth-century Malaya; the Origins of the British Political Control. London, New York, Oxford University Press, 1961. 286 p.; bibliography, maps, tables, index.     DS596.C6

*Text:* Originally prepared as a thesis in the University of London, the purpose of this study is to present an analysis of the way in which Britain came to intervene in the political affairs of the various Malay States in the 1870's. Furthermore, it considers the causes for such intervention which in time brought about a major change in Britain's foreign policy. To list a few of these causes: increased commercial interest in the Malayan peninsula, alteration in trade patterns, the disintegration of local Malay authority, and the need of the British settlements to take steps to protect their own internal security and their new trade. Very likely the most important factor in the development of a foreward policy in Malaya was the intent to prevent any other power from gaining an opening there, even "these contentious Chinese." The closing chapter summarizes very well in brief compass the steps how intervention in Malaya came about.

*Bibliography:* Divided into four parts: manuscript sources, official papers, newspapers, and books and published papers, pertaining to Malaya.

*Maps:* 19th- century Malaya. Perak in 1870's. Selangor in 1870's. Sungai Ujong and the neighboring Malay States in 1874.

*Tables:* Trade of Straits Settlements, Singapore, Penang and Malacca, 1865–73.

297. EMERSON, RUPERT. Malaysia: A Study in Direct and Indirect Rule. New York, Macmillan, 1937. xii, 536 p.; maps, tables, index.
     DS592.E5

*Text:* A careful inquiry into the comparative measure of failure and success of the British in dealing with the destiny of the Malay people and the Dutch in dealing with the Indonesian people, not only in terms of the imperialist design of the ruling nations, but also in terms of the interests and general welfare of the peoples themselves. The author, Professor of Government at Harvard, emphasizes the fact that the problems of direct and indirect government administration are peculiarly subject to local circumstances, and a true understanding of these problems comes only by personal contact with those peoples who have become subject to a foreign power.

An examination of the history, structure, and operation of the political systems established by the British in the Malay peninsula. By way of contrast the study also describes the different colonial policies adopted by the Dutch in Indonesia. Following this searching analysis, it is stated that no imperialist government—being by definition alien—can possess an intimate association with a subject people particularly in regard to their interests and culture, and that even if the foreign power should be endowed with the most lofty attributes of altruism, it would still fall short of interpreting the will of that people for their own destiny (p. 521).

*Maps:* Malaysia, $1'' = 500$ miles. British Malaya, showing political divisions.

*Tables:* Statistical data dealing with population, principal occupations, sources of government revenue, imports, and exports.

298. The Facts About Sarawak.* London, Printed by Balding and Mansell, [1946?]. 111 p.; map, appendices.     DS646.36.F3 1946a

*Text:* A collection of documents of James Brooke, Charles Vyner Brooke, the English rajahs of Sarawak. First part gives an outline of the history of Sarawak after James Brooke became its ruler.

*Map:* Sarawak showing principal cities.

*Appendices:* Last wills and testaments of the Brooke rajahs. Constitution of Sarawak, 1941. Letters and telegrams.

299. GULLICK, J. M. Indigenous Political Systems of Western Malaya. London, University of London, Athlone Press, 1958. 151 p.; bibliography, maps, charts, appendix, index. (London School of Economics. Monographs on social anthropology, no. 17)
     JQ692.G8

*Text:* Submitted as a thesis in anthropology at the University of London and issued in the series of Monographs on Social Anthropology with the purpose "to describe and analyse the political institutions of the western Malay States (Perak, Selangor, and Negri Sembilan) as they were in the period just before com-

*[The Bombay edition (1946?) has the name Anthony Brooke written in manuscript on cover.  DS646.36.F3 1946]

ing under British control in 1874." This account of indigenous Malay political institutions viewed by an anthropologist is based on unpublished administrative records including a long series of dispatches written by Governors of the Straits Settlements to the Colonial Office: Thomas Braddell, Hugh Clifford, Hugh Low, Frank Swettenham, and others.

*Bibliography:* Draws heavily on early issues of journals pertaining to Malaya in that period.

*Maps:* Show mining areas in Perak, Selangor, and Negri Sembilan.

*Charts* (selected): Lineage in a Malay village community. Sultans of Perak.

*Appendix:* Sources used.

300. HANRAHAN, GENE Z. The Communist struggle in Malaya. With an introduction by Victor Purcell. New York, International Secretariat, Institute of Pacific Relations, 1954. 146 p.; bibliography, appendices.

DS596.H33

*Text:* The author, a specialist in the study of guerrilla warfare and writer of *Chinese Guerrilla Tactics,* brings a special knowledge and understanding of the guerrilla tactics employed by the Communists in Malaya.

This study principally deals with the strategy and tactics of the Communist revolutionary movement in Malaya. Within the time span of 1924 through 1953, the historical account traces the origins and early development of Malayan communism, Communist activity, and the Malayan People's Anti-Japanese Army, the Communist guerrilla revolt after 1948, and the revolutionary course of Malayan communism in the postwar years. Special attention is given to the revolutionary doctrines and practices of the Malayan Communist Party, with emphasis on armed insurrection, revolutionary techniques, labor activities, and guerrilla warfare tactics—all of which are employed by Communists in carrying out a militant Bolshevik revolution.

At the time when this study was published, it appeared that the situation in Malaya was at a stalement, but the balance of power within Malaya might be altered by some radical change in the situation outside Malaya.

*Bibliography:* Many of the documents and sources used in this work are primary in nature. They include Japanese occupation records, Malayan Communist Party directives and histories, and guerrilla texts. These are among the monograph and periodical arti-

cle titles on communism in general and Malayan communism in particular which are listed.

*Appendices:* Six important Malayan Communist Party translated documents with explanatory notes include: Thesis of the Sixth World Congress of the Communist International on the revolutionary movement in the colonies. Constitution of the Malayan Communist Party. Iron discipline of the Party. Strategic problems of the Malayan revolutionary war. Supplementary views of the Central Political Bureau on strategic problems of the Malayan revolutionary war. Party directive of October 1, 1951. Biographical sketches of nearly 40 Malayan Communists.

301. HICKLING, HUGH. Sarawak and Its Government: A First Book in Civics. Kuchiang, Govt. Printing Office, 1954. xiii, 179 p.; illustrations, map, charts, appendices, index.

JQ642.A345

*Text:* Discusses the Council Negri—the lawmaking body of Sarawak, the written and unwritten laws of Sarawak, central and local governments, law and order, money in Sarawak, government departments, Chinese affairs, education, and foreign relations.

*Illustrations:* Opening of the Council Negri. Meeting of the Supreme Council. Sarawak Museum. Sarawak coat of arms.

*Map:* Sarawak, showing administrative divisions and principal towns.

*Charts:* 1954 proposals for a new Supreme Council and Council Negri. Certificate of birth.

302. JONES, STANLEY WILSON. Public Administration in Malaya. London, New York, Royal Institute of International Affairs, 1953. viii, 229 p.; index. (Published in cooperation with the International Secretariat, Institute of Pacific Relations) JQ715.J6

*Text:* This account of the administrative system in the territories of Malaya is divided into these 11 chapters: 1. The East India Company and the transfer to the colonial office. 2. Entry into the Malay States. 3. Federation of the Malay States. 4. Administrative development. 5. Constitutional history. 6. The administration of the law. 7. Emergence of political problems. 8. Conquest and reconquest of Malaya. 9. Rehabilitation. 10. Constitutional and political development. 11. The planning of economic and social development.

303. KENNEDY, JOSEPH. A History of Malaya, A.D. 1400–1959. London, Macmillan; New York, St. Martin's Press, 1962. viii, 311 p.; bibliography, illustrations, maps, tables, charts, index. DS596.K4 1962

*Text:* Serving as a supplement to *A History of Malaya and Her Neighbors* by Francis Moorhead, this work begins with the rise of the port-kingdom of Malacca in the early 15th century and gives a concise account of the principal events and main trends of Malayan history for the past five and a half centuries. Attention is given to the traditional patterns of life in the Malaya States and to their internal development as well as the varying influences exerted upon Malaya by various Western colonial powers.

The author, a teacher at the Malayan Teachers' Training College in Liverpool, gives a scholarly treatment of the historical data dealing with the Portuguese and the Dutch in the Malacca Straits, the English East India Company's settlement at Penang, the growth of Singapore economically and politically, the British intervention in the Malay States, the political and constitutional changes in the 20th century, the impact of Japan during World War II, and the achievement of nationhood in the postwar years.

*Bibliography:* Basic references, books, and official reports are arranged in chapter groupings.

*Illustrations* (selected): Early scenes of harbors at Penang, Malacca, and Singapore. Rubber plantation in Malaya.

*Maps* (selected): Sea routes to Malacca in 15th century. Malacca Empire in 1500. Penang, 1786. Singapore and adjacent islands. Siam and Malay States in 19th century. Malay States, 1909–41.

*Tables:* Time chart, 1512–1800. Population, Singapore and Malaya. Dates of events, Malaya and Singapore.

*Chart:* Family of Sultan Mohamed of Selangor.

304. KING, FRANK H. H. The New Malayan Nation: A Study of Communalism and Nationalism. With a foreword by Rupert Emerson. New York, Institute of Pacific Relations, 1957. xii, 89 p.; bibliography, map, appendices. JQ713.1957.K5

*Text:* A discussion of the knotty political problem of creating a strong, political organization or state out of a pluralistic society. Faces the issue as to whether the three principal communities—the Chinese, the Indians, and the Malays—will pull together to form a unified state or consider each other as adversaries struggling for communal victories.

Four chapters comprise the study: 1. The path to freedom. 2. The Constitution—framework of partnership. 3. The making of the Malayan nation. 4. The prospects for the Malayan nation.

*Bibliography:* Lists well-known sources, chapter by chapter.

*Map:* Federation of Malaya, showing tin, rubber, and rice areas.

*Appendices:* Citizenship charts. Excerpt from draft constitution about distribution of legislative powers.

305. MALAYA (FEDERATION). Draft Development Plan of the Federation of Malaya. Kuala Lumpur, Govt. Press, 1950. ii, 174 p.; illustrations, map, tables, appendices. HC497.M3A52

*Text:* Defines the objectives of social and economic policy for the period 1950–55 as presented to the Legislative Council of Malaya in July 1950. An underlying feature of the plan lies in the emphasis on rural development. Specific features are in these four chapters: 1. The development of social services. 2. The development of national resources and utilities. 3. The development of trade and industry. 4. Summary.

*Map:* Malay peninsula, showing states of Malaya.

*Tables:* Statistical tables on education, health, labor, agriculture, forestry, public works, and land settlement.

*Appendices:* Statistical tables.

306. MALAYA (FEDERATION). Malayan Constitutional Documents. Kuala Lumpur, Govt. Printer, 1959. xii, 311 p.; index. Law Gt. Brit. Malaya 1

*Text:* This collection of documents provides the principal constitutional instruments which in some way or other affect the Federal Constitution. The preface by R. H. Hickling gives a summary account of the modern constitutional government in Malaya from the Law of the Constitution granted in 1895 by the Sultan of Johore down to the present day.

Among the documents in this convenient one volume are: Federation of Malaya Independence Act, 1957. Federation of Malaya Agreement, 1957. Federation Constitution Ordinance, 1957. Proclamation of independence. Federal Constitution. Constitution of Penang. Constitution of Malacca.

307. MALAYA (FEDERATION). CONSTITUTION. The Federation of Malaya Constitution: Text, Annotations and Commentary, by L. A. Sheridan. Singapore, University of Malaya Law Review, 1961. 180 p.; index.    Law

*Text:* Analyzes the provisions in the Malayan Constitution pertaining to these selected subjects: religion, citizenship, the rulers' sovereignty, finance, elections, public services and subversion and emergency powers.

The work appeared earlier by installments in the University of Malaya Law Review in 1959 and 1960.

308. MALAYA (FEDERATION). DEPARTMENT OF PUBLIC RELATIONS. Anatomy of Communist Propaganda. Kuala Lumpur, Goverment Press, [1950]. vii, 60 p.    Orientalia

*Text:* An analysis of propaganda originating from Communist sources during the Emergency in Malaya, based upon recovered documents made available through the Police Department. Extracts from miscellaneous Communist propaganda are included to illustrate the typical kind of material employed.

The study is divided into three parts: I. A brief general survey of the Malayan Communist Party propaganda and method. II. The basic objectives. III. Propaganda lines in support of the basic objectives. This last part includes thirteen sections some of which are: Ideological appeals; Anti-British themes; Special propaganda lines to labor; Propaganda in support of bandit action; Appeals to security forces; Propaganda in opposition to the Malayan Chinese Association; Propaganda in support of a boycott of the press; Propaganda to students; and Special propaganda lines to Malays and Indians.

309. MALAYS (FEDERATION). DEPARTMENT OF PUBLIC RELATIONS. Communist Banditry in Malaya. Kuala Lumpur, Government Press, [1950]. 11 p.    Orientalia

*Text:* Contains extracts from the speeches by the High Commissioner, Sir Henry Gurney, delivered during the period of the Emergency. A good number of the statements are those made in the Legislative Council.

310. MALAYA (FEDERATION). DEPARTMENT OF PUBLIC RELATIONS. Communist Banditry in Malaya, the Emergency June 1948–December 1949. Kuala Lumpur, Printed at Economy Printers [1950]. 60 p.; illustrations, chart.    Orientalia

*Text:* Following a brief introduction regarding the pattern of the Communists' strategy in Malaya, two detailed chronologies of important daily events for the periods of June 1948 to December 1948 and January 1949 to December 1949 provide information about the violence which was agitated by the Communist-controlled Pan-Malayan Federation of Trade Unions.

*Illustrations:* Malayan and British troops used during the Emergency.

*Chart:* Increase in crime due to the Emergency.

311. MARKS, HARRY JULIAN. The First Contest for Singapore, 1819–1824. 's-Gravenhage, Nijhoff, 1959. 262 p.; bibliography, appendix. (Verhandelingen van het koninklijk Instituut voor Taal-, Land-en Volkenkunde, deel 27)    DS598.S7M34

*Text:* Gives the historical events of the British acquisition of Singapore, dating from the time when Sir Stamford Raffles signed an agreement with a Malay chief to establish a commercial trading center in Singapore, thus opening a five-year controversy with the Dutch over the trade of the region, until the Dutch-British treaty of 1824 whereby the British withdrew from Sumatra and the Dutch from India, Malacca, and Singapore.

*Bibliography:* Bibliographical footnotes which include articles and documents about the early years of Singapore.

*Appendix:* Treaty of 17 March 1824, and the Dutch and British treaty notes.

312. MILLER, HARRY. The Communist Menace in Malaya.* New York, Praeger, 1954. 148 p.; illustrations, map, glossary, index. (Books that matter)    DS596.M5 1954a

*Text:* A journalist's account and interpretation of the conflict with communism in Malaya beginning in 1948 and extending for the six year Emergency regime. Chapter one relates the birth of the Communist party in Malaya, and the succeeding chapters describe the jungle war, the uprooting of thousands of families, an account of the Communist leader Chen Ping, the "Briggs Plan" which led to the resettlement villages, the murder of Sir Henry Gurney—the High Commissioner, the defeat of the Communists, and the problems which emerged from the Communist conflict.

*Illustrations* (selected): General Sir Gerald Templer. Chen Ping, General of the Malayan Communist Party. Sir Henry Gurney. Sir Donald Charles Mac Gillivary.

---

*[Published in London by Harrap in 1954 under the title *Menace in Malaya*.]

*Map:* A sketch map of Malaya railroads and principal cities.

*Glossary:* Common Malay words used in the text.

313. MILLER, HARRY. Prince and Premier, a Biography of Tunka Abdul Rahman Putra Al-Haj, First Prime Minister of the Federation of Malaya. With a foreword by Tunku Abdul Rahman. London, Geo. Harrap, 1959. 242 p.; illustration, index.    DS595.6.A2M5

*Text:* This account gives a biographical sketch of Malaya's first Prime Minister. It was this man who brought about reform in the United Malays National Organization, thus making it a powerful political force in the newly independent country.

The account presents a person who is tolerant, friendly, and persuasive. By these qualities he was able to have the Chinese and Malays, the two dominant races in Malaya, to attempt to live together in political harmony; to persuade the nine Malay Sultans that independence was inevitable and that they would not lose their sovereign rights and privileges; and as the leader of the UMNO, persuaded the British Government to yield independence to Malaya without having to yield to violence.

This biographical account also tells about his early life as the son of a former Kedah Sultan, his educational training in England and relates his increase in political stature after being catapulted into Malayan politics thus bringing stability and confidence in the Malayan Government.

*Illustrations:* Tunku Abdul Rahman Putra Al-Haj.

314. MILLS, LENNOX ALGERNON. Malaya; A Political And Economic Appraisal. Minneapolis, University of Minnesota Press, 1958. 234 p.; bibliography, tables, index.    DS596.M53

*Text:* Emphasizes the significant, underlying fact that communal antagonism in Malaya was aggravated by the appearance of three nationalisms: Malay, Chinese, and Indian, and only by a shrewd alliance were they able to combat successfully the Communist imperialism. Shows on the economic side that Malaya demanded a higher standard of living but that only with Western aid, such as the Colombo Plan and investments of overseas capital, could the economic design in Malaya be realized.

Selected chapters are: 3. The Communist rebellion. 4. Communalism and self-government. 7. Malaya and

Commonwealth defense. 8. Natural and synthetic rubber.

*Bibliography:* Located in notes, chapter by chapter.

*Tables:* Acreage of rubber estates.

315. MOOREHEAD, FRANCIS JOSEPH. A History of Malaya And Her Neighbors. Volume one. London, New York, Longmans, Green, 1957. x, 245 p.; bibliography, illustrations, maps, charts, index.    DS596.M6

*Text:* Designed primarily as an introductory account of the early history of Malaya, the work is divided into two distinct parts: First, the events in the neighboring countries to Malaya, particularly Java and Sumatra, as they were related to the historical and political development of Malaya. Hence, one becomes aware of four dominating factors: the cultural influence of India which brought about the emergence of the Indianized states; the endeavor of these states to achieve political supremacy over each other; the political and economic influence of China; and the rise of Islam and its eventual dominance of the region—both Malaya and the Indian archipelago (Indonesia).

The second part deals with Malacca, the Sultanate which achieved a limited success by uniting a part of Malaya for the first time in its history, into a single state. Tells about how Malacca was a part of the Portuguese Empire in the Far East until the attacks by the Achinese from Sumatra and certain Sultans of the Malayan peninsula in the 16th century, and the fall of the colony into Dutch hands in 1641.

*Bibliography:* Arranged into two parts—to 1511, and 1511 to 1641.

*Illustrations* (selected): Portuguese ships of the 16th century. Afonso d'Albuquerque.

*Maps:* Early land and river routes across Malaya. Funanese Empire under Fan Cheman. Empire of Sri Vijaya and Javanese Kingdoms. Malacca and suburbs. The Moluccas in the 16th-century.

316. ONRAET, RENÈ HENRY DE SOLMINIHAS. Singapore—A Police Background. London, Dorothy Crisp and Co., 1947. 152 p.
                                         DS598.S7O5

*Text:* The author, a former Inspector-General of Police in the Straits Settlements, presents the problems involved in keeping law and order in Malaya during the first half of the 20th century. Against a background of the author's personal experiences and his observations of the political and social changes in

Malaya, he provides an anecdotal history of the development of the official police force in Singapore and Malaya and shows its importance when the commercial growth of Singapore was so rapid during the time of the immigration of thousands of Chinese from South China. Relates vividly some of the local conditions of crime, the difficulties of criminal investigation, and some of the requirements needed to established law and order and internal security.

Indicates in the chapter, Chinese secret societies in Singapore, that gang robbery, and subversive organizations to a very great extent depended on immigration from China and derived strength from Chinese societies. Chapter 8, A sketch of past subversive activities, tells how communism came to Malaya by the Chinese Communists with the main objective to create local Communist groups in Singapore and Malaya.

317. PARKINSON, CYRIL NORTHCOTE. British Intervention in Malaya, 1867–1877. Singapore, University of Malaya Press, 1960. xx, 384 p.; maps, appendices, index. DS596.P29

*Text:* This is the first volume in a series of about twelve historical monographs dealing with Malaya from the earliest times to the current era published in the Malayan Historical Studies. The focus of this study is on the Malay states of Perak, Selangor, and parts of Negri Sembilan, which came into the British Empire on the flood tide of British expansion. An introductory chapter debates the point whether the British were compelled to intervene in Malaya after a reasonable period of refusing an act of intervention, or whether it was part of the whole question of where British commercial interests lay.

The account is one which tells how the officers in the Straits Settlements were resolved to establish British influence over the Malay States, eventually to create a Malaya, thus opening for themselves and others in England a new field of investment and trade. Two interlocking elements which brought about the fulfillment of this colonial acquisition were the lack of any substantial Malay resistance and the Royal navy's implementation of naval blockades which were immediate and decisive.

*Maps:* Malay peninsula. Perak and Selangor. Negri Sembilan. The Perak River.

*Appendices:* Engagement entered into by the Chiefs of Perak at Pulo Pangkor, 20 January 1874. Agreements entered into by certain Chiefs of the Nine States on 23 November 1876. Despatches between Governor Jervois and Downing Street. Chinese secret societies.

318. PAYNE, PIERRE STEPHEN ROBERT. The White Rajahs of Sarawak. New York, Funk and Wagnalls, 1960. 274 p.; bibliography, illustrations, map, index. DS646.36.P3

*Text:* Based in part on the private letters of Sir Charles Brooke, Anthony Brooke, and Ranee Margaret Brooke, the account tells how James Brooke conquered Sarawak in the 19th century and with his descendants ruled the Dyaks and Malays as rajahs for over 100 years.

*Bibliography:* Brief list of references about the Brooke family and Sarawak.

*Illustrations* (selected) : Sir James Brooke, Sir Charles Brooke, Sir Vyner Brooke. The Ranee Margaret. Kuching, 1890.

*Map:* Sarawak, showing stages of its conquest.

319. PURCELL, VICTOR WILLIAM. Malaya, Communist or Free? Stanford, Stanford University Press, 1954. 288 p.; tables, index. (Published under the auspices of the Institute of Pacific Relations) DS596.P79 1954a

*Text:* An account of the political, economic, and social developments in postwar Malaya as observed by one who spent a quarter of a century as a member of the Malayan Civil Service and who is well known for the authoritative works: *The Chinese in Southeast Asia* and *Malaya: Outline of a Colony.*

Following four introductory chapters which provide historical background and which place Malaya in an international setting, the events of the Communist aggression in Malaya are carefully analyzed. The "reforms" of General Templer, the High Commissioner of Malaya, are also subjected to critical examination, with frequent quotations from various speeches of the High Commissioner.

Emphasis is given to the fact that it has been the British intention to help Malaya towards nationhood and self-government. With the advent of the emergency, however, it was decided that Malaya was looked upon primarily as a military problem and the clearing of the country of the terrorists took precedence over all political questions. As a result, there took place a complete departure from a century and a half tradition of colonial history in which the British possession of Malaya had been administered as a civilian trust and now was a strategic outpost in the "cold war."

*Tables:* Assessed incomes, Malaya and Singapore.

320. PURCELL, VICTOR WILLIAM. Malaya; Outline of a Colony. London, Nelson and Sons, 1946. vii, 151 p.; illustrations, maps, chart, index.    DS596.P8

*Text:* Outlines the early history of Malaya during the time of the Portuguese and the Dutch in Malaya followed by the establishment of British rule in Malaya. The achievement of Trusteeship is a chapter describing benefits which the British have given Malaya. Other chapters deal with tin, rubber, trade, agriculture, and finance.

*Chart:* Comparative populations in the diverse Malayan community.

*Illustrations:* Tin mines. Penang. Scenes of the country.

*Maps:* Chief products of Malaya. Sketch map of the Malay Archipelago.

321. PYE, LUCIAN W. Guerrilla Communism in Malaya; Its Social and Political Meaning. Princeton, Princeton University Press, 1956. xvi, 369 p.; chart, index.    DS596.P9

*Text:* As a case study of the Malayan Communist Party, significant insights are provided about the relationships of communism and Chinese culture, the political behaviour in economically underdeveloped societies, and the basic problems which must be overcome if the newly independent countries of Southeast Asia are to remain independent and not become Communist dominated or oriented.

With the view of understanding communism in Malaya, especially the Malayan Chinese who have joined the Malayan Communist Party, these topics are discussed in these chapters: 1. Communist doctrine and people's liberation parties. 2. From conspiracy to terrorism. 3. The Emergency. 4. Surrendered enemy personnel: a note on the sample. 5. Potential Communists. 6. The experiences of youth. 7. Understanding politics. 8. Perceiving the social environment. 9. Joining the Communist Party. 10. Adjusting to life in the Party. 11. Understanding the Communist movement. 12. Learning Communist theory. 13. Personal relations and promotions. 14. The process of disaffection. 15. The problem of political development.

*Chart:* Malayan Communist Party organization during the emergency.

322. RUNCIMAN, STEVEN. The White Rajahs: A History of Sarawak From 1841 to 1946. Cambridge, Cambridge University Press, 1960. xii, 320 p.; bibliography, illustrations, maps, glossary, index.    DS646.36.R9

*Text:* Written at the request of the Government of Sarawak and based on official papers and documents of the government archives, provides the history of Sarawak during the three regimes of James Brooke, Charles Brooke, and Vyner Brooke. Shows how a few Europeans were able, in time, to bring peace and contentment to a jungle country by means of interest in and sympathy for the people. Relates the historical events which brought about the order of the Privy Council in London to annex Sarawak, thus bringing to a close the rule of the British rajahs.

*Bibliography:* Official sources and other printed sources valuable for the study of Sarawak.

*Illustrations* (selected) : 1. Sir James Brooke. 6. Sir Charles Anthony Brooke.

*Maps:* 1. Far East in the 19th century. 2. Borneo in mid-nineteenth century. 3. Sarawak and Brunei, successive frontiers.

*Glossary:* Definitions on Malay names and titles.

323. SILCOCK, THOMAS H., and UNGKU ABDUL AZIZ. Nationalism in Malaya. New York, Internation Secretariat, Institute of Pacific Relations, 1950. 48 p. (Secretariat Paper no. 8, 11th Conference, Institute of Pacific Relations, Lucknow)    DS596.S54

*Text:* Following an introductory account of the population in Malaya with particular reference to the Chinese and Indian immigrants, there are chapters dealing with: the Chinese, Indian, and Malay nationalist movements; the impact of the Japanese occupation; the immediate postwar developments, with discussions of the United Malays' National Organization and the Communist Malayan Democratic Union; the political developments since early 1946; and, the Communist links with political groups and associations.

A study prepared by the Head of the Department of Economics of the University of Malaya.

324. SWETTENHAM, SIR FRANK ATHELSTANE. British Malaya; an Account of the Origin and Progress of British Influence in Malaya. London, Allen and Unwin, 1948. xxi, 380 p.; illustrations, map, appendices, index.

DS592.S9 1948

*Text:* Describes the circumstances under which the British assumed the administration of Malaya; the conditions which prevailed in the early days in Singapore, Malacca, Penang, and the different Malay States; and the gradual evolution of the system of administration in Malay, with some observations on the effect it has had on the neighboring British possessions. Besides the chapters which give an account of the early history of the Malays—those who were under British administration and those who were in other States of the peninsula—a most informative chapter on the customs, prejudices, arts, language, and literature of the Malay people is included.

First published in 1906, this revised edition concludes with the chapter twenty-five years after, telling about the ever-increasing industrial prosperity in Malaya with particular reference to exports and tin and rubber production.

The author was a Governor of the Straits Colony and a High Commissioner for the Federated States.

*Illustrations:* Sir Thomas Raffles. Government buildings in Singapore and Malaya. River and landscape views.

*Map:* Map of Malaya, showing political divisions, railroads.

*Appendices:* Extracts from an address delivered at the Annual Meeting of the Rubber Growers' Association, 1946.

325. TRAVERS, THOMAS OTHO. The Journal of Thomas Otho Travers, 1813–1820. Edited by John Bastin. Singapore, Govt. Printing Office, 1960. 226 p.; illustrations, maps, appendices. (Memoirs of the Raffles Museum, no. 4) DS643.T7

*Text:* Consists of lengthy passages from the Travers' journal, 1813–16 and 1818–20, the period when the Irish Captain Travers served with Sir Stamford Raffles in Java and western Sumatra, and in Singapore. The material presented here is drawn from a typescript copy of the journal prepared for use when the late C. E. Wurtzburg wrote his biography *Raffles of the Eastern Isles* (London, 1954).

The journal is divided into two parts: 1. Java, 1813–16. 2. West Sumatra and Singapore, 1818–20. It is an invaluable historical source for the historian concerned with the period when the British were in present-day Indonesia just prior to the British procurement and development of Singapore. Besides showing the characteristics of Capt. Travers, one also gathers interesting items worthy of note about Raffles, Fraser, Elliott, Farquhar, Flint, and others who played a part in the extension of British holdings in Southeast Asia.

*Illustrations:* Views of Buitenzorg, Fort Marlborough, Singapore, and Padang. William Farquhar. William Lawrence Flint. Thomas Otho Travers.

*Maps:* Map of 1801 showing Java, Sumatra, and Singapore, 1837 map of Singapore.

*Appendices* (selected): 1. Capt. Salmond's journey across Sumatra (1818). 2. Report on population of Marlborough (1821). 4. Bencoolen in 1823. 6. Singapore in 1823–24.

326. TREGONNING, K. G. Under Chartered Company Rule: North Borneo, 1881–1946. Singapore, University of Malaya Press, 1958. v, 250 p.; bibliography, illustrations, maps, index. DS646.33.T7

*Text:* The author, Head of the History Department at the University of Malaya in Singapore, presents a study which opens with a historical account of how Borneo was once an American colony prior to the emergence of the British North Borneo Company in the 19th century. The history of this Chartered Company is told here in full for the first time. Provides summary accounts of the government administration, economic development, labor, health, education, and the question of slavery which fluorished in the 19th century in Borneo.

*Bibliography:* Includes a long list of primary sources and a number of secondary articles and books on both the British North Borneo Company and the country of Borneo.

*Illustrations:* Sir Alfred Dent, founder of the Chartered Company. Views of port Sandakan. W. C. Cowie, Manager of Labuan Trading Company.

*Maps:* Borneo, 1878, North Borneo, 1941.

327. TSUJI, MASANOBU. Singapore; the Japanese Version. Translated by Margaret E. Lake. Edited by H. V. Howe. Introduction by H. Gordon Bennett. Sydney, Ure Smith, 1960. xxv, 358 p.; illustrations, maps, appendices, index. D767.5.T753 1960

*Text:* Col. Tsuji, the author, was the Japanese military commander of the group of officers who formulated the plans and tactics for the swift seventy-day campaign to take Singapore in the early part of World War II. It is recognized by the trained military technician that the remarkable conquest of Singapore by the Japanese was primarily due to the author's extraordinarily thorough and original planning, together with the research into the techniques of tropical warfare.

This account of the Malayan campaign from the Japanese standpoint is divided into seven parts which comprise 58 subsections describing the military campaign under these topics: whirlwind to the south; Army Commander Yamashita; a thrust through the jungle; the bicyclists; command of the skies; the blue signal flares; welcoming the Kigan festival.

*Illustrations* (selected) : General Yamashita. General Nishimura. Japanese use of bicycles. Surrender negotiations.

*Maps* (selected) : Japanese estimate of British dispositions in Malaya, 1941. Route of the invasion convoy. The Malayan campaign of the Japanese 25th Army. The capture of Singapore.

*Appendices:* 1. A pamphlet, *Read this alone—and the war can be won,* which was not included in the original Japanese version of this book. 2. East Asia Federation. 3. British garrison in Malaya.

328. WHEATLEY, PAUL. The Golden Khersonese: Studies in the Historical Geography of the Malay Peninsula Before A.D. 1500. Kuala Lumpar, University of Malaya Press, 1961. xxxiii, 388 p.; bibliography, maps, tables, diagrams, appendices, index. DS596.W45

*Text:* This historical geography of early Malaya, submitted originally as a thesis at the University of London, is one which is reconstructed from gleanings taken from foreign literature, principally early Chinese histories, encyclopedias, travel accounts and topographical studies; and Arabic and Persian records from the 9th century onwards. Supplementing these two principal sources, are scattered references in Indic writings and information revealed in Siamese and Javanese records.

The presentation falls into seven parts: Part one, China and the Malay peninsula; Part two, the Malay peninsula as known to the West; Part three, The Indians in Malaya; Part four, The Arabs in Malaya; Part five, Three forgotten kingdoms; Part six, The Isthmian age; and Part seven, A city that was made for merchandise: the geography of Malacca during the 15th century.

*Bibliography:* A long list of 40 pages which provide titles of many periodical articles pertaining to the history of Malaya.

*Maps* (selected) : Gold and tin deposits of the Malay peninsula. The rivers of the Malay peninsula. Voyage of the Sui envoys, A.D. 607–10. The Malay peninsula as known to Chinese mariners of the early 15th century. The Malay peninsula as known to Arab

pilots of the 15th century. The Sri Vijayan thalassocracy, A.D. 1150.

*Tables:* 13th-century trade between China and the Malay peninsula.

*Diagrams:* 15th-century Chinese compass card.

*Appendices* (selected) : Notes of Chinese texts. Tribute missions from the Malay peninsula to the Chinese court. Crawfurd's description of the ruins of ancient Singapore. Early Ptolemaic interpretations. Two 15th-century descriptions of Malacca.

329. WINSTEDT, SIR RICHARD OLAF. Malaya and Its History. London, Hutchinson's University Library, 1948. 158 p.; bibliography, index. DS596.W515

*Text:* The author, formerly of the Malayan Civil Service, and Reader in Malay at the University of London, presents in brief compass a reliable historical account of the events which occurred during the early days of Indian, Portuguese, and Dutch exploits in Malaya prior to the British occupation. Other chapters treat: the founding and development of Singapore; British administration in the Malay States and the relations of the Sultans to the State Councils; trade; industries; labor; education; public health; and events during and following the Japanese occupation of Malaya.

*Bibliography:* A briefly annotated list of titles to books and articles.

## ECONOMICS
(including: Agriculture, Commerce, Industry, and Labor)

330. AWBERY, S. S., and F. W. DALLEY. Labour and Trade Union Organization in the Federation of Malaya and Singapore. London, H. M. Stationery Office. Printed in Kuala Lumpur, Government Press, 1948. vi, 70 p.; tables, appendices. (Colonial no. 234) HD8689.M33A92

*Text:* A report on the labor and trade-union situation in Malaya, written by two experts in industrial relations who were sent to Malaya by the Secretary of State for the Colonies at the request of the Governments of the Colony of Singapore and the Malayan Union. Provides substantial information regarding wages and conditions of employment, housing, and costs of living, development of trade unions, labor legislation, and the Malayan Communist Party's relation to labor.

*Tables:* Labor distribution by races in Singapore and the Federation. Statistics of wages and hours of work, Malaya. Singapore prices, 1948.

*Appendices:* Press and broadcast statements by the authors. History of the harbor-board workers. Directive to the Trade Union Advisor.

331. BENHAM, FREDERIC CHARLES. The National Income of Malaya, 1947–1949 (With a Note on 1950). Singapore, Govt. Printing Office, 1951. 272 p.; tables, appendices.
HC497.M3B4

*Text:* A study, by the Economic Adviser to the Commissioner–General for the United Kingdom in Southeast Asia, which provides a large body of statistical data pertaining to: agricultural, forest, and mineral products; manufactured products; imports and exports; and government services. Endeavors to measure the national income of Malaya by output, by incomes received, and by the amount of consumption and investment.

Shows that approximately one-half of the net national product of Malaya—*i.e.,* the net value of the goods and services produced in Malaya—came from agricultural, forest, and mineral products. Of these, rubber is the most important and is reported to occupy seventy percent of the cultivated area in Malaya and provides employment for one quarter of the working population. The net national product for the years 1947, 1948, and 1949 is discussed in separate chapters, with attention given to natural and manufactured products, rehabilitation, distribution of retained imports, income from entrepôt trade, house rents, and taxes on output.

*Tables:* Statistical data about: agricultural, forest, and mineral products; manufactured products; the distribution of retained imports; free government services; and, imports and exports for 1947, 1948, and 1949.

*Appendices:* Appendix dealing with external trade and balance of payments provides considerable information on entrepôt trade—the re-export of imported goods.

332. FIRTH, RAYMOND WILLIAM. Malay Fishermen: Their Peasant Economy. London, Kegan Paul, Trench, Trubner, 1946. xii, 354 p.; bibliography, illustrations, maps, tables, charts, glossary, appendices, index. (Issued in cooperation with the Royal Institute of International Affairs and the Institute of Pacific Relations) HD9466.M32F5

*Text:* Presents a mass of basic information, systematically collected and correlated, regarding the way in which a Malay fishing economy ordinarily functions. It is the stated purpose of the author to "give some idea of the adaptative nature of these peasant economic systems, of the value of their traditional forms of cooperation, and of the claims of such types of society to survival in the face of pressure from forces which threaten to disrupt them while offering them no alternative forms of communal existence."

The eleven chapters carry the following headings: The fishing industry in Malaya and Indonesia; Economics of the industry in two Malay States (Kelantan and Trengganu); Structure of a sample fishing community; Planning and organization of fishing activities; Ownership of equipment and management of capital; The credit system in financing production; Marketing organization; The system of distributing earnings; Output and levels of income; Fishermen in the general peasant economy; and, Fisheries development and the Malay peasant.

*Bibliography:* List of references on sea fishing and allied occupations in Malaya.

*Illustrations:* Numerous views of different fishing methods employed by tropical fishermen. Types of fishing vessels. Peasant dwellings.

*Maps:* Communications and principal settlements in Kelantan and Trengganu. Land utilization and fishing in Kelantan and Trengganu. Approximate density of population in Kelantan and Trengganu.

*Tables:* Primary and secondary occupations. Summary of boats and fishing equipment.

*Charts:* Quantities and value of fish annually exported. Fishing output in Kelantan. Cycles of production in agriculture and fishing.

*Glossary:* Brief list of fishing terms in the Kelantan dialect of the Malay language.

*Appendices:* Note on problems and technique in a field study of a peasant economy. Variations in the scheme distribution in the major forms of fishing. Commoner kinds of fish taken in east-coast Malayan waters.

333. INTERNATIONAL BANK FOR RECONSTRUCTION AND DEVELOPMENT. The Economic Development of Malaya: Report of a Mission Organized by the International Bank for Reconstruction and Development at the Request of the Governments of the Federation of Malaya, the Crown Colony of Singapore, and the United Kingdom. Baltimore, Johns Hopkins Press, 1955. xix, 707 p.; maps, tables, appendix, index.　　　HC442.I5

*Text:* A general survey which assesses the natural resources in Malaya available for future development, considers just how these resources might best contribute to the social and economic development of Malaya and Singapore, and makes recommendations for practical measures to further this development. Addresses itself principally to broad issues of development and investment policies, and is not too concerned with the particular details of the issues and projects.

Divided into five precise parts. Part one, General contains an introduction to the physical, social and economic aspects of Malaya and the problems and prospects of a development plan. Part two, Productive sectors, deals with Malayan agriculture, mining, power, transport, communications, and industry. Part three, Social sectors, is devoted to social services, including education. Part four, Financing and organization of development, presents the financial resources available and proposals for organization and institutional needs. Part five, Technical reports, consists of twelve reports on agriculture and forestry, irrigation and drainage and river conservancy, land tenure, fisheries, mining, power, transport and communications, industrial development, education, public health, social welfare, and currency and banking.

*Maps:* Distribution of population, 1947. Transport. Geology. Land utilization. Malay reservations. Minerals.

*Tables:* Numerous statistical tables pertaining to the various subjects referred to above.

*Appendix:* Consolidated accounts of public authorities.

334. MALAYA (FEDERATION). RICE COMMITTEE. Final Report of the Rice Committee. Kuala Lumpur, Govt. Press, 1956. ix, 139 p.; tables, appendices.　　　HD9066.M3A5

*Text:* The report of a Committee appointed by the High Commissioner of Malaya to enquire into various matters relating to the economic status of padi culti-

vators in Malaya, and to make recommendations for measures calculated to assure an economic return to these cultivators.

Contents consist of these five chapters: 1. Review of available material. 2. Measures necessary to assure an economic return to the padi cultivators. 3. Methods to assure a remunerative price to padi cultivators. 4. Summary of findings and conclusions. 5. Summary of recommendations and minority reports.

*Tables:* Items of expenditures for padi cultivators in Kedah. Average yield of wet padi. Net cash returns for padi cultivators in Kedah.

*Appendices* (selected): State settlement schemes. Cost of production for padi planters. Estimates of total yield and cost of production for padi cultivators. Conclusions and recommendations of Thomson report on the marketing of rice in Malaya. Summary of irrigation schemes.

335. PUTHUCHEARY, JAMES J. Ownership and Control in the Malayan Economy: A Study of the Structure of Ownership and Control and its Effects on the Development of Secondary Industries and Economic Growth in Malaya and Singapore. Singapore. Published by Donald Moore for Eastern Universities Press, 1960. xxii, 187 p.; tables, charts, index.

　　　HC497.M3P8

*Text:* When considering the ownership and control of wealth in Malaya, this study contrasts the role of the small and medium-size producers with that of the large-scale capitalist in the fields of agriculture, rubber industry, import trade, and certain types of manufacturing. The important part which the agency houses or large firms have in connection with rubber plantations, export trade, and tin mining is emphasized. Notes distribution of resources and control among the various communities, and shows how Chinese capital is extremely important as a subsidiary to European capital.

Whereas part one deals with ownership and control, part two examines particularly the problems of capital supply for development of the Malayan economy.

*Tables* (selected): Earnings of padi planters. Size of farms and earnings of rice cultivators. Distribution of management estates. Agencies in the rubber industry. Import agencies.

*Charts* (selected): Interlocking directorships and agency houses.

336. SILCOCK, THOMAS H. The Economy of Malaya: An Essay in Colonial Economy. Singapore, Donald Moore, 1956. 55 p.; bibliography. (A background to Malaya book, no. 2)　　　HC497.M355 1956

*Text:* One of a series of brief monographs for the general reader with the purpose of explaining the three economies which constitute Malaya's economy: 1. The modified subsistence economy of rice and fish, of poverty and chronic debt, found mainly in the north and east and along the jungle fringes. 2. The mercantile economy of Penang and Singapore, an enduring economy involving monopolistic agencies, contractors, exchange controls, and distribution schemes. 3. The plantation and mining economy producing rubber and tin—Malaya's chief wealth.

Discussion of various aspects of these economies are outlined: working population, supplies of capital, role of the public sector.

*Bibliography:* Brief list of references on Malayan economy.

[Other studies in this Background to Malaya series are: 1. *A short history of Malaya* by C. H. Parkinson. 3. *The schools of Malaya* by F. Mason. 4. *Trade unionism in Malaya* by Alex Josey. 5. *The fishing industry of Singapore* by T. W. Burdon. 6. *Prehistoric Malaya* by M. W. F. Tweedie. 7. *Labour law in Malaya* by Victor Purcell. 9. *Problems of the Malayan economy* by Lim Tay Boh. 10. *Synthetic rubber and Malaya* by Charles Gamba. 11. *Social welfare in Malaya* by Kathleen Jones. 12. *Short history of the Nanyang Chinese* by Wang Gungqu. 13. *The development of Singapore's economy* by Lim Tay Boh.]

337. WILSON, JOAN. The Singapore Rubber Market. Singapore, Eastern Universities Press (Donald Moore), 1958. xii, 75 p.; bibliography, charts, glossary, index. (Malayan studies series, no. 1)*　　　HD9161.S5W5

*Text:* Deals with the most important market economically of Malaya and Singapore as it gives "an introductory outline for those with a non-professional interest in how the Singapore rubber market is organized and the contribution it makes to the commerce of Malaya and Southeast Asia." First in a series dealing with specific aspects of the economic life of Malaya and Singapore.

*Bibliography:* A few references dealing with the rubber industry as a whole.

---

*[Another item in this series is: *Rice Cultivation in Malaya* by Elena M. Cooke].

*Charts:* Graphically portray the economic characteristics of the rubber market.

*Glossary:* Terms used on the rubber market.

## SOCIAL CONDITIONS
(including: Anthropology, Education, and Health)

338. DJAMOUR, JUDITH. Malay Kinship and Marriage in Singapore. London, University of London, Athlone Press, 1959. 151 p.; bibliography, tables, charts, index. (London School of Economics. Monographs on social anthropology, no. 21)　　　GN635.M4D5

*Text:* As a shortened version of a thesis submitted to the University of London, presents the findings of fieldwork in a Malay fishing community on the southwest coast of Singapore Island, a mixed urban area of Malay, Chinese and Indian population. The specific problem studied is the instability of Malay marriage and the effects which this instability has on the divorced couples themselves, on their children, and on their respective kinsmen.

The study is divided into these seven chapters: 1. The structure of Singapore Malay society. 2. Kinship. 3. The household. 4. Marriage. 5. Children; birth, adoption, socialization. 6. Divorce. 7. Conclusion.

*Bibliography:* Consists mostly of books plus a few articles relevant to family and kinship.

*Tables* (selected): Occupation of Singapore Malays. Types of household. Household composition.

*Charts:* Saudara děkat (close relatives).

339. EVANS, IVOR HUGH NORMAN. The Negritos of Malaya. Cambridge, University Press, 1937. xiii, 323 p.; bibliography, illustrations, map, appendices, glossary, index.　　　DS595.E85

*Text:* An authoritative account of that branch of the Negritos living in the Malay Peninsula, providing information regarding their general appearance, domestic life, dress, weapons, government, music, art, religious concepts, superstitions, folk tales, language, shamanistic practices, and regarding numerous other topics pertaining to these aboriginal people.

*Illustrations:* Picture Negrito weapons, musical instruments, implements, art objects, and clothing.

*Glossary:* List of Negrito words.

*Appendices:* List of relationship terms used by the Jehai, speakers of a Negrito dialect.

340. FIRTH, ROSEMARY. Housekeeping Among Malay Peasants. London, Percy Lund, Humphries and Co., for The London School of Economics and Political Science, 1943. viii, 198 p.; illustrations, maps, tables, charts, appendices, index. (Monographs on social anthropology, no. 7)          DS598.K3F5

*Text:* A scientific inquiry into the organization, practices, and problems of the domestic life of Malay peasants in Kelantan, a Malay State on the northeast coast of the Federation, which is predominantly Malay in population.   Provides detailed information regarding their low standard of living as revealed by conditions of housekeeping, composition and resources of the household, the position of women, expenditure of money and use of the budget, the place of the child in the household, shopping and marketing, and the financing of ceremonial obligations.

*Illustrations:* Bazaar scenes.  Malay houses.  Communal practices.

*Maps:* Villages in Kelantan.   Perupok village plan.

*Tables:* Distribution of persons in household, and size of households.  Kinship composition of households. Occupations of women.  Economic position of polygamous men.  Family diets.

*Charts:* Average weekly expenditure per family. Variations in weekly expenditure on rice.  Family budgets.

*Appendices:* Case history of a polygamous establishment.  Cooking practices and recipes.  Analysis of weekly budgets.

341. FRASER, THOMAS M., JR. Rusembilan: A Malay Fishing Village in Southern Thailand. Ithaca, Cornell University Press, 1960. xviii, 281 p.; bibliography, illustrations, maps, tables, appendices, index. (Cornell studies in anthropology)          HN750.5.F7

*Text:* This study, based largely on field data gathered while living in a Malay coastal village in Thailand, is the first published account of any Malay community in Thailand or anywhere else designed to encompass the total socio-cultural organization and behavior of a Moslem Malay peasant group.  Endeavors to see how this community and other Malay communities are integrated into the natural structure of Thailand and how the social structure and cultural patterns reacted to points of stress in the process of integration.

The thirteen chapters are entitled: 1. Introduction. 2. The place and the people.  3. Historical background.   4. Maritime–economy.   5. Economy of the land.   6. Trade and commerce.   7. Rusembilan as part of the Thai nation.   8. Community organization. 9. Rusembilan as a Moslem community.  10. Belief in spirits.   11. The life cycle.   12. Patterns of a changing community.   13. Sociocultural change.

*Bibliography:* Comprised principally of book and article titles dealing with various community studies in Southeast Asia.

*Illustrations:* Various village scenes in Rusembilan, with reference to the economic life of the people.

*Maps:* Rusembilan tambon.

*Tables* (selected): Rainfall and temperature.  Population.   Land utilization.

*Appendices:* Introduction of motorboats at Rusembilan.   The language of Rusembilan.

342. GREAT BRITAIN.  COMMISSION ON HIGHER EDUCATION IN MALAYA.  Higher Education in Malaya.  Report of the Commission Appointed by the Secretary of State for the Colonies, June 1939.  London, H. M. Stationery Office, 1939.  vii, 151 p.; illustrations. (Colonial Office.  Colonial no. 173)
          LA1238.A5 1939

*Text:* Contains the findings presented as an official report to the Secretary of State for the Colonies of a Commission appointed to survey the status of higher education in Malaya.  It may be referred to as the McLean Report, since W. H. McLean was chairman of the Commission.

The work of the Commission was performed in 1938 and 1939, prior to World War II, which in turn prevented the implementation of the recommendations of the Commission.  This report served as a forerunner to the postwar Commission which studies higher education in Malaya in 1947–48. (See *Report of the Commission on University Education in Malaya,* London, 1948.)

The study includes valuable data on the following topics: The educational background of Malaya, Raffles College in Singapore (now the University of Malaya), King Edward VII College of Medicine, The future development of a University of Malaya, Higher technical education, The Sultan Idris Training College, English schools in Malaya, and Vocational education.

The summary consists of a condensation of each of the foregoing topics discussed in the text, and only indirectly makes recommendations.

*Illustrations:* Aerial view of Raffles College in 1939.
*Plan:* Simplified plan of the layout of the buildings of Raffles College.

343. GREAT BRITAIN. COMMISSION ON UNIVERSITY EDUCATION IN MALAYA. Report. London, H. M. Stationery Office, 1948. x, 150 p.; appendices, index.          LA1238.A5 1948

*Text:* Frequently referred to as the Carr-Saunders Report, since Sir Alexander Carr-Saunders was chairman of the Commission appointed in March 1947 for the purpose of investigating higher education in Malaya. The recommendation of the Commission to establish the University of Malaya at Johore Bahru, of which the King Edward VII College of Medicine and Raffles College would form part, was based on a study of the following problems: flow of students from secondary schools to the university; university entrance requirements; vocational needs in Malaya; courses of study to be offered; program for medical education; training of prospective school teachers; development of a university library; opportunities for research, student life, and welfare; and, the matters of the university constitution, administration, financing, staffing, and location.

Among the fifteen specific recommendations given concisely in the section Summary of recommendations, are provision for the creation of Departments of Malay Studies, Chinese Studies, and Tamil Studies and the establishment of a Scientific Advisory Council to co-ordinate various research organizations in Malaya.

In the words of the Secretary of State for the Colonies, A. Creech Jones, "This is a document of profound importance for all those who are concerned for the future of Malaya."

*Appendices:* Draft constitution of the University. Draft statutes of the University. Education in Malaya —a brief description of the main branches of schooling in Malaya. List of persons interviewed by the Commission.

344. HO, SENG ONG. Education for Unity in Malaya; an Evaluation of the Educational System of Malaya with Special Reference to the Need for Unity in Its Plural Society. Penang, Malayan Teachers Union, 1952. ix, 209 p.; bibliography, map, tables, charts, appendix. (Issued under the auspices of the *Malayan Educator*. Educational research series, vol. 1)          LA1236.H6

*Text:* As volume one in the Educational Research Series, it deals with the educational policy as projected by the Malayan Union Director of Education in his annual report for 1947. Contends that one of the best ways to weld together the various racial groups in the pluralistic society of Malaya is through the Malayan schools. This idea is developed in these selected chapters: 3. The Malayan educational system. 4. Does the Malayan educational policy and practice meet the need for unity. 5. A proposed plan of education for unity in the Malayan plural society. 6. Some implications of the proposed plan of education. 7. Summary of findings and recommendations.

*Bibliography:* Divided into three parts—A. General background on education and Malaya. B. Comparative education. C. Education in Malaya.

*Map:* Malaya—pre 1942, and postwar political units.

*Tables* (selected): Population of main racial divisions. Statistics on Malay, Chinese, Indian, and English schools.

*Charts* (selected): 2. Distribution of Malays, Chinese, and Indians. 3. Increase in population, 1921–47. 6. The educational system of Malaya, 1947.

*Appendix:* Questionnaire used to collect data.

345. JONES, KATHLEEN. Social Welfare in Malaya. Singapore, Donald Moore, 1958. iv, 45 p.; bibliography, illustrations. (Background to Malaya series, no. 12)*          HV394.M34T6

*Text:* Provides an account of the social service rendered to the various communities in Malaya by voluntary organizations and government-sponsored bodies. Sketches the kind of work which is done for children with abnormal home conditions, the physically and mentally handicapped, the sick and unemployed, the old people, the juvenile offenders, and needy communities—thus giving significant insight into the social conditions of Malaya. Relates the surveys and social research which is being done or which is sorely needed.

*Bibliography:* Lists a few references on various social problems in Malaya.

*[Other items issued in this series are: 1. *A short history of Malaya* by C. Northcote Parkinson (1957); 2. *The economy of Malaya: an essay in colonial political economy* by T. H. Silcock (1956); 3. *The schools of Malaya* by Frederic Mason; 4. *Trade unionism in Malaya* by Alex Josey (1958); 5. *The fishing industry in Singapore* by T. W. Burdon (1957); 6. *Prehistoric Malaya* by M. F. W. Tweedie (1955); 7. *Labour law in Malaya* by Charles Gamba (1957); 8. *The Chinese in modern Malaya* by Victor Purcell; 9. *Problems of the Malayan economy* by Lim Tay Boh; 10. *Synthetic rubber and Malaya* by Charles Gamba; 13. *A short history of the Nanyang Chinese* by Wang Gungwa (1959).]

*Illustrations:* Show health clinics, children's homes, blind welfare, and other relief work.

346. KAYE, BARRINGTON. Upper Nankin Street, Singapore: A Sociological Study Of Chinese Households Living in a Densely Populated Area. Singapore, University of Malaya Press, 1960. xvi, 439 p.; bibliography, illustrations, tables, charts, appendices, index.

HN690.S47K3

*Text:* Embodies the results of a year and a half of research undertaken by a social science research fellow at the University of Malaya in Singapore in the mid-fifties. This well-organized survey of the Chinese in a densely populated area of Singapore gives extensive data on The constitution of households; Living conditions; Date and place of birth and immigrant status; Dialect and education; Marital status; Occupation; and other topics related to the condition of a street in Singapore's Chinatown.

*Bibliography:* Brief list of books and articles pertaining to subjects of Chinese and social conditions in Singapore.

*Illustrations:* Exterior views of the buildings used by Chinese for housing and shops. Interior views showing living conditions of Chinese quarters or cubicles.

*Tables* (selected): Distribution of population in Upper Nankin Street according to age, sex, family size, living space, lighting conditions, language, occupations, type of household, education, marital status, time of working neighborliness, and other topics.

*Charts:* Typical plan of a shophouse. Population distribution.

*Appendices* (selected): House condition. Occupation. Classification of industries. Instructions to investigators.

347. LO, DOROTHY, AND LEON COMBER. Chinese Festivals in Malaya. Singapore, Eastern Unisities Press (Donald Moore), 1958. 66 p.; bibliography, illustrations, indices. (Malayan peoples and customs series)

GT4879.L6

*Text:* Describes the principal festivals celebrated in the Chinese community in Singapore, giving the origin and significance of the eight Chinese national festivals observed in Malaya. The festivals described are: Chinese New Year; Ching Ming festival; Dragon boat festival; Feast of the seven sisters; Feast of the hungry ghosts; Mid-autumn festival; Double-ninth festival; Winter solstice festival.

*Bibliography*: A few references on Chinese customs and legends.

*Illustrations:* Reproductions of original Chinese paintings on silk depicting the festivals.

348. MACDONALD, MALCOLM. Borneo People.* New York, Alfred A. Knopf, 1958. vi, 424 p.; illustrations.     DS646.36.M3 1958

*Text:* The former British High Commissioner of Southeast Asia describes the peoples which inhabit Sarawak providing vivid word pictures of the physical appearance of the country, life in a long-house, village ceremonies, the influence of Christianity on the people, customs, and traditions, and family life among the Kayans and Kenyahs. Other peoples described are the Land Dayaks, the Ibans, the Melanaus, the Malays and the Chinese.

*Illustrations:* Scenes of village life, housing, ceremonies, dress, and physical features of Sarawak.

349. MALAYA (FEDERATION). COMMITTEE ON MALAY EDUCATION. Report. Kuala Lumpur, Government Press. 1951. ix, 88 p.; tables, chart, appendices.     LA1236.A5 1951

*Text:* Present the findings of an education committee appointed by the High Commission of Malaya for the purpose of inquiring into the status of educational facilities available for Malays.

The frame of reference includes: the system of Malay vernacular education; the method of selection of students for admission to Malay Training Colleges; the means of raising the scholastic attainment and improving the training in pedagogy at the college level; the curricula of the Malay Teacher Training Colleges; the raising of the scholastic attainments of students in Malay schools; the necessary steps to accelerate the education of Malays in English; and, the ways of improving the organization within the local educational system.

Provides valuable information on what grounds Malay opinion holds the present educational arrangements to be inadequate, at what points and in what directions Malay opinion would desire to have educational changes made, and what motives and aims underlie the critical and dissatisfied Malay attitude with reference to education in Malaya. The closing chap-

*[Also published under same title: Toronto, Clarke, Irwin, 1956.  DS646.36.M3]

ter summarizes the recommendations and suggestions of the Committee relating to previous chapters in the report.

*Tables:* Enrollments in Malay schools. Malay pupils in English schools. Forecast of qualified teachers for national schools. Forecast of population in Malaya, 1953–1965.

*Chart:* Vernacular school system.

*Appendices:* List of persons interviewed by the Committee. List of documents received by the Committee.

350. MALAYA (FEDERATION). EDUCATION COMMITTEE. Report of the Education Committee, 1960. Kuala Lumpur, Govt. Press, 1958. x, 98 p.; diagram, appendices. In process

*Text:* An official document which will in time have considerable influence on the educational progress of Malaya. Following the discussion of the way in which the recommendations of the 1956 report were implemented, this report deals with these selected topics: recommendations for future development; new structure of the educational system; primary education; assistance to secondary schools; language medium of examinations; national and state education advisory boards; technical education; teacher training; Islamic religious instruction; national language; forecast of costs.

*Diagram:* Proposed education structure.

*Appendices* (selected): 1. Membership of consultative committees. Cost of implementing recommendations. Teacher training arrangements. Current education legislation. Papers submitted to the Education Review Committee.

351. PURCELL, VICTOR WILLIAM. The Chinese in Malaya. London, New York, Oxford University Press, 1948. xvi, 327 p.; bibliography, maps, tables, appendices, index. (Issued under the joint auspices of the Royal Institute of International Affairs and the Institute of Pacific Relations) DS595.P8

*Text:* Provides a consecutive account of Chinese social problems and politics, and the part the Chinese have played with the British in building modern Malaya. Part I consists of historical chapters describing Chinese immigration to Malaya, the Chinese in Malacca, Penang, Singapore, and in the Malay States in the 19th century. Part II tells of special aspects of the Chinese in Malaya—Chinese religion, Anglo-Chinese relations, secret societies, social problems, political

societies, education, and the place of the Chinese in Malayan industry. Part III gives information on recent developments: the Chinese activity in Malaya during the war period, the place of the Chinese in Malaya after the liberation, and, the Chinese and the Malayan Constitution in 1945.

*Bibliography:* Lists books, articles, and official documents related to the subject discussed.

*Maps:* Malaya—depicting political divisions, principal cities and railroads. Expansion of the Chinese population in Malaya—together with statistical tables regarding the Chinese and other racial groups in the political divisions.

*Tables:* Malaya population statistics. The population according to main racial divisions. Chinese schools, pupils, and teachers.

*Appendices:* The Baba language. Also above tables.

352. SINGAPORE. DEPARTMENT OF SOCIAL WELFARE. A Social Survey of Singapore: A Preliminary Study of Some Aspects of Social Conditions in the Municipal Area of Singapore. 1947. viii, 165 p.; maps, tables, appendices. HN690.S5A5 1947

*Text:* A study of the social conditions prevalent in Singapore, with data on population density and composition, characteristics of different households in various racial groups, occupation and education of wage earners, overcrowding and other housing problems, education of children, and the relation of immigrants (Indian and Chinese principally) with their homelands.

*Map:* Plan of the municipal area of Singapore showing survey wards, 1947, Scale—1½″ to 1 mile.

*Tables:* Statistical data relating to most of the problems discussed in the text.

*Appendices:* Information forms and manual of instruction used in the survey. Percentage distribution of survey households in different occupation groups, by earning category. Classification scheme of occupations. Numbers of school children in schools, by occupation groups of wage earners.

353. SKEAT, WALTER WILLIAM, and CHARLES OTTO BLAGDEN. Pagan Races of the Malay Peninsula. London, Macmillan, 1906. 2 vols.; bibliography, illustrations, maps, glossary, appendices, indices. DS595.S7

*Text:* A study in descriptive ethnography which presents a storehouse of information about the physical, racial, and cultural characteristics of different aboriginal tribes of Malaya.

Divided into four principal parts. Part one discusses the affinities of the various races and tribes, and the physical characteristics of each tribal group. Part two in a very detailed way deals with manners and customs as revealed in their food, dress, housing, hunting, modes of barter, weapons and implements, agricultural cultivation, arts and crafts, decorative art work, and social milieu. Part three presents their religious concepts in the customs and beliefs associated with birth, maturity, marriage and burial, and the place that music, feasts and folklore have in relation to their religious practices. Part four describes the numerous dialects and subdialects spoken by Semang, Sakai, and Jakun racial groups, with a detailed account of the past history of these languages and their relation to other languages.

*Illustrations:* Scores of views showing the various racial types. Cooking utensils. Articles of wearing apparel. Weapons. Art work. Houses. Musical instruments.

*Maps:* Distribution of the languages of the aborigines of the Malay peninsula. Principal Sakai districts. Position of the Mon-Annam dialects of eastern Indochina. Position of the various groups related to the Mon–Annam family.

*Glossary:* Comparative vocabulary of aboriginal dialects. Together with grammatical notes, extending over 250 pages.

*Appendices:* Tables and notes on racial affinities. Text of Semang songs collected in Kedah. List of place names and personal names. Materials and sources of the comparative vocabulary of aboriginal dialects.

354. SMITH, T. E. Population Growth in Malaya; an Analysis of Recent Trends. London, Royal Institute of International Affairs, 1952. viii, 126 p.; maps, tables, charts, appendices, index.                    HB3640.M3S6

*Text:* An abundant amount of statistical research and an intimate knowledge of Malaya and its people are revealed in this scholarly analytical study written by one who served for some years in the Malayan Civil Service. A study which describes the main outlines of demographic development, assesses the potentials for future population change, and indicates the nature of the problems to be encountered in Malaya. Shows how Malaya is an area where the population has had a marked increase because of immigration of

Indians and Chinese who have not become assimilated with the indigenous stocks.

The demographic characteristics of the three major communities—the Malaysians, the Chinese, and the Indians—are discussed in three principal chapters. Indicates the importance of the rate of increase of the population as a whole and of each community in relation to the economic, social, and political development of the country. Includes in outline form the most important economic activities of the different racial groups in Malaya and discusses the possible development of the economy in the next few years.

*Maps:* Malaya and its main industries. Internal migrations of Malaysians.

*Tables:* The occupational distribution of the major communities of Malaya. Acreages of agricultural crops in Malaya. Composition of population in Malaya. Percentage of literacy. Major occupations. Distribution of Chinese communities in Malaya.

*Charts:* Population of Malaya, 1947. Population growth, 1911–47. Population distribution, 1947.

*Appendices:* Statistical tables, noted above.

355. T'IEN, JU-K'ANG. The Chinese of Sarawak: A Study of Social Structure. London, Dept. of Anthropology, London School of Economics and Political Science, 1953. 91 p.; maps, tables, diagrams, appendix. (Monographs on social anthropology, no. 12) DS646.36.T5

*Text:* A small segment of the millions of overseas Chinese in Southeast Asia is described as the writer reviews the Chinese community in Sarawak, with particular emphasis on its social life. At a time when the whole of Southeast Asia is undergoing one of the most rapid processes of social change, the Chinese members of social groups, particularly Chinese associations, are faced with geographical, political, economic, and social challenges which are essentially different from those of China. Shows how these Chinese people—equipped with their Chinese social experience—respond to the challenge of the new environment, the constant changes, and the political pressures.

Analyzing the social environment of both rural and urban areas, these chapters are included: 1. The problem. 2. Emigration and emigrants. 3. The warp and woof of Chinese associations. 4. The nature of the Chinese community. 5. Clanship. 6. Rural economy and clan relationships. 7. Occupational identification and bazaar economy. 8. Bazaar economy and the rubber trade. 9. The problem of power. 10. Relationship with the mother country.

*Maps:* Sarawak, administrative divisions. 2. Provinces of Kwangtung and Fukien, from which many Chinese came. 3. Distribution of Chinese in the Kuching-Ban-Serian area.

*Tables* (selected): Statistical tables on Chinese associations in Kuching, clan relationships, dialect and occupation, dialect and economic status, and Chinese publications.

*Diagrams* (selected): Dialect differences among rubber dealers. Rubber transactions.

*Appendix:* Chinese population of Sarawak, dialect groups.

## CULTURAL LIFE

(including: Fine Arts, Language, Literature and Religion)

356. AHMAD MURAD BIN NASRUDDIN. Life at the Point of a Sword. Translated into English by Judith Rosenberg, and edited by John M. Echols. Kuala Lumpur, Printed at the Khee Meng Press, 1956. 96 p.   PZ4.A286Li

*Text:* The original of this work in English translation is entitled *Nyawa di huijong pedang.* It received first prize in a novel-writing contest sponsored by the Federation of Malaya Department of Information Services. Since its appearance in 1947, it has been issued in a Jawi or Arabic script edition and in a Rumi or romanized edition.

This example of Malay literature reveals grim experiences during the time of the Japanese occupation. It relates the horrible life of the prison camp, and at the same time manifests in the characters a firm belief in God and faith in his protection.

357. BEAMISH, TONY. The Arts of Malaya. Singapore, Donald Moore, 1954. 80 p.; bibliography, illustrations. (Malayan heritage series, no. 2)*   N7324.M3B4

*Text:* An introductory account of the various arts and crafts found in the culture of Malaya. Selected chapters: 2. Early arts and the Malaya contribution. 3.

---

*[Other items in this series are: 1. *Chinese ancestor worship in Malaya* by Leon Comber; 3. *Hantu bantu: ghost beliefs in modern Malaya* by J. N. McHugh; 4. *The adventures of Hang Tuah* by M. C. F. Sheppard; 5. *Chinese magic and superstitions in Malaya* by Leon Comber; 6. *Malay proverbs: bidal Melayu* by A. W. Hamilton; 7. *Fables and folk tales from an eastern forest* by W. W. Skeat; 8. *Malay pantuns: pantun Malayu* by A. W. Hamilton.]

Indian and Chinese contributions. 5. The visual arts: painting, sculpture and architecture. 6. Music and letters. 7. On the stage. 8. Silver and sarongs. 9. From pottery to puppets.

*Bibliography:* Cites a few books dealing with particular and local aspects of Malayan culture.

*Illustrations:* Depicts textiles, metal work, drama, music, and other arts of Malaya.

358. HENDERSHOT, VERNON EDWARDS. The First Year of Standard Malay. Foreword by Owen Lattimore. Mountain View, Calif., Pacific Press Publishing Association, 1943. 315 p.; bibliography, illustrations, maps.

PL5107.H4

*Text:* Within the opening sections of the book, the following subjects are discussed with clarity and understanding: the extent to which the Malay language is used in Southeast Asia, the types or varieties of the Malay language, the rise of the Malay language and certain tendencies in its development, Malay literature and written forms, pronunciation and orthography, and an outline of Malay grammar.

Twenty-five lessons which include exercises and vocabularies and comprise the basis of the book and are followed by sections on: conversations in Malay, Malay proverbs, selected reading in Malay, and letter-writing in Malay.

The Malay-English and English-Malay vocabularies which cover more than 125 pages are based on Sir Richard O. Winstedt's *Dictionary of colloquial Malay.* (Singapore, Kelly & Walsh, 1939.)

*Bibliography:* Lists dictionaries of the Malay language and other studies which discuss the Malay language and how to learn it.

*Illustrations:* Various scenes in the Malay archipelago where the Malay language is understood.

*Maps:* Sketch maps comparing the size of the Malay archipelago with the United States and Europe.

359. WINSTEDT, SIR RICHARD OLAF. The Malays; a Cultural History. New York, Philosophical Library, 1950. vii, 198 p.; bibliography, illustrations, appendices, index.

GN630.M3W55 1950a

*Text:* An authoritative account of the many-sided civilization of the Malay people as observed by a well-known student of Malay culture. Although the study is not a long one, its scope is broad enough to include valuable information regarding: origin, migrations, and early history of the Malay people; their beliefs and religion; social traditions and customs; political and legal systems; economic life; language and literature; and arts and crafts.

Inasmuch as practically all Malays in Malaya have been Muslims for several centuries, there is considerable data on: the beliefs and practices of Islam in Malaya, the way in which Muslim law and practice have conditioned Malay marriage and divorce, the influence which orthodox Muslim works have had on the Malay legal system, and the part which Muslim literature has played in Malay literature.

*Bibliography:* A highly selected list of references which include original sources.

*Illustrations:* Malay weapons. Malay village life. Malay silverwork.

*Appendices:* Malay text of certain passages cited in the chapters. Family relationships in Negri Sembilan.

# VI

# Indonesia

## GENERAL BACKGROUND

360. BRO, MARGUERITTE HARMON. Indonesia, Land of Challenge. New York, Harper, 1954. xiii, 263 p.; illustrations, index. DS644.B7

*Text:* The wife of an American Embassy officer relates her impressions of Indonesia's physical geography, history, education, health conditions, religious groups, food problems, economic situation, and foreign policy.

*Illustrations* (selected): Views of rubber industry, tea industry, salt industry, schools, children's clinics, and dancers. Dr. Roem, Mr. Hatta, Soetan Sjahrir, and Sultan Hamenku Buwono IX.

361. DOUWES DEKKER, NIELS A. Tanah Air Kita: A Book on the Country and People of Indonesia. 3rd ed. The Hague, W. van Hoeve, [1961] 315 p.; illustrations, maps, index. DS620.D613 1961

*Text:* A volume of colored and black-and-white photographs which depict the people, customs, geography, industries, and other subjects relating to the different islands comprising the Indonesian archipelago. A descriptive account of the principal parts of the country—Sumatra, Borneo, Celebes, The Moluccas, The Lesser Sunda Islands, East Java and Madura, and West Java—precedes the scores of pictures which follow. Each picture has clearly stated annotation.

*Illustrations:* Show the topography, volcanoes, shore lines, peoples, village life, dress, dance varieties, art, architecture, religious practices and festivals, flora and fauna, bazaar scenes, wedding ceremonies, palace scenes of the Sultans, Muslim mosques, sculpturing, musical instruments, bridges, roads, sports, and different industries—rice cultivation, fishing, shipping, mining, weaving, and rubber cultivation.

*Maps:* Indonesia. Sumatra. Borneo. Celebes. The Moluccas. The Lesser Sunda Islands. East Java and Madura. West Java.

362. GOODFRIEND, ARTHUR. Rice Roots. New York, Simon and Schuster, 1958. 209 p.; illustrations. DS625.G6

*Text:* Analyzes the causes and conditions underlying the crises throughout Asia, particularly Indonesia.

Contends that the masses of Asia are vaguely understood and thus frustrate Western comprehension. Purposes to offer Americans an insight into the "Asian mind," with reference to an American's role, responsibility, and opportunity in Asia's future.

These five reasons prompted the writer to study Indonesia: infant mortality, poverty, illiteracy, neutralism, and communism.

*Illustrations:* Indonesian children. Farmers at work.

363. HANNA, WILLARD ANDERSON. Bung Karno's Indonesia: A Collection of 25 Reports Written for the American Universities Field Staff. New York, American Universities Field Staff, Inc., 1960. Various paging; illustrations, tables, charts. DS644.H16

*Text:* Evaluates with keen insight the political, economic, and social trends in Indonesia taking place during President Sukarno's program of guided democracy. Among the 25 parts which comprise the compilation are these written between September and December 1959: 1. Backtracking a revolution. 3. The politics of mystification. 4. The economics of incongruity. 5. The indecision of the military. 6. The enigma of the Communists. 8. The Irian irritant. 9. The spoils of oil. 10. Bankers' quandry. 18. The case of Mochtar Lubis. 19. Politik bebas—independent policy or politics unlimited? 20. The Dutch cut their losses. 22. The Chinese take a second look. 23. The Russians are willing. 24. The United States is perplexed.

364. HONIG, PIETER and FRANS VERDOORN, eds. Science and Scientists in the Netherlands Indies. New York, Board for the Netherlands Indies, Surinam, and Curaçao, 1945. xxii, 491 p.; bibliography, illustrations, map, charts, supplements. Q127.D9H6

*Text:* Presents the development and status of a large number of branches of the natural sciences in Indonesia during the time of the Dutch regime. Although not a complete history of science in Indonesia during the 19th and 20th centuries, it nevertheless provides basic information about the scientific achievements of research workers in or around the Indonesian archipelago.

Among the articles dealing with various branches of science—agronomy, mineralogy, botany, meteorology, geology, geography, rubber cultivation, public health and medicine, demography, archeology, cinchona cultivation, and chemistry—are the following: On the climate of and meteorlogical research in the Netherlands Indies by C. Braak. Diversity and unity in Southeast Asia by J. O. M. Brock. A history of the visitors laboratory . . . of the Botanic Gardens, Buitenzorg, 1884–1934 by K. W. Dammerman. Prehistoric research in the Netherlands Indies by Robert van Heine-Geldern. Chapters on the history of cinchona by P. Honig, et al. Chapters on the history of chemistry in the Netherlands Indies by D. R. Koolhaas, et al. The geology of the Netherlands Indies by H. Stauffer. History of rubber cultivation and research in the Netherlands Indies by T. A. Tengwall.

*Bibliography:* Brief lists of references about rubber research, cinchona research, archaeology, zoogeography, medicine and health, and anthropology in Indonesia.

*Illustrations:* Volcanoes. Landscapes. Buildings of research institutes. Implements of the stone age. Botanic Gardens, Buitenzorg (Bogor)

*Maps:* Seismic map of the Netherlands East Indies. Population density in Southeast Asia. Zoogeographic borderlines in the Malay Archipalego. Volcanoes in Southeast Asia. Rainfall in Southeast Asia. Languages in Southeast Asia. Religions in Southeast Asia. Geology maps of Sumatra, Java, New Guinea, and the Celebes.

*Tables:* Mineral production. Rubber research programs. Rabies research.

*Charts:* International Rubber Regulation Committee. Hydrodynamic research.

*Supplements:* Scientific institutions, societies, and research workers in the Netherlands, by Frans Verdoorn and J. G. Verdoorn. Serta Malesiana: short articles, reports, and notes.

365. INDONESIA (REPUBLIC). DEPARTMENT OF FOREIGN AFFAIRS. Indonesia, 1962. Djakarta, [1962?] 174 p.; illustrations, map.

In process

*Text:* A general handbook covering various aspects of Indonesia. Selected chapters: Basic political structure. Indonesian socialism—principles and practice. Colonialism in West Irian. The 1961 census. Pioneers in an old land—transmigration in South Sumatra. Transformation of Djakarta Raja. Chronology of the years of independence.

*Illustrations* (selected): Views in Djakarta. Various industries. Military equipment. Sukarno addressing various groups.

*Map:* Outline map of Indonesia. Scale–1:10,000,-000.

366. INDONESIA (REPUBLIC). KEDUTAAN BESAR. U.S. The Cultural Life of Indonesia: Religion, the Arts, and Education. Washington, Embassy of Indonesia, Educational and Cultural Divisions, 1951. viii, 68 p.; illustrations, map. DS625.A5 1951

*Text:* A brief survey of Indonesian cultural life with particular emphasis on the ancient indigenous concepts which have persisted through the centuries, notwithstanding the uneven cultural developments in Indonesia due to environmental factors and the influence of foreign cultures.

These aspects of Indonesian life and culture are discussed: *adat* or customary law; religion; the arts; handicrafts; drama, dance, and music; language and literature; and education and science.

*Illustrations:* Religious temples. Wood carvings. Paintings. Textile arts—*batik* and *ikat* techniques. Puppets used in *wajang* kulit. The *djanger* and *bedojo* dances. The *gamelan* and *angklung* orchestras. Scenes from schools and laboratories.

*Map:* Indonesia in Southeast Asia, with the original Indonesian names used for the various islands.

367. KENNEDY, RAYMOND. The Ageless Indies. New York, John Day, 1942. xvi, 208 p.; maps, index. DS615.K4

*Text:* Represents a distillation of long personal experience in the Indonesian archipelago and years of subsequent research on the civilization of the Indonesian people by a former Professor of Anthropology of Yale University. Shows how the people of the island empire have withstood for centuries the successive intruders of foreign civilizations both of the Occident and of the Orient without losing their own cultural and social identity. Presents general background information about the geography and climate, population, languages, history, customs, and daily practices of the people as to food, clothing, handicrafts, music, religion, Dutch colonial government, and the economic wealth in Indonesia. The closing chapter, The Future, gives a faint outline of a plan for the extension of self-government in Indonesia and other countries in Southeast Asia. In the words of the author, this book is for "people [who] are awaking to the realization that they know next to nothing about these islands, their history and their inhabitants."

*Maps:* Peoples and tribes of the Indies. The East Indies, showing the names of the principal islands.

368. KENNEDY, RAYMOND. Bibliography of Indonesian Peoples and Cultures. Revised and edited by Thomas W. Maretzki and H. Th. Fischer. New Haven, Southeast Asian Studies, Yale University, by arrangement with Human Relations Area Files, 1962. xxii, 207 p.                                                    Z5115.K4 1962

*Text:* A reprint of a compilation which, in 1945, represented a close aproximation to complete coverage of all extant books and periodical articles, concerning Indonesia. Although the main foci of this list are anthropology and sociology, including ethnography, archaeology, linguistics, and studies of acculturation, titles to books and articles on geography, colonial administration, education, economics, and history have been incorporated. An index is sorely needed.

369. NETHERLANDS (KINGDOM). DEPARTMENT VAN ZAKEN OVERZEE. Report on Netherlands New Guinea 1954 . . . [The Hague, 1955?] various pagings. Illustrations, map, tables, charts, appendices.                          DU774.N35

*Text:* This annual, issued in Dutch from 1950 to 58 (9 vols. in 6) and also in English from 1954 to 58 (5 vols. in 3), was presented to the United Nations and published jointly by the Department van Zaken Overzee and the Departement van Buitenlandse Zaken.

This first volume in English is divided into four chapters covering many topics. I. General information: A. Geography. B. History. C. Population. D. Government; II. Economic situation: A. General economic situation. B. Agriculture and stock-breeding. C. Forestry. D. Fisheries, E. Mining. F. Power. G. Industry. H. Transport and communications. I. Public Finance. J. Banking and credit. K. Trade; III. Social conditions: A. General problems of race and culture. B. Human rights. C. Status of women. D. Labour and employment conditions. E. Cooperatives. F. Standard of living. G. Town and housing planning. H. Social security and welfare. I. Prevention of crimes. J. Public health; IV. Education: A. General education conditions. B. Administration of education. C. Structure of the educational system. D. Adult education. E. School buildings. F. Youth organizations. G. Cultural institutions. H.

Protection of nature. I. Development of education. J. Publicity.

*Illustrations* (selected): Hollandia harbor. Biak airport. Mokmer airfield. Agricultural station at Kota Nica. Technical training center at Sorong. Public health.

*Map:* Netherlands New Guinea, showing the six main divisions.

*Tables:* Temperature and humidity. Population. Port facilities. Financial expenditures. Income tax. Exports and imports. Government workers. Administration of justice. Hospitals and diseases. Educational institutions.

*Charts:* Organization of telegraph and telephone service.

*Appendix:* Besides tables above, ordinances enacted.

370. REITSMA, S. A. Van Stockum's Travellers' Handbook for the Dutch East Indies. The Hague, Van Stockum, 1930. xi, 613 p.; illustrations, maps, index.            DS614.R4

*Text:* Designed primarily to provide background reading for travellers who visit the Indonesian archipelago. Includes descriptive accounts of the geographical features, climate, population, language, religion, domestic life, history, government, education, agricultural production, mineral deposits, trade, and communications as generally found throughout the islands. A general review and detailed description of each of the islands of Java, Madura, Sumatra, Bali, Lombok, Borneo, the Celebes, and the Moluccas are included. Well indexed.

*Illustrations: Wajang priaji,* Indonesian drama. Batik cloth manufacture. Batak houses. Cremation ceremony.

*Maps:* Colored maps of each of the islands discussed in the text. Maps of the principal cities: Batavia, Buitenzorg, Bandoeng, Sourabaya, Medan, Padang, Semarang, and Djokjakarta.

371. "Special Number on the Netherlands Indies." *Far Eastern Quarterly,* February 1946, v. 5: 115–215, maps, tables, chart.

DS501.F274 1946

*Text:* A series of articles, brought together by the Publications Committee of the Southeast Asia Institute (formerly the East Indies Institute of America), devoted to a discussion of some of the postwar problems in Indonesia, insofar as these problems have affected the welfare and life of the Indonesian population. In most instances each article provides the necessary background for an appreciation of a given problem, and in some cases suggestions toward eventual solutions of the problem are considered.

The articles include: Man and resources in the Netherlands Indies by Jan O. M. Broek. Tanah Sobrang and Java's population problem by Karl J. Pelzer. Cross currents of culture in Indonesia by Adriaan J. Barnouw. Some proposals for postwar education in Indonesia by J. F. H. A. de la Court. The role of the Chinese in the Netherlands Indies by Bruno Lasker. One view on the position of the Eurasian in Indonesian society by H. Sjaardema. Labor law and legislation in the Netherlands Indies by A. Arthur Schiller. The development of marine resources in Indonesia by Martin D. Burkenroad. Japan's blueprint for Indonesia by Virginia Thompson. An analysis of nationalism in Southeast Asia by Rupert Emerson.

Brief biographical sketches of the contributors are included.

*Maps:* Netherlands Indies, showing the location of the principal minerals, principal export crops, cultivated rice areas, estate areas, and areas of shifting cultivation. Population densities of the Netherlands Indies.

*Tables:* Land use and densities of Indonesian population in selected districts of Java. Total area and forest area in Indonesia.

*Chart:* Survey of an educational system for the Netherlands East Indies.

372. U.S. NATIONAL SCIENCE FOUNDATION. Scientific Facilities and Information Services of the Republic of Indonesia by John O. Sutter. Honolulu, Published for the National Science Foundation by the Pacific Scientific Information Center, 1961. 136 p.; maps, tables, appendices, index. (Pacific scientific information, no. 1)    In process

*Text:* Presents significant data about the current status of scientific personnel, institutions, and research activity in Indonesia. In order to aid scientists in other parts of the world, it gives a résumé of what has taken place in postwar Indonesia with reference to scientific research and tells about research institutes being given new Indonesian names and now being manned by Indonesians after the Dutch left.

The six chapters, preceding the very worthwhile appendices with a wealth of information, discuss these matters pertinent to the scientific picture in Indonesia:

I. Indonesian background, in which the geographical setting, nature of the society, and government organization are sketched; II. Education for science, which tells about various aspects of Indonesian educational institutions, and the problems being faced; III. Manpower for science and research, emphasizes the shortage for scientists in all fields although the field of medicine is not as acute; IV. Indonesian scientific research institutions and publications, discusses scientific societies and the government control and ownership of these institutions; V. Council for Sciences of Indonesia, describes MIPI (Madjelis Ilmu Pengetabuan Indonesia), its officers, functions, publications and research promotion; VI. Reference works and equipment and international scientific assistance, which points out the importance of foreign publications, and translation services.

*Maps:* Outline maps of Indonesia and Java.

*Tables* (selected): Endemic diseases in Indonesia. Organizations for research and development in the Indonesian Government. Major scientific disciplines.

*Appendices:* Institutions of higher education providing science teaching and research. Research institutions. Scientific publications. Scientific societies. Biographic sketch of Sarwono Prawirohardjo. Conclusions of the 1959 conference of Indonesian scientists. Act establishing MIPI.

373. WALLACE, ALFRED RUSSEL. The Malay Archipelago: the Land of the Orang-utan and the Bird of Paradise; a Narrative of Travel, With Studies of Man and Nature. New York, Dover Publications, 1962. xvii, 515 p.; illustrations, maps, appendix, index.

DS601.W18 1962

*Text:* This volume is an unabridged republication of a book first published almost a century ago by an eminent naturalist who describes with enormous detail much of the natural life as well as the peoples discovered in most of the islands comprising the archipelago of Indonesia.

The work is divided into five systematic groups, according to island groupings, each of which provides an account of the natural history of those islands. The last chapter is a general sketch of the races of man found in the various islands.

*Illustrations:* Ferns, frogs, butterflies, mammals, and birds representative of the more than 125,000 specimens of natural history the author secured.

*Maps* (selected) : Route of expedition. Malay archipelago, showing volcanic belts.

*Appendix:* Languages of the races in the Malay archipelago.

374. WOODMAN, DOROTHY. The Republic of Indonesia. New York, Philosophical Library, 1955. ix, 444 p.; bibliography, map, index.
DS644.W65 1955

*Text:* Divided into four parts. Part one gives a geographical and general description of the principal islands—Java, Sumatra, Kalimantan, Sulawesi, Moluccas, West Irian and Bali; part two describes aspects of religious and political forces in Indonesian culture; part three is a historical account of the transition period during the Japanese occupation and the return of the Dutch; and part four continues the historical events leading up to the Indonesian independence and the problems facing the new republic, including communism.

Selected from the nineteen chapters are: 7. The pattern of Indonesian culture. 8. Islam, Marxism and nationalism. 9. Japanese interlude. 11. Indonesia and the United Nations. 12. The unitary state. 13. Education. 14. Cultural trends in the Republic. 15. Social welfare, public health and medicine. 16. Political parties and trade unions. 17. Building a new economy. 18. Meeting the world. 19. After nationalism.

*Bibliography:* Lists main reference works pertaining to the various chapters. Includes brief list of periodicals and official publications.

*Map:* Outline map of Indonesian archipelago.

375. YALE UNIVERSITY. GRADUATE S C H O O L. SOUTHEAST ASIA STUDIES. Area Handbook on Indonesia. Preliminary edition. New Haven, Southeast Asia Studies, Yale University, for the Human Relations Area Files, 1956.
DS615.Y3

*Text:* This composite product of a group of scholars presents a contemporary survey of the social, political, and economic aspects of Indonesia.

The three volumes contain 31 chapters which analyze various segments and problems of the society: 1. General character of the society. 2. Historical setting. 3. Physical geography. 4. Size and geographical distribution of the population. 5. Ethnic groups. 6. Languages. 7. Social structure. 8. Family. 9. Religion. 10. Social values and patterns. 11. Artistic and intellectual expression. 12. Education. 13.

Health and sanitation. 14. Public welfare. 15. Foreign minority groups. 16. The constitutional system. 17. Structure of government. 18. Political dynamics. 19. Socio-political instabilities. 20. Public order and safety. 21. Public information and propaganda. 22. Foreign policies. 23. Attitudes and reactions of the people. 24. Labor force. 25. Labor relations and organization. 26. Agricultural potential. 27. Industrial potential. 28. Taxation. 29. Banking and currency system. 30. Domestic and foreign trade. 31. Biographies of key personalities.

*Bibliography:* Includes various lists related to certain subjects covered in the survey.

*Maps* (selected) : Population. Ethnic groups. Languages. Provinces and areas. Exports, imports.

*Tables* (selected) : Growth of Indonesian and non-Indonesian population groups. Population and population density. Ethno-linguistic groups of Indonesia. Major languages. Indonesia's balance of trade.

*Charts* (selected) : School system, 1941. Organization structure of the Ministry of Information.

*Appendices* (selected) : Development of the central Indonesian National Committee. Enterprises registered according to law. Major Indonesian exports. Indonesian imports.

# HISTORY, POLITICS, AND GOVERNMENT

376. ANDERSON, BENEDICT R. O'G. Some Aspects of Indonesian Politics Under the Japanese Occupation, 1944–45. Ithaca, Southeast Asia Program, Department of Far Eastern Studies, Cornell University, 1961. ix, 126 p.; (Interim Reports Series, Modern Indonesia Project)
DS643.5.A5

*Text:* Provides significant data about the fiscal year of Japanese occupation of Indonesia, and discusses the events during the very early critical months of the independence when the revolutionary forces acquired their first institutional form. This account is admittedly based on written documentary materials available in America, and therefore gives only an initial part of a larger view of the entire revolutionary period (1945–49) which is now being explored by research in Indonesia.

Selected chapters are: 1. Japanese policies and perspectives. 6. The independence proclamation. 8. The final conflict with the Japanese and the beginnings of a new regime.

377. BENDA, HARRY JINDRICH. The Crescent and the Rising Sun; Indonesian Islam Under the Japanese Occupation, 1942–1945. The Hague, Bandung, W. van Hoeve, 1958. xv, 320 p.; bibliography, index. (Distributed in U.S.A. by Institute of Pacific Relations, New York) DS643.5.B4

*Text:* This contribution to the historiography of Indonesia is a well-documented account of Indonesian Islam, particularly the Islamic reform movement, during the regime of the Japanese occupation of Indonesia during World War II. This historical study with sociological insight does not present a full-scale historical account of the Japanese rule in Indonesia but provides a clear-cut analysis of the Islamic policy of the Japanese authorities.

Prior to the core of the study, the author describes a significant reinterpretation of the Islamic faith in Indonesia under Dutch colonial rule, emphasizing both the political and religious aspects of the movement.

Contents: 1. Indonesian Islam and the foundations of Dutch Islamic policy. 2. The renaissance of Indonesian Islam. 3. Challenge and response: Indonesian Islam in the closing years of Dutch rule. 4. Trial and error, April–December, 1942. 5. Indonesian Islam and the spirit of Dai Nippon. 6. The consolidation of Japan's Islamic policy during 1943. 7. The rise of Masjumi, November 1943–September 1944. 8. Towards independence, September 1944–August 1945.

*Bibliography:* Partially annotated list of valuable references, given in four parts—official documents; newspapers; periodicals, Dutch and Japanese; and books.

[Another study dealing with the Japanese occupation in Indonesian, more general in scope, is *Nederlandsch-Indie onder Japanse bezetting; gegevens en documenten over de jaren 1942–1945,* samengesteld onder leiding van I. J. Brugmans, door H. J. de Graaf, A. H. Joustra en A. G. Vromans. Franeker, T. Wever, 1960. 661 p.; illustrations. DS643.5.B4]

378. BENDA, HARRY JINDRICH, and RUTH T. McVEY, eds. The Communist Uprisings of 1926–1927 in Indonesia: Key Documents. Ithaca, Southeast Asia Program, Department of Far Eastern Studies, Cornell University, 1960. xxxi, 177 p.; maps, appendices. (Translation series, Modern Indonesian Project) DS643.B4

*Text:* Given limited circulation until now, these three significant reports give a fuller understanding of the uprising of the Communist Party in Indonesia and the conditions which nurtured it. The three reports are: Governor General's report in 1927 which provides information about the Indonesian Communist Party; the Bantam report which contains the findings of the Commission installed to investigate the causes of the disturbances in the residency of Bantam; and the West Coast of Sumatra report which tells about the Communist activities in Sumatra.

The long introduction by the editors both sketch the significance of the Communist revolts in the twenties and assess their intrinsic meaning.

*Maps:* Location of the Indonesian Communist Party in Indonesia.

*Appendices:* Crimes, taxes, religion, desa heads.

379. BONE, ROBERT C., JR. The Dynamics of the Western New Guinea (Irian Barat) Problem. Ithaca, Southeast Asia Program, Department of Far Eastern Studies, Cornell University, 1958. x, 170 p.; map, appendix. (Monograph series, Modern Indonesian Project) DS744.5.B6

*Text:* A scholarly approach to the relevant historical background which provides a rather full account of the contemporary factors, which shape the Dutch Indonesian problem. The author, having a substantial knowledge of modern history and contemporary politics of Indonesia and the Netherlands, with considerable residence in each of these countries where he could use the Indonesian and Dutch languages, is well qualified to prepare this study.

Recognizes that West Irian is an area which holds a symbolic value in excess of its intrinsic worth. The issue embodies the aspects of the colonial-anticolonial conflict, and represents for the Indonesian the fact that as long as the Dutch are in West Irian, the national revolution has not reached fulfillment. Adversely the Dutch consider it their moral mission to prepare the people of West Irian for self-government and believe that the area is valuable as a defensive bastion in the Pacific.

The five chapters consider: Background facts; The legal basis of the Dutch claims to West New Guinea; The origin and development of the Irian issue, 1946–49; The Irian issue in Dutch-Indonesian relations, 1950–53; The Irian issue in the world forum, 1953–58.

*Map:* The Moluccan Archipelago.

*Appendix:* Voting in the U.N. General Assembly on West Irian issue.

380. BRACKMAN, ARNOLD C. Indonesian Communism: A History. New York, Praeger, 1963. xvi, 336 p.; bibliography, tables, index. (Praeger publications in Russian history and world communism, no. 123)   HX402.B7

*Text:* Traces the strategy and tactics followed by the leaders of the Partai Kommunis Indonesia (PKI) during its history in Indonesia since the days of World War I. Examines the policy of Indonesian communism toward the August Revolution (1945), the Dutch regime and a colonial power, the Chinese question, Sukarno's "guided democracy," the explosive problem of West Irian. The closing chapter, A double game, analyzes the conflict between the PKI and the Indonesian army.

Considerable biographical data on the Communist leaders Tan Malaka, D. N. Aidit, Amir Sjarfuddin, and others is provided.

*Bibliography:* Brings together reference to books and articles on Communism and nationalism in Indonesia.

*Tables* (selected): Returns of Indonesia's first general election.

381. COLLINS, J. FOSTER. "The United Nations and I n d o n e s i a." *International Conciliation,* March 1950, no. 459: 115–200; maps, appendix.   DS644.C63

*Text:* Prepared by a former member of the United Nations Secretariat with the Committee of Good Offices, this survey describes the role of the United Nations in the Dutch-Indonesian problem from the day when the issue was first brought before the Security Council in February 1946 until the conclusion of the Hague Conference. The problems and political developments which engendered the dispute are related.

*Maps:* Political subdivisions in Indonesia after the Linggadjati Agreement. Political subdivisions in Indonesia after the Renville Agreement. Political divisions in Indonesia after the Hague Conference.

*Appendix:* Selected resolutions adopted by the Security Council on the Indonesian Question.

382. FEITH, HERBERT. The Decline of Constitutional Democracy in Indonesia. Ithaca, Cornell University Press, 1962. xx, 618 p.; maps, tables, index. (Published under the auspices of the Modern Indonesia Project, Southeast Asia Program, Cornell University)
DS644.F4

*Text:* The first major study of the postrevolutionary political development in Indonesia, describing and analyzing Indonesian government and politics during the crucial and formative period from the time of independence in 1949 until the time in 1957 when parliamentary democracy was overshadowed by "guided democracy." Relates the relevant historical background and the social and economic factors which have proved to be decisive influences in Indonesia's political course.

The kaleidoscopic complexity of Indonesian politics is clearly outlined in these eleven chapters: 1. The heritage of revolution. 2. The Hatta Cabinet, December 1949—August 1950: transition and unification. 3. The elements of politics. 4. The Natsir Cabinet, September 1950—March 1951: "Administrators" thwarted. 5. The Sukiman Cabinet, April 1951—February 1952: the slowing of momentum. 6. The Wilopo Cabinet, April 1952—June 1953: the breakthrough which failed. 7. From Hatta to Wilopo: some trends unfold. 8. The first cabinet of Ali Sastroamidjojo, July 1953—July 1955: the rise of the parties. 9. The Burhanuddin Harahap Cabinet, August 1955—March 1956: the elections and after. 10. The second cabinet of Ali Sastroamidjojo, March 1956—March 1957: the eclipse of the parties and the rise of their heirs. 11. Conclusion.

*Map:* Indonesia in December 1949. Indonesia in early 1957.

*Tables* (selected): Parties and parliamentary representation, March 1951. Natsir Cabinet. Sukiman Cabinet. Ali Cabinet. Harahap Cabinet. The results of parliamentary elections, 1956.

383. FISCHER, LOUIS. The Story of Indonesia. New York, Harper, 1959. x, 341 p.; bibliography, illustrations, index.   DS634.F5

*Text:* The opening chapters of part one present a rapidly moving but accurate historical account of Indonesia from the early times of Marco Polo down to the present decade of independence, including good summary accounts of the coming of the Portuguese and Spanish and the long colonial period under the British and the Dutch. Other chapters relate the Japanese invasion in 1942 and interpret clearly the subsequent bitter struggle of the Indonesians for their freedom from Dutch control.

Part two, comprising more than half of the text, deals with Indonesian persons, events, and problems that have emerged within the past decade of independence. Among the persons discussed at length are these who are currently prominent in Indonesia: Sukarno, Moh. Hatta, Wilopo, Abdul Nasution, Ali Sastroamidjojo, and Djuanda.

Indonesia, like the other liberated nations of Southeast Asia, now faces a variety of difficult economic, political and social problems. In discussing the problems of West Irian, the October 17 affair, industrialization and economic development, population growth and birth control, "guided democracy," pressure of communism, and the foreign policy of the United States toward Indonesia, this analytic journalist raises questions of deep importance to the West.

*Bibliography:* List of secondary sources for general background reading.

*Illustrations:* Sukarno, Moh. Hatta, General Nasution, Ruslon Abdulgani. General views of Indonesian life.

384. FURNIVALL, JOHN SYDENHAM. Netherlands India: A Study of Plural Economy. With an introduction by Jonkheer Mr. A.C.D. de Graeff. Cambridge [Eng.] University Press, 1939. xxii, 502 p.; bibliography, maps, tables, glossary, index.　　　　DS634.F8

*Text:* A study of the economic, political, and social developments in Indonesia during the Dutch regime, with particular reference to the nature of a "plural society"—a society in which distinct social orders exist separately, side by side, within the same political unit. Depicts the various stages from the 17th to the 20th centuries in the history of the political and economic development of Indonesia, and traces in each stage the course of economic progress and the principal features of the social economy.

Among the topics discussed are the "culture system" employed in the 19th century; the indigenous movement of "Barihat Islam"; industrial disputes and communism; agricultural production; mineral production; industry; communications; commerce; labor and trade unionism; education; finance; the Chinese community; effects of the crisis in 1929; and, nationalism in a plural economy.

*Bibliography:* Each chapter concludes with a brief list of references. A longer list of books, official documents, and periodicals concludes the study.

*Maps:* Netherlands India, including leading cities and seaports.

*Tables:* Deal with imports and exports in the 19th century; agricultural capital in Java and Sumatra; crop production; irrigation in Java; mineral produc-

tion; growth of population, 1852–1930; and pupils in educational institutions, 1930–31.

*Glossary:* Brief list of terms used in text.

[Also published in 1944 with same title by Macmillan Co. in New York]

385. GOETHALS, PETER R. Aspects of Local Government in a Sumbawan Village (Eastern Indonesia). Ithaca, Southeast Asia Program, Department of Far Eastern Studies, Cornell University, 1961. vii, 143 p.; bibliography, map, glossary. (Monograph series, Modern Indonesia Project)　　　JS7205.S6G6

*Text:* Presents selected aspects of an Indonesian village government, which reveal certain post-colonial social and political changes. Based on two years of intensive research in the Moslem village of Rarak in western Sumbawa, an island east of Java, the study will be of particular interest to the political scientist or the sociologist who desires information on village civil government, village religious authority, problems related to marriage, kinship structure, and relevant topics.

*Bibliography:* Lists books and articles dealing with village structure and patterns of behaviour in various parts of Southeast Asia.

*Map:* Outline map of Sumbawa Island.

*Glossary:* Lists Indonesian, Sumbawan, Dutch, Japanese, Arabic and Makassarese words used in the text.

[Another item in the Monograph Series dealing with local village government is *Some social-anthropological observations on gotong rojong practices in two villages of central Java* by Koentjaraningrat. Translated by Claire Holt, 1961.]

386. GOULD, JAMES W. Americans in Sumatra. The Hague, Nijhoff, 1961. vii. 185 p.; bibliography, tables, index.　　E183.8.S75G6

*Text:* Based on a thesis written at the Fletcher School, it provides a historical account of the relation which America has had with Sumatra through the activity of both individual Americans or American commercial and industrial firms.

The five chapters are entitled: 1. The growing interdependence of Sumatra of the United States, 1873 to the present. 2. Black gold: the history of American enterprise in Indonesian oil development. 3. Wealth from trees: the history of American enterprise in Indonesian rubber. 4. American contributions to education, religious and secular. 5. Scholar-adventurers.

*Bibliography:* Lists American writings on Sumatra.

*Tables* (selected): U.S. Counsulor officers in Sumatra, 1833–1960. Growth of American investment in Sumatra, 1909–59. U.S. imports of rubber from Netherlands Indies. American missions in Sumatra, 1960.

386a. HAAR, BAREND TER. Adat law in Indonesia. Translated from the Dutch by George C. O. Haas and Margaret Hordyk, and edited by E. Adamson Hoebel and A. Arthur Schiller. Djakarta, Bhratara, 1962. xvi, 280 p.; bibliography, map, tables, indices.          Law

*Text:* Formerly published in 1948 by the Institute of Pacific Relations, this study is a translation of the major part of a book entitled *Beginselen en stelsel van het adatrecht* (Groningen, Batavia, J.B. Wolters, 1939) by a Dutch jurist who prepared the book originally for persons interested in the study of *adat* law, particularly for students of the Law College in Batavia.

The study has two principal approaches: first, to describe the characteristic features of Indonesian legal institutions, legal relations, and legal acts in such a way that the principles and the system of *adat* law become clear and understandable; and second, to indicate the factors that affect the nature and modification of *adat* law, and the social circumstances which promote or counteract particular characteristics of it. A fairly copious survey is also provided of the structure of the autonomous communities, which, the author states, are the foundation of the territorial structure on which *adat* law acts.

The fifteen chapters which comprise the study deal with the social organization of the autonomous communities; land rights, and land transactions; obligations involving land; the law of family relationship; laws pertaining to marriage, divorce, and marital property; inheritance; the relation of statutory criminal law and *adat* law; and the time factor in *adat* law.

The lengthy and well-documented introduction by Professor Hoebel, Associate Professor of Anthropology at New York university, and Professor Schiller, Associate Professor of Law at Columbia University, seeks to place in proper setting the subject matter presented by Mr. ter Haar. The editors emphasize certain legal aspects of the customary practices of the Indonesian people by discussing the place of law in the native culture and the place of *adat* law in the legal system.

*Bibliography:* Chapter fifteen, *Adat* law literature, gives in essay form the works dealing with Indonesian customary law under five heads: the studies of van Vollenhoven, case law, *adat* law areas, *adat* law topics, and *adat* law policy.

*Map:* Law areas of Indonesia.

*Tables:* Administration of justice over native inhabitants. Geographical table of administration of justice.

387. INDONESIA (REPUBLIC). DEPARTMENT OF INFORMATION. Handbook on the Political Manifesto: Two Executive Directions of Manipol. Djakarta, [1961]. 160 p.
          In process

*Text:* This official document issued by the Government of Indonesia outlines the basic guidelines of Indonesian foreign policy as unanimously adopted by the Provisional People's Consultative Assembly and the Supreme Advisory Council. The document consists principally of these two addresses by President Sukarno: "The march of our revolution," given in Djakarta on 17 August anniversary, and "To build the world anew," given before the U.N. General Assembly. The West Irian issue is the principal focus in the first address.

388. INDONESIA (REPUBLIC). DEPARTMENT OF INFORMATION. The Indonesian Revolution: Basic Documents and the Idea of Guided Democracy. Djakarta, 1960. 122 p.
          JQ763 1960.I6

*Text:* Following an introduction on how the various documents emerged, the translated text of these Indonesian documents are given: The birth of Pantja Sila. The Djakarta charter. The proclamation of Indonesia's independence. The 1945 Constitution. Elucidation of the Constitution of the State of Indonesia. The idea of guided democracy. Some of these documents, *e.g.,* The birth of Pantja Sila, are addresses of President Sukarno.

389. KAHIN, GEORGE McTURNAN. "Indonesia." In *Major governments of Asia* edited by George McT. Kahin. Ithaca, Cornell University Press, 1961. p. 471–607; bibliography, table, chart.          JQ5.K3

*Text:* Part five in a study of comparative government devoted to the five largest states of Asia—China, India, Japan, Indonesia, and Pakistan. Presents a succinct survey of Indonesian government from the time of pre-Dutch control down to the present day, with these chapter headings: 19. The precolonial and colonial background. 20. The revolution and the revolutionary government. 21. The postrevolutionary setting. 22. Government and politics in postrevolutionary Indonesia. 23. Some major problems. Following a clear discussion of indirect rule by the Dutch and the emergence of Indonesian nationalism, the emphasis is upon the development of governmental structure and policies in postwar Indonesia.

*Bibliography:* Ten pages of significant titles dealing with the subject of government, including foreign policy.

*Table:* Assessments for purposes of income tax, 1925–40.

390. KAHIN, GEORGE MCTURNAN. Nationalism and Revolution in Indonesia. Ithaca, N.Y., Cornell University Press, 1952. xii, 490 p.; bibliography, maps, index. (Published under the auspices of the International Secretariat of the Institute of Pacific Relations and the Southeast Asia Program, Cornell University) DS644.K32

*Text:* This comprehensive and well-documented study traces the development of the Indonesian nationalist movement from the time when the Saminist movement was organized in the very late 19th century down to the unitarian movement in early 1950.

Contents: 1. The social environment of Indonesian nationalism. 2. Genesis of the Indonesian nationalist movement. 3. History of the nationalist movement until 1942. 4. The Japanese occupation. 5. Outbreak of the revolution. 6. The internal politics of the revolution until the first Dutch military action. 7. War and United Nations intervention. 8. Aftermath of the Renville Agreement. 9. The internal struggle for power from Renville through the Communist rebellion. 10. Ideological orientations and the development of internal politics, October–December 19, 1948. 11. The second Dutch military action and the United Nations' reaction. 12. The strategy and tactics of indirect rule. 13. The final struggle and the Republic's victory. 14. The Unitarian Movement. 15. Achievements and prospects.

*Bibliography:* Located in the voluminous footnotes.

*Maps:* 1. Netherlands East Indies. 2. Java showing Renville truce line. 3. Federal Indonesia. 4. Unitary Indonesia.

391. LEGGE, JOHN DAVID. Central Authority and Regional Autonomy in Indonesia; a Study in Local Administration, 1950–1960. Ithaca, Cornell University Press, 1961. xiii, 291 p.; bibliography, maps, tables, charts, glossary, appendices, index. (Published under the

auspices of the Modern Indonesia Project, Southeast Asia Program, Cornell University) JS7193.A8L4

*Text:* A study which addresses itself to the problem of fashioning democratic institutions at the local level in Indonesia where government has been traditionally the task of a body of professional Dutch administrators. Particular attention is given to the attempt of the Indonesian Government to devise a system of local government within the unitary state which would satisfy local needs, and at the same time counteract tendencies toward regional separatism.

*Bibliography:* Cites the legislation relating to basic laws concerning regional government, regional representative councils, and the laws in the various regions in Indonesia.

*Maps* (selected): First level regions of Indonesia, 1960. Federal Indonesia.

*Tables* (selected): 1. Population of individual provinces. 4. Distribution of central taxes.

*Charts:* 1. Organization of health services in East Java. 2. Organization of the office of *bupati/kepala daerah* in East Java.

*Glossary:* Indonesian terms used in text.

*Appendices:* A. Seats held by the four main parties, 1956–1957. B. Extracts from Law 22 of 1948 relating to the position of *Kepala Daerah*. C. Extracts from Law 1 of 1957. D. Extracts from Presidential Edict no. 6 of 1959.

[Also published in 1944 with same title by Macmillan & Co. in New York]

392. MCVEY, RUTH THOMAS. The Development of the Indonesian Communist Party and Its Relations With the Soviet Union and the Chinese People's Republic. Cambridge, Center for International Studies, Massachusetts Institute of Technology, 1954. 97, 32 p.; bibliography. JQ779.A5K65

*Text:* Traces the history of Indonesian communism in the context of the Indonesian Communist Party's relation to the international Communist movement with reference to the Soviet Union and the Chinese People's Republic. This study of the only Communist Party in non-communist Asia which supports the government in power follows the party policy through the three principal stages of Indonesian history during this century: the colonial period, when communism achieved the leadership of the non-cooperative Indonesian nationalist movement; the period of the rebellion, when the Communist Party reached its greatest power; and the current period, when the Communists occupy a powerful position as the champions of Indonesian ultra-nationalism.

*Bibliography:* A list of over 150 references in newspapers and periodicals, and official Communist documents.

[Two corollary publications are: *Summary of the development of the Indonesian Communist Party and its relations with the Soviet Union* by Ruth McVey. Cambridge, Center for International Studies, M.I.T., 1954, 10 p.; JP1779.A5K652. *The Soviet view of the Indonesian revolution; a study in the Russian attitude towards Asian nationalism.* Ithaca, Modern Indonesia Project, Southeast Asia Program, Cornell University, 1957. iii, 83 p. (Interim report series) DS640.R8M3]

393. NEDERLANDS GENOOTSCHAP VOOR INTERNATIONALE ZAKEN. Indonesia's Struggle, 1957–1958, a report prepared under the direction of B. H. M. Vlekke. The Hague, 1959. 76 p.; tables, charts. (Distributed in cooperation with the Institute of Pacific Relations, New York) DS644.N4

*Text:* Following a series of events in 1957 and 1958 which resulted in a fierce and more heated controversy between Indonesia and the Dutch, and later the outburst of civil war, this booklet presented an evaluation of the political, the economic, and the constitutional and social problems of Indonesia.

The three articles, written by three persons are as follows: The political situation in Indonesia by Vishal Singh. The high cost of political instability in Indonesia, 1957–58 by Douglas Paauw. The campaign against nationalist Chinese in Indonesia by V. Hanssens.

*Tables:* Election results in 1955, 1957–58.

*Charts:* 1. Money supply, 1957. 2. Food prices, 1956–57.

394. PALMIER, LESLIE H. Indonesia and the Dutch. London, New York, Oxford University Press, 1962. xii, 194 p.; bibliography, maps, table, index. (Issued under the auspices of the Institute of Race Relations, London)
DS640.N4P3

*Text:* Serving as a supplement to *Nationalism and revolution in Indonesia* by Kahin, this study brings into focus most of the events related to the Indonesian nationalist movement during the decade from 1952 to 62.

Selected chapter headings are: 4. Education for discontent. 6. Japan in occupation. 8. Sovereignty

comes to Indonesia. 9. Indonesian-Netherlands links under strain. 10. The end of the Hague agreement. 11. The final rupture. 12. The Western New Guinea dispute. 14. Internal disorders. 15. External symptoms.

*Bibliography:* Lists mostly well-known secondary works.

*Maps* (selected): Indonesia, showing ethnic groups. Dutch first police action. Republic of the United States of Indonesia, 1949.

*Table:* Ethno-linguistic groups of Indonesia.

395. PAUKER, GUY. The Role of the Military in Indonesia. Santa Monica, Calif., Rand Corporation, 1961. 65 p. (Rand Corporation Research memorandum RM–2637–RC)
Q180.A1R36 RM 2637

*Text:* Constitutes one chapter in a forthcoming volume on the role of the military in underdeveloped areas. Also, this monograph is one in a series on the emerging political structure of Indonesia.*

Contends that the instability, both political and economic, which is manifest in present day Indonesia is due to military authoritarianism and intrigue. It appears that military officers have been awarded important cabinet posts and other ministerial positions.

396. PRINGGODIGDO, A. K. The Office of President in Indonesia as Defined in the Three Constitutions in Theory and Practice. Translated by Alexander Brotherton. Ithaca, Southeast Asia Program, Dept. of Far Eastern Studies, Cornell University, 1957. ix, 59 p.; appendices. (Translation series, Modern Indonesian Project) JQ771.P7

*Text:* Because Sukarno has been the most prominent leader of the Indonesian revolution and successful struggle for independence and simultaneously has been the nation's first president for well over a decade, the office of the Indonesian presidency has become a highly important institution in Indonesia—rivaled in few countries, Western or Asian.

This examination of the constitutional status of the Presidency and the role of the President in state affairs is divided into these three parts: The provisions of the 1945 Constitution and the application of these provisions; The provisions of the 1949 Constitution;

*[Indonesian images of their national self (P–1452–RC). The role of political organization in Indonesia (P–1514–RC). Recent Communistic tactics in Indonesia. (RM–2619–RC).]

and the 1950 Constitution and the application of these provisions.

*Appendices:* Extracts from reports of Chamber of Representatives committees on expenditures allocated to the President and the Vice President for 1951. Extracts from the government statement in reply to reports of Chamber of Representatives committees on expenditures allocated to the President and the Vice President for 1951.

397. ROUND TABLE CONFERENCE, THE HAGUE, 1949. Results as Accepted in the Second Plenary Meeting Held on 2 November 1949 in the "Ridderzaal" at The Hague ['s Gravenhage, 1949]. Secretariat-General of the Round Table Conference, 1949. 126, 56 p.; map, appendices. DS644.R67 1949d

*Text:* This volume is a documentary sourcebook which provides the agreements arrived at during the Round Table Conference in late 1949 when the Indonesian and Dutch delegations met to determine the way to transfer real, complete, and unconditional sovereignty to the Republic of the United States of Indonesia in accordance with the Renville principles.

The draft agreements include: (1) the draft Charter of Transfer of Sovereignty. (2) the draft Union Statute including special agreements on the principal subjects of future cooperation. (3) the draft Agreement on Transitional Measures, including special agreements on the settlement of those subjects, which require provisions as a result of the transfer of sovereignty.

Within the Exchange of Letters section are letters of the Chairman of the Netherlands Delegation, the Chairman of the Republican Delegation, and the Chairman of the Delegation of the Federal Consultative Assembly, which were written on the subject of the above draft agreements.

All of these documents were also issued elsewhere, in the Dutch and Indonesian languages.

*Map:* Naval base at Surabaja.

*Appendices:* List of trade and monetary agreements in which Indonesia participates. Draft Constitution of the Republic of the United States of Indonesia (full text).

398. SCHILLER, A. ARTHUR. The Formation of Federal Indonesia, 1945–1949. The Hague, Bandung, W. van Hoeve, 1955. x, 472 p.; bibliography, tables, indexes. JQ762.S35

*Text:* A description of the steps taken in the formation of the structure for the federal state of Indonesia from 1945 to 1949. For purposes of background there is included a summary statement of the policies and institutions during the Dutch regime and the military government at the time of the war. Although the author gave his impressions as gathered from government officers in the central Secretariat, the negara ministries, and in local councils, the core of the book is primarily an explanation and interpretation of the abundance of documents he used.

The five chapter headings: 1. The concept of the Federal State. 2. The central government. 3. Local government. 4. The distribution of the powers of government. 5. The administration of justice.

*Bibliography:* A list of book and periodical articles cited more fully in the voluminous notes to the text.

*Tables:* List of abbreviations used for government bodies and organizations. Technical terms and designations in English, Dutch, and Indonesian.

399. SCHILLER, A. ARTHUR. Legal and Administrative Problems of the Netherlands Indies. New York, International Secretariat, Institute of Pacific Relations, 1945. [iii], 43 l. (Secretariat paper no. 7, 9th Conference, Institute of Pacific Relations, Hot Springs, Va.) JQ763 1945.S3

*Text:* A document prepared for a conference of the I.P.R. by a Professor of Law at Columbia University who has done considerable study of Indonesian *adat* law.*

Comprised of three chapters of distinctively different nature, which present valuable information regarding Indonesian law and government administration. Chapter one, Problems of political autonomy in Indonesia, treats of one significant factor in public law: Indonesia's right "to complete self-government in the shortest possible time, and that the people of Indonesia are the ones who shall decide the means by which that autonomy shall be accomplished". Chapter two, Pluralism and conflict of laws, outlines the problems to be faced in a society formed of heterogeneous elements, and deals with private international law, interregional law, interracial law, and interlocal law. Chapter three, Labor law and legislation, shows the structure of a particular field of law as it has evolved in a plural society, and states the essential facts in the status of labor laws before 1926 and the conflict problems in labor legislation.

-------
*[See *Adat law in Indonesia* by Barend ter Haar.]

400. Selosoemardjan. Social Changes in Jogjakarta. Ithaca, Cornell University Press, 1962. xxvii, 440 p.; bibliography, map, tables, charts, glossary, index. (Published under the auspices of the Modern Indonesia Project, Southeast Asia Program, Cornell University)

HN707.S4

*Text:* The focal theme of this study is centered on the changes which have taken place in the Special Region of Jogjakarta in central Java subsequent to the Dutch colonial period (1755–1942), commencing with the Japanese occupation period from 1942 to 1945, and continuing through the struggle for national independence from 1945 to 1949.

This specialized study of social and political change in Central Java is divided into 5 parts with 11 chapters: I. Changes in the administration of Jogjakarta: 1. The habitat. 2. Jogjakarta under the Dutch regime. 3. The Japanese occupation period. 4. Jogjakarta since independence. II. Administrative political parties and society. 5. Administration and society since independence. 6. Political parties, and society. III. Social change and economic development. 7. The peasant agriculture. 8. Foreign enterprises. 9. Social problems of economic development. IV. Education and social change. 10. Education and social change. V. Conclusion. 11. Theoretical comments.

*Bibliography:* Bibliographical references in footnotes.

*Map:* Daerah Istimewa Jogjakarta, Special Region of Jogjakarta.

*Tables* (selected): 3. Bureaus and offices in Kulon Progo.

*Charts:* 1. Jogjakarta's administrative organization during Dutch colonial period after 1918. 2. Jogjakarta's administrative organization in 1946 prior to reorganization. 3. Jogjakarta's administrative organization, 1946–58. 4. Jogjakarta's administrative organization based on Law no. 1/1957 realized in 1958. 5. Jogjakarta's administrative organization based on Presidential decree no. 6/1959.

*Glossary:* Javanese and Indonesian terms used in text.

401. Sjahrir, Soetan. Out of Exile. . . . based upon letters by Soetan Sjahrir rewritten and edited in Dutch by Maria Duchâteau-Sjahrir. Translated with an introduction, by Charles Wolf, Jr. New York, John Day, 1949. xxiii, 265 p.; glossary. (An Asia book)

DS644.S513 1949

*Text:* The author is a prominent person in the story of the Indonesian Revolution: the one who presented the case of the Indonesian Republic at the Security Council of the United Nations, and an individual Indonesian thinker competent to compare, analyze, and interpret both Eastern and Western culture.

The volume is composed mainly of the letters written by this Indonesian nationalist during a part of his long period of imprisonment, 1934—42. The letters in Part one were written to his Dutch wife in Holland, later to be published by his wife in 1945 under the pseudonym Sjahrazad (*Indonesische Overpeinzingen,* Amsterdam, Bezige Bij). Although written in Tjipinang, Boven Digoel, and at Banda Neira—the places where he was imprisoned—the letters are not bitter toward the Dutch nor colored with a morbid melancholy but give his analysis of the attributes and weaknesses of the rationalism and science of the West and the mysticism and fatalism of the East. The writings contain his discussions of the prewar colonial policy of the Dutch in Indonesia and show how colonial society in Indonesia was undergoing marked changes fully a decade before the war came to Indonesia.

Part two, written by Sjahrir in 1947, outlines the historical events in Indonesia after the outbreak of war in Europe during World War II. Whereas the letters came from an idealist, the historical part is that of a pragmatist.

*Glossary:* Unfamiliar names used in the text.

402. The South Moluccas: Rebellious Province or Occupied State, by J. C. Bouman, and others. Leyden, A. W. Sythoff, 1960. 196 p.; bibliography, map, biographical sketches.

DS646.6.S62

*Text:* Comprises a series of papers in English setting forth the basis of the struggle for independence desired by residents of various islands in the eastern portion of the Indonesian archipelago called the South Moluccas.

The chapters, by professors, lawyers, engineers, and others are: 1. Location, history, forgotten struggle by J. Prins. 2. Political aspects of the struggle for independence by J. A. Manusama. 3. The legal position according to international law by Gesina H. J. van der Molen. 4. Relation to the United Nations by N. J. C. M. Kappeyne van der Copello. 5. An existing state by H. J. Roethof. 6. The strategic importance in the world picture of present and future by H. J. Kruls. 7. The strategic position by D. E. L. Helfrich. 8. Ecclesiastical aspects by W. H. Tutuarima. 9. Social-psychological aspects by Jan. C.

Bouman. 10. Anthropological aspects by Gerard Louwrens Tichelman.

403. SUBANDRIO, HURUSTIATI. Indonesia on the March: The Collected Speeches of H. E. Dr. Subandrio Delivered While Ambassador of the Republic of Indonesia to the Court of St. James, 1950–1954. Djakarta, Djambatan, 1959. 146 p.; illustrations.        DS644.S75

*Text:* Describes the changes and developments of Indonesia and her relationship with other countries. Also reveals the manifold problems confronting Indonesia and the other newly independent nations of Asia.

Selected titles of speeches include: A new approach to Southeast Asia. Trial of communism and Western democracy in Southeast Asia. State and peasantry in Indonesia. Contemporary problem of Southeast Asia. The future of Southeast Asia.

404. SUKARNO, PRESIDENT OF INDONESIA. "Pantjasila—the basic philosophy of the Indonesian State." *Indonesian Review.* January 1951, p. 11–18.        DS611.I526 1951

*Text:* Discusses the five principles underlying the Indonesian State and the Indonesian Constitution: national consciousness or nationalism—the belief in the national unity of all Indonesia; humanity or internationalism—a respect for all humanity throughout the world, and a desire to unite with the peoples of all nations to promote world peace; democracy—the principle of representative government; social justice—a belief in social, economic, and political equality, whereby all members of the state work together to secure prosperity for all; and belief in God—the basic foundation of religious freedom, whereby every person is free to worship according to his own religious faith.

These principles are summed up in the term of *gotong royong*, or "Mutual assistance," the basic spirit of the ancient Indonesian philosophy.

405. SUKARNO, PRESIDENT OF INDONESIA. Toward Freedom and the Dignity of Man: A Collection of Five Speeches by President Sukarno of the Republic of Indonesia. Djakarta, Dept. of Foreign Affairs, [1961]. 163 p.; appendix.        In process

*Text:* The five addresses are entitled: 1. The birth of Pantja Sila, an outline of the Five Principals of the Indonesian State, June 1, 1945. 2. Address to the joint session of the U.S. Congress, May 17, 1956. 3. The rediscovery of our revolution, political mani-

festo, August 17, 1959. 4. "Like an angel that strikes from the skies," the march of our revolution, August 17, 1960. 5. To build the world anew, September 30, 1960.

*Appendix:* Supreme Advisory Council decision respecting specification of the political manifesto of the Republic of Indonesia of 17 August 1959.

406. TAYLOR, ALASTAIR MacDONALD. Indonesian
407.     Independence and the United Nations. With a foreword by Lester B. Pearson. Ithaca, Cornell University Press, 1960. xxix, 503 p.; bibliography, maps, chronology, appendices, index. (Published under the auspices of the Carnegie Endowment for International Peace)        JX1977.2.I5T3

*Text:* Records the struggle which occurred during the postwar years when Indonesia made the transition from the colonial era to independent sovereign status. It is not a complete review of the history of Indonesian nationalism, but an analysis of the basic issues in the Indonesian-Netherlands relations and how the United Nations brought the whole question into the international arena to resolve the dispute.

Besides the use of U.N. official documents, the writer has drawn on his own first-hand experience as a member of the U.N. Secretariat serving with the Security Council's field office in Indonesia thereby augmenting his information by interviews with individuals possessing specialized knowledge on the Indonesian Question.

*Bibliography:* Important U.N. documents on the Indonesian problem supplemented with secondary sources in books and articles.

*Maps:* 1. Netherlands East Indies showing Southeast Asia and Australian Commands in 1945. 2. Results of the first Police Action. 3. United States of Indonesia; 1949.

*Chronology:* Events in the Indonesian Question, August 17, 1945 to April 3, 1951.

*Appendices* (selected): 1. Resolutions on the Indonesian Question adopted by the Security Council. 3. Text of the Linggadjati Agreements. 4. The Renville political principles. 5. Comparison of the Cochran Plan and Netherlands counter proposals. 7. The debt position of Indonesia at the time of the transfer of sovereignty, 1949.

[An official Indonesian publication on this same subject is *The Question of West Irian in the United Nations, 1954–1957,* issued by Kementerian Luar Negari or Ministry of Foreign Affairs in 1958 at Djakarta]

408. UNITED NATIONS. SECRETARIAT. DEPARTMENT OF PUBLIC INFORMATION. Peaceful Settlement in Indonesia. New York, 1951. 20 p.; map. (United Nations publications. 1951.I.6) DS644.U23

*Text:* Tells in a succinct and clear manner the part which the United Nations played in bringing about the independence of Indonesia from the time when the Republic of Indonesia proclaimed its independence, just after the Japanese surrender in August 1945, to the time when Indonesian sovereignty was formally transferred to the United States of Indonesia in December 1949.

Summarizes the salient facts relevant to the achievement of Indonesian independence, emphasizing the pact which the Committee of Good Officers made (later the UNCI—United Nations Commission for Indonesia) in bringing about the Renville Agreement, and various talks which led to the Round Table Conference in The Hague.

A chronology of events concludes the account.

*Map:* Pictorial map showing the principal products of Indonesia.

409. VANDENBOSCH, AMRY. The Dutch East Indies, Its Government, Problems and Politics. Berkeley and Los Angeles, University of California Press, 1941. 2nd ed. xii, 446 p.; bibliography, map, tables, appendices, index. DS615.V3 1941

*Text:* A comprehensive account of the Dutch colonial policy, administration, and economic progress in Indonesia up to World War II. Following a few introductory chapters dealing with the land and people, population, economic stratification along racial lines, and religion, the main part of the study deals with the colonial policy of the Dutch in the development of the East Indian Company, the constitutional changes and parliamentary control, the powers and responsibilities of the Governor-General, the Volksraad, the governmental organization and the position and powers of the native states, and the preservation and study of *adat* or customary law. The social and economic development is presented in sections dealing with the educational system, commercial policy, land tenure, constructive social measures, labor problems, taxation and finance, Indonesian nationalism and political parties, national defense, and the place of Indonesia in world politics.

A closing chapter tells of Japanese-Indonesian relations.

*Bibliography:* An extensive list which includes official documents, books, and pamphlets, the major portion of which are in Dutch.

*Map:* The Dutch East Indies, superimposed on a map of the United States.

*Tables:* Distribution of population by racial groups. Income—taxpayers according to racial groups, 1936. Value of imports and exports, 1913–39. Sources of revenue as affected by the depression (1932–37).

*Appendices:* The economic situation in the Netherlands Indies in 1939. Statistical tables regarding imports and exports.

410. VLEKKE, BERNARD HUBERTUS MARIA. Nusantara: A History of Indonesia. rev. ed. The Hague, van Hoeve; Chicago, Quadrangle Books, 1960. viii, 479 p.; bibliography, illustrations, maps, appendix, index.

DS634.V55 1960

*Text:* A historical study of the development of Indonesian civilization and the effect of three hundred years of slow and steady growth of Dutch influence on this "Empire of the Islands." Discusses the arguments for and against many controversial historical points and deals at length with matters of government administration and the Dutch economic policy.

Provides detailed accounts of the outstanding Indonesian and Dutch persons who have influenced the history of Indonesia in the past three centuries: Gajah Mada, the founder of the Javanese empire; Jan Pieterszoon Coen, the founder of the Dutch commercial empire; Herman Willem Daendels, a prominent military leader; Thomas Raffles, the founder of Singapore; and Johannes van den Bosch, a pioneer in a system of government controlled agriculture. The chapter, The end of a colony and the birth of a nation, is an excellent epitome of the development of Indonesian nationalism. The concluding chapter tells of the part of Indonesia in World War II. Well documented throughout.

*Bibliography:* Notes to each chapter include many valuable bibliographical references.

*Maps:* Extension of Hindu influence. Java in the Hindu-Javanese period. Java in the 16th century. Principal states in the 17th century. Archipelago in the 19th century.

*Appendix:* Chronology of the principal events in Indonesian history, including the names of the rules of Java.

411. VLEKKE, BERNARD HUBERTUS MARIA. The Story of the Dutch East Indies. Cambridge, Mass., Harvard University Press, 1945. xvii, 233 p.; illustrations, maps, index.

DS634.V56

*Text:* A simple but authoritative narrative of the outward trend of events in Indonesian history which provides the most significant aspects of past and present Indonesian civilization and of the inter-exchange of Dutch and Indonesian cultures. Designed for the general reading public.

*Illustrations:* Relate various aspects of Indonesian culture: the ceremonial dance, religious temples, the *wayang* theater, Balinese dances, and village life. Views of different cities in Java.

412. WIRJOSUPARTO, SUTJIPTO. A Short Cultural History of Indonesia. Djakarta, Indira, 1959. 45 p.; bibliography, illustrations.

DS625.W5

*Text:* Written primarily as collateral reading for Indonesian students taking a course in Indonesian history and archaeology, the booklet provides a brief survey of the growth of Indonesian culture.

*Bibliography:* Lists items in Indonesian, English, and Dutch pertaining to Indonesian history and archaeology.

*Illustrations* (selected): 2. Javanese shadow play. 6. Borobudur movement. 8. Mosque at Sendang Dukur.

413. WOLF, CHARLES. The Indonesian Story; the Birth, Growth and Structure of the Indonesian Republic. New York, John Day, 1948. xi, 201 p.; appendices, index. (Issued under the auspices of the American Institute of Pacific Relations)

DS644.W6

*Text:* Traces the historical development of the Republic of Indonesia from its beginning on August 17, 1945, to the early part of 1948, when the Security Council of the United Nations endeavored to reach a settlement of the Dutch-Indonesian problem. Deals with the political and economic struggle which ensued in Indonesia during the turbulent postwar period when opposing political, economic, and sociological forces were met partly by diplomatic persuasion and partly by military pressure. Tries to present an objective analysis of both sides of the controversy as viewed by the Dutch and Indonesians.

The significant events relating to the British occupation in 1945–46, the Linggadjati agreement, the political organization and the new economic problems of the Republic, and the failure to implement the Linggadjati agreement are discussed in detail.

Biographical data on Soekarno, Soetan Sjahrir, Mohammad Hatta, Amir Sjarifoeddin, and other Indonesian leaders are included. Well indexed.

*Appendices:* Preamble and Constitution of the Republic. Political manifesto of the Indonesian Government. Text of the Linggadjati (Cheribon) Agreement. The truce agreement between the Netherlands and Indonesia, signed January 17, 1948. Radio address of Queen Wilhelmina on February 3, 1948.

414. WULFFTEN PALTHE, P. M. VAN. Psychological Aspects of the Indonesian Problem. Leyden, E. J. Brill, 1949. 58 p. DS644.W8

*Text:* The author, a noted Dutch psychiatrist, and formerly rector of the University of Indonesia in Djakarta, would show certain psychological predispositions within the Indonesian mind, which he contends were factors underlying the turbulent political developments in Indonesia. He analyzes the violence and the revolutionary movement prevalent in Indonesia in the postwar years, and indicates these three distinct aspects of the problem: the phenomenon of the traditional Javanese band who periodically give themselves to *rampok,* or robbery accompanied with violence; the psychological frustrations and confusion appearing during the Dutch colonial rule and the Japanese occupation; and the outlook of the Indonesian intellectuals.

The study concludes with the contention that regardless of past events or of future happenings, the bonds between Holland and Indonesia are indissoluble; never should Indonesians or Hollanders feel like "aliens" in each other's country. "The new political structure has to provide for a regulation in order that Netherlands and Eurasians of Netherlands' extraction may continue to live and to work in Indonesia with a concrete senses of 'belonging' and the same ought to be true for Indonesians who live and work in Holland, where they must feel themselves at home." (p. 57)

# ECONOMICS

(including: Agriculture, Commerce, Industry, and Labor)

415. Boeke, Julius Herman. The Structure of Netherlands Indian Economy. New York, International Secretariat, Institute of Pacific Relations, 1942. x, 201 p.; tables, index. (Issued in cooperation with the East Indies Institute of America I.P.R. International research series) HC447.B67

*Text:* A study by a distinguished Professor of Tropical Economics at the University of Leiden, which presents the basic economic problems in Indonesia just prior to the Japanese occupation of that area.

Divided into three parts—Characteristics and component factors of colonial society, Economic contact between the colonial groups, and Vital colonial questions. Attention is given to these subjects: the village community; social and economic needs in the village; landlordism and sharecropping; place of money in the economy; general characteristics of the economic contact between Indonesian and Western colonial groups; land tenure; labor market; population problems; and the relationship of native production to colonial capital.

*Tables:* Types of property holdings. Population density in Java and Madura. Imports and exports in relation to colonial capital and private enterprise.

416. Broek, Jan Otto Marius. Economic Development of the Netherlands Indies. New York, International Secretariat, Institute of Pacific Relations, 1942. xv, 172 p.; map, tables, index. (I.P.R. inquiry series) HC447.B7

*Text:* Depicts the problems of production and trade in Indonesia in the decades just prior to World War II and relates the changes in economic policy as introduced by the Dutch during and following the depression in the thirties. Introductory chapters deal with the historical background and the critical agrarian population problem in Java and other islands. The position of Indonesia in the quantity and the diversity of production and her place in the world market are related in detail. The chapter, The foreign trade of the Indies, discusses the shift in trade currents and tells of the export-import trade with leading countries of the world. A survey which will prove valuable for an understanding of the problems in a realistic planning of the economic postwar structure of Indonesia.

*Map:* The Netherlands Indies.

*Tables:* Agricultural colonization of the Outer Provinces. Value of agricultural exports, 1894–1940. Production of important minerals. Trade within certain economic blocs. Volume of foreign trade (1928–39). Imports by continents and major countries of origin. Exports by continents and major countries of destination.

417. Cator, Writser Jans. The Economic Position of the Chinese in the Netherlands Indies. Chicago, University of Chicago Press, 1936. xi, 264 p.; bibliography, tables, index.

DS632.C5C3 1936

*Text:* An account of the origin and growth of the Chinese community in Indonesia, with particular reference to the ever-growing influence which that community has exercised upon almost every phase of industry, commerce, trade, and agriculture of the islands. Includes a discussion of the economic, social, cultural, and political questions affecting the Chinese in Java, Sumatra, Borneo, Bangka, and other islands of the archipelago. Attention is given to government edicts which have a bearing on the Chinese prior to World War II.

*Bibliography:* The bibliographical list of approximately 100 titles is organized in relation to the various chapters.

*Tables:* Distribution of Chinese in Indonesia according to Chinese provinces from which they came. Chinese attending schools. Incomes of Chinese. Chinese population in the various regions. Professions engaged in by the Chinese.

418. Charlesworth, Harold Carr. A Banking System in Transition: The Origin, Concept and Growth of the Indonesian Banking System. Djakarta, New Nusantara, 1959. 224 p.; map, tables, appendices, index.

HC3304.C5

*Text:* A factual picture of the growth and development of the Indonesian banking system established by the Indonesian government since independence.

Selected chapter headings indicate the scope of the study: 2. The present-day banking system. 4. Credit facilities granted by foreign exchange banks. 5. The five state banks of Indonesia. 7. Indonesian private foreign exchange and non-foreign exchange banks. 8. Specialized governmental credit agencies.

*Map:* Population distribution. Bank Rakjat Indonesian branches throughout Indonesia.

*Tables* (selected): Money supply in Indonesia. Indonesian commercial banks. Monetary balance sheet.

*Appendices* (selected): Statute of the Bank of Indonesia. Government ordinance bearing upon the supervision of the credit system. Regulation no. 1, year 1955, covering the conduct of the credit institutions.

419. CHECCHI AND COMPANY. Washington, D.C. Report on Indonesian Cooperatives. Washington, 1956. 2 vols. (iii, 22–41) bibliography, tables, appendices.  HD3544.A4C5

*Text:* Prepared for Freedom Fund, Inc., the study deals with the nature and problems of the cooperative movement in Indonesia, together with information on the political, social, and economic setting in which it operates; and an exploration of possible action which might strengthen the cooperative movement in Indonesia and thus increase its ties to the cooperative movement in the United States and other countries of the Free World.

*Bibliography:* Principally articles dealing the the subject.

*Tables:* (Indicated by * in appendices).

*Appendices* (selected): *2. Official cooperative statistics, 1954. *3. Miscellaneous cooperative statistics, 1927–54. 15. Text of Cooperative Ordinance of 1949.

420. DE MEEL, H. "Demographic dilemma in Indonesia." *Pacific Affairs,* September 1951, v. 24: 266–283; tables.  DU1.P13 1951

*Text:* Gives certain facts concerning population developments before 1930, the year when the last official census was taken in Indonesia; records the scanty recent population data and estimates; considers the causes for current trends in the population movements; and discusses the alternative courses open to Indonesia in the endeavor to deal with the problem of an overabundant population.

Contends that the immediate problems of population pressure cannot be solved by either agricultural improvements, migration, or industrialization. Believes that a practicable approach to the problem of lowering birth rates among primitive, uneducated peasants should follow these two lines of endeavor: to postpone the age at which people marry by instituting compulsory education for girls between the ages of thirteen and nineteen years, and to establish numerous health centers as part of a far-reaching program of public hygiene by the popular dissemination of knowledge and means of birth control.

The writer is a member of the staff of the Australian National University, and formerly was in the Indonesian Planning Department.

*Tables:* Comparison of certain statistics in the 1920 and 1930 census data. Increase of population (1905–51).

421. GOVERNMENTAL AFFAIRS INSTITUTE, Washington, D.C. Indonesian Labor; a Management Survey. Washington, 1961. [82 1.]; tables, appendices. (International Studies. Foreign Labor Practices Series)  HD8706.G6

*Text:* One of 28 such surveys of various countries prepared by the Institute in the Foreign Labor Practices Series of its International Studies. Comprises these five chapters: 1. The society and worker behaviour. 2. The governmental system. 3. Manpower resources and recruitment. 4. Employment conditions and personnel management. 5. Labor relations.

*Tables:* (indicated by * in appendices).

*Appendices* (selected): *1. Ethno-linguistic groups of Indonesia. *2. Schools, teachers and pupils in Indonesia, 1956–57. *3. Population of Indonesia. *6. Jobs classified according to industry and status, 1958.

422. HAWKINS, EVERETT DAY, LESLIE H. PALMIER, and HAROLD W. GUTHRIE. Entrepreneurship and Labor Skills in Indonesian Economic Development; Symposium. Introduction by Benjamin Higgins. New Haven, Yale University Southeast Asia Studies; distributed by Cellar Book Shop, Detroit, 1961. 140 p.; tables. (Yale University Southeast Asia Studies. Monograph series, no. 1)  HC447.H39

*Text:* Comprises three essays which discuss manufacturing and labor problems in Indonesia which significantly relate to the economic growth and development in Indonesia. The three essays are entitled: The batik industry by Everett Hawkins. Batik manufacture in a Chinese community in Java by Leslie Palmier. The development of a skilled labor force in Indonesia by Harold Guthrie.

*Tables:* Statistical data on various aspects of Indonesian labor in cottage industries and other manufacturing.

423. HIGGINS, BENJAMIN. Indonesia 1970: Political and Economic Prospects. Santa Barbara, Calif., Technical Military Planning Operation, General Electric Co., 1959. 66 p.; tables, appendices. (TEMPO report. Research memorandum, RM 59TMP–93)

HC447.H516

*Text:* The economic future of Indonesia during the next decade is forecast in the words which appear in the summary: "Given the lack of economic sophistication of the present government, and the antagonism to 'national capitalism,' private enterprise is likely to be hampered without being replaced by vigorous public enterprise . . . . It is unlikely that Indonesian per capita real income will be more than ten or twenty percent above present levels by 1970, and Indonesia's relative importance among Asian countries is likely to decline."

Contents: 1. Economic importance of Indonesia to the United States. 2. Indonesia's role in international relations. 3. The political outlook. 4. The problem of unification. 5. The starting point: the Indonesian economy in 1959. 6. Economic development under the first five-year plan. 7. Prospects for Indonesian exports. 8. Entrepreneurship, political, elite, and prospects for development. 9. Economic prognosis.

*Tables:* 1. Indonesia, regional imports and export. 2. National income.

*Appendices:* 1. Net national product by sources of origin. 2. Consumption of goods and services available in Indonesia.

424. HIGGINS, BENJAMIN. Indonesia's Economic Stabilization and Development. New York, Institute of Pacific Relations, 1957. xxii, 179 p.; bibliography, tables, appendices.

HC447.H52

*Text:* Undertaken originally as a paper for the Kyoto Conference of the Institute of Pacific Relations, the study was enlarged at the Massachusetts Institute of Technology Indonesia Project to present some major findings which reveal the economic policy of the central Indonesian Government between the transfer of sovereignty in 1949 to the opening of the first elected parliament in the spring of 1956.

These five parts comprise the study: 1. Short-run problems and policies: stabilization. 2. Long-run problems and policies: development. 3. Political aspects of economic development. 4. Political stability, security and economic development. 5. Conclusions: outlook for stabilization and development.

*Bibliography:* Indicated by * in appendices.

*Tables:* Indicated by * in appendices.

*Appendices:* 1. Draft bill on foreign investment. 2. Indonesian foreign trade regulation. *3. Select bibliography. *4. Statistical tables.

424a. KLAVEREN, J. J. VAN. The Dutch Colonial System in the East Indies. [Rotterdam? Printed by Drukkerij Benedictus] 1953. 212 p.; bibliography, maps, charts, index.

JQ762.K45

*Text:* Basically an economic history of the Dutch in Indonesia, the study tells about the controlling power and deep seated influences on Indonesian economy brought about by the Dutch companies Vereenigde Oost-indische Compagnie and the Nederlandsche Handel-Maatschappij, and the Culture System which made the land-rent system possible and revolutionized the whole economy.

Selected chapters include: 3. Native civilizations. 6. The V.O.C. as a merchant-monopolist. 7. The V.O.C. as a sovereign. 13. The Nederlandsche Handel-Maatschappij. 14. The Cultuur Stelsel (Culture System). 17. Trial and error period of parliamentary colonial policy, 1848–70. 20. Ethnical government vs. exploitation.

*Bibliography:* Largely official publications and books in the Dutch language.

*Maps* (selected): Tropisch Nederland, 1619–1898. Plantation region of Sumatra's east coast.

*Charts* (selected): Sales of produce by the N.H.M., 1824–1924.

425. KONINKLIJK INSTITUT VOOR DE TROPEN. Indonesian Economics: The Concept of Dualism in Theory and Policy. The Hague, van Hoeve, 1961. xii, 446 p.; bibliography, glossary, index. (Selected studies in Indonesia by Dutch scholars, vol. 6) HC447.K65

*Text:* A symposium by a number of prominent Dutch economists which describes the Dutch economic policy in prewar Indonesia. Includes four studies by the late Dutch economist J. H. Boeke, based on his extensive experience in Indonesia both as an economics teacher and as an advisor to the government, which have been translated into English for the first time.

Among the contents are these chapters: Colonial economics and theoretical economics by G. Gonggrijp. The economics of the tropical colony by J. van Gelderen. Dualistic economics by J. H. Boeke. Brown and white economy, unity in diversity by G. H. van der Kolff. Village reconstruction by J. H. Boeke. Over-population and the emancipation of the village by Th. A. Fruin.

*Bibliography:* Includes a long list of Boeke's works and many other items on Indonesian economics and economic theory.

*Glossary:* Indonesian terms used in the text.

425a. LEUR, JACOB CORNELIS VAN.   Indonesian Trade and Society: Essays in Asian Social and Economic History.   The Hague, Bandung, W. van Hove, 1955.   xix, 465 p.; bibliography, glossary, index.   (Selected studies on Indonesia by Dutch scholars, v. 1)

HF3805.L45 1955

*Text:* This volume is one in a series* of selected studies on Indonesia being designed and published by the Royal Tropical Institute in Amsterdam under a grant from the Netherlands Organization for Pure Research, at The Hague.

The basic purpose of the book is to bring together—for the first time in English—these significant writings of a Dutch scholar who has made an important contribution in the years past to a better understanding of certain aspects of Asian history and the historical relation between Europe and certain sectors of Asia.   Employing the methodology of sociology and economic history developed by Max Weber, the author arrived at certain surprising and revolutionary conclusions. He takes issue with the traditional Dutch colonial historians, and he would break loose from the Europe-centered view dominating Western historical writing on Asia.

In the section dealing with early Asian trade, the reader is provided with new light on the Hinduization and the Islamization of Indonesia.   The section entitled The world of Southeast Asia: 1500–1650, is

---

*[Other studies within this series of selected studies on Indonesia by Dutch scholars, and included in this compilation, are as follows: 2. *Indonesian sociological studies: selected writings, part one* by B. Schrieke (1955); 3. *Indonesian sociological studies: selected studies, part two.   Ruler and realm in early Java* by B. Schrieke (1957); 4. *The Indonesian town: studies in urban sociology* (1958); 5. *Bali: studies in life, thought, and ritual* by J. L. Swellengrebel and others (1960); 6. *Indonesian economics: the concept of dualism in theory and practice* by J. H. Boeke and others (1961).   Volume no. 7, *Indonesia's history between the myths* by G. F. Resink is now in preparation.]

a rich storehouse of data dealing with varying aspects of early trade routes, Dutch East India Company, products traded, conflicts for power, and other topics.

*Bibliography:* Contains over 250 items, including a number of books of the 19th century.

*Glossary:* Indonesian terms associated with trading.

426.   PAUKER, GUY J.   The Indonesian Eight-Year Over-All Development Plan.   Santa Monica, Calif., Rand Corporation, 1961.   vii, 35 p. (Rand Corporation.   Research memorandum, RM–2768)        Q180.A1R36 no. 2768

*Text:* The Indonesian National Development Council (DEPERNAS) produced in 1960 an eight-year over-all development plan for Indonesia which received the approval of the Provisional National Assembly.   This monograph evaluates this seventeen-volume Indonesian document of DEPERNAS, giving particular attention to the "A" projects which are designed to improve the standard of living, and the "B" projects which are supposed to provide the needed capital to put the developmental and economic projects into effect.   A summary statement on Indonesian socialism is included.

427.   SUTTER, JOHN O.   Indonesianisasi: Politics in a Changing Economy, 1940–1955.   Ithaca, Southeast Asia Program, Department of Far Eastern Studies, Cornell University, 1959.   4 vols.   (xxi, 1312 p.); tables, glossary, appendices.   (Data paper no. 36)   HC447.S89

*Text:* Presents a comprehensive coverage of politico-economico-social developments in postwar Indonesia. Provides a competent survey of the economic history of Indonesia from 1940 through the decade following World War II, with particular reference to the way in which the economy has been Indonesianized.   This Indonesianization process reflects significant major Indonesian political currents closely linked to nationalism.

The four volumes are divided into these four parts: 1. The Indonesian economy at the close of the Dutch period.   2. Reorganization of the Indonesian economy under the Japanese.   3. The Indonesian economy split by revolution.   4. Sovereign Indonesia strives for a national economy.

*Tables* (selected): Agricultural landholdings, 1930–40.   Petroleum producers, 1940.   Coal producers, 1940.   Investments by nationality, 1937.   Investments of Dutch capital, 1940.   Organization of the

Ministry of Prosperity, 1946. Industrial projects, Sumitro Plan. Bank Rakjat Indonesia credits, 1950–55.

*Glossary:* Dutch, Indonesian and Japanese names and abbrevations used in the text.

*Appendices* (selected): Agricultural lands under cultivation. Java Central Advisory Council. Committee to investigate means of preparing for independence. Foreign policy manifesto, 1945. Proposed ten year reconstruction plan, 1947. Decisions of the Inter-Indonesian Conference, 1949. Financial and economic agreement, 1949. Constitution of the Federal Republic of Indonesia, 1949. Provisional constitution of the Republic of Indonesia, 1950. Government policy statement on foreign investment, 1954. Regulations affecting government officials in business.

428.  Tedjasukmana, Iskandar.  The Political
429.  Character of the Indonesian Trade Union
430.  Movement. Ithaca, Southeast Asia Program, Department of Far Eastern Studies, Cornell University, 1958. x, 130 p. (Monograph series, Modern Indonesia Project)
HD6822.T4

*Text:* The author, Minister of Labor in three different Indonesian cabinets and chairman of the Political Bureau of the Indonesian Labor Party, traces and identifies the ideological influences, especially Communist and socialist influences, which have caused the trade union to pursue long-range political aims and economic gains. With reference to Marxist and Leninist influences in Indonesia, the importance of the Communist victory in the Chinese mainland is noted.

The six chapters are entitled: Short history of the Indonesian trade union movement. The current status of the Indonesian trade union movement. The impact of political ideologies. Relationship of the trade unions to political parties. Political activities of the trade unions. Conclusion.

## SOCIAL CONDITIONS
(including: Anthropology, Education and Health)

431.  Bone, Robert C.  The Role of the Chinese in Indonesia. Washington, Dept. of State, Foreign Service Institute, 1951. 155 p.; bibliography, tables, appendices.  DS632.C5B65

*Text:* An account of the Chinese who became established in Indonesia long before the Dutch arrived and who remain to hold a dominant economic position while the Dutch conclude their three and one-half centuries of domination of Indonesia.

Following a brief introductory statement, part II deals with the development of the Chinese immigration to Indonesia, its historical background, geographical sources, economic political motivations, the growth of the Indonesian-Chinese population, and restrictions on Chinese immigration. Part III deals with the Chinese in the Indonesian community; their economic role, social role, and political role. Part IV emphasizes the ability of the Chinese to prosper and flourish and to withstand cultural amalgamation into the Indonesian population. Part V discusses the future of the Indonesian-Chinese.

*Bibliography:* Lists the books and articles used in making the study.

*Tables* (selected: Chinese population, 1860–1930. Laboring groups in various occupations.

*Appendices* (selected): Chinese immigration, 1900–33. Civil condition of Indonesian-Chinese, 1930. Chinese longevity. Chinese-language press of Indonesia.

432.  Cunningham, Kenneth Stewart.  The Educational System of Indonesia; Outline of Structure and Terminology. Djakarta, Printed by Technical School of Printing, 1957. 20 p.; diagrams.  LA1271.C8

*Text:* This booklet gives a brief introduction and guide to the main features of the national education system of Indonesia, and was prepared by the Unesco Adviser to the Indonesian Ministry of Education in Teacher Training and Educational Research.

The topics discussed are: general system of control, mass education, Department of Culture, Department of Higher Education, Bureau of Libraries, higher education—the faculties and universities, teacher training colleges.

*Diagrams:* 1. Administrative structure of education in Indonesia. 2. Susunan pendidikan tehnik (system for technical training).

[An interpretation of the problems in Indonesian education is the Sir John Adams lecture given at the University of California by Marnixius Hutasoit, *Problems and potentials of Indonesian education.* Los Angeles, University of California, 1961. 22 p.]

433.  "The development of national education in Indonesia." *Indonesian Review,* October–December 1951, v. 1: 393–399.  GPRR

*Text:* Outlines the new basis of education which is now being put into operation in Indonesia—a system which lays emphasis on the development of character, having as its goal the creation of a nation consisting of people with initiative, with a sense of responsibility towards society, and with a spirit of independence and citizenship. Discusses the types of schools offering higher education—many of which have been newly established since the Dutch regime concluded. Compares the present Indonesian educational system with the educational system during the Dutch colonial period.

434. DJAJADININGRAT, LOEKMAN, *radan*. From Illiteracy to University: Educational Development in the Netherlands Indies. New York, 1944. 68 p.; illustrations, charts, appendix. (Bulletin 3 of the Netherlands and Netherlands Indies Council of the Institute of Pacific Relations)　　　　LA1271.D58 1944

*Text:* An account of the history, methods, problems of education in Indonesia in the years prior to World War II. Divided into three parts—oriental education, occidental education, and vocational education—the study discusses elementary, intermediate, secondary, and university education as found in the dual system of vernacular schools and Dutch schools, and describes trade schools, business schools, teacher training schools, and training schools for government officials, as integral parts of the vocational educational system.

Revised edition of *Educational developments in the Netherlands Indies,* a paper prepared for the Eighth Conference of the Institute of Pacific Relations, Mont Tremblac, Quebec, 1942, by the Director of Education and Public Worship in the Netherland Indies at that time.

*Illustrations:* Medical College in Batavia (Djakarta). Javanese dance in education. Law college in Batavia (Djakarta).

*Charts:* Organization of oriental and occidental education in Indonesia. Courses offered in higher elementary schools.

*Appendix:* The battle against illiteracy by Charles O. van der Plas, former Governor of East Java. A chart of the Indonesian educational system.

435. EMBREE, EDWIN R., MARGARET SARGENT SIMON, and W. BRYANT MUMFORD. Island India Goes to School. Chicago, University of Chicago Press, 1934. 120 p.; illustrations, tables, chart, index.　　　　LA1271.E55

*Text:* An analysis of the educational system and schools in Indonesia (in Java and Bali) established during the Dutch regime, with particular emphasis on the motives and objectives which prompted Western educators at the expense of indigenous culture.

The study was made by: Mr. Embree, President of the Julius Rosenwald Fund, who had a lifelong interest in racial questions and in education as a means of cultural growth and racial adjustment; Margaret Simon, also associated with the Rosenwald Fund, and a teacher and writer; and, Mr. Mumford, Superintendent of Education in the British Colonial Service in Tanganyika Territory where he directed a school experiment in education based on native culture.

Following a rather lengthy introductory account of the natural scene, the religions, the daily life, the music and dance, and the Western influences in Java and Bali, a thorough historical account is given of the Dutch development of a dual educational organization—a vernacular school system and a European school system. The principal criticism is that the schools took so little account of the history and culture of the peoples of Indonesia. The Western educational method "tends to disinherit a people from its own traditions and ways of life which assumes that 'progress' means Western civilization, which ignores all the beauty and expression and communal assets of the East." (p. 72)

*Illustrations:* Gamelan and Balinese dancer. Desa, secondary, and technical schools. Views of the landscape.

*Tables:* Statistical analysis of the vernacular and Dutch schools as to students, teachers, and budget.

*Chart:* The dual educational organization in Java.

436. GEERTZ, HILDRED. The Javanese Family: A Study of Kinship and Socialization. New York, Free Press of Glencoe, 1961. 176 p.; diagrams, appendices, index.　　　　GN480.G4

*Text:* Contends that kinship plays an important role in the traditional social structure in the *desa* bringing to bear considerable influence on the economic, political, and the religious behaviour of the Javanese villagers. At the same time, it is emphasized that kinship plays a secondary role in the overall Javanese social structure. Considerable attention is directed to the process of socialization: the way in which standard continuity is maintained from generation to generation. Reveals that the deepest and most cherished Javanese values are retained both by socialization techniques within the family and by the very structure of the Javanese kinship system.

The two principal divisions are: The structure of

the Javanese kinship system and The functioning of the Javanese kinship system. Selected chapters therein discuss: Kinship terminology; household composition; property holding; marriage, courtship, and wedding rituals; customs surrounding childbirth; social relationships during childhood; aspects of adulthood; and Javanese values and the Javanese family.

*Diagrams:* 1. Javanese kin terms, with reference to generation and seniority. 2. Javanese kin terms, with reference to linguistic etiquette system.

*Appendices:* 1. Javanese kinship terminology. 2. Methods of research.

437. HUTASOIT, M. Compulsory Education in Indonesia. Paris, UNESCO, 1954. 111 p.; tables, appendices. (Studies in compulsory education, 15) LC136.I55H8

*Text:* Like the other studies in the Unesco series on education in various countries this is designed to show how the principle of universal, free and compulsory education can be applied in Indonesia, to illustrate some of the problems encountered in developing a satisfactory educational system in that country, and to indicate the solutions which have been achieved or are being tested currently. For the most part the volume is factual, with a minimum of interpretations. It summarizes the history of education in Indonesia during the Dutch period and then relates in detail various aspects of education in Indonesia today, including the abolition of illiteracy, Muslim education, Chinese education, and provisional teacher-training courses.

*Tables:* Curriculum of Indonesian schools. Primary schools in 1951–52. Primary schools in the Dutch period. Literacy courses, 1951–52. Muslim education.

*Appendices:* Ministers of education with their educational programmes after the declaration of independence of Indonesia. Annual development of the 10 year programmes preparatory to the introduction of free compulsory primary education in 1960–61.

438. INDONESIA. PANITIA CHUSES PENJELIDIKAN PENDIDIKAN TEHNIK. (Special Study Committee on Technical Education). Technical Report. Editors: William J. Micheels and Warren E. Philipps. Bandung, 1959–1960. 11 reports in 3 vols.; maps, tables. LC1047.15A56

*Text:* The eleven reports are: A–1 The work of the Committee. B–L Pedoman pendidikan tehnik. Directory of technical education. B–2 Design and administration of the status study. B–3 The current structure, status, and facilities of technical education. B–4 A study of technical school teachers and directors. B–5 A study of technical school students and graduates. B–6 A study of workers in small industries and selected large industries. C–1 Working theses for developing technical education in Indonesia. C–2 Foundations of committe deliberations. C–3 The recommendations of the committee. C–4 Digest of committee reports and recommendations.

*Maps* (selected): Technical schools in Sumatra. Technical schools in Java. Technical schools in Kalimantan and Sulawesi. Technical schools in Moluccas.

*Tables:* Provide statistical data about schools, students, curriculum, students costs, national budgets, and other topics.

439. JOSSELIN DE JONG, P. E. DE. Minangkabau and Negri Sembilan: Socio-Political Structure in Indonesia. The Hague, Nijhoff, 1952. vii, 208 p.; bibliography, illustrations, maps, table, diagrams, index. GN635.D9J6

*Text:* An anthropological study which presents data about certain aspects of the social and political organizations of the Minangkabaus who inhabit the western part of central Sumatra and the emigrants from Minangkabau who settled in Negri Sembilan, a Malay state on the west coast of the Malay Peninsula.

Using mostly contemporaneous data as a starting point, the study endeavors to see how these facts are integrated into one cohesive cultural pattern. The author ventures into the historical field as he finds it necessary for background information with which to reconstruct the social system of the Minangkabau people. The patterns of kinship and the social organization which are considered with much detail show clearly that the Minangkabau social organization implies a system of double descent with pronounced matrilineal stress. The study gives a large amount of information about the fundamental rules governing marriage relations and customs, property holding, kinship terminology, and the place of *adat* law as practiced by the Minangkabaus. Chapters on modern trends show how Islam and modern European influence have changed Minangkabau culture.

*Bibliography:* An extensive list of references used in the study.

*Maps:* Sketch maps of Sumatra and the Malay Peninsula showing location of Minangkabau and Negri Sembilan.

*Table:* Minangkabau kinship terms.

*Diagrams:* Relating to matrilinear or patrilinear decent.

440. KARTINI, *raden adjeng.* Letters of a Javanese Princess. Translated from the original Dutch by Agnes Louise Symmers; with a foreword by Louis Couperus. New York, Knopf, 1920. xviii, 310 p.      DS646.23.K3

*Text:* These letters of Princess Kartini, a daughter of a Javanese Regent, written to her Dutch friends in the Dutch language from the age of 20 to the time of her death just five years later, describe vividly Javanese life and manners. The letters reveal the intense urge which the young princess felt for feminine freedom, particularly the freedom which was forbidden by rigid Moslem canons of feminine behavior and practice. As a result, Princess Kartini, posthumously, had a profound effect on the feminist movement and female education in Indonesia.

The introduction provides a biographical sketch of Princess Kartini.

[A French edition was published in 1960 under the title *Lettres de Raden Adjeng Kartini; Java en 1900.* Paris, Mouton.]

441. KOENTJARANINGRAT, *raden mas.* Some Social-Anthropological Observations of Gotong Rojong Practices in Two Villages of Central Java. Translated by Claire Holt. Ithaca, Southeast Asia Program, Department of Far Eastern Studies, Cornell University, 1961. viii, 67 p.; bibliography, maps, appendices. (Modern Indonesia Project. Monograph series)      HD3543.A4K63

*Text:* Shows how the Indonesian term *gotong rojong,* meaning cooperation between members of a community, operates in villages of central Java and engenders cooperative endeavor among the villagers in a variety of situations. Other information about village practices and concepts of interest to the sociologist is given: kinship ties, hamlet bonds, land ownership, and daily habits.

*Bibliography:* A few selected references of books and articles in Dutch and English.

*Maps:* The villages of Tjelapan and Wadjasari where the surveys were made.

*Appendices:* Cases of *gotong rojong.* Work diaries of those making surveys.

442. KONINKLYK INSTITUUT VOOR DE TROPEN. The Indonesian Town: Studies in Urban Sociology. The Hague, Bandung, van Hoeve, 1958. xxvi, 379 p.; bibliography, maps, tables, charts, glossary, index. (Selected studies on Indonesia by Dutch scholars, vol. 4)      HT147.I54K6

*Text:* This work of particular concern to demographers and sociologists comprises four significant writings which deal with the complex problem of urban development in Indonesia. Part one, Town development in the Indies, is an official Dutch report setting forth policies and explanations about a town-planning ordinance for municipalities on Java. Part two, The living conditions of municipally employed coolies in Batavia in 1937, reveals the hygienic, housing, and living conditions in one section of the capital city. Part three, Differential mortality in the town of Bandung by W. Brand, discusses the European, Chinese, and Indonesian population groups in the resort city of Bandung. Part four, Kuta Gede by H. J. van Mook, describes the developmental changes of the Javanese community of Kuta Gede located in central Java not far from Jogjakarta.

*Bibliography:* A lengthy list of references, articles and books, mainly in Dutch, dealing with cities and towns of Indonesia.

*Maps* (selected): Lay out of an average regency seat showing the location of public buildings, craftshops, and population groups.

*Tables* (selected): Deal with population, labor conditions, wages, educational facilities, family economics, housing conditions, occupations, and mortality rates, 1918–39.

*Glossary:* Indonesian terms used commonly in the text.

443. NEFF, KENNETH LEE. National Higher Technical Education in Indonesia, Recent Trends. Washington, Dept. of Health, Education, and Welfare. Office of Education, 1961. 67 p.; bibliography, table, appendices. (Studies in comparative education)      T163.I6N4

*Text:* An evaluation of the experimentation that Indonesian educators are conducting at Gadjah Mada

University and the Bandung Institute of Technology with the purpose of utilizing the methods of technical education during the colonial period and the methods needed to meet present aspirations in Indonesia.

*Bibliography:* Brief lists of Indonesian publications on education.

*Tables:* Curriculum in Indonesian secondary education.

*Appendices:* 1. Patterns of Indonesian higher education. 2. Glossary of Indonesian terms and abbreviations pertinent to technical education. 3. Study plan at Gadjah Mada University. 4. Study plan at Bandung Institute of Technology.

444. PALMER, LESLIE H. Social Status and Power in Java. London, University of London, Athlone Press; New York, Humanities Press, 1959. 168 p.; bibliography, maps, tables, charts. (London School of Economics. Monographs on social anthropology, no. 20) HN710.J3P3

*Text:* Data gathered during two field trips in Indonesia and later used for a thesis at the University of London presents an illuminating account of the social structure in Javanese society. Among the topics discussed are: 4. Social characteristics of a small town. 6. Status and kinship among the Javanese nobility. 7. Regents and wives. 8. Maternal status, kinship, and appointments. 9. Poverty and honour. 10. Javanese-Chinese relationships. 12. The Provisional Regional People's Representative Assembly. 14. The public recognition of status. 15. The transmission of power.

*Bibliography:* A few well-known references.

*Maps:* Indonesia on Europe. The small town.

*Tables:* Marriages contracted by a Javanese regent.

*Charts:* Javanese kinship terminology used by the nobility. Wives of a line of Javanese regents.

445. SCHRIEKE, BERTRAM JOHANNES OTTO. Indonesian Sociological Studies: Selected Writings. The Hague, van Hoeve, 1955–57. 2 vols., bibliography, maps, appendices, index. (Selected studies on Indonesia by Dutch scholars, vols. 2 and 3) HN703.I5S3

*Text:* These two volumes bring together some of the works of a highly respected Dutch ethnologist and historian who pioneered in various fields of reserach on Indonesia.

Volume one consists of an article, an official report, and two monographs heretofore published only in Dutch. The article, The shifts in political and economic power in the Indonesian archipelago in the sixteenth and seventeenth centuries, describes the rise and fall of Javanese trade from the 13th to the 17th century. The official report, The causes and effects of communism on the west coast of Sumatra, relates the development of the Communist movement in Sumatra, and describes the Minangkaban society.

One monograph, The native rulers, was a lecture on the position of the regents from the time of the Dutch East India Company to the Constitutional Regulation of 1854. The other study, Some remarks on borrowing in the development of culture, is enlightening on the process of acculturation.

Volume two, entitled Ruler and realm in early Java, is a study previously unpublished, and is a detailed historical account of Javanese history from the 13th to the 18th century.

*Bibliography:* A lengthy list of monograph and periodical references on Javanese history.

*Maps* (selected): Java and Madura. Sumatra.

*Appendices* (selected): The rise of Islam and the beginnings of Hinduism in the archipelago.

446. SMITH, BRUCE LANNES. Indonesian-American Cooperation in Higher Education. East Lansing, Institute of Research on Overseas Programs, Michigan State University, 1960. xxii, 133 p.; bibliography, appendix, index. LB2285.I55S6

*Text:* Part of a series of studies of relations between universities in the United States and universities in other countries: being a "country study" which analyzes the relations between American universities and their opposite institutions in Indonesia.

Following these three chapters—1. Backgrounds of the Indonesian educational system. 2. University education in post-revolutionary Indonesia. 3. Indonesian-American interuniversity relations—recommendations are presented concerning curriculum and organizational patterns with respect to affiliated American universities and affiliated Indonesian universities.

*Bibliography:* An annotated selective list of references on education in Indonesia, America, and other places for comparative purposes.

*Appendix:* Descriptive list of nine American university affiliations in Indonsesia, 1958–59.

447. SWELLENGREBEL, JAN LODEWIJK, ROELOF GORIS, VICTOR EMANUEL KORN, CHRISTIAAN JOHAN GRADER, and HENDRICUS JACOBUS FRANKEN. Bali: Studies in Life, Thought, and Ritual. The Hague, van Hoeve, 1960. xii, 434 p.; bibliography, maps, tables, diagrams, glossary, index. (Selected studies on Indonesia by Dutch scholars, vol. 5)

DS647.B2B3

*Text:* A selection of articles, papers, and monographs by Dutch scholars, formerly not in English, together with the introductory essay, constitute a concise account of the pattern of Balinese life and society.

Selected chapter headings are: Balinese history and the elements of Balinese culture. Religious practices of the family and the individual. Some religious problems of today. The religious character of the village community. The temple system. Holidays and holy days. The consecration of a priest. The state temples of Mengwi. The festival of Jayaprana at Kalianget. The village republic of Tenganan Pereringsingan.

*Bibliography:* Lengthy list of book and periodical titles which these authors and others have written.

*Maps* (selected): Bali, showing towns and villages.

*Tables* (selected): Population of Bali, 1930 and 1954. Ethno-religious breakdown of Indonesian population on Bali.

*Diagrams* (selected): System of water distribution.

*Glossary:* Indonesian and Balinese terms used in text.

448. VAN NIEL, ROBERT. The Emergence of the Modern Indonesian Elite. The Hague, van Hoeve; Chicago, Quadrangle Books, 1960. vii, 314 p.; bibliography, index.

HN703.V3 1960

*Text:* Provides a careful analysis and evaluation of selected historical events which took place in colonial Indonesia during the first quarter of the twentieth century. The principal emphasis is not upon political events per se, but upon social change, particularly the social change manifested among the leader group of Indonesian society. The author's stated purpose is to analyze and interpret Dutch colonial practices, policies, and attitudes and to show their effects upon Indonesian society, while at the same time to evaluate the dynamics of Indonesian society and their part in forming the social foundation for political independence decades later.

*Bibliography:* Divided into documents, government reports, official speeches, books and pamphlets, periodical and newspaper articles.

449. VREEDE-DE STUERS, CORA. The Indonesian Woman: Struggles and Achievements. The Hague, Mouton, 1960. 204 p.; bibliography, illustrations, maps, tables, appendices, index.

HQ1752.V713

*Text:* Shows how the birth of the feminist movement and the struggle for liberation from the narrow bonds of a traditional society in Indonesia during the time of Kartini have been intimately allied to the national awakening. Presents the part played by the woman in the traditional society of various regions of Indonesia. Also portrays the influence of Islam on the customs, especially those which concern the matrimonial system and the education of women.

Contents: 1. Adat and Islamic law. 2. The precursors of the feminist movement. 3. The national awakening: modern education for women. 4. The Indonesian novel: reflections of the old and glimpses of the new. 5. The women's movement: colonial period. 6. Matrimonial legislation: colonial period. 7. The women's movement in Indonesia. 8. Matrimonial legislation: contemporary period. 9. Vocational training. 10. The Indonesian women today.

*Bibliography:* Documents, books, and pamphlets arranged by chapters, a large number in Dutch.

*Illustrations:* Pictures of women who have distinguished themselves in the women's movement. Views of the various types of vocational training.

*Maps:* Outline map of Indonesia showing principal cities. Indonesia compared in size with Europe and the U.S.

*Appendices* (selected): Various formulae of the ta'līḳ aṭ ṭalāḳ (right of repudiation). E. Resume of the articles written by nine Indonesian women for the report on the improvement of the position of women. F. The Oath of the Youth, pronounced at the Second Congress of Young Indonesians held in Djakarta in 1928. G. List of women members of the Provisional Parliament of Indonesia. H. List of women members of the first parliament of Indonesia. Biographical notices of Indonesian women.

[Also issued in French. *L'émancipation de la femme indonésienne.* Paris, Mouton, 1959.]

450. WERTHEIM, WILLEM FREDERIK. Effects of Western Civilization on Indonesian Society. New York, International Secretariat, Institute of Pacific Relations, 1950. 83 p.; bibliography. (Secretariat Paper No. 11, 11th Conference, Institute of Pacific Relations, Lucknow)　HN703.D8W4

*Text:* A brief historical-sociological analysis of the effects of Western civilization on Indonesian culture and society with special reference to contemporary Indonesian nationalism, prepared by a Professor of Sociology at the University of Amsterdam. Although some attention is given to economic developments, special treatment is given to these social processes: changes which have evolved in class structure, urban development and the problems of urban growth, and modernization of Islam during a period of Islamic reform. The study concludes with a chapter on Indonesian nationalism and the accompanying problems of freedom.

*Bibliography:* Extensive list of references relating to the individual chapters of the text.

451. WERTHEIM, WILLEM FREDERIK. Indonesian Society in Transition; a Study of Social Change. The Hague, Bandung, van Hoeve, 1956. xiv, 360 p.; bibliography, maps, tables, index.　HN703.W45

*Text:* As an enlargement of a former paper *The effects of Western civilization on Indonesian society,* this volume deals primarily with Indonesian social history as it describes the social background of Indonesian nationalism, the changes in class structure, the urbanization processes, and the modernization of Indonesian Islam.

Selected chapters: 3. A cursory survey of some social developments in South and Southeast Asia. 4. General outline of Indonesian political history. 5. Shifts in the economic system. 6. The changing status system. 7. Urban development. 8. Religious reform. 9. The changing pattern of labour relations. 10. Cultural dynamics in Indonesia. 11. Nationalism and after.

*Bibliography:* Short subject bibliographies follow each chapter.

*Maps:* Indonesia, an outline map. Peoples and tribes of Indonesia.

*Tables:* Principally statistical data pertaining to economics and labor.

452. WILLMOTT, DONALD EARL. The Chinese of Semarang; a Changing Minority Community in Indonesia. Ithaca, Cornell University Press, 1960. xii, 374 p.; tables, appendices, index. (Published under the auspices of the Modern Indonesia Project, Southeast Asia Program, Cornell University)

DS632.C5 W52

*Text:* Presents a comprehensive view of the Chinese minority in a rapidly changing Indonesian community, based on extended research in the field with actual residence in Semarang in central Java. Supplementing the descriptive account, an analysis and interpretation of the social and cultural change of both Chinese and Indonesian people is given. The opening chapters provide the necessary geographic, demographic and historical data for a better understanding of the social conditions.

The ten chapters are entitled: 1. The city and its people. 2. Sources of new currents in the Chinese community. 3. Occupations and economic activities. 4. Ethnic group relations. 5. Chinese community structure. 6. Organizations. 7. Leadership. 8. Schools and education. 9. Religion and magic. 10. Family and kinship.

*Tables:* Chinese occupations. Language distribution. Religious preferences.

*Appendices:* An approach to theories of sociocultural change. The questionnaire survey. Municipal statistics. The interview survey. Statistical procedures.

453. WILLMOTT, DONALD EARL. The National Status of the Chinese in Indonesia, 1900–1958. Ithaca, Southeast Asia Program, Department of Far Eastern Studies, Cornell University, 1961. xi, 139 p.; appendices. (Monograph series, Modern Indonesia Project)

Law

*Text:* One of the first of several studies relating to the Chinese minority in Indonesia carried out by persons in the Cornell Modern Indonesia Project. It is the product of a 16-month field study in Indonesia made by one who had a command of both the Indonesian and Chinese languages and one who had a substantial knowledge of Indonesian and Chinese cultures.

Although a large portion of the study is about the legal aspects of the Chinese minority in Indonesia, particularly the dual citizenship problem, the social conditions of the Indonesian Chinese are included.

*Appendices* (selected): 1. Main provisions of the Indonesian citizenship act of 1946. 5. Act no. 62 of the year 1958 concerning Republic of Indonesia citizenship. 6. Agreement on the issue of dual nationality between the Republic of Indonesia and the People's Republic of China. 8. Summary of Government regulation no. 20, 1959, concerning the implementation of the dual citizenship treaty between Indonesia and China.

## CULTURAL LIFE

(including: Fine Arts, Language, Literature and Religion)

454. BATESON, GREGORY *and* MARGARET MEAD. Balinese Character: A Photographic Analysis. New York, New York Academy of Sciences, 1942. xvi, 277 p.; bibliography, illustrations, glossary, index. (Special publications, vol. II) GN671.B3B3

*Text:* Issued in commemoration of the one hundred and twenty-fifth anniversary of the founding of the New York Academy of Sciences, the volume presents the findings of two years (1936–38) of anthropological research in Bali by stating the intangible relationships among different types of culturally standardized behavior side by side mutually relevant photographs. Depicts various aspects of Balinese culture in a most systematic manner—village organization, ceremonial rites, the trance, painting, carving, shadow-play puppets, death rituals, and child behavior. Tells about different Balinese customs and practices connected with religion, amusements, courtship and marriage, and parental-child relationships.

*Bibliography:* Lists the manuscripts and publications actually referred to in the preparation of the work.

*Illustrations:* Each picture illustrating children at play, cock fights, the trance, Balinese dance, the funeral, marriage ceremony, and other activities is accompanied by a general statement telling about the contextual setting in which the photographs were taken and defining the theoretical points which the picture conveys.

*Glossary:* A statement about Balinese names and a glossary of Balinese words used in the text.

455. BERNET KEMPERS, AUGUST JOHAN. Ancient Indonesian Art. Amsterdam, van der Peet, 1959. vi, 124 p.; bibliography, illustrations, diagrams, glossary, index. N7325.B4

*Text:* A former director of archaeology in Indonesia presents in this volume of archaeological documentary

material a large collection of photographs published for the first time from a mass of negatives of the Archaeological Service of Indonesia. The stated purpose of the presentation is "to give a general and up to date survey of prehistoric, Hindu-Indonesian and early Islamic art in Indonesia." The text accompanying the photographs gives explanatory data about the monuments and sculpture reproduced, introductory remarks, and a historical survey.

*Bibliography:* A comprehensive list of references on Indonesian archaeology appearing as books, articles, or chapters in books.

*Illustrations:* 353 plates showing Hindu, Buddhist, and Islamic monuments, temples, figures, reliefs, and decorative friezes.

*Maps:* Showing location of monuments in Java and other islands.

*Diagrams:* Ground plans of temples.

*Glossary:* Indonesian words with their definitions alphabetically in the index.

456. COVARRUBIAS, MIGUEL. Island of Bali. New York, Knopf, 1937. xxv, 417 p. x p.; bibliography, illustrations, glossary, index.
DS647.B2C6

*Text:* Presents a bird's eye view of the life and culture of the Balinese people who continue to retain their own traditions and their own manner of life. Twelve chapters tell of the history, legal system, organization of the village, language, rice culture, labor, domestic life, family, art, music, drama, dance, religious rites, festivals, and beliefs in witchcraft as found in this exotic island east of Java.

*Bibliography:* List of books and articles dealing with various aspects of Bali.

*Illustrations:* Portray scenes of the coastline, vegetation, rice fields, religious festivals, wayang shadow plays, gamelan orchestra, and village life.

*Maps:* Pictorial map of the island. Sketch map of Indonesia.

*Glossary:* Indonesian words used in the text.

457. Cultureel Indie. Onder redactie van de Afdeeling Volkenkunde van het Koloniaal Instituut. Leiden, E. J. Brill, 1939–1948. 8 vols.; bibliographies, illus., musical scores, maps. DS611.C8

*Text:* Comprises numerous articles dealing with various aspects of Indonesian cultural life which have been published in annual volumes by the Department of Ethnology of the Colonial Institute in Leiden. The subjects discussed include drama, dancing, painting, history, language, handicrafts, literature, temples, music, religious practices, customs, and other topics. Also throughout the series, biographical accounts of these prominent persons in the history of Indonesia are included: George Webb (1787–1837); Governor-General D. J. de Eerens (1781–1840), Junghuhn (1809–1864).

From among the many articles within these eight volumes the following few are cited: Bijdrage tot de geschiedenis van de Mardjid Lama te Palèmbrang by J. W. J. Wellan (1:305–314). Bataksche maskerplastiek by G. L. Tichelman (1:378–388). Ardjoena Wiwaka by Z. H. Mangkoenagara VII (2:65–80). Onde en nieuwe kunst op Bali . . . by H. Paulides (2:169–185). Uit mijn dagboek; feesten op Bali by Margarete Zueler (3:12–16). 's Lands Plantentuin te Buitenzorg, 1817–1942, by W. M. Docters van Leeuwen (489–104). Noengoenangé van Wonga Wéa by P. Heerkens (5:1–24). De omgeslagen prauw (Tangkoeban Prahse) . . . by C. Steinmetz (5:197–213). Van kotoen tot ikat-doek. Studie over het ikatten onder de Sikaneezen op Flores by P. Heerkens (6:1–19). De betekenis van het sanskrit voor de Indische archipel by J. E. van Lohuizen-de Leeuw (6:66–84) De eerste schipvaart der Nederlanders naar Oost-Indië en terug 1595–97 by C. Steinmetz (7:43–62).

*Bibliography:* Many of the articles conclude with a brief list of references related to the subject discussed. In some instances the bibliographical lists are rather extensive.

*Illustrations:* All of the articles include photographs. There are illustrations related to history, handicrafts, drama, temples, music, dancing, archaeology, and many other subjects.

*Musical scores:* Music in Flores (5:138–140).
*Maps:* Semarang in 1756 (4:216). Sumatra, early sketch map (4:199). Early maps of Batavia and Buitenzorg by C. J. J. G. Vosmaer (5:134–135).

458. DE LEEUW, ADÈLE LOUISE. Indonesian Legends and Folk Tales. Edinburgh, New York, Nelson, 1961. viii, 160 p.; glossary.
GR320.D4

*Text:* A collection of twenty-six legendary tales known in Java, Sumatra, and other parts of the Indonesian archipelago. The tales have a variety of settings and provide many insights into Indonesian life and thought.

*Glossary:* List of common Indonesian words used in the text.

459. ECHOLS, JOHN M., comp. and ed. Indonesian Writing in Translation. Ithaca, Southeast Asia Program, Department of Far Eastern Studies, Cornell University, 1956. 178 p.; glossary. (Monograph series. Modern Indonesia Project) PL5095.E1E3

*Text:* Compiled primarily for use in a course on Southeast Asian literature in translation, this anthology brings together Indonesian poetry, short stories, and essays written originally by Indonesians and thus makes available to the Western reader a beginning knowledge of modern Indonesian literature. Brief biographical sketches of the Indonesian writers are included. Among the authors chosen are the famous Indonesian poet, Chairil Anwar, and the well-known journalist, Mochtar Lubis.

*Glossary:* Indonesian words and abbreviations used in the text.

460. ECHOLS, JOHN M. *and* HASSAN SCHADILY. An Indonesian-English Dictionary. Ithaca, Cornell University Press, 1961. xvi, 384 p.
PL5076.E25

*Text:* Meets the longstanding need for a practical, comprehensive dictionary of modern Indonesian terms with English equivalents designed primarily for those who deal with contemporary Indonesian materials. It is more than the traditional bilingual word index in that it provides illustrative phrases and sentences to explain words and idioms in modern usage.

461. GEERTZ, CLIFFORD. The Religion of Java. Glencoe, Ill., Free Press, 1960. xv, 392 p.; map, appendix, indices. BL2120.J3G42

*Text:* The first of a series* of descriptive monographs about various aspects of contemporary Indonesian life in eastern Java. Based on field work in the community of Modjokuto, a commercial, educational, and administrative center for eighteen surrounding villages,

---

*[Other scheduled monographs to appear in this series are: *Village life and rural economy* by Robert Jay. *The market* by Alice Dewey. *Administrative organization* by Donald Fagg. *Family organization and socialization* by Hildred Geertz. *The Chinese community* by Edward Ryan. The above publication, *The religion of Java,* was issued by M.I.T. in 1958 under the title *Modjokuto: religion of Java.*]

this study presents the salient aspects of Islam under these three religious traditions: the *abangan*, the *sentri*, and the *prijaji*. These three respective sections describe the ritual feast called the *slametan* which involves an extensive and intricate complex of spirit briefs; the basic rituals of Islam and the social, charitable, and political Islamic organizations; and the Hindu aspects related to the bureaucratic elements in Javanese society. Emphasis is placed on the antagonism among these various religious groups which appears to have increased markedly in this country, has sharply intensified since the Revolution, and is probably still increasing. These conflicts are manifested in three ways: ideological conflicts, class conflicts, and political conflicts.

*Maps:* Town of Modjokuto. District of Modjokuto.

*Appendix:* A note on methods of work.

462. KRAEMER, HENDRIK. From Missionfield to Independent Church: Report on a Decisive Decade in the Growth of Indigenous Churches in Indonesia. With an introductory note by W. A. Visser 't Hooft. London, SCM Press, 1958. 186 p.    BR1220.K7

*Text:* Consists of reports written from various areas of Indonesia between 1922 and 1935 which have been brought together here as one treatise to describe the condition of the Christian Church in Indonesia. Although the author does not make the claim of being a cultural anthropologist, information on Amboina, Minahasa, Batak, East and West Java will be of interest to the cultural anthropologist.

Discusses at length the need for a radical change in the relation of the Western Church to the Missionfield in order to bring about self-governing and self-responsible Christian churches in Indonesia.

463. KUNST, JAAP. Music in Java: Its History, Its Theory and Its Technique. 2d rev. and enl. ed. Translated from the Dutch language by Emile van Loo. The Hague, Nijhoff, 1949. 2 vols.; bibliography, illustrations, maps, charts, diagrams, appendices.

ML345.K95 1949

*Text:* A scientific study of Javanese music, based on twenty-eight years' careful observation and actual tone measurements by the Curator of the Ethnological Department of the Royal Institute for the Indies. Over one-fourth of volume one is devoted to a detailed analysis of the tone sequences and scale systems used in Javanese vocal and instrumental music. Includes

a thorough investigation of Javanese musical instruments, with particular attention to the gamelan. A comparison of Sundanese music with Javanese and Balinese music, both instrumental and vocal, appears in volume one. An extensive bibliography of 407 entries.

Volume two includes the photographs, bibliography, and appendices.

*Bibliography:* An extensive list of 407 references dealing with various aspects of Javanese music.

*Illustrations:* Prehistoric and modern bronze kettle drums. Reliefs found on the temple of Barabudur. Various Javanese musical instruments. The gamelan.

*Maps:* Three maps which show (1) the spread and mutual relation of *pélog* and *sléndro* orchestras in Java and Madura, as expressed in the tuning of orchestras and in vocal music; and, (2) the density of gamelan property in Java and Madura.

*Appendices:* Numerous musical scores. Detailed table showing the spread of the gamelan and the wayang, and the two tonal systems in Java and Madura. List of gramaphone records mentioned in the text.

464. MELLEMA, R. L. De Islam in Indonesië (in het bijzonder op Java). Amsterdam, 1947. 52 p.; illustrations, index (Koninklijke Vereniging "Indisch Instituut." Madedeling, no. 77 Afd. Volkenkunde, no. 25)

BP65.I5M4

*Text:* Describes the outward manifestations and practices of Islam principally on the island of Java-architecture used in mosques, religious rituals, marriage customs, the Koran, the Moslem calendar, and religious meetings.

*Illustrations:* Types of mosques. Marriage costumes. Public meetings.

465. NAERSSEN, FRITS HERMAN VAN. Culture Contacts and Social Conflicts in Indonesia. Translated from the Dutch by A. J. Barnouq. New York, Southeast Asia Institute, 1947. 18 p.; bibliographical notes. (Occasional papers no. 1)    DS625.N313

*Text:* Shows that the relations between modern ways of the West and traditional ways of life and thought in Indonesia have produced a certain degree of acculturation and at the same time a sense of loss, uncertainty, and deculturation. This is illustrated at length with a discussion of the Hindu and Islamic colonizations in Indonesia centuries ago. The examination would indicate that there was an acceptance on the part of the Indonesians of certain aspects of foreign cultures and a rejection of other aspects of those same cultures. Concludes that a new acculturation process is now taking place and that Indonesian society is passing through a phase of cultural lag.

The author, a Dutch ethnologist, is Rector of the Agricultural College at Wageningen.

*Bibliography:* Consists of notes to the text and includes references to certain unpublished theses dealing with Indonesian culture.

466. NIEUWENHUIJZE, CHRISTOFFEL ANTHONIE OLIVER VAN. "The Dar ul-Islam movement in western Java." *Pacific Affairs*, June 1950, v. 23: 169–183. DU1.P13

*Text:* A discussion of a certain revolutionary movement which has influenced a segment of Indonesian life in the course of the postwar years, and which, from the very outset of the Indonesian revolution, failed to conform to the pattern set by the nationalist movement. Indicates that the aims of the Dar ul-Islam movement in Indonesia are shared widely, beyond its formal limits, among the Indonesian Moslem community. Shows that the ideal of the movement to realize a Moslem state of the standard set by Moslem canon law as incorporated in the Koran and in tradition cannot be realized in Indonesia without difficulties. Discusses the relation of the two leading Moslem political parties in Indonesia—the Masjumi (Madjlis Sjuro Muslimin Indonesia) and the P.S.I.I. (Partai Serikat Islam Indonesia)—to this movement, and tells about S. M. Kartosuwiryo, an active Indonesia politician who embraced the ideal of Dar ul-Islam. Concludes that while the movement will ultimately die of military and economic exhaustion, the Dar ul-Islam ideal will become increasingly real, "as the need for an ideal to complete the personality of the national state becomes more acutely felt."

The author was once attached to the Moslem Affairs Department of the postwar Netherlands Indies Government, and wrote *Samou 'l-din van Pasai: bijdrage tot de kennis der sumatraansche mystiek* (Leiden, Brill, 1945) and other studies on Indonesian cultural history and contemporary affairs.

467. RASSERS, WILLEM HULBERT. Pañji, the Culture Hero; a Structural Study of Religion in Java. Introduction by J. P. B. de Josselin de Jong. The Hague, Nijhoff, 1959. ix,

304 p.; illustrations, glossary. (Koninklijk Instituut voor Taal-, Land-en Volkenkunde. Translation series, 3) MH

*Text:* On the premise that there is an unbreakable unity of myth, ritual, and social structure in a particular cultural environment, the author interprets four facets of Indonesian culture in these four previously published articles: On the meaning of Javanese drama. Siva and Buddha in the East Indian archipelago. On the origin of the Javanese theatre. On the Javanese kris.

*Illustrations: Kayon* figures in the wayang. Temples.

*Glossary:* Long list of Indonesian terms in cultural anthropology.

468. SUPATMO, RADEN. Animistic Beliefs and Religious Practices of the Javanese. Unpublished lectures. Mimeographed. [45 l.] Orientalia

*Text:* A series of lectures given by a Javanese at the plantation of the United States Rubber Company in Sumatra for the purpose of giving its Sumatra staff information about the language, folklore, customs, and religion of the Indonesian people, specifically of the Javanese.

The subjects discussed are: The beliefs of the Javanese in good and evil spirits; The exercising of evil spirits and the influence of the *dukun* [native healer]; The *dukun;* Something about the Islamic religion and the Javanese people; and The significance of Islam for its adherents in Netherlands Indies.

Emphasizes the fact that although the people generally have been influenced by Hinduism, Buddhism, and Islam, the religion of the Javanese is a peculiar mixture of animistic worship of the natural elements, with the religious concepts introduced from the West. Indonesian terms for numerous indigenous spirits, daily rituals, various diseases, festivals, different months of the Moslem year, practices of magic, types of worship, and certain Moslem doctrines are used throughout the text.

469. VAN NIEUWENHUIJZE, C. A. O. Aspects of Islam in Post-Colonial Indonesia: Five Essays. New York, Institute of Pacific Relations, 1958. xii, 248 p.; index. BP63. I5N5

*Text:* A collection of five essays which present some valuable insights into the nature and future of Islam in Indonesia. A significant chapter is the one on

Dar ul-Islam which has one of its leading ideals: the realization of an Islamic state in Indonesia.

Contents: 1. Background of Islam in Indonesia: the self-enclosed traditionalism of the "closed" community. 2. Islam in a period of transition in Indonesia: an essay on tendencies and possibilities. 3. Japanese Islam policy in Java, 1942–45. 4. The Dar ul-Islam movement in western Java till 1949. 5. The Indonesian state and "deconfessionalized" Muslim concepts.

470. WAGNER, FRITS A. Indonesia: The Art of an Island Group. Translated by Ann E. Keep. New York, McGraw-Hill, 1959. 257 p.; bibliography, illustrations, maps, chronology, index. (Art of the world; the historical, sociological and religious backgrounds.)

N7326.W297 1959

*Text:* Starting with the time of the emigration of the Indonesian people from Yunnan in Southern China (The Neolithic Age) between 2500 and 1500 B.C., it is shown how the important cultural and religious influences of the Dong-Son culture, Hinduism, Buddhism, and Islam made an impact on the historical development of Indonesia.

Selected chapters are: 4. General observations on decorative art in Indonesia. 5. Applied art in islands other than Java and Bali until circa 1850. 8. Literature within the area of Hindu-Javanese civilization. 9. Influence of Buddhism and Hinduism upon architecture, sculpture and wayang plays. 10. Cultural progress during the Islamic period to the beginning of the 19th century. 11. Music and dancing on islands other than Java and Bali. 12. Bali. 13. Indonesia in the 19th and 20th centuries.

*Bibliography:* (Indicated by * in appendices)

*Illustrations:* Colored plates of architecture, wayang figures, weaving, wood carvings, and other crafts.

*Maps* (selected): Antiquities in central Java. Spread of Islam in Indonesia.

*Appendices:* Chronological table, 2500 B.C. to 1949. Bibliography of selected books on Indonesian art and culture. Glossary of technical terms.

[Also issued in French: *Indonésie; l'art d'un archipel.* Paris, A. Michel, 1961].

# VII

# Philippines

## GENERAL BACKGROUND

471. BLAIR, EMMA HELEN and JAMES ALEXANDER ROBERTSON, eds. The Philippine Islands, 1493–1898: Explorations by Early Navigators, Descriptions of the Islands and Their Peoples, Their History and Records of the Catholic Missions, as Related in Contemporaneous Books and Manuscripts, Showing the Political, Economic, Commercial and Religious Conditions of These Islands From Their Earliest Relations With European Nations to the Close of the Nineteenth Century. Cleveland, Arthur H. Clark Co., 1909. 55 vols.; map, index. DS635.B63

*Text:* This encyclopedia made its appearance soon after the entrance of the United States into the arena of world politics, occasioned by the establishment of American authority in the Philippines archipelago. The work, extending to 55 volumes including the two index volumes, presents information selected and arranged from a vast mass of printed works and unpublished manuscripts. In order to furnish authentic and trustworthy material for a thorough and scholarly history of the islands up to the present century, contemporaneous documents which constitute the best original sources of Philippine history are reproduced in English translations.

In tracing the course of history in the archipelago through a period of more than three centuries—comprising the greater part of the Spanish regime—the scope of the work has been made commensurate with the breadth of the field. Attention has been given to the political relations, social and religious conditions, and economic and commercial factors which characterized the history of the Philippines prior to the American regime.

All classes of writers are represented: early navigators, civil and military officials, ecclesiastical dignitaries, and priests. The documents include letters, reports, narratives, descriptive accounts, papal bulls, royal decrees, and many other papers.

The many subjects discussed include: the early Chinese in the Philippines; commerce and trade; government administration by the Spanish; educational institutions in the Philippines; the growth and influence of the Catholic Church in the Philippines; social customs, mythology, religious beliefs, marriage practices, esthetic life, languages, and intertribal relations of the Filipinos; history and description of Manila, Catholic missions; the social life, customs, religion, and government of the Moro tribes.

*Map:* Philippine Islands, especially prepared to illustrate this encyclopedia, with inset of the city of Manila.

472. CHICAGO. UNIVERSITY. PHILIPPINE STUDIES PROGRAM. Area Handbook on the Philippines. Supervisors: Fred Eggan, Evett D. Hester, Norton S. Ginsburg. Directors of Research: Robert B. Fox, Frank Lynch; Research Staff: Jacques Amyot, Moises Bello, Charles D. Callender, John Donoghue, Charles R. Kaut, Melvin Mednick, Stella Paluskas, Richard K. Pope, Willis E. Sibley, George H. Smith, Jr. Chicago, University of Chicago, for the Human Relations Area Files, 1956. 4 vols.; bibliography, maps, tables, charts. (Human Relations Area Files, Inc. Subcontractor's Monograph, HRAF 16) DS655.C45

*Text:* Provides a survey of the social, political and economic organizations of the Philippines together with basic information on the cultural background and the significant social institutions of the Filipino people.

Organized in five parts, the handbook presents: an Introduction covering the general characteristics of Philippine society, geographical features, and cultural and modern history; a Sociological section on the peoples, languages, demography, settlement patterns, social organization, religion, education, communication, and artistic and intellectual expression in the Philippines; a Political section covering political structure and dynamics, and health and sanitation; an Economic section covering the history and character of the economy, agricultural patterns and problems, fishing, mining, forestry, industry, transportation, and trade; and a final section which includes two sample studies of cultural—linguistic groups—the Ilokano and the Moro.

*Bibliography:* Lists the sources utilized for each chapter and for the volume as a whole.

*Maps* (selected): Political divisions. Rainfall zones. Cultural-linguistic groups. Population distribution. Concentrations of population. Ecclesiastical territories of the Catholic church. Literacy in the Philippines. Major mineral resources. Principal roads.

*Tables* (selected): Beyer's hypotheses of prehistoric migrations into the Philippines. Increases in the population, 1799 to 1948. Summary of intercensal growth in barrios. Population growth of Manila, 1571–1948. Public education, 1898–1954.

*Charts:* Schematic structure of Philippine social class. Religions and rice cycle calender of the Tagalog area. Organization of the Bureau of Public Schools.

473. FORBES, WILLIAM CAMERON. The Philippine Islands. rev. ed. Cambridge, Mass., Harvard University Press, 1945. xv, 412 p.; illustrations, map, index.          DS685.F62

*Text:* Provides a clear description of the Islands; summarizes early Filipino history; describes events during and immediately following the American occupation; and tells about the organization of the government, the maintenance of public law and order, the system established for revenue collections, the organization of Philippine courts and the administration of justice, the problems of health and education, the tribal peoples with particular reference to the Moros, and the policy of "Filipinization" of the government with special attention to the administration of General Leonard Wood. The chapter, The independence movement, contains a summary of events leading up to December 7, 1941.

*Map:* Philippine Islands—showing political divisions, railroads, and principal cities.

*Illustrations:* President Sergio Osmeña. President Manuel Quezon. Gov. Gen. Luke Wright. Gov. Gen. Leonard Wood. Rice cultivation. Village life. Views in Baguio and Manila and Insular coastlines.

474. HAYDEN, JOSEPH RALSTON. The Philippines, a Study in National Development. New York, Macmillan, 1942. xxviii, 984 p.; bib-liographical notes, illustrations, maps, appendices, index.          DS686.H3

*Text:* An authoritative and well-documented study of the elements which have entered into the development of the Philippine nation, with particular reference to the American policy of entrusting the Filipinos with genuine political power, and thus enabling them to develop an experienced native leadership in national and local affairs. Shows how Philippine culture rests upon the substrata of pre-Spanish Malayan law, religion, literature, and art, and yet at the same time how the institutions of the Commonwealth have stemmed from both Spanish and American roots.

Following an introductory chapter on the land and people, a detailed examination is made of the origin and development of: the Philippine Constitution; the executive, legislative, and judicial branches of the government; the civil service; the administrative organization; the political parties; the social services of education and health; the problems of literacy; a national language; national defense, finance, and economic readjustment; and, foreign relations policy of the country, with particular reference to China, Japan, and the United States.

The American policy and administration in the Philippines and the effects of colonial status upon the Islands and their peoples have been examined.

Based mainly on primary and secondary historical sources, the author supplements the basic source material with an account of his personal experience of 20 years in the Philippines.

*Bibliographical notes:* Almost 100 pages (p. 861–955) contain valuable bibliographical data and footnotes to the text of the 31 preceding chapters.

*Illustrations:* John Chrysostom Early. President Manuel L. Quezon. Francis B. Sayre. Sergio Osmeña. Manuel Roxas. Eulogio Rodriguez. General Emilio Aguinaldo. General Douglas MacArthur. Paul V. McNutt.

*Maps:* The most important mineral locations of the Philippines. Commonwealth of the Philippines (color). The languages and dialects of the Philippines. The Philippines and the Pacific Mindanao and the Sulu Archipelago.

*Appendices:* The Philippine Commonwealth and independence law (Tydings-McDuffie Act). Constitution of the Philippines.

475. SPENCER, JOSEPH EARLE. Land and People in the Philippines: Geographic Problems in Rural Economy. Berkeley, Los Angeles, University of California Press, 1954. xviii, 282 p.; bibliography, illustrations, maps, tables, indexes. (Issued under the auspices of the International Secretariat of the Institute of Pacific Relations)   HD2087.S6

*Text:* The questions of land reform, rural credit, crop improvement, and agricultural extension work have been recognized by both the United Nations and America in its rural reconstruction and economic aid as administered by the MSA and the USOM programs. The present volume provides much valuable data on various aspects of the rural Philippines and its vital need for improvement.

These chapter headings are selected: 1. Basic structure of the economy. 3. Population growth and standards of living. 9. Land ownership, tenancy, and credit problems. 12. Rural mechanization. 14. The problem of rural health. 16. Corporate participation in rural economy. 17. Government services in the hinterland.

*Bibliography:* Lists books and periodical articles pertinent to the rural Philippines.

*Illustrations:* Views of Filipino villages, upland rice cultivation, terraced farming, coconut groves, manila hemp, bazaar scenes, and transportation.

*Maps* (selected): 2. Philippine provinces and provincial capitals. 4. Rainfall regimes and water supply. 6. Population. 7 and 8. Crops. 10. Food deficit areas, land tenancy, and settlement projects.

*Tables* (selected): 1. Area and population. 2. Comparative census data by provinces. 3. Physiologic density of population by provinces. 8. Distribution of tenancy, 1939. 12. Balance of foreign trade. 18. Postwar investment, 1945–49.

## HISTORY, POLITICS, AND GOVERNMENT

476. ABAYA, HERNANDO. Betrayal in the Philippines. With an introduction by Harold L. Ickes. New York, A. A. Wyn, 1946. 272 p.   DS686.4.A7

*Text:* A Filipino journalist, who served the late President Quezon as confidential secretary before World War II and who was a member of the Free Philippines guerrilla organization during the Japanese occupation, gives a summary of the events which took place in the Philippines from 1941 to 1946—with the political and economic ramifications clearly emphasized.

Describes the activities of these Filipino political leaders in their relationship to Japan and the United States: Manuel Quezon, José Laurel, Jorge Vargas, Sergio Osmeña, Claro Recto, and others. The strongly worded account accuses the late President Roxas and his associates of not only being collaborators with the Japanese during their occupation of the Philippines, but also of setting up a dictatorial regime in the Philippines which was backed by General MacArthur and American industrial interests.

An important part of the account in the struggle between the Hukbalahaps (short for the Tagalog Hukbo ng Bayan Laban sa Hapon—"United Front Against the Japanese"), the peasant resistance movement organized soon after the Japanese invasion of the Islands, and the Roxas administration in which the peasants demanded far-reaching agrarian and social reforms.

477. ABUEVA, JOSÉ C. Focus on the Barrio; the Story Behind the Birth of the Philippine Community Development Program Under President Ramón Magsaysay. Manila, Institute of Public Administration, 1959. 527 p.; bibliography, illustrations, tables, appendices, index. (Studies in public administration, no. 5)   HN713.A25

*Text:* One of a series of studies published by the Institute of Public Administration to provide a comprehensive and realistic description of the political system in the Philippines. Besides giving an administrative history of the establishment of a major government program during the first two years of the Magsaysay administration, many aspects of Philippine political life, such as shifting party alignments, and charismatic leadership, and are related to the issue of public policy.

The chapter, U.S. aid and the Cabili-Yen Mission, tells of the part which U.S. and U.N. aid had in the development of a program of rural improvement in the Philippines.

Throughout the study is the political personality and unorthodox administrative work habits of President Magsaysay before his tragic death in the spring of 1957.

*Bibliography:* Extensive list of public documents, letters and memoranda, unpublished materials, books and other materials bearing on public administrations.

*Illustrations* (selected): Various views of President Magsaysay in the villages. Village scenes. Members of Community Development Planning Council.

*Tables* (selected): Accomplishments of the community school program. U.S. aid to the Philippines, 1954–55. Summary budget of community development project.

*Appendices* (selected): Philippine Who's Who. Chronology of events in Philippines, 1948–56.

478. BACLAGON, ULDARICO S. Lessons From the Huk Campaign in the Philippines. Manila, M. Colcol, 1960.* 272 p.; appendices.

DS686.5.B3 1960

*Text:* Relates the military action taken by the Armed Forces of the Philippines to clear the country of the Huks (Hukbalahap for Hukbo ng Bayan Labon sa Hapon or United Front Against the Japanese), a wartime group against the Japanese which later became a Communist-led dissident, anti-government body. Besides the military tactics, presents the problems, the difficulties, the need, and the practical methods of combatting communism at the grass-root level in the barrios.

The author, a military historian, presented the material originally as articles in Manila newspapers and periodicals.

*Appendices:* Brief history of the Communist movement in the Philippines. Information on local Communist and Huk leaders.

479. BEYER, H. OTLEY. Early History of Philippine Relations With Foreign Countries, Especially China. Manila, National Printing Co., 1948. 17 p.; bibliography, table. Orientalia

*Text:* Professor Beyer of the Museum and Institute of Archaeology and Ethnology at the University of the Philippines, tells about China's relations with the Philippines as gleaned from historical documents and Chinese dynastic annals. Discusses briefly the prehistoric period—when Neolithic cultures came into the Philippines from China and Indochina, and then outlines the historic relations of the Philippines with the Chinese and peoples of Southeast Asia—during the Southern Sung and Yuan periods (12th–14th centuries), and during the late Yuan and early Ming periods (14th–15th centuries), after the introduction

of Islam during the Javanese control of the Philippines and early Arab trade in the 15th century. Shows that certain other pre-Spanish relationships besides the Chinese and Arab traders included trade with India, Cambodia, and Thailand.

Concludes with an outline of European relations with the Philippines, principally the Spanish and Portuguese.

*Bibliography:* Lists the printed and manuscript works used in the preparation of the study.

*Table:* Summary of the racial history of the Philippine population, originally prepared for the Philippine Census of 1918, with the latest revision in 1942.

[Originally printed as an "Historical introduction" to E. Arsenio Manuel's *Chinese elements in the Tagalog language* (Manila, 1948).]

480. "Constitution of the Philippines." *Philippine Review,* October, 1943, v. 1: 49–57.

AP7.P46

*Text:* Presents the official text of the Constitution which was adopted by the Preparatory Commission for Philippine Independence in its plenary session held in Manila on September 3, 1943.

481. CORPUZ, ONOFORE D. The Bureaucracy in the Philippines. Manila, Institute of Public Administration, University of the Philippines, 1957. xv, 268 p.; bibliography, tables, index. (Studies in public administration, no. 4)

JQ1347.C6

*Text:* An historical account of the evolution of bureaucracy in the Philippines, showing how the Spanish regime centralized the political life of the numerous native communities, and how the American colonial administration established a modern civil service. How the civil service gradually came to occupy a nonpolitical position in its process of evolution is revealed in these two chapters: 9. The Filipinization of the American colonial service, 1913–35; 10. The Philippine civil service, 1935–55.

*Bibliography:* Besides voluminous footnotes, titles, public documents, books and articles are listed.

*Tables* (selected): Annual receipts and expenditures in the Central Government, 1880–95. Separations of Americans from the civil service in the Philippines.

---

*[Issued under the same title for instructional purposes at the Infantry School, Philippine Army Training Command, Fort Wm. McKinley, in 1956.]

---

*[The President of the Philippines at the time of the framing of the Philippine Constitution, José P. Laurel, interprets certain measures of this important document in the article "Commentary on the Constitution" in *Philippine Review,* October 1943, p. 57–59.]

482. FALK, STANLEY L. Bataan: The March of Death. New York, Norton, 1962. 256 p.; bibliography, illustrations, maps, appendices, index. D805.J3F27

*Text:* A historian in the Office of Military History of the Department of the Army, provides for the first time a full account of the event known as the "March of Death" on the Bataan peninsula on the island of Luzon during the Philippine campaign in early 1942. The narrative relates what happened to the thousands of American and Filipino troops who were captured by the Japanese 14th Army at the time of the fall of Bataan: describing the torture, hard work, ill-health, and finally the death which they had to endure.

Endeavoring to give both the Japanese viewpoint and the viewpoint of the prisoners, the account is based on American and Japanese army records, the trial of General Masaharu Homma, the commander of the Japanese army in the Philippines, and diaries and letters of survivors of the horrible event.

*Bibliography:* Brings together in essay form the sources used for the research on this particular event in the Philippine campaign.

*Illustrations:* Scenes of the conditions before and during the march. General Masaharu Homma. Surrender of General King to Colonal Motoo Nakayama.

*Maps:* Route of the death march. Bataan peninsula.

*Appendices:* A. Japanese Army regulations for handling prisoners of war. B. Senior command and staff on Bataan—American and Japanese.

483. GRUNDER, GAREL A. and WILLIAM E. LIVEZEY.
484. The Philippine and the United States. Norman, Oklahoma, University of Oklahoma Press, 1951. xi, 315 p.; bibliography, illustrations, maps, index. DS685.G75

*Text:* A study of the origin and development of the policy of the United States towards the Philippines during the half-century between the time of the annexation of the Islands and the time the Philippines became an independent republic. It is a historical account of the Philippines only to the degree that it refers to U.S. administration of the Philippines and the extent to which their national development affected American foreign policy. Activities of the executive and legislative branches of the United States Government pertaining to the Philippines are discussed at length in the chapters: Establishment of civil government, Governing the Philippines, 1902–13, The Democrats Administer the Philippines, The Hawes-Cutting-Hare Independence Bill, and, Establishing the Commonwealth. Particular attention has been given to the economic relationships between the two nations, the evolution of Philippine Government institutions, and the development of the independence question.

*Maps:* The Philippine Islands. Railroads in the Philippines. The Philippines and the Pacific. United States bases in the Philippines, obtained under 99 year lease in 1947.

*Bibliography:* The long list of references (p. 286–305) presents the titles of United States Government publications, the Philippine official publications, books and articles used in the preparation of the study .

*Illustrations:* General Emilio Aguinaldo. Elihu Root. William Howard Taft. General Leonard Wood. President F. D. Roosevelt and the Philippine Mission (1935). General Douglas MacArthur. Sergio Osmeña.

485. MALCOLM, GEORGE ARTHUR. First Malayan Republic, the Story of the Philippines. Boston, Christopher Publishing House, 1951. 460 p.; illustrations, index. DS655.M36

*Text:* A survey of the Philippine Islands which will serve as a companion volume to Hayden's work *The Philippines* . . . . The author was resident in the Philippines over 35 years and served as a dean of the College of Law in the University of the Philippines, a justice of the Supreme Court of the Philippines, and a staff member of the Office of the U.S. High Commissioner to the Philippines.

The study, consisting of 25 chapters, gives data on: physical features and climate; the Negritos, Indonesians, and Malayans, as the ancestors of the Filipinos; characteristics and the position of Filipino women; the minority groups—with considerable emphasis on the form of government established by the United States in the early 20th century; biographical sketches of José Rizal, Emilio Aguinaldo, and other nationalist leaders who were prominent in the development of Philippine nationalism; the transition from the status of the Commonwealth of the Philippines to the Republic of the Philippines; the Constitution, the Presidency, the Congress, and the Judiciary; international relations—with special reference to other countries in the Far East; local government as found in Quezon City, Baguio, Cebu, and Zamboanga, and political parties; finance, trade, and economic resources; national defense; public welfare—with emphasis on education; religion and Philippine culture. Well-documented and indexed.

*Illustrations:* President Manual Roxas. José Rizal. General Aguinaldo. Governor General Frank Murphy. General MacArthur. Justice Recto, President of the Philippine Constitutional Convention. President Elipidio Quirino. President Sergio Osmeña. Ambassador Carlos Romulo. Dr. José Laurel, President of the Occupation "Republic of the Philippines." President Manuel Quezon, first President of the Commonwealth.

486. PALMA, RAFAEL. The Pride of the Malay Race: A Biography of José Rizal. Translated from the original Spanish by Roman Ozaeta. New York, Prentice-Hall, 1949. x, 385 p.; illustrations, appendix, index.

DS675.8.R5P32

*Text:* Depicts the events in the life of the foremost hero of the Philippines, relating his life, works, words, deeds, and above all his ideas which have continued to influence Filipino thought particularly related to nationalism.

*Illustrations:* José Rizal. Rizal's parents. Leonor Rivera. Execution of Rizal.

*Appendix:* Address of President Manuel Roxas on the commemoration of the Rizal fiftieth anniversary.

487. POBLADOR, FILEMON. Important Documents Illustrative of Philippine History. Manila, Mrs. P. Aruallo Poblador, Research and Editorial Service, 1936. 172 p.; appendix.

DS653.P6

*Text:* Consists of the following documents: The constitution of the Philippine Republic—the Malolos Constitution of 1899; Treaty of Paris, treaty of peace of December 10, 1898; The President's [McKinley] instructions to the Commission; Act creating the Philippine Assembly; The "Jones Law" (1916); Tydings-McDuffie Law, (1934); and the Constitution of the Philippines (1935).

*Appendix:* Delegates to Constitutional Convention (1935).

488. PHELAN, JOHN LEDDY. The Hispanization of the Philippines: Spanish Aims and Filipino Responses, 1565–1700. Madison, University of Wisconsin Press, 1959. xiv, 218 p.; bibliography, illustrations, maps, appendix, index.

DS674.P5

*Text:* Describes how the Spanish culture in the Philippines envisaged a radical transformation of native Philippine society. Assesses the sweeping social reforms—religious, political, and economic—which the Spanish launched in the Philippines in the late sixteenth century with the design of reorganizing Philippine society. Relates the way in which the Filipinos showed creative social adjustment by adapting many Hispanic features to their own indigenous culture.

This ethno-historical account is divided into these eleven chapters: 1. The Spaniards. 2. The Filipinos. 3. The Spanish missionaries. 4. The "spiritual geography of the Philippines." 5. The imposition of Christianity. 6. The "Philippinization" of Spanish Catholicism. 7. Exploitation of labor. 8. Ecological and economic consequences of the conquest. 9. Political Hispanization. 10. Patterns of resistance. 11. In retrospect.

*Bibliography:* Bibliographical essay discusses printed sources and manuscript sources.

*Illustrations:* Pictures from manuscripts showing people in various provinces.

*Maps:* Outline map of Central and Southern Philippines showing Catholic centers. Luzon, showing Catholic centers.

*Appendix:* List of Jesuit, Augustinian, Franciscan, and Dominican parishes shown on maps.

489. PHILIPPINES (REPUBLIC). CONGRESS. HOUSE OF REPRESENTATIVES. SPECIAL COMMITTEE ON UN-FILIPINO ACTIVITIES. Communism in the Philippines. Manila, Bureau of Printing, 1952. 29 p.          JQ1419.A5C62

*Text:* Outlines the beginnings, growths, and status a decade ago of the Communist party in the Philippines. Includes a description of Communist methods: infiltration, use of front organization, subversive propaganda, pretended support of liberal causes, nationalism, guerrilla warfare, murders, and others. Designed primarily for the use of lecturers and groups studying techniques of communism at work in the Philippines.

490. QUEZON, MANUEL LUIS. The Good Fight . . . Introduction by General Douglas MacArthur. New York, London, Appleton-Century, 1946. xxiv, 336 p.; illustrations, maps, index.          DS686.3.Q4

*Text:* An autobiographical account of the first President of the Philippine Commonwealth written with the stated purpose "to keep alive in the memory of the American people the service rendered by the Philippine Army in the heroic defense of Bataan and Corregidor . . . and to offer, inferentially, a pattern which

142

may be followed if the redemption of the teeming millions of subjugated peoples is ever to be attempted" (Preface).

Gives the history of a Filipino who was born during Spanish régime in the Philippines, became an insurrectionist who fought first against Spain and later the United States for the independence of the Philippines at the close of the 19th century, and describes the early events after the Japanese attack of the archipelago in World War II.

As the book was not finished at Quezon's death in 1944, the closing chapters, Through the blockage from Corregidor and To Australia and the United States, were prepared respectively by Governor General Francis Burton Harrison, adviser to the late President Quezon, and by Colonel Manuel Nieto, President Quezon's principal military aide.

*Illustrations:* President Quezon. The Quezon family. Mrs. Quezon. General Douglas MacArthur. President Quezon addressing the U.S. House of Representatives. President Roosevelt and President Quezon. Scenes of Manila water-front. Malacañan Palace, and other government buildings in Manila.

*Maps:* Sketch maps (on lining papers) of the Provinces of Tayabas and Bataan.

491.  QUIRINO, CARLOS.  Magsaysay of the Philippines.  Manila, Alemars, 1958.  xiii, 266 p.; illustrations.        DS685.6.M3Q5

*Text:* A biography of the third President of the Philippines, Ramón Magsaysay written soon after the fatal air crash in March 1957, in which the head of the Philippine Government and political leader in Southeast Asia was killed. The first biographical account appeared previously in serial form in the Philippine Free Press.

This account portrays the highlights of a man who did much to clear the Philippines of the Communist threat when he was Secretary of National Defense, which in turn opened the road to the Philippine Presidency. Selected chapter headings: 1. Man of the masses. 4. Congressman from Zambales. 5. Fighting the Huks. 6. Policing the 1951 elections. 7. Road to the Presidency. 8. The great political crusade. 11. Problems of the President. 13. Nemesis of Communism.

This sketch is one which will serve as a guide to future historian-geographers writing accounts that will delve more deeply into his career, reveal the origins of his character and personality, and assess the achievements of his short life.

*Illustrations:* Magsaysay at various stages of his military and political career.

492.  ROMULO, CARLOS PENA.  Crusade in Asia: Philippine Victory.  New York, John Day, 1955.  309 p.; appendices.        DS686.5.R6

*Text:* A vivid, fast-moving account of the way in which the Huk movement in the Philippines was reduced from a major national threat to the nation to a movement of insignificant proportions. Includes a fair appraisal of the important part which President Magsaysay had in ridding the country of this Communist menace to the security and stability of the Philippine Republic. Tells about Luis Taruc, the top Communist leader of the Hukbalahaps.

*Appendix:* Text of the Southeast Asia Collective Defense Treaty (SEATO).

493.  ROMULO, CARLOS PENA and MARVIN M. GRAY.  The Magsaysay Story.  New York, John Day, 1956.  316 p.; illustrations, index.
DS686.6.M3R6

*Text:* A biographical account of a Filipino who rose from the humble, poor surroundings as a farm boy to become both the leader of his country as the President of the Philippines and the person who saved the Philippines from the spread of communism propagated by the Huks.

*Illustrations:* Ramón Magsaysay on various occasions during his lifetime.

494.  SCAFF, ALVIN HEWITT.  The Philippine Answer to Communism.  Stanford, Stanford University Press, 1955.  165 p.; bibliography, illustrations, map, appendix, index.
DS686.5.S35

*Text:* The eight-year struggle, initiated in 1946 by the Communist Huk rebellion against the young Philippine Republic, forms the subject of this book. It traces chronologically the steps taken to quell the uprising, to isolate the Communist leaders, and to encourage the participation of the ex-Huks in representative government and in democratic communities. At the heart of the ambitious campaign, in the author's opinion, lay the desire of Ramón Magsaysay, then Secretary of National Defense, to win the Huks to support of the government by means of a positive program of social reform. The project for developing self-respecting farmers through land settlements was organized under the guidance and discipline of the Economic Development Corps of the Army.

Based in large part upon interviews held by the author with ex-Huks in all the settlement areas and with still-imprisoned former Communist leaders, this report introduces an array of individuals from all social and intellectual levels. These people revealed their grievances against the old regime and their reasons for succumbing to Communist direction.

This work demonstrates an experience in democracy in a country where force, backed by understanding and opportunity, has defeated communism, and has fashioned an effective program for strengthening all of its democratic institutions.

*Bibliography:* Bibliographical notes on sources used in the study.

*Illustrations:* Results of Huk terrorism. EDCOR (Economic Development Corps) communities, and how they were made.

*Map:* Islands of Luzone and Mindanao showing "Huklandia," the area of the main strength of the Huk forces.

*Appendix:* Charts of the National Organization of the Communist Party of the Philippines: the national administrative committees, military organization, the organization department, education department, the finance department, party control of finances.

495. SMITH, ROBERT AURA. Philippine Freedom, 1946–1958. New York, Columbia University Press, 1958. vii, 375 p.; map, appendices, index.                    DS686.5.S5

*Text:* Traces in a lucid manner principally the political events and trends in Philippine politics prior and subsequent to the death of President Magsaysay. Particular attention is focused on the significant way in which the United States cooperated with the Filipinos in what the author cites as "an unusual political and social experiment." The opening chapters trace the origins of the concept of Philippine freedom, and the successive chapters describe how the so-called "Asian experiment" encountered numerous cross-purposes, conflicts, and misunderstandings, thus necessitating a new evaluation of the future. A serious threat to the democratic way was the Hukbalahap revolt which is summarized in chapter six—Democracy in disrepute: subversion on the move.

*Map:* An outline map of the Philippines naming the principal islands.

*Appendices:* A. The Jones Act. B. The Tydings—McDuffie Act. C. Amendments to the Tydings—Mc-

Duffie Act. D. Constitution of the Philippines. E. Philippine trade agrement revision Act of 1955.

496. SMITH, ROGER M. and MARY F. SOMERS. Two Papers on Philippine Foreign Policy: The Philippines and the Southeast Asia Treaty Organization; The Record of the Philippines in the United Nations. Ithaca, Southeast Asia Program, Department of Far Eastern Studies, Cornell University, 1952. 79 p.; bibliography, tables. (Data paper, no. 38)
                    DS686.5.T85

*Text:* Friendship with America and with the free nations of Asia has been a common denominator in the Filipino foreign policy in its untiring support of and participation in both the SEATO pact and the United Nations. Both studies also point out the sense of need in the Philippines for "collective security" in view of the Communist push in Southeast Asia.

*Bibliography:* Lists primarily United Nations documents.

*Tables:* Indicates the voting record of the Philippines before the U.N. General Assembly of the Philippines on various issues.

496a. "Special Number on the Philippines." *Far Eastern Quarterly,* February 1945. v. 4:91–181; maps.        DS501.F274 1945

*Text:* A series of articles, brought together by the Publication Committee of the East Indies Institute of America*, provides information about the Filipino people so diverse in racial backgrounds and cultural levels and discusses social and economic conditions, giving particular emphasis to education, public health, and agrarian matters. Although the contributions do not follow a systematic plan designed to cover in logical sequence all of the major subjects relating to the area, each of the articles provides basic information for the appreciation of the subject covered.

The articles include: Races and peoples in the Philippines by Herbert W. Krieger; Cultural trends in the Philippines by Felix M. Keesing; Central Mindanao—the country and its people by Fay-Cooper Cole; The Moros in the Philippines by Edward M. Kuder; The shadow of unfreedom by Bruno Lasker; An unparalled venture in education by W. W. Marquardt; A basic problem in Philippine education by Pauline

---

[*The name of this Institute was changed to Southeast Asia Institute, which, in turn, ceased to exist in 1948.]

Crumb Smith; Public health and medical services in the Philippines by Zygmunt Deutschman; Philippine fisheries and their possibilities by Albert W. Herre; Farm tenancy and cooperatives in the Philippines by Leopoldo T. Ruiz; and The Philippine Bill of Rights by Robert Aura Smith.

Brief biographical sketches of the contributors are included.

*Maps:* Language map of the Philippine Islands. Bukidnon Province and adjacent territory.

497. STARNER, FRANCES LUCILLE. Magsaysay and the Philippine Peasantry: the Agrarian Impact on Philippine Politics, 1953–1956. Berkeley, University of California Press, 1961. ix, 294 p.; bibliography, maps, tables, charts, appendices, index. (University of California publications in political science, v. 10)
JA37.C3 vol. 10

*Text:* Correlates the relationship between the 1953 election when Magsaysay won the Philippine presidency and the agrarian problem against the background of the Communist movement. These ten chapter headings denote the issues and conflicts: 1. Philippine political democracy and agrarian reform. 2. The agrarian setting. 3. The presidential campaign of 1953. 4. The election of 1953. 5. Peasant attitudes and political behavior. 6. The role of the peasant unions. 7. A program of action. 8. Partisan politics and tenancy reform. 9. Enactment of the Land Reform Bill of 1955. 10. A summary and an evaluation.

*Bibliography:* Cites numerous official documents, monographs, and articles relevant to the Magsaysay administration and agrarian reform.

*Maps* (selected): 2. Tenancy distribution in the Philippines, 1948. 3. The presidential election of 1949. 4. The presidential election of 1953.

*Tables:* Key provisions of 1954–55 land tenure bills.

*Charts* (selected): Magsaysay's land reform and rural development program.

*Appendices* (selected): 1. 1949 elections. 2. 1953 elections. 3, 4, and 5. Acts in agrarian reform.

498. URIARTE, HIGINIO DE. A Basque Among the Guerrillas of Negros. Translated from the original Spanish version by Soledad Lacson Locsin. Bacolod City, Civismo Weekly, 1962. xx, 323 p.; illustrations, maps, appendices.
D802.P5U713

*Text:* An account of a Spanish Basque who joined the Filipino guerrillas during the years of the Japanese occupation of the Philippines, and lived the life of the guerrillas in the Negros Occidental and Negros Oriental provinces in connection with the resistance movement in Negros. Tactics employed in guerrilla warfare are described in detail, and the conditions under which the men had to live from day to day are clearly shown.

The thirty-two chapters are divided into these four parts: 1. Guerrilla background. 2. I join the guerrillas. 3. The resistance movement. 4. Intelligence missions to occupied Philippine zones.

*Illustrations* (selected): Gen. Wainwright giving surrender orders. Currency during Japanese occupation. Col. Ernesto Mato. Col. Salvador Abcede. Col. Edwin Andrews. Governor Alfredo Montelibano. Major Jesus Villamon. Views in southern Negros.

*Maps* (selected): Positions of enemy and guerrilla forces on Negros Island.

*Appendices:* Letter of Gov. Confesor to Dr. Fermin Caram. U.S. forces in the Philippines at La Carlota, Negros. Civil government roster, Negros. Col. Andrews' letter to Commissioner Elizalde.

499. VALERIANO, NAPOLEON D. and CHARLES T. R. BOHANNAN. Counter-Guerrilla Operations: the Philippine Experience. New York, Praeger, 1962. 275 p.; bibliography, charts, appendices. (Books that matter)
U240.V3

*Text:* Presents the experience of those who participated in guerrilla warfare in the Philippines and thus reveals how this type of warfare depends on careful planning and at the same time is the result of accidental circumstances. Endeavors to outline the basic principles and practices of successful counterguerrilla operations as experienced in the rugged terrain of the Philippines. Throughout the text references are made to the Huks, the Communist forces in the Philippines.

Selected chapter headings: 2. Characteristics of guerrilla movements and operations. 3. Approaches to counterguerrilla warfare. 4. The situation and the terrain. 5. Know thine enemy: estimate of the enemy situation. 6. Know thyself: analysis of friendly forces.

*Bibliography:* Indicated by * in appendices.

*Charts:* Indicated by * in appendices.

*Appendices:* Patrol for counterguerrilla operations. *2. Suggested special warfare battalion, with charts showing organization. *3. Bibliography— an arbitrary selection of references on guerrilla warfare in various parts of the world.

500. WOLFF, LEON. Little Brown Brother: How the United States Purchased and Pacified the Philippine Islands at the Century's Turn. Garden City, N.Y., Doubleday, 1961. 383 p.; bibliography, illustrations, maps, index. DS682.A1W6

*Text:* An account of the Spanish-American War which led to the American acquisition of the Philippines. Besides relating the military and political events in both America and the Philippines, valuable data is given about the Filipino nationalists—Emilio Aguinaldo, Apolinario Mabini, Antonio Luna, and Gregorio del Pilar.

*Bibliography:* Secondary sources together with U.S. congressional documents.

*Illustrations* (selected): Emilio Aguinaldo and other Filipino nationalists. President McKinley. Admiral Dewey. Judge Wm. Taft.

*Maps:* Philippine archipelago. Central Luzon Plain. Manila and suburbs, showing troop positions.

501. ZAIDE, GREGORIO F. History of the Katipunan. Manila, Loyal Press, 1939. xiii, 206 p.; bibliography, appendices, index. DS678.Z25

*Text:* An account of the history, development, and activities of the Kataastaasan Kagalanggalang Katipunan ng mga Bayan (Highest and Respectable Association of the Sons of the People), a Philippine nationalist secret society, commonly known as the Katipunan, which was active in the latter part of the nineteenth century, in opposition to the Spanish regime. Includes biographical data about Bonifacio, who has been referred to by the author as "The Father of the Philippine Revolution."

*Bibliography:* Lists the many primary and secondary sources cited and used in the preparation of this work.

*Appendices:* Documents on the history of the Katipunan—Antonio Luna's denunciation of Katipunan existence. Letters of Fr. Mariano Gil to Wenceslao E. Retana. Affidavit of Fr. Mariano Gil regarding the discovery of the Katipunan plot. The Tejeros Convention, March 22, 1897, from the revolutionary memoirs of General Artemio Recarte. Letters of Bonifacio to Emilia Jacinto. Record of the court martial of Andres and Procopio Bonifacio. The execution of Andres and Procopio Bonifacio.

502. ZAIDE, GREGORIO F. The Philippines Since the British Invasion. Manila, R. P. Garcia Publishing Co., 1949. xiv, 507 p.; bibliography, index. DS668.Z315

*Text:* Describes the principal historical events of the sweeping and dramatic tale of the Philippines since 1762, the year of the British invasion of that archipelago. It tells about not only the military phase—the wars, the battles, and the revolutions—but also the political, economic, social, and cultural aspects which, in the long view, show the real signs of national progress.

This analysis of Philippine events, divided into 25 chapters, gives data on the following subjects: the British invasion and the period of reconstruction which followed; Governor Basco's economic policy in the late 18th century; the religious question and the rise of the Filipino clergy; social life and progress during the Spanish regime; intellectual and cultural progress during the Spanish period—Spain's educational policy, introduction of Latin alphabet and Spanish language, and Spanish influence on Filipino literature; the birth of Filipino nationalism; the twilight of Spain's colonial administration; Rizal and the Katipunan; the Philippine revolution and the war of Philippine independence; the American occupation of the Philippines and the growth of Philippine self-government; social life and progress under the American administration; intellectual and cultural progress during the American regime—educational policy and advances in the educational system; the independence movement following World War I, and the Commonwealth of the Philippines; the part of the Philippines in World War II; the birth of the Republic, and the Roxas administration.

*Bibliography:* A long bibliographical list of references dealing with history of the Philippines from 1762 to 1949.

## ECONOMICS

(including: Agriculture, Commerce, Industry, and Labor)

503. GOLAY, FRANK H. The Philippines: Public Policy and National Economic Development. Ithaca, Cornell University Press, 1961. xviii, 455 p.; bibliography, tables, index.

HC455.G6

*Text:* An examination of the role of government policy in the postwar national economic development of the

Philippines. Emphasizes the fact that national economic development is poorly approximated by economic growth, that is increase of per capita income and elevation of the national standard of living. Also, indicates in Philippines that economic nationalism, industrialization, economic sovereignty, and external stability may come into substantial conflict with the pursuit of economic growth. Although primarily descriptive in nature, a rather severe appraisal of government policy is given with reference to comprehensive economic plans for accelerated economic growth.

Selected chapters from this long study are: 1. The role of the State. 3. Structure of the economy. 5. Dimensions of economic progress. 7. Exchange control and the supply of foreign exchange. 11. Industralization policy. 12. Agrarian reform and agricultural development. 13. Foreign aid and reparations policy. 17. The welfare state.

*Bibliography:* Presented in essay style, and includes the principal source materials on Philippine government as it relates to the economic life of the nation.
*Tables:* These are among the subjects for which statistical data are provided: agricultural products, land colonization, export trade, import trade, taxation and revenues, investment requirements of certain plans.

504. A Half-Century of Philippine Agriculture. Written by men of the Bureau of Agriculture and its successors, the Bureau of Plant Industry, the Bureau of Animal Industry, and the Feber Inspection Service. Manila, published for the Bureau of Agriculture Golden Jubilee Committee by Graphic House, 1952. xix, 376 p.; bibliography, illustrations, tables.
S471.P6H3

*Text:* From among the 31 chapters in this specialized agricultural compilation these are selected: 2. Control of plant pests and diseases in the Philippines. 10. Rice industry and scientific research. 11. Fifty years of rice research. 12. Philippine sugar. 14. The tobacco industry. 17. Problems of the Philippine cottage industries.
*Bibliography:* Certain chapters have lists of references pertaining to the chapter's subject.
*Illustrations:* Views pertaining to the plant industry, animal industry, and the fiber inspection service.
*Tables:* Statistical data on various crop production and the livestock industry.

505. HARTENDORP, A. V. H. History of Industry and Trade of the Philippines. Manila, American Chamber of Commerce of the Philippines, 1958. xx, 743 p.; tables
HC453.H35 1958

*Text:* Based on a series of articles published in the *American Chamber of Commerce Journal* (Manila), dating from August 1952 to June 1953, and from September 1955 to September 1957. The author, who was editor of the *Journal,* has written 35 chapters covering a wide range of topics, including these selected ones: the Japanese occupation, war damage and American aid, foreign affairs, the Huks, public works, education, labor, agriculture, taxation, import control, exchange control.
*Tables:* Scores of tables offering statistical data on a wide range of economic subjects.

506. JENKINS, SHIRLEY. American Economic Policy Toward the Philippines. With an introduction by Claude A. Buss. Stanford, Stanford University Press, 1954. viii, 181 p.; appendix, index.
HF3126.J38

*Text:* An analysis of factors and motives in the Philippines and in the United States is made in this study, to explain the situation in which the Philippines has achieved political independence and at the same time is unable to meet the demands of economic conditions from the turn of the century, following acquisition of the archipelago by the United States, to the present, with the particular emphasis on the trade and tariff policy leading to Philippine independence.

The Philippine Trade Act, known before 1946 as the Bell Bill, is thoroughly discussed in three different chapters to show how it established a pattern for future economic relations between the United States and the independent Philippine Republic. The analysis indicates that underlying the act was the basic assumption that Philippine economic survival depended on restoring trade with the United States and stimulating a flow of American investment, thus causing Philippine-American economic relations to retain a quasi-colonial character.

Granting that the economic policy of the United States was not the sole, or even the primary, determining force in recent Philippine economic history, the study emphasizes that the failure of the newly independent nation to alter inefficient production, low income, and uneven distribution of wealth cannot be separated from the past failure of the United States to attack effectively these and other problems related to

Philippine economy and to promote a solid basis for political independence.

*Appendices:* (Selected tables)—Philippine foreign trade, 1880–1948. U.S. trade with the Philippines, 1937–1950. Principal crops, 1940–50. Cost-of-living index.

507. JOINT PHILIPPINE-AMERICAN FINANCE COMMISSION. Communication from the President of United States Transmitting the Report and Recommendations of the Joint Philippine-American Finance Commission, Dated June 7, 1947, and a Technical Memorandum Entitled "Philippine Economic Development." Washington, U.S. Govt. Printing Office, 1947. xiv, 222 p.; tables, appendices.  HG188.PJ56

*Text:* Following the request of President Roxas on behalf of the Philippine Government for substantial budgetary and rehabilitation loans from the United States Government, a joint finance commission comprised of three Filipino and three American members was formed for the purpose of: (1) considering the financial and budgetary problems of the Philippine Government; and (2) making recommendations to the respective Governments with reference to taxes, budget, public debt, currency and banking reform, exchange and trade problems, reconstruction and development.

Outlines a financial, monetary, fiscal, and trade program designed to facilitate the achievement of economic rehabilitation and recovery in the Philippines following World War II, and presents recommendations for instituting sound and efficient governmental financial policies and practices. With the view to realize additional revenue and achieve the most effective use of the Philippine Government's actual and potential financial resources, the Commission gave consideration to the following matters: the adoption of new tax measures; the reduction of expenditures for nonessential government activity; the floating of internal loans; the establishment of a central banking system; the freeing part of the present currency reserves with an adequate margin of safety; and the effective use of foreign exchange resources for internal reconstruction.

The technical memorandum which is a part of the report was prepared by Thomas Hibben, and proposes a broad balanced economic program, namely: (1) domestic production of all goods now imported for the manufacture of which the principal raw materials can be made available locally; and (2) the production

of Philippine export products at prices which will permit competition in the world's markets.

*Tables:* Statistical data on Philippine balance of payments, Philippine imports and exports in 1946, national income, wages of laborers, government receipts and expenditures, monetary and banking business, communications, mining, and rice milling.

*Appendices:* Exchange of notes between Philippine and United States Governments. Statistics of above tables.

508. KURIHARA, KENNETH K.  Labor in the Philippine Economy. Stanford, Stanford University Press, 1945. xi, 97 p.; bibliography, illustrations, tables, index. (Issued under the auspices of the American Council, Institute of Pacific Relations)  HD8714.K8

*Text:* Shows the development of Philippine labor problems against the background of the national economy, with brief reference to the backward agrarian economy, slow industrial development, population and labor supply, and women and child labor. Discusses the objectives, policies, and problems of industrialization in the Philippines. Tells of the conditions of labor: standards of living, wages in industry and agriculture, hours of work, accident, and unemployment. Describes the history, organization, partisanship, and problems of the labor movement in the Philippines, and relates the agrarian reforms of the government under the Social Justice program.

*Bibliography:* Lists official documents, books, and articles dealing with Philippine labor.

*Illustrations:* Kinds of industry—mining, hemp, tobacco, and sugar.

*Tables:* Workers engaged in manufacturing and mechanical industries. Labor disputes and workers involved. Growth of labor organization, 1918–34.

509. PHILIPPINES (COMMONWEALTH). TECHNICAL COMMITTEE TO THE PRESIDENT. Report of the Technical Committee to the President of the Philippines. Washington, n.p., 1944–45. 5 vols.; bibliographies, maps, tables, charts, appendices.  HC451.A53 1945

*Text:* Presents the findings of the Technical Committee created by the Secretary of Finance in 1944 to make an extensive research and detailed study of the numerous problems of Philippine relief and rehabilitation and to submit specific proposals and recommendations pertaining specifically to the agricultural, financial, commercial, and industrial reconstruction and future development of the Philippine economy.

Vol. 1. *American-Philippine trade relations*, deals with the historical development of Philippine-American trade, gives a detailed analysis of the principal Philippine exports and imports, shows the influence of the United States tariff arts, and shipping laws on Philippine shipping, and measures the advantage to each country of the trade relations between the United States and the Philippines.

Vol. 2. *Certain phases of Philippine relief and rehabilitation*, discusses the food requirements of the Philippines for the first six months of relief, the preliminary estimates of the clothing requirements of the Philippines for the three six-month periods, the requirements of medical, dental, and veterinary supplies for relief, and the requirements of agricultural rehabilitation in the Philippines.

Vol. 3. *Program and estimated requirements for welfare services in the Philippines*, presents background information about prewar Philippine welfare services and organization, and outlines the basic needs as to personnel, equipment, new community service projects, and training and supervision of the welfare program in the Philippines.

Vol. 4. *Farm machinery and equipment requirements for relief in the Philippines*, provides estimates for new farm machinery and the necessary equipment for the repair of agricultural machinery and tools. A Philippine community canning program is outlined.

Vol. 5. *Preliminary estimates of Philippine property war damages and losses*, presents an over-all estimate of the war damage to property of all types in the Philippines, with particular attention given to the rehabilitation of the lumber industry and shipping, and the cost of repairing and restoring public property damaged or lost during World War II.

*Bibliographies:* Official documents giving agricultural surveys in various provinces. References dealing with welfare programs.

*Maps:* Density of areas cultivated, 1939. Density of production of sugar, 1939. Density of production of abaca (Manila hemp), 1939. Density of production of tobacco, 1939. Location of sawmills, 1940. Manila, nerve center of the Far Eastern trade. Location of welfare establishments. Distribution of community canning centers. Operating Philippine sugar centrals and their location, 1941.

*Tables:* Statistical information pertinent to all the subjects discussed in each volume.

*Charts and graphs:* Philippine imports and exports. Percent of total Philippine commerce with foreign countries. Volume of Philippine sugar exports. Volume of Philippine coconut products exports. Volume of Philippine abaca and cordage exports.

*Appendices:* Statistical tables referred to above.

510. PHILIPPINES (REPUBLIC). DEPARTMENT OF COMMERCE AND INDUSTRY. BUREAU OF THE CENSUS AND STATISTICS. 1948 Census of the Philippines; Population Classified by Province, by City, Municipality and Municipal District, and by Barrio. Manila, Bureau of Printing, 1951. 245 p.; illustrations, maps, tables, appendix. In process

*Text:* Presents statistical data about the population of the different political subdivisions of the Philippine Islands as enumerated on the latest Census Day, October 1, 1948.

The total population, over 19,000,000, is distributed systematically in descending order by province, municipality, and barrio, or village—the smallest political subdivision unit of the Philippines—with all provinces appearing alphabetically. Shows how the increase of population has led to the organization of new political units, with particular reference to the increases over the 1939 census of 983 municipalities compared with 923, of 21 chartered cities as compared with 9, and 18,859 barrios as against 18,115. Manila is presented as a province, subdivided into districts.

Includes a list of the government officials associated with the Bureau of Census and Statistics.

*Illustration:* President Elpidio Quirino.

*Maps:* Republic of the Philippines, 1950 (color), showing provinces, provincial capitals, chartered cities, airfields, mines, railroads, highways, and steamer routes. Population distribution map of the Philippines, census of 1948. Population density map of the Philippines by province, census of 1948. Total population map of the Philippines by province, census of 1948.

*Table:* A table, preceding all the many provincial tables, lists all the provinces in descending order according to population.

*Appendix:* Alphabetical list of congressional districts with population figures.

511. U.S. ECONOMIC SURVEY MISSION TO THE PHILIPPINES. Report to the President of the United States. Washington, Government Printing Office, 1950. ii, 107 p.; tables. (Dept. of State. Publication 4010, Far Eastern series 38)          HC455.A43 1950

*Text:* A survey of the principal aspects of Philippine economy, with particular reference to the current financial and economic problems, together with clearly stated recommendations for improving financial conditions and the general standard of living. Commonly referred to as the "Bell Report."

Following the summary and recommendations, part one presents: the current economic difficulties as noted in prices, wages, and national income; government finances; monetary and credit policy; international payments, and import, exchange, and price controls. Part two describes: development problems and policies as found in agriculture, fisheries, and forestry; industry, utilities, and trade; fiscal, investment, and credit policy; commercial and exchange policy; labor, health, and education; and public administration and technical assistance. Specific recommendations regarding United States aid conclude the report.

A list of the members, advisers, and other persons in the Mission is included.

*Tables:* Production of principal foods, 1940–49. Estimated investment in the Philippines, 1945–49. Wages rates for agricultural laborers. National government receipts, 1946–50. Money supply of the Philippines, 1940–50. Assets and liabilities of commercial banks and the Central Bank. Principal exports and imports of the Philippines, 1938–40. Estimated tax collections under new program.

## SOCIAL CONDITIONS
(including: Anthropology, Education and Health)

512. BARTON, ROY FRANKLIN. The Kalingas: their Institutions and Custom Law. With an introduction by E. Adamson Hoebel. Chicago, University of Chicago press, 1949. 275, p.; illustrations, maps, tables, diagrams, glossary, index. (Social anthropological series)          Law

*Text:* A study of the Kalingas, a tribe living in the northern part of Luzon, which was made on the field while the author was engaged in educational work in the Kalinga Subprovince and on another occasion when he returned to that area just prior to World War II in the Philippines.

The author tells about these primitive people of the Philippines both from the viewpoint of an anthropologist and as one interested in jurisprudence. He relates their customs and folkways as they are particularly conditioned by customary law. He describes what actually takes place in this primitive society when certain social norms are violated or deviated from. Detailed information is provided about: the relation of Kalinga customary law to the household and kinship group—marriage customs, husband and wife relations, parent and child relations, adopted relatives, and *dagdagas* or concubines; the Kalinga economic life and customary law—classification of wealth, landlord and tenant relationship, transfer of property, inheritance, interest rates, payment of debts, and the right of seizure; local government and customary law—the position of the *pangat* or the influential men of the wealthy class, the importance of peace pacts and alliances; and civil and criminal law practice among the Kalingas.

*Illustrations:* Village scenes. Houses. Racial types. Burial customs.

*Maps:* Ethnographic map of northern Luzon. Distribution of trading-partner relationships and peace pacts in the mountain province.

*Tables: Pangats* (leaders with influence) in Lubwagan region. Lubwagan pact-holders.

*Diagrams:* Kalinga kinship group.

*Glossary:* Extensive list of Kalinga terms used in the text.

[The author has published other ethnological studies about certain mountain peoples in the Philippines: *Ifugao law.* Berkeley, University of California Press, 1919; *Ifugao economics.* Berkeley, University of California Press, 1922; *The half-way sun: life among the headhunters of the Philippines.* New York, Brewer and Warren, 1930; *Philippine pagans: the autobiographies of three Ifagaos.* London, G. Routledge, 1938.]

513. BEYER, H. OTLEY and F. D. HOLLEMAN. A Collection of Source Material for the Study of Philippine Customary Law; From the Beyer Collection of Manuscript Sources in Philippine Ethnography (1912–1931) and Other Sources. Selected and classified by F. D. Holleman, under the auspices of the Philippine Section of the Committee on Indonesian Customary Law of the American Council of Learned Societies and the Union Académique Internationale. Manila, 1912–1931. 10 vols; bibliography.          Orientalia

*Text:* Comprises 255 individual papers on the customary law of the numerous racial groups in the Philippines, which have never been published but which were brought together between 1912 and 1931 by Professor H. Otley Beyer of the Institute of Archaeology and Ethnology at the University of the Philippines, and later classified by F. D. Holleman at that time the Secretary to the Government of the Netherlands East Indies. The collection is usually referred to as the *Beyer-Holleman series on Philippine customary law.* The first two volumes were originally referred to as the *Beyer collection of original sources in Philippine ethnography.*

The papers were written by numerous persons over a long period of years and offer a wealth of information on the ethnological aspects of Filipino culture as found in the customary law of the Philippines. The classification of the papers was not according to customary law provinces; temporarily, they were arranged primarily by geography and only partly on ethnographical division.

From among the papers within the ten-volumes these following few are cited: A brief history of the study of Philippine customary law . . . by H. Otley Beyer (no. 1); General Philippine customary laws . . . by H. Otley Beyer (no. 3); Marriage customs of the Filipinos by Tarcila Malabanan (no. 143); The religion of the Kiañgan Ifugao by Roy F. Barton (no. 244); Various papers dealing with Philippine economic life (vol. 8); papers giving court decisions which have a bearing on Philippine customary law (vol. 9); and, throughout the volumes, numerous papers on the customary law of these peoples: Bisaya, Bicol, Tagalog, Sambali, Pampañgan, Iloko, Moro, Palawan, Igorot and others.

*Bibliography:* List of the literature relating to Philippine customary law abstracted or listed in the Leyden Adatrechtbundels (vol. 1).

*Appendices:* Volume one contains these documents: Report of the secretary on the organization of the first Philippine Committee. Documents concerning the International Academic Union and its interest in Indonesian customary law.

514. BUNYE, ALFREDO M. The Philippine Prison System. Unpublished thesis, University of Santo Tomas, Manila, 1952. Various paging; bibliography. HV9808.B8

*Text:* A penological study by one who spent almost a quarter of a century in active prison administration and for some years has been the Superintendent of Bilibid Prison, the central national penal institution

of the Philippines. Records the important historical data regarding the development and progress of the Philippine prison system drawn from a very limited amount of literature on prisons, penology, and criminology in the Philippines and from personal observation and experience.

The scope of the study is indicated by these chapter headings: New Bilibid Prison, a transition; Prison conditions in the early parts of the American regime; Correctional institution for women; San Ramón Prison and penal form; Iwakig penal colony; Davao penal colony; Provincial jails; Parole system; Juvenile delinquency as a prison problem; Philosophy of prison administration; and Accomplishment of the prison system.

*Bibliography:* Lists numerous references, the majority being official documents and reports, which deal with various aspects of the prison system in the Philippines.

515. ISIDRO Y SANTOS, ANTONIO. The Philippine Educational System. Manila, Bookman, Inc., 1949. ix, 463, p.; illus., bibliography, tables, charts, appendix, index.

LA1292.I7 1949

*Text:* A volume designed as a textbook for normal schools and colleges in the Philippines by a Professor of Education at the University of the Philippines and former Educational Consultant and Officer-in-Charge in the Bureau of Private Schools. A large proportion of the data within the book was taken from memoranda, circulars, courses of study, bulletins, and other publications issued by the Department of Education and the Bureau of Public Schools.

Following historical account of Philippine education during the Spanish, American, and Japanese regimes, the discussion turns to these topics: the objectives of Philippine education; the organization and administration of the Philippine school system; elementary, secondary, and higher education; the teacher and his profession; the need for vocational education; methods of financing education; and the concluding chapter gives an appraisal of the Philippine school system.

The full text of the Philippine Teacher's Code of Ethics is included in the chapter on The teacher and his profession.

*Bibliography:* Each chapter concludes with references on some phase of education.

*Tables:* Growth of secondary school population. Secondary academic curriculum. The general curriculum. Salary scale for educational administrators.

*Charts:* Organization of the national system of education. Administration set-up of the public schools. Field administration and supervision of the public schools.

*Appendix:* Sample forms used in the Philippine public schools.

516. ISIDRO Y SANTOS, ANTONIO, JUAN C. CANAVE, PRISCILLA S. MANALANG, and MATILDE M. VALDES. Compulsory Education in the Philippines. Paris, UNESCO, 1952. 84 p.; bibliography, tables.  LC136.P518

*Text:* One of a series of studies by UNESCO which provide a survey of particular problems found in the Philippines in its system of education and with compulsory, free education.

Following a brief historical sketch of education under the Spanish and American regimes, these chapters follow: Present status of compulsory education; The tasks ahead; General factors influencing compulsory education; Overcoming obstacles to compulsory education.

*Bibliography:* Lists books, articles, laws, executive orders, and school regulations on education in the Philippines.

517. KEESING, FELIX MAXWELL. The Ethnohistory of Northern Luzon. Stanford, Stanford University Press, 1962. vi, 326 p.; bibliography, maps, tables, appendix, index. (Stanford anthropological series, no. 4)  DS688.L9K38

*Text:* What began as a study of a single racial group, the Isneg, and an examination of historical documents pertaining to them developed into a synthesis of the ethnographic data on various racial groups located in Northern Luzon. Describes the interrelations of lowland and mountain peoples in northern Luzon in an endeavor to test existing theories of migrations and relationships within the area.

After stating the problems, the successive thirteen chapters consider the peoples in three broad geographic areas which include the Pangasinan, the Ilocos, and the Cagayan.

*Bibliography:* Lists books and articles pertaining to the racial groups in Luzon.

*Maps:* Detailed maps of the Pangasinan, Ilocos, and Cagayan areas.

*Tables:* Population tables for the peoples in the three areas studied.

*Appendix:* Agricultural census, 1948.

518. KEESING, FELIX MAXWELL and MARIE MARTIN KEESING. Taming Philippine Headhunters: A Study of Government and of Cultural Change in Northern Luzon. With an introduction by Theodore Roosevelt, Jr. London, Allen and Unwin, 1934. 288 p.; bibliography, illustrations, maps, tables, index.

DS688.L9K4

*Text:* This study was prepared as part of a research project dealing with dependencies and native peoples in the Pacific, conducted under the auspices of the International Research Committee of the Institute of Pacific Relations.

Shows the Spanish influences since the late 16th century and the more recent American and Filipino controls to which the mountain people of northern Luzon have been subjected. A study in cultural contact and assimilation which was prepared from information gathered by the authors as they lived in the mountain region in direct touch with the people. The districts where close study was made include: Bontoc, Lepanto, Apayao, and Benguet.

Among the topics discussed are: native agriculture, government, socio-economic organization (the *baknang* system), education, trade and commerce, communications, handicrafts, health conditions, influence of Christian missions, judicial system, status of women, marriage customs, and native political system.

*Bibliography:* List of references dealing with the Igorots, Ifugaos, and other mountainous people in the Philippines.

*Illustration:* A Bontoc village.

*Maps:* Ethnic areas in northwest Luzon. The mountain province showing political divisions and communications. Northwest Luzon—topographical sketch.

*Tables:* Population statistics of the Apayao, Kalinga, Ifugao, Bontoc, and Benguet peoples. Exports and imports of the mountain people.

519. KRIEGER, HERBERT W. Peoples of the Philippines. Washington, Smithsonian Institution, 1942. iv, 86 p.; bibliography, illustrations, maps. (War background studies, no. 4. Publication 3694)  GN4.S6 no. 4

*Text:* The author, an ethnologist at the U.S. National Museum, presents principally information about the cultural life of the various peoples of the Philippines. Intermingled with history, geography, and population, the study tells about: cultural influences on the Philippines from India, China, and Indonesia; racial ancestry of the Filipino; principal characteristics of the Malay, the Moro, and the Negrito; and, principal everyday practices and customs as revealed in houses, weapons, food and agriculture, language, government, head hunting and human sacrifice, and religion.

*Iluustrations:* Street scenes in Manila. Agricultural practices. Houses and village life of the Negritos, Igorots, and Tinguians. Handicrafts. Various racial types.

*Maps:* Density of population by provinces, 1939. Races and tribes of the Philippines. Ethnic areas in the southwest Pacific. Languages of the Philippines—listing languages in the Luzon groups. Bisaya groups, Mindoro and Palawan groups, and Mindanao and Salu groups.

520. PHILIPPINE ISLANDS. BOARD OF EDUCATIONAL SURVEY. A Survey of the Educational System of the Philippine Islands. Manila, Bureau of Printing, 1925. xviii, 677 p.; illustrations, maps, tables, charts, graphs, index. LA1292.A3 1925

*Text:* This document, known as the "Monroe Report," by Paul Monroe, the Director of the Educational Survey Commission, is an indispensable document for the research scholar interested in Philippine education. Comprises the report of the Board of Educational Survey and the report of the Survey Commission to the Board of Educational Survey. These reports provide a wealth of information on the measurement of the results of instruction, elementary education, secondary education, teacher training, health education, physical education, private schools, general education administration, finance and the educational program, and the University of the Philippines. Throughout the text there are scores of tables, charts, and graphs which illustrate the text.

*Illustrations:* Various types of school buildings, handicrafts in schools, agricultural schools.

*Maps:* Christian and non-Christian Malayan groups. Provinces in which pupils were tested.

*Tables:* Statistical data pertinent to the topics discussed in the text.

*Charts and graphs:* Growth of the Philippine school system. Cost of public education and its growth. Measurements of reading, spelling, and language comprehension. Organization diagram of the Bureau of Education.

521. PHILIPPINES (REPUBLIC). PRESIDENT'S ACTION COMMITTEE ON SOCIAL AMELIORATION. Philippine Social Trends: Basic Documents Pertinent to Long-Range Social Welfare Planning in the Philippines. Manila, Bureau of Printing, 1950. 50 p.; tables, charts. HV406.A52 1949a

*Text:* Presents the findings of the President's Action Committee on Social Amelioration (PACSA) and the social affairs services of the United Nations program pertaining to the social problems of a predominately rural and agricultural population in the Philippines exposed to economic dislocations manifested in inadequate income, unemployment, and low standards of living. A study and analysis of various aspects of Philippine social problems, their root causes, and the implications in the whole structure of the national system, it gives in perspective the direction and trend that these problems are expected to take in the future.

In considering an organized and systematic program of uplifting the Filipino people who are forced by circumstances to a substandard of living and of meeting the deficiencies in the social and economic conditions of their country, the account includes data about pertinent economic factors relevant to social welfare: food production, population distribution, wages, labor and trade unions, cooperative associations, inheritance laws, land conservation, population movements and their effect on family life, and the need for an improved educational system in the Philippines, as well as postwar social factors.

*Tables and charts:* Statistical tables and pictorial charts throughout the text were prepared by the Philippine Bureau of Census and Statistics.

522. U.S. DEPARTMENT OF HEALTH, EDUCATION, AND WELFARE. Higher Education in the Philippines, by Arthur L. Carson. Washington, 1961. xiii, 251 p.; bibliography, illustrations, map, tables, charts, appendices. (Bulletin 1961, no. 29) In process

*Text:* The discussion is divided into these 9 chapters: The islands and the people; The development of an educational system; Higher education—the public institutions; Higher education—the private institutions; Programs of study; Students, teachers, and teaching; International Cooperation; Problems, plans, and progress; A philosophy of education.

The author was for 14 years the President of Silliman University at Dumaguete City, and was the founder of the Association of Christian Schools and Colleges in the Philippines.

*Bibliography:* Lists documents on education in general but principally cites studies pertaining to education in the Philippines. Also includes Philippine periodicals and university publications relating to education.

*Illustrations:* Scenes of various university buildings and laboratories.

*Map:* Provinces and principal cities.

*Tables* (selected): Religious adherents in the Philippines. Principal language groups. Number of Philippine public schools. Enrollment in public schools. University of the Philippines enrollment. Growth of private schools. Exchanges with the Philippines under the Fulbright Act.

*Charts* (selected): Educational system of the Philippines. National organization for education. Department of Education. Bureau of Public Schools. Bureau of Private Schools.

*Appendices* (selected): Degrees and certificates granted by the University of the Philippines, 1909–1959. Private colleges and universities in the Philippines.

523. U.S. INTERNATIONAL COOPERATION ADMINISTRATION. A Survey of the Public Schools of the Philippines, 1960, by a Staff of Americans and Filipinos Chosen by the International Cooperation Administration of the United States and the National Economic Council of the Republic of the Philippines. Manila, U.S. Operations Missions to the Philippines, 1960. xxii, 594 p.; illustrations, tables, charts, appendices.     LA1291.82.U53

*Text:* A product of Filipino-American concerted effort to survey, under the leadership of J. Chester Swanson of the University of California, the problems, organization, personnel, curriculum, and finanical management of the elementary, secondary, vocational, and teacher training schools in the Philippine Islands.

*Illustrations:* The survey team personnel. Views of various activities in the public schools.

*Tables:* Scores of statistical tables on enrollment, teachers, achievement tests, distribution of schools, employment status, student skills, and a host of other topics dealt with in the text.

*Charts* (selected): Enrollment trends. Vocational education organization. Philippine apprenticeship program.

*Appendices* (selected): Criteria for the evluation of the elementary school program.

524. U.S. OPERATIONS MISSION TO THE PHILIPPINES. EDUCATIONAL DIVISION. The 6th Milestone: ICA and Education in the Philippines. [Manila? 1959?] 344 p.; bibliography, illustrations, maps, tables, charts, appendix.     L601.U5

*Text:* This report is the result of six years of cooperative effort of Filipino and American educators in their study of three principal areas of Philippine education: vocational education, general education, and the University of the Philippines. Each chapter presents a background for specific projects; analyzes briefly the circumstances surrounding the present situation; and provides pertinent information concerning project purposes, organization, and staff.

The section on vocational education is thus divided: first agricultural education for rural Philippine youth; and second, trade and industrial education for youth of the urban population. The section on general education covers a program in elementary education and a companion program in secondary education. The part on the University of the Philippines describes the College of Education, College of Engineering, College of Business Administration, and a program of new emphasis in the future.

The voluminous six-year summary concludes with fourteen specific recommendations which will affect Philippine education in all of its phases.

*Bibliography:* Lists materials, published and unpublished, which are available in connection with the work of the Education Division of the ICA in Manila.

*Illustrations:* Views of school buildings, agricultural projects, industrial projects, educational facilities, graduation exercises, and university projects.

*Maps:* Schools approved for foreign aid. Secondary education improvement projects.

*Tables:* Statistics pertaining to various segments of education, and materials used in school projects.

*Charts* (selected): Secondary trade schools. Trade and industrial educational division. Organization of Bureau of Public Schools. Illustrative secondary education.

# CULTURAL LIFE

(including: Fine Arts, Language, Literature and Religion)

525. ACHUTEGUI, PEDRO S. DE and MIGUEL A. BERNAD. Religious Revolution in the Philippines: the Life and Church of Gregorio Aglipay, 1860–1960. Manila, Ateneo de Manila, 1960. xiv, 578 p.; bibliography, illustrations, table, appendices, indices.
BX4795.I5A42

*Text:* A historical account of how the Philippine Independent Church emerged at the time of the Filipino struggle for political freedom. The ecclesiastical leader, Aglipay, appointed by General Aguinaldo as "military vicar general" or head of an independent Catholic Church in the Philippines was to be the guiding power. Describes events in re the Filipino clergy's renunciation of their allegiance to the Roman hierarchy, the struggles with Roman authorities, the conflict with the American Government, the eventual schism with the established church at Rome, and the organization and official doctrines of the IFI (Iglesia Filipino Independiente).

The life of Aglipay, as related to the Philippine Independent Church—from the time of his excommunication by the Roman Church to the decline of Aglipayanism and his closing years—is an integral part of Philippine history at the time of the Philippine political revolution.

*Bibliography:* An extensive list of references on politics and religions in the Philippines: manuscript sources, published documentary material, Aglipayan sources, and general works.

*Illustrations:* Gregorio Aglipay of Labayan. Aglipay's guerrilla band. Isabelo de los Reyes.

*Table:* Chronology of Aglipay's life.

*Appendices:* Aglipay's mission to the insurgents. The incident at Sagada. Religious revolution in three towns, Jiminez, Misamis, and Batac.

526. AGCAOILI, T. D., editor. Philippine Writing: an Anthology. With an introduction by Edith L. and Edilberto K. Tiempo. Manila, Archipelago Publishing House, 1953. xxxi, 351 p.; appendix.
PS9992.P4A7

*Text:* An anthology which provides students interested in Philippine literature with a representative body of creative writing by current Filipino writers in the field of short stories, poetry, and critical essays.

The critical and analytical introduction by Edith and Edilberto Tiempo, both teachers at Silliman University at Dumaguete, gives a valuable survey of Philippine literature.

*Appendix:* Biographical notes on the writers contributing to the volume.

527. BERNAD, MIGUEL ANSELMO. Bamboo and the Greenwood Tree: Essays on Filipino Literature in English. With an introduction by Alfred Stirling. Manila, Bookmark, 1961. 128 p.; appendices.
PR9797.P6B4

*Text:* A collection of essays, formerly published in periodicals in Manila or Australia, which present aspects of Filipino culture unseen before. In the main chapters are commentaries on Philippine literature as a whole, and on particular Filipino writers.

*Appendices:* 1. Awards and anthologies of Philippine writing. 2. Writers talk back.

528. FREI, ERNEST J. The Historical Development of the Philippine National Language*. Manila, Bureau of Printing, 1959. v, 92 p.
PL5507.F7

*Text:* A dissertation prepared at the Hartford Theological Seminary by one who has lived in the Philippines for many years. Provides an extensive survey of the literature dealing with Tagalog and its selection as the national language of the Philippines.

Cites the magnitude of the task of changing over an educational system from one medium of instruction to another, *i.e.,* from English to Tagalog. Discusses at length the language problems during the Spanish regime in the Philippines, telling about the important relations of language to the educational system.

*[Appeared earlier in the *Philippine Social Sciences and Humanities Review* (December, 1949) under the same title.]

529. OSIAS, CAMILO. The Filipino Way of Life: The Pluralized Philosophy. Boston, Ginn, 1940. xiv, 321 p.; bibliography, illustrations, maps, appendices, index.
DS664.O8

*Text:* Written by one who was the first Filipino Division Superintendent of Schools, a former Philippine Resident Commissioner to the United States, and the author of other books on Philippine education,* this

[*Barrio life and barrio education* and *Education and religion in the Philippines.*]

volume is designed to give information and guidance to the Filipino teacher and others engaged in the task of character education, discusses the *Tayo* (Tagalog) concept, or pluralized concept, which is basic in the Filipino philosophy of life. Contends that a people who shoulder the obligations of leadership must exercise proper initiative and intelligent self-direction, and that they need to demonstrate those elements of character essential in a progressive democracy—such as self-control, self-reliance, self-discipline, initiative, self-assertion, and self-direction. The author seeks to lay the foundation for the formulation of a guiding philosophy for the Filipino people.

Various aspects of Filipino culture are outlined in these chapters: The Philippines, a cultural laboratory; Specific educational aims and goals; Finding the soul of a nation—Filipino traits; Harmonizing the cultural streams; and, Philippine institutions and constitutional ideals.

*Bibliography:* List of references dealing with character education, civic education, philosophy, and general background books on the Philippines.

*Illustrations:* Malacañan Palace, Manila. Scenes of Philippine schools. Legislative building, Manila. Roads in Baguio. Manual L. Quezon. Sergio Osmeña.

*Map:* Philippine Islands, showing principal cities.

*Appendix:* Constitution of the Philippines (1935).

530. PAVÓN, JOSÉ MARÍA. The Robertson Translations of the Pavón Manuscripts of 1838–39. Chicago, Philippine Studies Program, Department of Anthropology, University of Chicago, 1957. 4 vols. (Philippine Studies Program. Transcript no. 5A–5D)   GR325.P3

*Text:* "The Pavón documents are among the most important of the small number which have survived, since they contained translations of earlier accounts preserved in Bisayan or collected by preceding scholars." A Catholic priest by the name of José María Pavón of Araguro compiled in 1838–39 in written form the stories and legends of the Bisayan island of Negros, together with his personal account of the customs of the Indio people who lived on Negros. They were later translated into English by James A. Robertson, who was in charge of the Philippine Library at the time when the manuscripts were acquired for the Philippine Government.

The translations are presented in these four parts: Stories of the Indios of this island (Negros). Stories of the Indios of the olden time and of today. The ancient legends of the island of Negros, book first. The ancient legends of the island of Negros, book second. These folk tales present concepts on superstitions about the dead, creation of the world, the origin of man, how fish were first made, the calendar, the marriage of the Negritos and other island peoples, and the use of herbs for the cure of diseases.

531. RIZAL Y ALONSO, JOSÉ. The Lost Eden (Noli me tangere). A completely new translation for the contemporary reader by Léon Ma. Guerrero. Foreword by James A. Michener. Bloomington, Indiana University Press, 1961. xviii, 407 p.   PZ3.R5285

*Text:* The first English translation of the famous novel and acknowledged masterpiece of Filipino literature written by the Filipino hero while he was travelling in Germany where the original Spanish edition was published in 1887. Presents a vivid picture of conditions in 19th-century Philippines: the ignorance and superstitions of the people, their poverty and the bad social conditions, and the abuses committed by Spanish Government officials and religious orders. This novel, smuggled into the Philippines, was read widely by the Filipino people, and it became the *Uncle Tom's Cabin* for the historic revolutionary movement and marked Rizal as a dangerous man in the eyes of the Spanish.

532. RIZAL Y ALONSO, JOSÉ. ". . . Where Slaves Are None . . ." Translated by Alfredo S. Veloso. Manila, Far Eastern University, 1961. xi, 148 p.; musical scores. In process

*Text:* Taking its title from a phrase in what is generally looked upon as Rizal's poetic masterpiece, *Mi ultimo adiós,* this volume presents the complete poems of Rizal in both Spanish and English. The translation into English was done as a project of the Institute of Arts and Sciences, Far Eastern University.

Although translations can never take the place of the original poems, this volume in translation of Rizal's complete poems places within the reach of the English-speaking generation which has been alienated from Rizal because of the language barrier.

*Musical Scores:* "A Orillas del Pasig"—the words by José Rizal, the music by B. Echegoyen.

533. WHITTEMORE, LEWIS BLISS. Struggle for Freedom: History of the Philippine Independent Church. Greenwich, Conn., Seabury Press, 1961. xi, 228 p.; bibliography, table, index.
BX4795.I5W5 1961

*Text:* Provides an account of the religious revolution which has been taking place in the Philippines from the time of Gregorio Aglipay in the late 19th century through the first six decades of this century, thus placing the Philippine Independent Church in a true perspective of its historical relation to the Roman Catholic Church from which it emerged. Included also is a discussion of the proposed Concordat between the Protestant Episcopal Church in America and the Philippine Independent Church.

*Bibliography:* Bibliographical notes, chapter by chapter.

*Table:* Catholic directory of the Philippines, 1960.

534. YABES, LEOPOLDO Y., The Ilocano Epic; a Critical Study of the "Life of Lam-ang," Ancient Ilocano Popular Poem, With a Translation of the Poem Into English Prose. Introductory remarks by Dr. José P. Bantung. Manila, Carmelo and Bauermann, 1935. xi, 60 p.; bibliography. Orientalia

*Text:* The first of a series of studies on the more important works in Ilocano literature, which literature, next to the Tagalog, scholars consider the richest and most highly developed in the Philippines. The author, a professor at the University of the Philippines, states that the "Life of Lam-ang," the ancient Ilocano popular poem, is valuable in that it reflects the life and culture of the early Ilocanos, and is about the only work in the vernacular which gives any firsthand information about how those ancient people lived in the northern Philippines. According to Professor Bantung of the University of Santo Tomas in his introductory remarks, the writing is a highly valuable ethnological document which describes the regional customs, the ancient industries, and the outstanding characteristics and virtues of the Ilocano people.

The epic is based upon a popular legend of the Ilocanos well-known in the early days of the Spanish occupation of the Philippines. The theme concerns the successful wooing by an Ilocano youth, who displays almost superhuman strength and courage as a hero of many battles, of the most beautiful Ilocano maiden of his time—Doña Ines Kannoyan—daughter of the richest and most influential family in northern Ilocos, over scores of other rivals, many of whom were Spaniards of great wealth and handsome features and coming from distant places. A closing chapter describes the heroine of the epic, providing much data gathered by the author.

The translation by the author, appearing side by side with the Ilocano words, is the first English translation of the poem ever made. Abundant footnotes define many Ilocano words.

*Bibliography:* Brings together the fragments from various publications dealing even in an indirect manner with the poem.

535. YABES, LEOPOLDO Y. In Larger Freedom: Studies in Philippine Life, Thought and Institutions. Quezon City, University of the Philippines, 1961. vii, 471–612 p.; bibliography. (Philippine studies series, no. 6)
DS664.Y32

*Text:* A series of essays on a variety of subjects which serve as a collective plea for a wider freedom of thought both within the university atmosphere and throughout the Philippines as a whole. Emphasizes "independent thinking is most important in the strengthening of our democratic institutions because it is the independent thinker that can fight most effectively the enemies of freedom and democracy both on the left and on the right."

Selected essays in the collection include: The state of Philippine literature. The Philippine press and its democratic tradition. A great sage, teacher, and benefactor of humanity (Rizal). Mutual appreciation of Eastern and Western cultural values. The independence and integrity of the university. Higher education in the humanities.

*Bibliography:* List of references on Rizal follows the essay about him.

# Index

This index includes names of authors, titles, and selected subjects. The numbers refer to entries, not to pages.

Gurney, Henry, 309
Gurney, Natalie, 158
Guthrie, Harold, 422

## H

Haar, Barend ter, 386a
Haas, C. O., 407
*A half-century of Philippine agriculture,* 504
*The half-way sun: life among the headhunters of the Philippines,* 512
Hall, Daniel G. E., 29, 46, 115
Halpern, Joel, 217, 231, 278
Hamilton, A. W., 357
Hammer, Kenneth, 10
*Handbook on the political manifesto: two executive directions on Manipol,* 387
Hanna, Willard, 363
Hanrahan, Gene, 300
Hanson, Ola, 128
Hanssens, V., 393
*Hantu bantu: ghost beliefs in modern Malaya,* 357
Hardiman, J. P., 89
Harnett, Joseph, 218
Harrison, Brian, 46
Harrison, Francis, 490
Hartendorp, A. V. H., 505
Harvey, Godfrey, 104
Hatta, Mohammed, 382, 383, 413
Hauser, Zelda, 284
Hawkins, Everett, 422
Hay, Stephen N., 5
Hayden, Joseph, 474
HEALTH AND MEDICINE, 14, 67, 68, 76
   Borneo, 284
   Burma, 86, 121
   Cambodia, 211
   Indonesia, 360, 362, 363, 369, 372, 374, 375, 442
   Laos, 198a, 206, 278
   Malaya, 333, 345
   Philippines, 472–475, 496a, 509, 511, 533
   Thailand, 151, 163
   Vietnam (North), 214
   Vietnam (South), 215, 267, 272
Heine-Geldern, Robert van, 364
Helfrich, D. E. L., 402
Hendershot, Vernon, 358
Henderson, E. J., 136
Henderson, William, 267
Hendry, James, 267
Herre, Albert, 496a
Hester, Evett, 472
Hickey, Gordon, 201
Hickling, Hugh, 301
Higgins, Benjamin, 423, 424
*Higher education in Malaya,* 342
*Higher education in the Philippines,* 522
*Higher education in Vietnam,* 269
*The hilltribes of Northern Thailand: a socio-ethnological report,* 185
Hilsman, Roger, 255
HINDUISM, 48
*The Hispanization of the Philippines: Spanish aims and Filipino responses, 1565–1700,* 488

*Histoire ancienne des états Hindouises,* 222
*Histoire du Vietnam de 1940 à 1952,* 224
*The historical development of the Philippines national language,* 528
HISTORY AND CULTURE, 9, 11, 14, 15, 28, 29, 40, 41, 59, 69, 81, 84
   Borneo, 282, 287, 291, 293, 326
   Brunei, 282, 287
   Burma, 29, 35, 41, 58, 61, 81, 88, 89, 90–92, 100, 101, 103, 104, 107, 108–111, 113, 115, 116, 136
   Cambodia 59, 198, 211, 222
   Indochina, 208, 212, 222, 226, 234, 248, 277
   Indonesia, 35, 41, 58, 59, 81, 222, 315, 325, 360, 367, 369, 371, 374, 375, 377, 379, 383, 384, 394, 397, 398, 401, 406, 408, 409, 410, 411–413, 425a, 440, 445, 448, 451, 455, 457
   Laos, 29, 59, 198a, 201, 206, 221, 231, 242, 247, 254
   Malacca, 29
   Malaya, 35, 41, 58, 61, 296, 297, 300, 302, 303, 315, 317, 320, 324, 325, 328, 329, 336, 359
   Philippines, 35, 471, 472, 473, 475, 476, 479, 483, 485, 487, 488, 491, 494, 500, 501, 502, 518
   Sarawak, 287, 298, 318, 322
   Singapore, 41, 295, 311, 327
   Thailand, 35, 58, 81, 150–153, 155, 159, 161, 162, 166, 168, 169, 170, 186, 187, 193, 194
   Vietnam, 35, 199, 204, 205, 220, 223, 224, 229, 230, 232, 233, 240, 241, 249, 253, 272
*History and philosophy of Caodaism: reformed Buddhism, Vietnamese spiritism, a new religion in Eurasia,* 276
*A history of Burma,* 100
*History of Burma from the earliest times to 10 March, 1824, the beginning of the English conquest,* 104
*A history of communism in East Asia,* 34
*History of French colonial policy, 1870–1925,* 241
*History of industry and trade of the Philippines,* 505
*History of Laos,* 254
*A history of Malaya, A.D. 1400–1959,* 303
*A history of Malaya and her neighbors,* 315
*A history of Siam: from the earliest times to the year 1781,* 170
*A history of Southeast Asia,* 29
*History of the British residency in Burma, 1826–1840,* 101
*A history of the diplomatic relations between Siam and the United States of America, 1833–1929, 1929–1948,* 160
*History of the Katipunan,* 501
*History of the territorial dispute between Siam and French Indochina, and postwar political developments in the disputed territories,* 158
Hla Maung, U., 76
Hla Pe, U., 136
HO CHI MINH, 29, 56, 199, 224, 239, 249
Ho, Seng Ong, 344
Hoang van Chi, 204, 271
Hobbs, Cecil, 129
Hoebel, E. Adamson, 386a, 512
Hoffman, Bernard, 145
Holland, William, 31
Holleman, F. D., 513
Honey, P. J., 204
Hong phuc Vo, 201
Honig, Pieter, 364

167

U.S. GOVERNMENT PRINTING OFFICE:1964